BULLETPROOF BUDDHISTS AND OTHER ESSAYS

D1738091

INTERSECTIONS

Asian and Pacific American
Transcultural Studies

Russell C. Leong
General Editor

University of Hawai'i Press
Honolulu

in association with
UCLA Asian American
Studies Center
Los Angeles

BULLETPROOF BUDDHISTS AND OTHER ESSAYS

Frank Chin

For Ishmael Reed
"Writing is fighting."

© 1998 *University of Hawai'i Press*
All rights reserved
Printed in the United States of America
03 02 01 00 99 98   5 4 3 2 1

Library of Congress
Cataloging-in-Publication Data

Chin, Frank, 1940–
Bulletproof Buddhists and other essays /
Frank Chin.
p.   cm. — (Intersections)
ISBN 0-8248-1999-3 (cloth : alk. paper).—
ISBN 0-8248-1959-4 (pbk. : alk. paper)
1. Chinese Americans—Social life and
customs. 2. Chin, Frank, 1940–   .
3. Chinese Americans—Biography. I. Title.
II. Series: Intersections (Honolulu, Hawaii)
E184.C5C473   1998
305.895'1—dc21   97–39399
                                    CIP

University of Hawai'i Press books are
printed on acid-free paper and meet the
guidelines for permanence and durability
of the Council on Library Resources

Design by Barbara Pope Book Design

Contents

I AM TALKING TO THE STRATEGIST SUN TZU ABOUT LIFE WHEN THE SUBJECT OF WAR COMES UP

Sun Tzu says: Life is war. War is the state of being the big fuck-up. Life or death. The road to glory or extinction. Therefore, before you go to war, study it. Study hard.

War leaves no doubt about who your friends are. That's why war is my friend and, from time to time, my only friend. There is no war when I am ordered to appear for my preinduction physical in Iowa in 1961. I am free, yellow, twenty-one, and in Iowa. *Iowa.* Corn. Pork. Dubuque and Davenport, Iowa. The Mississippi River. And Iowa City and the strange empire of organized hokum, the Creative Writing Workshop, a kind of Shangri-la, a Loopy Land of legalized loonies and weirdos in the southeastern quarter of the state, right on I-80. I'm happy to get out of Berkeley, where crazy people are going on campus with guns looking for Commies and shooting my friends down. Other friends looking for poetic genius beyond madness are trying to go crazy and succeeding. One recites Rudyard Kipling, borrows a gun from a friend, kills his girlfriend

Talking to Sun Tzu

in the Bancroft Library with a dumdum shell. Then he pops another round into his head. The bullet doesn't expand and blow his brains out the way it should, but spins around the inside of his skull, and exits his brain through his right eye.

In Iowa, I see my recovery and recuperation are failing, as the state is full of white women, all strangers to me who sit down next to me and ask me, "What are you?" and refuse to believe me when I tell them I'm a Chinaman.

The coffee in the student union is no better, no worse than coffee anywhere else in Iowa City, or any other coffee I've had in Iowa. I read in the student paper that my friend who'd shot his girlfriend dead, and shot out his right eye and lived, is the last man California executed in the gas chamber before abolishing capital punishment. Thanks, Iowa. Iowa: all of it is at war with me. It isn't their biggest war. It might be their dippiest war, it is stupid, but it is against me. What are these Iowa whites treating me like the ugly duckling for? Why is it so important for them to convince me that I am too tall to be Chinese? Why do I have to be an Indian?

Study war in terms of the five fundamental factors: (1) moral influence; (2) weather; (3) terrain; (4) command; and (5) doctrine.

Therefore, if you say which ruler possesses moral influence, which commander is the more able, which army obtains the advantages of nature and the terrain, in which regulations and instructions are better carried out, which troops are stronger, which has the better-trained officers and men, and which administers rewards and punishments in a more enlightened matter, I will be able to forecast which side will be victorious and which defeated.

Even hiding out in the only Chinese restaurant in Iowa City, with chopsticks and the wispiest, Fu Manchuiest mustache ever seen east of the Rockies, some crazy Iowan sits down next to me and, as if he and his wife are my disappointed Father Flanagan, sternly ask me what I am doing in a Chinese restaurant. John Wong, the owner, has three daughters, one three years old, one five, and one ten, who like to watch and listen whenever this happens. I call them the Three Monkeys: See No Evil, Hear No Evil, Speak No Evil. They throw stuff at me. "No! No! Go to the cash register and throw money at me," I yell.

All warfare is based on deception.

Therefore, when capable, fake impotence; when active, fake inactivity.

I never hit anybody in John Wong's restaurant. He and his family live here in Iowa City. I don't. I will be better soon and be gone. I'm just passing through, hanging out at the State University of Iowa, wondering why so many Iowans want me to be a Native American. It's as if the idea of a Chinaman six feet tall offends their religion, shakes their faith, and sorely dislocates the shoulders of their reality. I tell one young Iowa lady stranger, "I'm not really six feet tall, I am five foot twelve with my walking boots on, and my skinniness adds the look of an inch or two. Barefoot I stand three foot six."

"Chinese are never taller than five foot six."

"I think Chiang Kai-shek is six foot," I say, having no idea how tall Chiang is.

"Chiang converted to Christianity," they say. I know better than to ask what Christianity had to do with Chiang's height. So I begin telling them I am a tall Japanese. I don't expect any of them to say, "Don't try that old trick on me." But that is what they say, believe it or not. Is there a tall Japanese in Iowa City? Does he also refuse to be converted into an American Indian to fit in with traditional Iowa culture?

Talking to Sun Tzu

Victory is the main object of war. Win fast and sure, or your weapons will go dull and your morale go down. When troops take cities house by house, their strength is exhausted.

I appear for my draft physical in Cedar Rapids. I am naked with a Manila folder in my hand, in a line of naked men with Manila folders of blank paperwork to be filled in. Mine armed with letters from my doctor that say I am so afflicted with asthma and hay fever I would be useless to the army. The floor is warm. The seats are cold. I have no idea listing and explaining the traffic tickets and juvenile arrests will take me more than an hour and cause a delay of the intelligence test. I write as fast as I can and explain my being arrested and taken out of circulation in Cuba as a U.S. spy, while the other preinducted physical bodies watch and wonder if I am an Indian. Because I am six feet tall. Finally they start the intelligence test without me.

The intelligence test is multiple choice, read the questions and mark the appropriately numbered row of answer boxes on the piece of odd-feeling paper that looks like the engineering-drawing-of-a-cheese-grater kind of test I haven't seen since high school and the Kuder Occupational Aptitude Test, which tells me I am destined to become a forest ranger, and the Minnesota Multi-Phasic Personality Inventory, which flunks me, tells me I have no personality at all and I should hie my ass to Minnesota to get some multi-phasic personality in my life. Interesting, I think; they're telling me I'm invisible, but I'm the only one out of all the high school kids they're offering a free trip to Minnesota, to be studied. I know something they don't know, and they want to get it out of me. I decide to keep it that way and graduate high school with a personality that doesn't show up in the tests for one. I have the stealth personality.

I don't like taking tests where the only choice is between

Frank Chin

one blank that looks just like the other, so I look at the page of the answer sheet, and go for the graphic design of the thing, and don't bother reading the questions and the choice of stupid answers, and finish the test ahead of everyone else after all. Then the sergeant appears, and sends the others on, and tells me to stay in the room while a Marine lieutenant in the green, not the nice dress blue with red piping, and an army captain of the MPs walk in and look anxious to talk to me about something.

"Would you care to tell us why you went to Cuba, Mr. Chin?" Captain MP asks in perfect Jack Palance. They swallow the drool of anticipation behind closed and hardened lips, and their eyes shine, tensing for the kill. They turn the seat-desk combo packs around to face me and sit to hide their hard-ons. What do they think they have in me? I wonder.

To troops on the move, ground is by nature (1) accessible, (2) entrapping, (3) indecisive, (4) constricted, (5) precipitous, (6) and distant.

To the commander looking for throwing his troops into a fight, the ground is (1) dispersive, (2) frontier, (3) key, (4) communicating, (5) focal, (6) serious, (7) difficult, (8) encircled, and (9) death.

The Cuba story begins in Berkeley in 1960. Lunch. An ad in the *Daily Cal* asks if I want to go to Cuba, spend two weeks, and come back to the States, all travel between Miami and Cuba, and back, food and lodging in Cuba at the Riviera, Meyer Lansky's luxury hotel, all travel in Cuba, for only $250. They recommend two bills spending money for food not provided and goodies. Why not? I think. I can buy a couple of guitars in Cuba. There has to be at least one flamenco club in Havana, and the Chinatown of Havana is the largest collection of Chinese outside Asia, second only to San Francisco.

Talking to Sun Tzu

There is no good reason to spend Christmas in the Bay Area, or the United States. I buy a pocketbook-sized hardback beginning Spanish textbook used, at Cal Books, walk upstairs to my friend's apartment, and use his phone to call my mother.

Ma gives me the $250, plus another hundred as a Christmas present. Pa says something wise and fatherly to set me on the road of life, like, "Now you got what you ask for, get out!" I understand the old man. We can always talk. He doesn't want me to just go away. He wants me to go away mad. Neither Ma nor Pa really understand I have no problem with either coming or going mad.

I take three of the five hundred I have in the bank for pocket money and hook up with three others from the Berkeley area, making for Miami and the Fair Play for Cuba Committee tour. The car is a '52 two-tone white-top, orange-body Chevrolet. It looks like it used to be owned by the old Key System that ran the Oakland streetcars and the Oakland–San Francisco electric train. It is actually owned by a late thirtyish longshoreman, a big man, six foot plus, with thinning red hair and Van Gogh red beard. He wears a new dark fuzzy-bodied yellow leather–sleeved Cal jacket over a white T-shirt, and new khaki pants, and low-topped Wellingtons on his feet.

The other riders are Blum and Hay, a couple of poli sci white liberals in horn-rims and tweed jackets who know each other, sit in the backseat together all the way to Miami because they don't know how to drive, but are willing to pay a little larger share than mine to the red-bearded longshoreman, who doesn't talk much and doesn't mind me driving or the way I drive. When I'm not driving, I sleep or read the Spanish textbook and learn Spanish to stay out of the Marxist-Leninist dreamworld the poli sci liberals talk up to each other in preference to everything they see on the road.

Frank Chin

Ground to which access is bottlenecked, where the way out is "tortuous," and where a small enemy force can strike my larger one is called "encircled."

Texas looks like the end of the world to me. Driving in Texas is no fun, nothing to look at, nothing to look for. I might as well be kayaking in the middle of the ocean. Every dead armadillo by the road is an event to the boys in the backseat. But the straight road and flat, skinned, and dried landscape hypnotizes. They're asleep when I drive up on a buzzard that lifts its head outside the bloody open body of a rabbit, and snaps its wings and muscles a few beats, and is up and over the car, slipping its shadow over the hood as I miss the rabbit. Redbeard grunts and nods his head once, as if meaning had happened.

"Why run over a dead rabbit?" I say, answering his grunt.

"Why not run over a dead rabbit?" Redbeard asks. "It's my car."

If the army is confused and suspicious, neighboring rulers will cause trouble. This is what is meant by the saying, "A confused army leads to another's victory."

The Ph.D. candidates want to spend the night over in El Paso so they can go whoring in Juarez. I advise them to stash their wads of money someplace safe, this side of the border, before looking for cheap nookie in Mexico. They shoot me a look of contempt and resentment. After getting hotel rooms, I leave them and go out sniffing for the Chinatown action, following clues collected from the letters of Diego Chang, the Chinaman king of gringo flamenco now in the Air Force servicing F-105 Thunderstreaks, in Oklahoma. I follow his nose to an El Paso class Chinese restaurant with a large wooden Kwan Kung watching the door, a nice dragon and phoenix on the back wall, and an owner with wild-eyed generosity for out-of-

Talking to Sun Tzu

town Chinamen and beautiful daughters serving drinks, tending bar, and waiting tables. Blum finds me there. His look says it all. He needs me to help him rescue Hay, the other white poli sci whiz.

We find Hay, and he's drunk, angry, ashamed. He didn't know what he was doing. He didn't want us to know he was a virgin; then his first fuck turns out to be a blow job from a twelve-year-old girl. He came in her mouth. She was only twelve; he shakes his head. "What kind of life is that for a twelve-year-old girl, sucking dick all night long?"

"What if she was fifteen?" I ask. "That make it okay?"

"What has age got to do with it?"

"Okay, age means nothing. What if she was twenty-eight?" I shout hard into his face. "You went in there to stick your dick into a whore's mouth. You crossed the border to break *Yanqui* law and do immoral dirty things you wouldn't want your mother to know about. So what's her age got to do with anything?"

"He'd *feel* better if she'd been older. Let's have a little consideration for his feelings. All right with you?" Blum says.

"So if you came in the mouth of a twenty-eight-year-old woman or a thirty-year-old, that would have made it a real orgasm for you? You don't think the twenty-eight-year-old whore was once twelve? You should be happy you were one of the first thousand to come in her face, man. Who knows, maybe you were in the first ten. Or the very first!"

"This isn't what going to the whorehouse was supposed to be like."

"Wow, think of it, man. It was your shot of cream down her throat that taught her what it was all about!" I say, and he goes crazy enough to justify me punching him in the face in the film noir about me, but Redbeard pulls me away.

"We have to rescue her," the Crushed Cherry says. "Pool our money! Buy her from the whorehouse!"

Frank Chin

To stop him screaming and attracting attention to us stupid gringos, I say, "You're right! Let's get the car and go rescue her."

I get in the back with the liberals, close the door, and tell Redbeard to head for El Paso, it's past our bedtime. Mr. Crushed Cherry says, "Wait! You said . . . ," lurches forward, and I put my left hand against my right fist and batter him in the solar plexus with the right elbow hard. He gasps and crumples. I rip his sweater off and tie his wrists to his ankles with it, like hog-tying a steer at the rodeo. I sit on his lap, and stick a ballpoint pen, clicker end first, up his left nostril, and click the point out, and click it in. "You be cool, and just shuddup. We're not going to kidnap a Mexican twelve-year-old and take her into the United States, and I am not giving up my Christmas vacation in Cuba! You two have been endangering my ass ever since we pulled up to the first gas station with segregated rest rooms. Stop it! This is the South, boys. This white-and-orange Chevy with California plates is no place to hide. You two don't talk like local good old boys. You don't look local either. If you want to get to Miami in time to catch our plane, save the desegregation of the South till after you get back from Cuba.

There are tears in their eyes. Crushed Cherry weeps. Thin snot slinks shiny out of his nose down the barrel of the ballpoint pen onto my fingers. Blum weeps too. He looks at me as if I'd hit him in the eyes.

The ultimate in disposing one's troops is to be without discernible shape. Then the most penetrating spies cannot pry in, nor can the wise lay plans against you.

Iowa City in the late spring is hot and muggy. There's a view of the Woolworth's under the long red-and-gold Woolworth sign across the street I'm not looking at. My eyes are closed. The gauze curtains aren't wafting. I'm sleeping on top

Talking to Sun Tzu

of my bed in the daytime, three floors up, with all the doors and windows open, in my holey T-shirt and holey jockey shorts, trying to keep cool. My feet are toward the door. My head near an open window. I fall asleep imagining a breeze coming up the stairs, through the open door, and crossing all the little piggies bulging on my feet, and up my body, and out the window. The tall poetry workshop grad student downstairs plays blues guitar and has family all over Iowa City. He took me by his grandmother's house, and she kicked me out. He had never thought of his grandmother as a white racist. "Maybe she thought I was an Indian," I say, not sure what just happened.

I wake up to a fourteen-year-old white girl and her fourteen-year-old girlfriend kneeling at the side of my bed staring at my hard-on through the holes in my jockey shorts. They don't notice me open my eyes. They're looking at my dick like it's a hand puppet and it's talking to them. They just walked in my open door while I was asleep, sat down, and stared at my dick. Two little white girls in Iowa City.

"What have you done to my dick!" I sit up screaming. "How'd it get so big? Oh, no! No! It's all stiff! It won't move! What am I going to do with my big dick sticking out like that? How'm I going to piss? You've fucked up my dick! My poor dick!"

They run downstairs to the poetry workshop grad student who plays blues guitar. The dark-haired girl is his cousin. The girls anxiously tell him everything they've seen like they've been on a field trip to study the dick of the animal upstairs. What if I hadn't woken up when I did? What did wake me up? It's hot and muggy. I lay back down on top of the bed and go to sleep.

The five winners:
One who knows when it's time to fight and when it's not will be victorious.

Frank Chin

One who knows how to use both large and small forces will be victorious.

One whose ranks are united in purpose will be victorious.

One who is prudent, and lies in wait for an enemy who is not, will be victorious.

One whose generals are able and not interfered with by the sovereign will be victorious.

In New Orleans the liberals in the back want to spend a day watching the National Guard protect Negro children integrating the junior high school—and catch the sights. They buy film for their cameras and talk about protection from tear gas. I tell them again, We have out-of-state plates. We ride in a car that stands out. We stand out. I am not white. When they start a riot at the junior high school, I don't want to be anywhere around. They ask me if I am a latent white racist, a lackey of the imperialist oppressor.

"I am the Lone Chinaman is what I am. Mr. Supervisible! Even after you run off and melt into a crowd of whites, redneck peckerwoods they may be, but still white enough for you to disappear, they can find me. So drop me someplace, and I'll meet you the morning after tomorrow, and we'll travel on to Miami again," I say.

"What you're trying to say is, 'When in Rome, do as the Romans do.'"

"That should be your tactic, man," I say. "You can pass. Me, I don't look like any Roman to these fucking Romans."

They drop me off at a corner in the French Quarter. We agree to meet on this same corner at eight in the morning day after tomorrow.

Apparent confusion is a product of good order; apparent cowardice, of courage; apparent weakness, of strength.

Welcome to New Orleans; it's supper time, and dark. I'm hungry, and look into the big front windows of crowded

Talking to Sun Tzu

restaurants, and look at the crowd and what's dripping off their forks and the looks on their faces and the looks of their clothes, and make little decisions about what looks like a place where I can afford to eat and what place looks like it serves food that won't scare my stomach. I walk into a restaurant down in the fish market, and the white boys aren't with me to make it easy on the management. I look from side to side and see the many faces at the white counter look up and the few faces at the black counter look up and don't know which side to sit on. I wait between the black side to my left and the white side to my right, and I wait and wait, and make a step toward the white side. The white woman watching me crackles into motion, shaking her head, nodding at her white customers, who nod at me, as she shuffles out from behind the counter wiping her hands on a kitchen towel. "What do you want?" she asks as if we've been arguing for hours and is really sick of it.

"I want to sit down and buy myself dinner," I say in the same tone and accent, and it's too late to say I didn't mean it, I don't mean to make fun.

"Well you know better 'n to try and eat on this side of the restaurant. Go on over to the other side. They'll be happy to see to you over there," she says in a tone that tells me they won't be that happy to see me at all.

A black man with white in his hair looks up from his food when I sit at the counter. "Shit!" he shouts, throws his spoon on the floor, gets off his stool, and walks out. I do not offer to pay his abandoned bill. Some of the customers are insulted. Do they think I'm trying to pass for colored? Do they think I'm white? I order the deep-fried catfish. The catfish fillet is hot and flaky inside, a hot blobular doughnut. Canned peas and carrots. French fries. Lemonade. When the waitress drifts past me, I ask the way to the rest room. The dishwasher lifts his hands out of the water and says he'll show me. I'm grate-

Frank Chin

ful for the company. I would hate to insult and surprise sensitive Negroes standing at the urinals in the colored rest room. It is cold. We stand at urinals next to each other and piss. I think that's pretty friendly.

He tells me he makes fourteen to eighteen dollars a week. He wants to save up enough money to buy a good suit and get something for his mother, then join the navy. Yeah, when things get better, I'm leaving you, Ma. I'll buy you a new coat so you'll be warm. I know that movie. But he says he wants to live as a navy ascetic, save his money, and come back. "Why?" I ask. "You say Louisiana is a hard place for Negroes. Life is a constant insult. So why don't you leave when you leave, man?"

"I don't want to leave. I can't leave. This is my home!" he says. I've never had his sense of home.

Nothing is more difficult than the art of maneuver. What is difficult about maneuver is to make the devious route the most direct and to turn misfortune to advantage.

Outside again, walking in what they call the French Quarter, I feel like I'm in Chinatown Frisco with a few lights out. I'm still hungry. I don't savor whatever it is I ate at the fish market. Around the French Quarter I look into storefront restaurants with whites and blacks sitting at tables eating together. Gay joints. The food looks good. The prices on the menu are reasonable. I choose one and eat like a king.

I step into a near empty bar across the street for a drink and to sketch the front window of the restaurant worth remembering for the food. A woman in a little tight dress with lots of buttons down the front and a fake fur coat feels my leg and asks me to buy her a drink and she'll show me a little tit. I say, "I'll be glad to buy you a drink and happy to look at any tit you want to show. But I'm a poor traveler. No money. No ambition. I'm just here for a drink."

Talking to Sun Tzu

"Okay, buy me a beer, and I'll keep you company," she says and watches me sketch over a couple pages of my bound pad. "Do you think you could draw my picture?" she asks.

"Sure, but you see I don't draw things exactly realistic looking. My stuff is a lot of messy stuff herded into some kind of sense," I say. "I have water running around on the page making the paper bumpy and oops! a little pool of water right here, see. And the ink on the pen or brush is unpredictable because it likes to blob up and then plop onto the paper. So I don't draw with any kind of photographic lifelikeness."

"I know what you mean," she says. "I like the way you draw. You have a lot of feeling."

I do a few more sketches of her between sketches of action in the window across the street. She brushes off a white man wanting her attention with a bitchy snarl. I offer to trade her a drawing for her couch for the night. Much to my surprise, she accepts. "Don't get the wrong idea, now. I'm a working girl. All you get is the couch for the night."

"That's all I'm looking for, babe. And all you get from me is drawings. I'm just a poor artist."

"Don't call yourself poor."

"I am poor."

"No, I think you're a very good artist," she says. She thinks more of my drawings than me.

She has a baby and a roommate. I walk the baby, a baby girl, much of the night, and sing her Harry Belafonte's "Banana Boat Song (Day-o)," and put everybody to sleep.

To foresee a victory that the ordinary man can foresee is not the acme of skill.

To triumph in battle and be universally acclaimed expert is not the acme of skill, for to lift an autumn down requires no great strength; to distinguish between the sun and the moon is no test of vision; to hear the thunderclap is no indication of acute hearing.

Frank Chin

The boys have taken off their glasses and are asleep in the backseat with a suitcase and Val Pak making a cushioned wall between them. The night's not over, and I have driven the white-and-orange Chevy out of Mississippi into Alabama, and the South goes on and on. I hate eating with these guys. Every café we stop to eat, sitting on the white side because they're white, they talk loud about the stupidity of the place, the boorishness of segregated rest rooms, the ickiness of the South, as if everyone in the South is deaf. I'm tired of telling them to cool it and have them bring me back takeout while I wait in the car and listen to the radio and see if we made the news.

The ultimate in disposing one's troops is to be without ascertainable shape. Then the most penetrating spies cannot pry in, nor can the wise lay plans against you.

The radio is sucking Wolfman Jack's fifty thousand mighty pirate watts out of the night from Del Rio, Texas, he says, and I'm alone at last, and don't have to rubberize my nerves against anyone saying something stupid, and can breathe. Redbeard opens his eyes next to me and looks over his shoulder for a look at the boys sleeping in the back. "Frank, I've been thinking about what you've been saying, and how you talk to people, and I have to say, I like your style," Redbeard says. "You give good advice on how to travel when you're on a mission."

"A mission?"

"So to speak," Redbeard says. "You know what I mean. I haven't had four years of college like these fellas, but you know what I mean."

"So to speak," I say.

"Well, I don't mean to get personal or pry into your personal business, but I feel you're the kind of man I don't mind telling. I've been a card-carrying member of the Party for three years now."

Talking to Sun Tzu

It is according to the shapes that I lay the plans for victory, but the multitude does not comprehend this. Although everyone can see the outward aspects, none understands the way in which I have created victory.

One night in Iowa City I pass the pizza parlor and start across the alley to pass under the marquee of the local neon bijou that extends out over the sidewalk, on my way home, and five big, big Iowa boys step out of the alley and surround me. "We're going to beat the shit out of you," the leader says.

"You'd better hurry up because I have someone waiting for me at home," I say. I look at his chest. I keep my hands down and open, my shoulders loose.

"You keep talking like that, I'm going to knock your head off," the biggest of the big guys says.

"Well, I wish you'd hurry up and do it, so I can be on my way. All right?" I say, and am ears away, and hear myself pumping crazy. My teeth feel hard and full of radar. My eyes seem to throw light on what I'm looking at. Their hands. Their feet. Their hips. Their eyes.

"Do you know why we're going to beat the shit out of you?" the leader asks.

"Oh, there's a reason why?" I say. "Sure, tell me why." And the fighting fire's gone cold. They're listening. They're thinking. They're not punching and kicking me.

"You said you were going to beat the shit out of us," the leader says.

I laugh. People inside the pizza parlor stand inside the glass door and watch. They won't come out. The movie lets out, and nobody steps out beyond the marquee. "I said I was going to beat you up? Even if I said that, you believed me?" I say. "How much do you weigh?" I ask the six-foot-two leader.

"Two fifty," he says.

"I weigh a hundred and forty," I say. I look around at each

guy in the eye. "You all weigh at least two hundred each, right? You all have fifty or sixty pounds over me, right? Yeah, I can see how just the thought of a one hundred and forty pound kid jumping the five of you guys really kept you all up late at night with the cold sweats, I bet."

I give them no reason to move. I stand and talk. They talk back. I keep the talk simple, in friendly simple sentences, try to be funny and keep them listening and standing till police cars twirling their red lights screech up to the alley from both ends of the street. The door to the pizza parlor opens, and people stream out. The crowd under the marquee of the movie house moves. I fade into the crowd between the cops and am gone before the five guys notice.

Therefore, when I have won a victory, I do not repeat my tactics but respond to circumstances in an infinite variety of ways.

There are hundreds of students in the airport, from all over the country, milling around the Cubana Airlines counter. A group of anti-Castro Cubans heckles us as we line up with our letters and receipts from the Fair Play for Cuba Committee at the Cubana Airlines desk. An American tourist steps in line wearing a fatigue uniform complete with combat boots. Cubana Airlines officials take him aside and ask him to change his clothes. I say good-bye to the liberals, and tell them to keep away from me and not to look me up in Berkeley afterward, and lose them in the crowd.

I travel light. A zip bag with a change of jeans, a sweatshirt, three T-shirts, a shirt, and three pairs of socks. In an olive-drab army-surplus gas-mask bag, I carry a Chinese inkstick and inkstone, a plastic bottle for water, a cheap set of Japanese watercolors in a little wooden box, a wad of rags, and the Spanish textbook. I plan to come back with more than I'm taking in. Two guitars more. One for me. One to sell.

Talking to Sun Tzu

I get a seat on a plane that carries none of the guys I rode with across the country. Cubana flies me over in a twin-engined turbo-prop Convair.

Off the plane in Havana, we're herded into a glass-walled warehouse-sized room where an American speaking as a tour boss tells us we will be traveling in twenty-five buses and lays down the rules and describes details of the tour I don't like at all. There are no guitar shops on the itinerary. No flamenco. No Chinatown. No raw, unprocessed, unrehearsed Cubans. The tour boss tells us to form lines in front of the row of desks for processing by Cuban customs and a short interrogation by men in green fatigues. I hang back and watch to see how the others get through and which interrogators work fast and which don't. I follow the tour boss at a distance through the crowd to see who she talks to and who talks to her. And see who's here. A few act like celebrities of some kind. Poets? Writers?

The uniforms and the guns catch my eye. On the other side of the glass, where Cuba begins, everyone carries an M-1 carbine or a side arm. I unlimber my pad, ink, and water and sketch with brush and stick, looking for action, looking for someone who looks like he wants to get away from this tour as much as I do, who speaks Spanish. I haven't learned enough Spanish crossing the country in Redbeard's Chevy to try anything out loud.

The nine variables:
  In low-lying ground: do not make camp.
  In communicating ground: unite with your allies.
  In desolate ground: do not linger.
  In enclosed ground: you'd better be a genius.
  In death ground: fight.
  There are some roads not to follow; some troops not to strike; some cities not to assault; and some ground that should not be contested.

Frank Chin

I meet Leon in the crowd of tourists waiting for some kind of processing in Havana. He is blond, pale, thin. He speaks Spanish and knows Latin American history, country by country. He is tall, skinny, and more obnoxious than me without bullshit in several languages. He is happy I notice and tells me he is a little irritated at me not recognizing him from Barnhart's political science class, the Edward N. Barnhart of tenBroek, Barnhart, and Matson, authors of *War, Prejudice, and the Constitution*. I only notice him now because he speaks Spanish like a Cuban. I just want to use him.

"You're right, I tell him. I want to use you. And you can use me," I say. "They plan to load us in twenty-five buses and haul us around Cuba like freight. I want to get out and on my own till it's time to catch the plane home. And you do too, but you don't have the balls to do it on your own, and I don't have the Spanish. Follow me, and we shall see Cuba and meet Cubans. We'll have an adventure!"

When the troops continually gather in small groups and whisper together, the general has lost the confidence of the army.

I look up from sloshing water on a page of my big bound book of blank white drawing paper and see a man shorter than me, chunkier than me, in a light blue denim shirt and blue trousers, what looks like the uniform at some juvenile detention camps. But he wears a web belt, and a leather holster with a military .45 automatic in it hangs from the belt. He's no prisoner. The black beret he wears like an artist is part of his uniform. He motions me to the glass wall and points to the crack between the locked double doors. He lowers his head on his side, and I lower my head and put my ear to the crack on my side. He asks to see my drawings. I hold the pad up and flip the pages. "I am an artist, too," he says. He waves to the soldier in green fatigues stepping up to tap me on the shoulder. I step away, and the soldier bends to the short man's

Talking to Sun Tzu

mouth. The soldier takes me away, gets an officer, and takes me back to the short man in the black beret and two-tone blue. After a short conversation at the crack between the locked doors, the officer unlocks the doors and lets the short man in.

"Hello," the short man says in English. "Are you from People's China? I notice you are using Chinese brushes and Chinese ink. I, too, am an artist. I was a commercial artist before the Revolution. Now I am a captain in the militia and chief of a group of artists for the Revolution."

"People's China? No, I'm an American from the United States. My ancestry is Chinese."

"I understand perfectly," he says. "I ask too many questions. But as one artist to another, in the spirit of brotherhood around the world, I would like to trade you one of my drawings for one of yours."

"I would be honored, *usted*, . . ." I say, attempting a word of Spanish, and already it's wrong.

"Oh, no more *usted* in Cuba. The language is now without class distinctions. Everything is the *tu*, the familiar, brotherly form. The Cuban Revolution is total."

"Artist to artist, brother to brother, I would like to escape this tour and see the simple Cuba. Visit a guitarmaker's shop and perhaps buy a guitar or two, go to a flamenco club."

"And see the spot where they shot Hemingway's *Old Man and the Sea*."

"Ah, my friend James Wong Howe, a Hollywood Chinese, photographed that movie."

"It is a beautiful place to sketch. Especially for someone who uses watercolor washes and pen and ink like you."

It is the business of a general to be serene and inscrutable, impartial and self-controlled.

He should be capable of keeping his officers and men in ignorance of his plans.

Frank Chin

He prohibits superstitious practices and so rids the army of doubts. Then until the moment of death there can be no trouble.

I open the window of the bus on the way into Havana and get my first whiff of Cuba. The land, the breath of the jungle, smells like aged venison and rye whiskey. I can smell the land crawling with life. I want to breathe this air through my mouth and chew it and swallow it, maybe carve it up into loaves and bake it.

The Fair Play for Cuba Committee tour is being housed by the state at the Riviera Hotel and Casino. Half a blue angel food high-rise layer cake with two king-size beds in every huge room, a bathroom larger than a room at Motel Six, with a bidet and two double-size sinks besides the flush toilet, the tub and shower combination, and the first Jacuzzi I have ever seen. Leon knows the history of the place. Built by Meyer Lansky, Jewish gangland power behind Lucky Luciano in New York and gambling czar of Cuba with Batista in his pocket. The Riviera was the jewel in Lanksy's Cuban money machine. After registering and dumping our stuff in the room, we ride down to the lobby and look into the big casino room. The dealers and croupiers and floor managers stand at parade rest at their gaming tables. No one, not one person, is playing anything tonight. If the Cubans are looking to the Fair Play for Cuba Committee tour as a gambling junket, they are going to be disappointed, I think.

The next day the artist picks us up in his Studebaker and takes us to a little coffee stand not far from the hotel for coffee and a pastry breakfast. The sky shines. The sea shines. The air is juicy, a kind of breathable cheese, and brighter than real. I sketch the stand and the shoe-shine stand next to it for an hour or more. The artist militia captain is in no hurry. Leon learns that the Russian Folk Ballet is housed in the little hotel across the street. Yes, the captain has tickets for us to tomorrow night's performance. Cojimar, where Jimmie Wong Howe

Talking to Sun Tzu

shot *Old Man and the Sea* and got the Oscar for color photography, is beautiful water I don't know how to paint or draw. I scratch flesh and bone, nerves and human weight, with brush and pen all over my paper, and sometimes in a little blotchy thing with a few scrawls of the pen is the beginning and end of a face. Architecture and the sea are beyond me.

After a couple of hours peering around, astounded by the sea and the light, we drive back into Havana and meet Gavilán at his guitar shop. He is not only a guitarmaker but a fine guitar player. He smokes dark tobacco Partagas cigarettes and plays a *requinta*, a guitar cut off at the fifth fret, a little short-necked high-tinkling machine. Friends hang about the dimly lit shop, bitching about the government it sounds like to me. Leon plays it cool, listens to the music, and smiles. I play several guitars, trade a few flamenco licks with Gavilán. I buy the best guitar I can for $90.00, and a case for $20.00 for my friend back in Berkeley, and say I'll be back tomorrow to play some more.

"And tomorrow after the Russian Folk Ballet we'll all go to a flamenco club," Gavilán says.

The militia captain artist lets us off back at the Riviera around supper time. We'll meet here at about this time tomorrow to go to the Russian Folk Ballet and have dinner afterward at the flamenco club.

We follow the desk clerk's directions to the letter and get to Chinatown Havana by bus. In downtown Havana, where we are waiting to change busses, I see all the men in green fatigues and blue militia uniforms on the streets, window-shopping or walking the mains with their girlfriends, and families, carrying guns. They carry tinny black machine guns and lots of M-1 carbines with clips taped together; all kinds of pistols and revolvers hang along their legs in leather holsters. I feel us catch in their eyes, and they nod and smile back when I nod and smile. Most glance over us and pretend not to see

Frank Chin

that Leon and I do stand out in this crowd. We are obviously not of Cuba. I get the feeling we make them feel embarrassed about the guns in their hands and on their belts. They would rather let us act like fools, run around snatching purses and picking pockets, than shoot us. "Arming the masses has made the mob humble and tolerant," Leon says.

"Be cool about quoting Gabby Hayes out loud in public places, man," I say. "We play stupid friendly tourist."

"Did Gabby Hayes say, 'Arming the masses has made the mob humble and tolerant?'" Leon asks.

"Yeah, man. *Sagebrush Buccaneers!* Roy and Dale tie bundles of dynamite onto the pack saddles of a mess of donkeys, man, remember? Roy lights the slow-burning fuses and sends those donkeys mingling with the mob grumbling around the jail, right?" I say. "And the mob disperses, and calm is restored. And Gabby Hayes turns to Roy Rogers and says—"

"'Arming them asses has made the mob humble and tolerant.'" Leon says.

"See, I knew you've seen that movie."

The experts in defense conceal themselves as under the ninefold earth; those skilled in attack move as from above the ninefold heavens. Thus they are capable both of protecting themselves and of gaining a complete victory.

There's a statue to the Chinese who fought in the revolution against the Spaniards. Before the Revolution against Batista Chinatown Havana was second only to Chinatown San Francisco. Now the Chinese are gone. The lights of the electric signs are off. The town looks dark. Everyone seems hiding from me.

Thus a victorious army wins its victories before seeking battle; an army destined to defeat fights in the hope of winning.

Talking to Sun Tzu

The good restaurants are closed forever, the old men above a closed good restaurant tell me in Cantonese. The floor is without inner walls. Pillars hold up the roof. Factory lamps hang from chains high over the floor. It's like a factory floor stripped bare of rows of looms or sewing machines or tables where people rolled cigars. A few old men look like things left behind and forgotten. They sit scattered over the floor, grouped around empty five-gallon cans. The empty lard and cooking oil cans catch the spills and squirts from large-mouthed two-foot-long bamboo water pipes the old men load with coarse tobacco and smoke.

I don't see any bowls, dishes, chopsticks. No evidence of food. I see teacups. There are thermos bottles of tea. Strange to see no food. The owners of the good restaurants fled the country with their money before their restaurants could be nationalized by the Revolution. The best Cuban Chinese restaurants are in New York and New Orleans now, the old men say. The best restaurant still open is the Mariposa.

The Mariposa is a classic greasy spoon in plate-glass walls. The big U-shaped counter is covered with linoleum. It is the first Chinese greasy suey I have seen with an espresso machine. The menu Spanish for Chinese food I've only eaten in American English is a surprise to my stomach. Suddenly I am more comfortable speaking Spanish than Cantonese or English. After serving Leon and me tea the waiters stay away from us and whisper to each other in the doorway to the kitchen.

A little sliding door between the kitchen and the dining room opens up, and a potbellied sixtyish Chinaman with thin, graying hair looks out at me as he washes his arms, changes his undershirt, combs his hair, blows his nose, puts on a thin short-sleeved white shirt, and closes the sliding door before he steps out of the kitchen through the doorway and goes and sits behind the cash register without passing close to me. He watches me from the cash register. A waiter goes to the cash

Frank Chin

register and makes a show of telling the sixtyish man, the obvious boss, in loud Cantonese that I speak Cantonese, and I speak Spanish with a North American accent, and Leon speaks Spanish like a Cuban but looks like a Russian. The old man nods and picks up the phone. I raise my hand and in loud Spanish say, "Let's order up and get to eating!"

Leon snaps out of his tropical reverie and steam trip and doesn't know how to say he wonders what I just said. "They think we're some kind of spies. Yankees posing as Chinese and Russians. He's calling the cops."

"Oh."

"Let's order up. They won't let us get arrested before we pay up. And I'm not paying for anything I don't eat," I say.

We catch a bus, any bus, back, and I recognize nothing outside the windows. The bus is full. People ride standing in the aisles. I rehearse the Spanish I'll use to ask which bus we should take to get back to the Riviera Hotel, look around for a friendly face, and ask a thin man standing in the aisle. I reduce the problem of getting back to the hotel to the simplest question I have a chance of asking in Spanish and being understood. Pardon me. I'm looking for the Riviera Hotel. Can you help me? "Con permiso, señor. Yo busco el Hotel Riviera. Puede usted ayudarme?"

"Eres China Popular? Are you from People's China?" the skinny man says, and waves his hands, and turns round and round shouting, "Stop the bus! Stop the bus! We have two students from our sister People's Republics of China and the Soviet Union. They have lost their way in our beautiful city of Havana. It is our patriotic duty and honor to help these foreign students who have come to help us!"

Now the elements of the art of war are, first, measurement of space; second, estimation of quantities; third, calculations; fourth, comparisons; and, fifth, chances of victory.

Talking to Sun Tzu

The bus squishes to a stop, and people mob us. They hand us books and pieces of paper and ask for our autographs. They ask if I am from People's China and won't believe I come from the USA, from California. They are sure Leon is a blond Russian. He speaks Russian when the one Russian speaker on the bus aims Russian his way. He enjoys the confusion the pair of us inspire. No, we are not from People's China and the Soviet Union. "Of course! Of course!" the Cuban who stopped the bus says. "You are no China Popular and USSR. Weee understaaaaand!" he says with a bow.

A short balding man in a dark suit, white shirt, and no tie says to get off the bus at the next stop, where he will wait to see us onto the right bus bound for the Riviera Hotel. Leon takes over speaking for the both of us, thanks the man, and we follow him off, waving at the people on the bus like freaks. He motions us to the counter. He doesn't seem to understand Leon's Spanish, even as he answers Leon. He orders *café con leche* for the three of us, and the man in the light inside the stand sets an espresso-cappuccino machine hissing and guzzling.

Of the five elements, none is always predominant; of the four seasons, none lasts forever; of the days, some are long and some short; and the moon waxes and wanes.

The bus stop is by a corner coffee stand. The short man is nervous. I wonder if he's carrying a gun, if he's Cuban fuzz. Perhaps he wonders if we are some kind of secret police, a test of his faith. The street is lit and dark. We seem to be the only people on foot in this part of town. Out of the dark walks a wiry young man bare chested under a windbreaker jacket. He looks me in the eye as he walks toward me. I step closer to the counter, thinking I'm in his way, and turn to read the signs over the espresso machine. He taps me on the shoulder. I turn, not knowing what to expect.

Frank Chin

"Eres existencialista?" he asks. "Are you an existentialist?"

"Yes, of course, I'm an existentialist," I answer.

"Me too. I'm an existentialist!" he says, "My name is Justo. I want to buy you a cup of coffee and a cigar."

"From one existentialist to another," I say.

"I, too, am an existentialist," Leon says.

"Of course, I buy coffee and cigar for you too," Justo says, shaking Leon's hand. Then to me, "Are you from People's China?"

"No," I say.

"Are you from USSR?" Justo the existentialist asks Leon.

"Also, no," Leon answers.

"I am the national kayak champion of Cuba," Justo says. He points to the crossed paddle insignia on his windbreaker.

"Did he say 'national kayak champion of Cuba'?" I ask Leon in English. The world has been a very funny, very odd, twitching and swooning western movie with fifties cars all around me since I don't speak Spanish in a Spanish-speaking world.

"Yes, that is what the existentialist said," Leon says. Even to Leon, who speaks Spanish and processes his languages fast, the idea of a national kayak champion of Cuba is unexpected.

We thank the dapper little man in the double-breasted suit for his help and the coffee, and let him catch the next bus home to his wife, and hang out with Justo the existential kayak champion of Cuba. Justo takes us home to his apartment, where he lives with his mother, sister, and a couple of little brothers. His mother serves us thin pieces of round steak, beaten even thinner and fried, ripe plantains, potatoes, and sliced green tomatoes and onions with oil and vinegar. A feast. The apartment looks like nothing unexpected in a modern concrete building; then I offer to wash the dishes, and Justo tells me there's no sewer, no plumbing, no water in the building.

Talking to Sun Tzu

Justo makes what he calls "the Cuban rocket" out of a paper match, an unfolded paper clip, and a bit of foil from the lining of a cigarette pack. He seals the match head up in foil, and wraps it into the rocket body, and folds out a little fin on the bottom. He leaves a little opening at the bottom, and slips the rocket onto the angled paper clip, and puts a lit match under the rocket. The match head inside ignites and burns slowly, rocketing the little foil thing across the room with a little sniffing sound. We all laugh and applaud.

He rides us back to the Riviera on the buses and asks if he can have a look at our room. He has never been inside the Riviera before. A little clutch of Americans is playing something in the casino. It's a party in the lobby. The elevator to the fourteenth floor is full of tipsy American girls who leap on Justo as soon as we introduce him. They follow him to our room, start a party, fill our room with women, and disappear with Justo.

Justo walks back through our open door bare chested and shaking his head. "I didn't know she was a virgin," he says. "We have a saying here. He who takes it, pays for it."

"We have that same saying North America," Leon says.

"So you gave her your Kayak Club jacket?" I ask.

"I wouldn't have done it if I'd known she was a virgin," Justo says. "I thought she was experienced. She acted like she was experienced."

"I thought you were an existentialist," I say. "Come on. Albert Camus. She's *The Stranger*. She's not in love. She's horny. You are a gratuitous act. Forget it. She has."

"Maybe I'm in love with her!" Justo says, beating his chest.

"Maybe you are drunk, my friend," Leon says.

Justo falls out on a couch. Leon flops on the king-size closest to the window. I step out to check the action in the lobby and on the other floors and find nothing but Americans chasing Americans, Americans chasing Cubans, and various ide-

Frank Chin

alogues, gurus, and ultra people holding court in their signature symbolic hats, gloves, earrings, moustaches, and style. Justo pops awake around six and wakes us up to thank us. He has to get to work. I give him a white shirt to wear out of here and ask him to come downstairs to the dining room to have a decadent North American–style gut-busting greasy breakfast with me. Link sausage, or ham or bacon, or a hamburger patty or a steak and eggs, fried, poached, shirred, scrambled, or omeletted. Fried potatoes, grits, toast, English muffin, the works. "You have to start the day with a good breakfast, man," I say.

But, no. He has to run. He seems afraid of me and Leon. I fade back to sleep for a couple of hours.

It is because of disposition that a victorious general is able to make his people fight with the force of suddenly released pent-up waters plunging down into a bottomless abyss.

The guitar shop is all soft worn wooden edges. The air smells and feels like old leather and hot hide glue, with a hint of turpentine. Gavilán is a good guitarist and today is more interested in playing than building or repairing guitars. Tomorrow Leon and I bus off to Trinidád to see a country town on the other coast of Cuba. To see a bit of the old Cuba. Cuba before modernization. We'll be gone for about a week. I tell Gavilán I'll buy a flamenco from him if he can have it made and ready to travel in a week.

"Of course, I can," he says. "Five hundred dollars."

"I am prepared to pay only three hundred," I say, and spread the money out on the little table by his right elbow. We finally settle on three fifty. He is a very generous man. He buys all the coffee we drink and treats me and Leon to lunch. Captain Artist meets us at the guitar shop, and Leon and I ride in his old Studebaker. Gavilán follows with his wife in his old Buick.

Talking to Sun Tzu

We have standing room along the left wall of the auditorium at the Russian Folk Ballet. I recognize the Fair Play for Cuba Committee people in the front and center sections of the theater. Two balconies above us are full of cheering people. I am where everybody claps and shouts for everything. Every act does two or three encores.

At the flamenco club I drink too much wine and eat paella till my face is hot. I play on the flamenco guitarist's second guitarist's guitar. It is a flamenco with cypress sides and back and a nice spruce top, an exact copy of a Ramírez made by Gavilán. Of course. Gavilán is showing off his work.

The guitar is six years old and plays very well. Gavilán and the second guitarist begin clapping, and I'm committed to playing my bit of fifties Frisco gringo flamenco *bulerías* out and hope I don't fuck it up. I don't seem to for here comes the club maestro joining in and trading verses to test me. It's *bulerías*. It's fun. Gavilán has brought along another guitar. "Try this one," he says. "This one is mine."

I pass the second guitarist's guitar back to the young guitarist and take up the guitar Gavilán holds precariously over the table of rice and saffron chicken and shrimp stew. It isn't a new guitar. It isn't a copy of a Ramírez. Cypress sides and back. Tight, tight pinstripe spruce top. Gavilán has also brought his *requinta,* and we all capo at the fifth fret. The club maestro, the young second guitarist, Gavilán, and I have played for the dancers, played for the singers, played for each other for a little more than an hour when the artist militia captain says it is time for us to get back to the Riviera.

Around midnight Leon and I walk over to the corner coffee stand and find it open and full of the Russian Folk Ballet. The roundly muscled blonde dancer with blonde hair in her armpits is sweaty in a blouse at the bar. The night is hot and humid. Leon speaks a little Russian. They speak no English,

Frank Chin

no Cantonese, and their Spanish is as unintelligible as mine. I strike up a conversation with the man next to the sweaty blonde. He is a thin man in a tailored double-breasted dark blue suit. We draw cartoons and doodle on napkins and point at pictures of postcards to accomplish a kind of conversation. He buys Leon and me a beer. I buy a round of beer for the dancers. The bartender pries the caps off the bottles of warm beer with pops and fizzes, to loud wordless cheers. The blonde wearing her hair in braids goes ahhh at the bottle of beer pressed into her hand. She looks to the man in the double-breasted suit. He tells her I'm buying this round. She catches my waiting eye. I raise my bottle and smile. The thin man makes me understand she wants to know my name. I point to myself and say, "I am Frank Chin."

She takes a rose from the bouquet at her left elbow, looks me in the eye and sniffs the bud, and hands it to me and says something in Russian that ends with her saying my name and giving me a kiss on the air between us. I have seen this movie, too.

When campaigning, sweep like a sudden wind; march as majestic as the forest; raid and plunder like fire. Stand as rooted as the mountains and unfathomable as the clouds. Move like a thunderbolt.

At breakfast in the Riviera's dining room someone at the next table has a newspaper and says, "We should have been at the flamenco club last night. They say an agricultural expert from People's China enchanted everyone by playing passionate flamenco guitar."

Catch a bus into the mountains, to Trinidád, a little town on the other side of the island in the Santa Clara Mountains.

We sit at the restaurant where the bus drops us, and two young men having beers a few tables over ask if they can buy us a beer. They wear short-sleeved shirts and khaki trousers, combat boots. They each carry a small holster on their belts under their shirts. Leon invites them to sit.

"Eres China Popular?" one asks.

"No," I say, "I am not from People's China. I am a literature student in North America."

They are two lieutenants in the army and would be honored to buy us lunch. No. No, we can't allow that. Is Leon from the Soviet Union? No, we say. They say they understand perfectly. They say their uncle is just back from seventy-two days of fighting counterrevolutionaries in the jungle. The officers are having a party for him at his house on the edge of town. He would like to meet us, the lieutenants say. Why don't we accompany them right now?

"We heard in Havana there was no more counterrevolutionary action," Leon says innocently.

"Propaganda for the city," one of the lieutenants says. "You understand."

"We haven't settled into a hotel yet," I say. "I want to get my stuff put away, change my shirt, and wash a little after the bus trip. Then we'll be happy to go party with your uncle."

The lieutenants walk us to the hotel and do all the talking with the desk clerk. We take two rooms that turn out to be two corner suites. High ceilings. Ceiling fans. Arched doorways. A sitting room with a fireplace. A bedroom. A small bathroom. A balcony overlooking the street. My room is a movie set. I can't wait to get back to it, hear how the $90.00 Gavilán guitar I bought sounds here, and be me about my room in Cuba, in *The Movie about Me.* Maybe I'll stay here a month.

Those who do not know the conditions of mountains and forests, hazardous defiles, marshes and swamps, cannot conduct the march of an army.

Frank Chin

Those who do not use local guides are unable to obtain the advantages of the ground.

The house is small, whitewashed stucco. The M-1 carbines are piled on a table just inside the dining room. I check my guitar with the carbines. The side arms stay on the hip. We stand looking stupid while the young lieutenants introduce us to the men at the big table. Uncle is a big man with a skinny gigolo moustache and a big black cowboy hat. A big red-skinned poached fish sits right side up on a platter. Men all around Uncle grab pieces of fish with big thick soda crackers and crunch cracker-and-fish sandwiches with lots of beer and lots of rum and Coke. "Sure I speak American," Uncle says, waving us in to sit at his table. "Fuck you!" he says and laughs.

Uncle says he'll take us up the mountain to the officers' club, where the technical commandante is entertaining his girlfriend. He says the technical commandante will want to meet us, and we eat and drink for another hour before we step out into the warm fleshy air and climb into the lieutenants' jeeps. We start up and drive a few yards and stop. A lieutenant jumps out of the front jeep with his carbine and walks up to me riding shotgun in the jeep behind. He asks me to pull my guitar case all the way into the jeep. Sticking out it looks like a gun, he says. I sit the guitar on the floor between my legs and hug the neck. We drive higher and deeper into the Santa Clara Mountains.

Big Uncle Blackhat crashes the technical commandante's party. The technical commandante dances with his girlfriend on an empty dance floor as her mother sits, watches, and knits. An officer wobbles and croaks rhythmically, if not sensibly, at the piano. The technical commandante is also the military commandante of the area. He is a curly-headed, muscular man just an inch or two shorter than me. His wrists are thicker than mine. He seems happy to see us. With a few more people it seems more like a party. There's so much counter-revolutionary activity around the officers don't hang out at the officers' club. No, we are not from People's China and the USSR. No matter, he is happy to see us and wants to show us the secret projects he's built up here in the mountains. It's too late to drive us back to Trinidád, and anyway we would just have to drive back up to the mountains to see his work, so we will spend the night at his work camp, on the site of one of his secret projects.

Ground that both we and the enemy can traverse with equal ease is called "accessible." In such ground, he who first takes high sunny positions convenient to his supply routes can fight advantageously.

The secret projects the technical commandante built look like big freeway intersections to me. Big cement X's laying flat on the ground. I look off into the jungle for some sign of roads coming out from somewhere to hook up with the clover-leaf intersection. Where is the work being done? Turkeys and children walk all over the secret projects, and nobody seems to be doing any building or paving. This seems a very strange way to build roads to me, but who am I to say?

The technical commandante brings us borrowed clothes and boots to change into for a tour of his territory by horseback. We ride out across high meadow, along a river, by his girlfriend's house, by parts of his secret projects I don't understand at all, and back to the big cement X. We climb in his jeep and head to town for lunch.

The commandante walks us through the whole town past every doorway looking for lunch. We cross a square, pass a fountain-birdbath thing in the center, and are climbing a shallow staircase when Arminda grabs my hand. I stop, and she grabs hold with her other hand and smiles into my face. Apple cheeks. Baby fat. Big round breasts in a tight shirt tucked into

Frank Chin

blue jeans. "I'm so happy to see you," she says, as if I'm right on time.

"I'm happy to be here too," I say. "Why don't you join us for lunch?"

"Are you from People's China?"

"Oh, you think I'm from People's China," I say. "I'm sorry to say I am not from People's China."

"Oh, you have to be from People's China. I would be so happy if you were from People's China," Arminda says, explaining the many strange women of Iowa City to me without realizing it. Or are they explaining her? Will she give me my dream if I give her hers?

"Join us for lunch, anyway. This is the technical commandante of the area. And this is Leonardo, my brother student-tourist from Berkeley, California, of the United States. I am Frank."

"I am Arminda. I am a lieutenant in the militia. I was in the Revolution in the mountains when I was fifteen. I recognize the commandante."

Blood and innocence. Leon looks at her as if she's a religious experience. She holds my hand with her two, wishing real hard I am from People's China and not Berkeley, California.

Sun Tzu says: Ground easy to get out of but difficult to return to is entrapping. The nature of this ground is such that if the enemy is unprepared and you sally out, you may defeat him. If the enemy is prepared and you go out and engage but do not win, it is difficult to return. This is unprofitable.

Home in Iowa City is hard to come by. For the first time in my life I am ordered out of a house because I am a China-man. People are very open about despising anyone not white. The only place I can rent is a house. I get the poet to split the house with me. The house is next door to the local commander of the American Legion. He's a Korean War vet. The two things this man hates are Chinese and beatniks. He ties his dog to the front porch of my house. I use the back door. He goes to the university and gets a dean to call me in for violating a university rule against single male students renting single-family dwellings.

The dean tells me I piss out my second-floor window, sleep on the sidewalk, harass my neighbor's dog.

"It's a real shame you're not involved in education. I thought this was a university, not a Nazi police state," I say. My white housemate pulls on my sleeve and in a low voice tells me to calm down.

"I resent that. I have a master's in education," the dean says.

"You didn't ask me if I piss out my second-floor window. You accused me. You didn't ask if I slept on the sidewalk. You told me. What kind of education is that? You learn that as Socratic dialogue in the Gestapo school of education? I resent you!" I say. And when the dean sits up, flashing his stinkeye, I say, "I want you to put the purpose and content of this meeting in writing. I want you to write that rule against me renting a house next door to the local commander of the American Legion down in a letter on university letterhead. And I want you to sign it, please. And then and only then, after consulting with my lawyer, will I consider looking for another place to rent."

"The rule against single male students renting single-family dwellings is to respect the Christian . . . ," the dean babbles.

"Christian! Yeah, be sure to put that down, too. The university takes federal money, right? A land grant university, right? When the feds see you don't separate church and state and discriminate against Chinamen, your federal funds will resent it, too. You do know how to write what you speak, don't you? You're a graduate of a school of education! Come

Frank Chin

on!" I stand and throw down his letter ordering me and my housemate to appear at his office. "This won't do. I resent it," I say. "If I don't hear from you in a week, I will assume this whole matter and your stupid rule are forgotten." I pull my housemate up by his arm and haul him out with me.

"If you're going to go crazy, don't include me next time . . . ," White Blues Guitar says.

"I didn't let him get to the part where he says the Christian rule is against homosexuals. He called us both in. The rule is against single men, not single women, renting a single-family dwelling," I say, and watch him click and think a breath, and say, "I saved you the embarrassment of seeing how crazy I go when a dean calls me a queer just because I'm your friend."

"You really think? . . ."

"We can forget the dean, man," I say. I'm right, but my housemate, the white poet who plays blues guitar, doesn't see the fun and is pissed at me. He moves. I find a married couple to rent the house with me. I never hear from the dean again.

Years later, my Iowa housemate and his wife visit me in Seattle and stay for a year.

Ground equally disadvantageous for both the enemy and ourselves to enter is indecisive. The nature of this ground is such that although the enemy holds out a bait, I do not go forth but entice him by marching off. When I have drawn out half his force, I can strike him advantageously.

Every hundred yards along the curving road up the mountain to the secret town of Meyer, there's a machine-gun nest with an air-cooled thirty-caliber machine gun behind a bunker of sandbags. Every fifty yards a pair of riflemen. All the soldiers at the machine guns and patrolling the spaces in between know the commandante's jeep and the commandante and

Talking to Sun Tzu

wave. He waves. I wave. Leon waves. Arminda waves. I begin to see mortar batteries beside the machine-gun nests. What do they expect to come up this road? I wonder.

If I first occupy constricted ground, I must block the passes and await the enemy. If the enemy first occupies such ground and blocks the defiles, I should not follow him; if he does not block them completely, I may do so.

In the town of Meyer, the secret town. The G-2 military intelligence office is in what looks like a duplex apartment building. A black captain in green fatigues takes all our papers and wallets and doesn't seem to like me at all. He goes off to radio Havana. The shortwave is busy with voices of patrols in the field. The technical commandante assures us everything is fine. He is getting us permission to visit his secret projects, but first we have to get permission from the G-2, but to get permission from the G-2 we have to come to this secret town that we have no permission to visit. Don't worry, he says. I don't worry.

I smoke cigars with the guards. They tell me about planes in crates from the Soviet Union. The militia guards give me a cigar, spread out an army blanket, and disassemble their weapons for me. Their rifle is about as long as the U.S. M-1 Garand, but the gas tube and piston are on top of the barrel and not under it, like the Garand. The bayonet on this rifle folds flat against the front hand grip and is not a separate piece. It takes clips of ammo that click into the underside of the receiver.

They tell me the Skoda machine gun is a killer. They don't like it. If you drop it, it's likely to go off and keep firing and spinning around till it's out of ammo. The captain is in the radio room, on the radio to Havana spelling my name. The guards tell me they have airplanes, bombers in crates. I ask them why keep them in crates when they can take them out and put the wings on. They don't have wings, they tell me.

Frank Chin

Airplanes without wings. I nod knowingly and am sure it is my faulty Spanish.

We move to another apartment, I think for supper with the officers. They tell me to follow the noncom while they talk with Leon.

The noncom is making a little bed, two feet wide, six feet in the closet off the bathroom. Sheets and an olive-drab army blanket. "You won't be here long. The last man we had here wasn't here long." This is the first I hear we are under some kind of arrest and detention.

"How long was that?" I ask.

"Only six months."

"I'll miss my finals," I say. "Are we under arrest?"

"You are under investigation."

"Oh. And the reason why we are being kept here and not in the jail is . . ."

"No one knows where you are."

"No one?"

"No one like your collaborators, for example."

"Oh, them."

"You have collaborators?" The noncom stands up alert.

"No, I thought you might have located some for me," I say, and laugh. "I speak the Spanish of the stupid. My friend Leon outside does all the talking. Where is Leon going to sleep, by the way?"

"This bed is for the both of you," the noncom says.

"Oh, we both sleep on this bed."

"Outside the door will be two guards with machine guns," the noncom says. "The window is very high, and we have barbed wire and traps under the window."

"Keeping us together makes us easier to watch," I say. "I understand." Then ask, "What about Arminda? If she's being detained with us . . ." I catch the look in his eye and smile the rest off.

Talking to Sun Tzu

"We put the girl in the other room."

"Ah, there is another room, just like this."

"Her room is a little more spacious."

"She who is not a foreign spy, but is being detained to keep her from spreading the news of our arrest, gets the big room," I say. "And you hope to woo the secrets of us foreigners by putting two of us in a space designed for less than one. I like your mathematics."

A step from the bed through the door and I'm in the all-tile bathroom. No window. A high skylight and an electric bulb high up the tile walls. Sit on the toilet, and look up, and the ceramic showerhead looks ready to squirt in my face. The controls to the shower are in easy reach of me sitting on the toilet. I can take a dump and shower at the same time. The whole room is the shower room. There's a large drain in the floor directly under the showerhead. No tub. No medicine cabinet. Leon and I won't be able to be in here at the same time showering and brushing our teeth unless we're both willing to shower. The bathroom is not designed for a married couple. This is not an apartment converted into a prison where suspected spies vanish. This was built as a prison disguised as an apartment.

Sun Tzu says: Now when troops flee, are insubordinate, are distressed, collapse in disorder, or are routed, it is the fault of the general. None of these disasters can be attributed to natural causes.

The black G-2 captain in the green fatigues seems in charge. He does most of the talking, gives all the orders. The white officer in the blue jeans shirt and blue black trousers and black beret of the militia slinks and curls his lip at me a lot, then sits at my side and stares at the edge of my right eye. Interrogation. Beyond the white militia officer's short hairs, I see two militiamen in their blue uniforms sitting next to each other

Frank Chin

holding their rifles upright by their left leg with their left hand, a matched set of thin, wiry old men, in black berets, on a couch upholstered in a floral print. The light on them through the big picture window is just the right Caribbean rosy bright to make the old men in two-tone blue and floral couch look like glazed porcelain.

"Why did you choose to come to Trinidád of all the places in Cuba?" the black G-2 captain asks in slow Spanish.

"We heard Columbus landed here," I say.

"Columbus landed all around Cuba," the captains barks.

"Of course. We weren't thinking," Leon says. "Columbus landed all over Cuba. He was an explorer, right?"

"Quien es Jorge?" the white officer asks into my face like a Jap in a World War II movie. No! Not *Purple Heart!* Wrong movie. I am not Dana Andrews in *The Movie about Me.* No! Dana Andrews dies! Wrong movie.

"Who is Jorge?" I ask, playing stupid *Yanqui* for stupid time. "I give up. Who is Jorge?"

"Are you saying you don't know anyone named Jorge?" the black G-2 officer in green fatigues gruffs.

"That's what I'm saying," I say.

"Then why do I find this note signed Jorge in your coat pocket?"

"My coat pocket?"

"I found all these notes in your coat pockets," the G-2 officer says, opening his hands over little pieces of paper piled in front of him on the table like potato chips.

What is called "intelligence" cannot be divined from spirits, nor from gods, nor by analogy with past events, nor from hocus-pocus of calculations. Intelligence is obtained from men inside the enemy situation.

Now there are five sorts of secret agents: (1) native; (2) inside; (3) doubled; (4) expendable; (5) living. Use them all.

Talking to Sun Tzu

"Oh, those notes!" I say. I recognize those notes. "I recognize those notes. See, I don't speak Spanish. And when I'm drawing and sketching, I can't understand Spanish and draw at the same time, so when I'm drawing and sketching at this coffee stand every morning, people who want to ask me questions write me little notes, and when I'm done drawing, I read and answer their questions."

"You say you draw pictures? You know how to draw pictures?" the G-2 officer barks at me like a drill instructor on parade.

"Yes, he draws very well," the technical commandante says. My pal. "I have his book of drawings in my jeep. I'll go down and get it. You'll see."

"Wait!" the G-2 officer barks. He stinks his eyes into mine as he tears a corner off the top page of the yellow legal pad he uses for his notes. The corner is less than two inches square. He plants it in front of me. "Draw!" he commands.

I smile stink in his stinkeyes back into his head and reach over and take his yellow legal pad from him. I glance at his notes, fold the page back, peel off a clean whole page, and hand the pad back to him. He lifts his pencil. I take it from him and wave it at him. "Just go on talking. I can draw as you move. It'll just take a little longer to finish, that's all. But I have the time."

"All right, I'll sit as still as I can. But hurry up. I don't have the time," he says, and I draw his picture, on his paper, with his pencil. The guards stand up from the couch to watch from a distance. The white militia officer steps off to my right, makes a show of unsnapping his holster flap, and stands off watching from a nice spot to shoot me behind the right ear, should he feel like it.

The technical commandante watches over my shoulder, and smiles and raises his eyebrows at the black officer, and nods his head reassuringly, as if his reputation rests on the offi-

Frank Chin

cer liking the portrait I do in twenty minutes. I flip the picture over to the G-2 captain and ask the room for a cup of coffee. The army noncom, who seems in charge of our apartment jailhouse when the officers aren't here, says I deserve a coffee and goes to make coffee with Arminda. The G-2 captain puts the drawing in his pad, and his pad in his briefcase, and tells the technical commandante to go down to the jeep and get my drawing pad and bag of ink and paints. He leans back.

The commandante is happy to go. Leon looks like his life depends on my drawings. As the commandante's feet scuff down the steps to the jeep, Captain G-2 lays a card with a chess piece knight and "Have Gun Will Travel . . . Wire: Paladin, San Francisco" printed on it.

"You still say you are a student from North America?"

"See, it's a joke."

"A joke!" Captain G-2 slams his fist on the table.

"I mean a publicity thing. Coca Cola sponsors a North American TV show set in the North American west they call "Have Gun Will Travel." And the show always opens with someone taking out this card. So everyone who watches this show knows this card from watching that show. And one day Coca Cola was outside the entrance to the university passing out these cards and free Coke." I look around, realizing how stupid this would sound in English, and feel this has to sound stupid in the Spanish of the stupid I'm speaking. "And that's how I happen to have a 'Have Gun Will Travel' business card. I'm not Paladin," I say. And if this is the end of my life, I am going to have a good time, and take no shit, and say, "Paladin is an assassin played by Spencer Tracy, the actor. You know Spencer Tracy. He played the old man in the movie of *The Old Man and the Sea* they photographed over in Cojimar."

"Oh, Spencer Tracy. *Old Man and the Sea*. Hemingway," the white militia officer says behind my right ear.

Captain G-2 flips the card over, and there is a phone number in my hand on the back. He asks the obvious question, "Whose phone number is this?"

"I don't know," I say. "Why don't you go to Berkeley and try dialing it?"

"Hmmmmm," Captain G-2 says.

That night Leon's asthma strikes. I recognize it because I have it. But mine is quiet in Cuba. I like the air. I like the cigars, and I like the strong cigarettes. His asthma is bad. His lungs sound like plastic bird whistles tweetering full of water as he fails to breathe. He doubles up. There's no real standing room between the bed and the wall to the bathroom. I beat on the door and cuss in good old American English.

"Shuddup!" Captain G-2 growls and kicks the door from the other side.

"Hey! Hey!" I shout. "Enfermo! Enfermo! Sick! Sick! Mi amigo enfermo! Fuckhead! Asthma!"

"Shuddup!"

"Baaad! Black plague! Sick! Cancer! Death! Disease! Asthma! Asthmaaaaa!" I shout, and feel him outside listening at the door. "Open the door. Abre el fucking puerto y mirar! Come on!"

Captain G-2 unlocks the door, and a guard pokes his rifle at me. There's no place for me to step back to, so I go into the bathroom, to make room for Captain G-2 to look at Leon.

"You know what sickness he has?" Captain G-2 asks.

"Yes. Asthma."

"Write it down here," he says, offering me his yellow legal pad. I write the word *ASTHMA* in all capital letters on his pad. About an hour later he's back with pills to give Leon. I see Leon gets his pills down, and Captain G-2, standing some distance from me in the kitchen, asks me to step out to the front room, and the guard directs me with little nods and swings of his rifle. I sit at the table by the big picture window, and Captain G-2 says, "Your collaborators just dropped a

Frank Chin

number of these to you." He stands a number of brass tubes packed in holes drilled into blocks of wood on the table and packs the mess in an olive-drab box about the size of a pack of cigarettes. "Recognize these?" he asks, and hands the box to me. I refuse to touch it.

"I don't know what that stuff is," I say.

"Booby trap," Captain G-2 says. "You make booby traps."

"I draw pictures. I play the guitar. I do not make booby traps."

"We shall see what you do or do not make."

"I want a typewriter," I say. "I also write. It looks like we are going to be here awhile, so I want a typewriter, a hundred sheets of paper, some carbon paper. You can read what I write. I don't care. But what I write here, I take with me when I go."

"Why should I get you a typewriter?"

"I'm not asking for a gun. I can do nothing threatening with a typewriter. I'm no danger to anybody and easy to guard if I'm sitting at the typewriter all day."

"Are you certain you are not from People's China?" Captain G-2 asks. "We are expecting agricultural experts from China."

Sun Tzu says: All things being equal, if a force attacks one ten times its size, the result is flight.

When troops are strong and officers weak, the army is insubordinate.

When the officers are valiant and the troops ineffective, the army is in distress.

When the general is morally weak and his discipline not strict, when his instructions and guidance are not enlightened, when there are no consistent rules to guide the officers and men, and when the formations are slovenly, the army is in disorder.

When a commander unable to estimate his enemy uses a small

Talking to Sun Tzu

force to engage a large one or weak troops to strike the strong, or when he fails to select shock troops for the van, the result is rout.

When any of these six conditions prevails, the army is on the road to defeat. It is the highest responsibility of the general that he examine them carefully.

Conformation of the ground is of the greatest assistance in battle. Therefore, to estimate the enemy situation and to calculate distances and the degree of difficulty of the terrain so as to control victory are virtues of the superior general. He who fights with full knowledge of these factors is certain to win; he who does not will surely be defeated.

When I wish to give battle, my enemy, even though protected by high walls and deep moats, cannot help but engage me because I attack a position he must succor.

When I wish to avoid battle, I may defend myself simply by drawing a line on the ground; the enemy will be unable to attack me because I divert him from going where he wishes.

I am guarded by a fourteen-year-old boy in a militia uniform armed with a Skoda machine gun. Every try at a few words with the kid makes him flop sweat and point the gun at me. No, thanks. I look out the window at the tall grass in the alleyway between the backs of the buildings. Even here the red meat-headed condors fly down easy, low, and very slow. Their wing tips almost brush the walls.

The porcelain twins come to get me. They take me into the front room, where Leon sits on a metal folding chair. "I told them you should be here if they were going to ask questions about you."

"¿Cómo te parece Secretary of State Herter?"

"Me parece Herter es un ass," Leon says.

"¿Cómo?"

"Un burro," Leon says. "Ass en Español es burro."

Frank Chin

"Culo," I say, using the Spanish word for *cunt*. Arminda jumps up.

"Do you know what you've just said?" she asks, giggling and crying. Strange.

"Yes, I know what I have said is a curse word in Spanish. That is why I used it. Where we come from, *ass* is a curse word, indicating the same part of the body as the word *culo*. Understand?"

Arminda understands. She laughs, perhaps giddy about the longest bit of sustained Spanish I have accomplished thus far in my Spanish-speaking career. And she weeps, angry, insulted by my lack of consideration. She laughs, growls, stamps her feet, and runs to her room and slams the door. The officers glower at me and blink.

Leon's asthma hits again. Some odd pollen from the jungle perhaps. He wheezes back to the little narrow bed. The white bread officer tosses the "Have Gun Will Travel" card across the table at me. "Only decadent capitalists would even think of prospering on the story of an assassin."

"Don't call me a decadent capitalist, you backward Marxist. I am more radical than you. I'm an anarchist. I don't owe my heart to any society or any state."

"Have you read *Das Kapital?*" White Bread in Blue asks. "You?"

"You call yourself a Communist, and you're still clicking out Marx and Engels like some kind of antique record player? Don't talk to me about that old obsolete stuff!" I say. "Have you read Gabby Hayes on the phoniness of the class struggle?"

"Gabby Hayes? Who is Gabby Hayes?"

"Who is Gabby Hayes?" Captain G-2 asks White Bread.

"You don't know Gabby Hayes?" I laugh. "You're going to tell me about radical socialism and theory, and you don't know Gabby Hayes? Marx is obsolete because of Gabby Hayes!"

Talking to Sun Tzu

"Marx is obsolete?" White Bread whines. "That's ridiculous!"

"Marx is an intellectual chump like you," I say.

"That will be enough interrogation for today," Captain G-2 says, and packs his briefcase. The officers leave the militia guards sitting on the floral print couch.

I stay and clack away at the typewriter the black captain got me. No curtains on the big picture window, full of a big picture of the jungle on a hillside across the valley and the baby blue sky. Here and there on the road by this building a palm tree fingers up from the ground and splatters green fronds from the tip. I look out of the window down on the back and spread black wings and fanned tail of a condor sailing low over the road. It glides amazingly slow, big shouldered and graceful, over the blacktop. The secret town in the mountains has blacktop roads and apartment buildings with plumbing, sewers, water, and electricity.

One of the guards stands up from his couch and comes over to my table, pulls up a chair, and sits. He shifts his rifle to his left hand, and makes a loose fist with his right hand, and wobbles his wrist. "Do you know what this means?" he asks me, and wriggles his wrist again.

"No," I say. "What does that mean?"

"Do you know what this means?" He puts the index finger and thumb of his left hand together into an *O* and pokes the straight index finger of his right hand through it.

"Yes," I say, "I know what that means."

"In Cuba, this," he wriggles his wrist, "means this," he pokes his finger through the *O*.

"Do you know what this means?" I ask the guard, and curl my index and ring fingers against my extended middle finger and make the bird.

"No," the guard says, "I don't know what that means."

Frank Chin

"In the USA, this," I make the bird, "means this," I poke my index finger through the O.

"Ahh," he says.

"I'm surprised you don't know what we call 'the bird' in my country," I say. "I thought North Americans were all over Cuba before the Revolution."

"They don't come to the countryside. They stay in Havana," the thin guard says. "I'm a forty-year-old man. The Revolution taught me how to read a year ago."

"You're forty years old?" I say, and look surprised. He looks seventy to me. All my aunts and uncles in their sixties look younger than this old man.

"I have an eighteen-year-old son."

"Oh, you do!" I say, amazed.

I watch the shadows and colors change in the jungle as the sun lowers behind us. Different depths of the air take on different glows as the sun goes down. The forty-year-old old man with the Soviet rifle tells me of the times of his life. Working hard at the sugarcane. Getting drunk. Chasing women. Dancing in the streets. Afro-Cuban music. He has brought along a bottle of rum to warm the opportunity to get acquainted. The other porcelain twin stays on the couch. The old man and I drink and talk dirty stories to each other. The beautiful women who melted around our pulsing, straining cocks. The animals who have threatened us with death. The nights in the jungle. Stories we tell with lots of wagging the wrist and flipping the bird. Our lives and the lies we tell are very ordinary. The secrets we tell each other are the same old secrets we keep only from our mothers, and fathers, and wives. The mistresses, mistakes, and adventures we secretly want our children to discover and whisper about.

Therefore the skilled commander seeks victory from the situation and does not demand it of his subordinates. He exploits the situ-

Talking to Sun Tzu

ation and does not demand accomplishment of those who have no talent.

New Year's Eve. We're supposed to be in Twenty-sixth of July Square in Havana having dinner with Fidel and fifty thousand people. Instead we're listening to the crowd in Havana waiting for Fidel over the shortwave radio. A rifle shot, and I hear the bullet twirl by the big window and make it shudder. There are no shades or blinds or curtains. I jump up and snap the lights off. Fidel clears his throat at the microphone. Another shot outside. A little further away. I don't hear this bullet whiz. A machine gun sounds like a faint popcorn machine in the dark. I see the silhouettes of twin-engined B-26 bombers flying in pairs and fours against the sky. I can't hear their engines. They fly toward the mountains, flashing as shadows in the flame of explosions too far away to hear.

Fidel clears his throat. His voice echoes out of the speakers around the outdoor square. The crowd chants, "Fidel! Fidel! Fidel!" And Fidel clears his throat and says, "La Revolución!" And the crowd chants louder, "Fidel! Fidel! Fidel!"

One of the guards jumps up from the couch and fills his pants. The apartment fills with the smell of his shit. He limps off to the bathroom off the closet where we sleep. We stare at the little lights of the dials on the shortwave radio. Fidel clears his throat. The chanting crowd does not quiet. "La Revolución Cubanaaaaa!" Fidel intones and clears his throat again. And the crowd chants louder. Their voices echo into the microphone and out of the speakers and make feedback. Arminda complains about the smell and weeps because her comrade is so scared he crapped his pants. Fidel and I clear our throats together and, in duet, trill from the gut, "La Revolución Cubanaaaaa!" The noncom in charge jumps up and snaps off the radio. There are several popcorn machines popping outside. Perhaps if I listened hard, I might hear some-

Frank Chin

thing of the explosions attached to the flashes of bombs or artillery in the mountains I see bring the shape of peaks breaking suddenly out of the dark and fading out slow. The shots I hear around have no rhythm, no regularity; nothing holds them together. There's a shot. Then a long silence. Then a shot and another silence. It's like hunting. They're not celebrating the New Year. I walk over to the typewriter on the table closer to the window, sit down at the little machine, and look out the window. Everything is dark. It is definitely not party time outside.

I see jeep headlights bobbing down the road and hope it passes, as I imagine some counterrevolutionary with a mortar choosing his spot to plunk this stupid jeep, and it stops at the bottom of the stairs. Captain G-2 and White Bread trot up the stairs. Captain G-2 throws the door open and snaps on the lights. He has a bottle of rum in each hand. Behind him White Bread has shopping bags full of groceries. "Hoppy New Yeeaaarrrr!" Captain G-2 shouts. "Rum and beefsteak for everybody!"

Captain G-2 and Arminda cook the steaks in the kitchen. The guard who crapped his pants is ordered to clean up his track of shit through the kitchen and the front rooms of the apartment. Whew! I thought one of us might be ordered to clean it up. The white militia officer sits down at the table in front of me just as I am contemplating the wisdom of sitting in the light, in front of a big window, without curtains or shades.

"Draw my picture," White Bread says.

"What?"

"Draw my picture. You drew his picture and gave it to him. I want you to draw my picture and give it to me."

"Draw his picture," Arminda wails. "I wouldn't be here if I hadn't seen you in the square and approached you in the spirit of international brotherhood." She weeps.

Talking to Sun Tzu

"It's almost over. Before they didn't allow us to all be together. Now we're partying. They're done with us," I say.

I toast White Bread with the rum Captain G-2 poured me and begin to draw with water, brush, and ink. It's one of those rare nights when I can hold my liquor, and slowly, with sneering disrespect, I move him into matching me drink for drink as he drools over the portrait of him in his black beret shaping up on the paper, and he teases Arminda to keep reminiscing about life in the mountains singing around the campfire with the guerrillas during the Revolution till he woozes out.

I keep my drawing of him. That's my revenge.

Two days later Captain G-2 tells us the United States broke diplomatic relations with Cuba on New Year's Day. Captain G-2 gives us newspapers from Havana and the provincial capital of Santa Clara.

The next day they move Leon and me to the garrison that also serves as the orphanage. We never see Arminda again.

We are put in the charge of Little Caesar, an eighteen-year-old orphan with the Beretta pistol they call the adjutant while the captain is out on patrol. The freeway intersections the technical commandante built must be a key to something. Why else are the counterrevolutionaries focusing all their action here? Are they out there in the jungle stopping the roads from coming through to meet the intersections? Are these roads so important all the officers and men of this Trinidád garrison are out in the woods leaving the garrison in the hands of the orphans? During the day all the troops around the garrison are too tired and hurt to be aware of Leon and me. Especially Leon. Leon sleeps and stares all day. On his back in an asthmatic pillhead hyperwooze.

The punk adjutant tries to convert me with stupid newspaper headlines. I tell him he's scared of me and I know it. The third day he says he's taking us to the provincial capital of Santa Clara. He opens a desk drawer and takes a little Beretta out of its holster and tries to load a clip in backward. I grab the pistol and clip out of his hand, load the thing for him, and hand it back.

He plans to take us by cab around to the hotel to pay our bill and collect our luggage and back to the work site to get our clothes. Leon says he won't survive the ride. His asthma is making him a pain-in-the-ass invalid. "I think you have to shoot Leonardo. If you just leave him here, he might escape."

"Shoot him?"

"What if his asthma gets better while we're out in the cab?" I ask.

"You're correct." He puffs up and goes to ask one of the off-duty soldiers to keep an eye on Leon.

No matter I was a mad dog prisoner and dangerous spy, the cabbie is in the biz for the money and gives everybody a ride who has the money. We arrive at the bus stop ready for our last trip to the provincial capital of Santa Clara, site of a famous battle of the Revolution, with two chickens, a goat, young girls, and old women sitting on our laps, and Little Caesar the junior adjutant ready to shoot them all.

A platoon of the local women's militia marches to a stop on the unpaved hard dust outside the bus terminal, stands at ease, and falls out. The thirty women in black berets and two-tone blue pull bottled pop and juice out of the coolers, and some walk over to the espresso machine. I decide it's time for a *café con leche* and a little flight of my Spanish in the familiar tense, get up, and sneer at orphan honorary adjutant when he leans forward and goes for his gun.

"I'm going to escape over that way by the coffee machine, okay, Capitán?" I say, knowing he knows *Capitán* is a Cuban way of affectionately calling a Chinaman a lucky-charm leprechaun-like creature, or a waiter. And in that flicker of wonder about what I heard him say and when I heard it, I am across the dull linoleum floor to the counter, among the mili-

Talking to Sun Tzu

tia women waiting for their coffees. The man at the coffee machine nods my way. I order a *café con leche,* and women notice my accent, my looks.

"Are you from People's China?" a thirtyish woman asks me with a smile, and I feel the others listening.

"No, no. I am a student from North America. I was born in the western state of California in the USA," I say, "But my friend, the blond one over there, is from the USSR, if you understand my meaning." I smile at Leon and wave him over.

"We want to buy a coffee for our comrades from abroad," the thirtyish woman says as Leon joins us. I talk the women into inviting us out to dinner in the spirit of international brotherhood. As we walk out arm in arm with the women's militia, Capitán Adjutant jumps out of his seat with his little Beretta drawn. "Stop!" he shouts. "These are dangerous *Yanquí* spies, and I will not allow them to escape!" He fires his pistol into the air and blows a little hole in the tin roof above his head. Dust dribbles through the hole onto his shoulder. I laugh. Leon sits down fast and puts his head between his legs. The women's militia scatters.

The junior adjutant falls asleep on the bus ride to Santa Clara. The sailor at the back of the bus wearing a white web belt and a nickel-plated .45 automatic in a leather holster asks me to touch his pistol.

"No, you'll shoot me," I say.

"No. No. Just touch it, you'll see."

I reach down and touch the butt of his .45 with two fingertips. It's hot. "It's hot," I say.

"I'm sitting right on top of the engine," the sailor says. "And I can't take off my pistol."

Little Caesar delivers us to an army officer in green fatigues and a black beret outside a building that looks most like an old New York firehouse. Inside, on what would have been the

Frank Chin

garage, partitions are up, walls that do not reach all the way to the ceiling. In the innermost office without any ceiling is the provincial commandante, a thirtyish dark-haired white man with a thick mustache, who sits behind his desk in green fatigues. Behind him, sitting on a cabinet with one foot up on a table, a man in white trousers, green short-sleeved shirt, and straw hat twirls a nickel-plated .45 automatic with Cuban flags on the pistol grips and puffs on a cigar.

"What you make in Cuba?" the provincial commandante asks me.

"What I make in Cuba?" I ask back and don't understand. "Ask me in Spanish."

"¿Que hacéis en Cuba?"

"Oh, what am I doing in Cuba. I'm a tourist," I say. "Somos turistas. We're tourists."

"¿Cómo te parece Mao Tse-tung?"

"I think Mao is the only proper leader of China," Leon says in Spanish.

"Me parece Mao es un hombre muy formidáble," I say.

"¿Cómo te parece Chiang Kai-shek?" the commandante asks.

"Me parece Chiang es un hombre muy formidáble," I say.

"Don't listen to him," Leon says. "Chiang is a *Yanqui* puppet. A criminal."

"How can you say Mao is a formidable man and Chiang is formidable man?" the commandante asks.

"Chiang owes his very existence to the U.S. Seventh Fleet, and still he has the nerve to blackmail the USA and make them pay their troops stationed on Taiwan in U.S. dollars. That makes him a fairly formidable man."

"Yes, I see. Good thinking," the commandante says. "Do you think we are Communists in Cuba?"

"It doesn't matter. I myself am a Communist," Leon says.

Talking to Sun Tzu

"I was arrested at the House Un-American Activities Committee riots in San Francisco," he says, and pulls clippings of his arrest out of his wallet.

"I'm an anarchist. I don't like any form of government."

"Well, I guess you can both go."

"I'm not going anyplace until you, the government of Cuba, give me, a poor student from North America, twenty dollars," I say.

"Twenty dollars? Why?"

"Before we were detained, we took rooms at a hotel in Trinidád. Before we were put on the bus to Santa Clara, we went back to the hotel to collect our luggage, and we paid our bill for rooms we had never occupied."

"Why didn't you occupy them?"

"We were being detained in the G-2 apartment and the garrison."

"Were you badly treated?"

"We didn't get to go where we wanted, and we didn't get to do what we wanted," I say. "I don't think it is proper for the people's revolutionary government of Cuba to make me pay for our own arrest and discomfort."

The man in the straw hat stops twirling his nickel-plated .45 auto and looks me over. The commandante picks up the phone and dials a number, says, "Patria o muerte, Fatherland or death," and tells the ear on the other end he has two North American students in his office. We have been held awhile, and he's interrogated us, and we've answered all his questions satisfactorily. We like Mao Tse-tung. We don't like Chiang Kai-shek. We don't think they're all Communists. And we want twenty dollars. Should he give it to us?

He listens awhile, then covers the mouthpiece and asks if we want twenty dollars altogether or twenty dollars apiece.

"Just give him twenty dollars. I don't want anything. I'm happy," Leon says.

Frank Chin

The commandante gives me twenty dollars out of his wallet and says we can go.

"Go where? Point us to the bus station. We'll catch a bus back to Havana."

"I'll take you," the commandante says. He gives us a ride in an old white-and-orange '53 Chevrolet. He drives us to the bus station.

Leon flies back to Miami as soon as he can get his stuff out of the Riviera. The FBI picks him up for questioning as soon as he comes off the plane. I stay over another week at Gavilán's, hanging out in the guitar shop in the day, and hanging out with him drinking coffee and rum, and smoking cigars, and going to the whorehouses, and playing the guitar at night.

Every American corporation office still open, like United Air Lines and Kodak, has a bunker of sandbags and a machine gun mounted on a tripod manned by the Cuban army out front. The window of Kodak features stills from *La Historias de La Revolución!* draped in rolls of exposed thirty-five-millimeter film. A banner reads, "Cuba's first feature film, *La Historias de La Revolución!* was made with Kodak film!"

The tactical variations appropriate to the nine types of ground, the advantages of close or extended deployment, and the principles of human nature are matters the general must examine with the greatest care.

I land in Miami with two guitars stuffed with Cuban newspapers, magazines, a copy of Che Guevara's manual of guerrilla warfare, a Spanish translation of Alvah Bessie's novel *The Un-Americans,* and the roses the Russian folk dancers sniffed and passed to me the night I bought them rounds of beer. I see the sign over the U.S. customs inspection stations, prohibiting the entry of plants. I hang back and look for the friendliest customs inspector and take my chances on the neat gray-haired woman. She opens up a guitar case and sees the dried roses.

"Oh, you know you're not allowed to bring any plants into the country . . . ," she says.

I nod and sigh. "My mother . . . ," I begin, but she raises her hand.

"I understand," she says, and snaps the case closed, and doesn't look into the other guitar case or my suitcase or bag of inks and paints, and passes me through.

I hitchhike out of Miami. A blond Elvis in shades and a convertible runs me about an hour out of town and leaves me under a light in the dark. Hours later a half-ton truck carrying the U.S. mail picks me up. "I knew right away you was Chinese," the driver says. "You shouldn't be walking along this road at night. And if I hadn't seen you was Chinese, I wouldn't have picked you up."

"I gave up hanging my thumb out. Nobody was picking me up."

"Thought you was a nigger, most likely, the way you was walking."

"Oh."

"You know, you couldn't get me to walk along that road at night for half an hour if you gave me five hundred dollars!"

"Why's that?"

"Don't you know that's the Everglades!"

"The Everglades?" I say. "The swamp?"

"It's got wild animals all over it."

"Wild animals! I stepped over a snake," I say.

"There's rattlesnakes, cottonmouths, snakes like that. Alligators. Panthers. Bobcats."

"Bobcats? They're small," I say, "just a little bigger than house cats, right?"

He drops open the door to the glove compartment and shows me a shiny nickel-plated short-barreled .357 magnum.

Frank Chin

"I've never heard of 'em attacking a human being, but they attacked this truck three times. And after I hit 'em with the truck and stopped, you know, they still tried to kill it, and I had to shoot 'em every time."

He drops me at a truck stop by a turn he makes just before dawn. At the truck stop a waitress tells me they'll serve me out back. There is no out back. I go back to the highway through the Everglades and start walking.

A couple hours after dawn a white four-door '49 Cadillac pulls up and stops ahead and waits for me. As I walk up to the open window on the passenger side, a black man in a khaki garrison cap with blue piping reaches across the woman riding shotgun and pokes his finger in my face. "I know what you are! You're Chinese!" His wife looks terrified of Chinese. The kids in the backseat can't believe their eyes. The woman won't let me get in the backseat, where there's room, or even put my guitar cases back there. So we all ride in the front, the man in the garrison cap, his wife, my two guitars, zip bag, canvas bag of inks, and me. They drop me at the nearest Greyhound connection, a little tin shanty by the road, and I buy a bus ticket back to Berkeley.

Ground in which the army survives only if it fights with the courage of desperation is called "death."

"The Cubans thought you were a spy?" the Marine Corps captain asks.

"Yessir," I say.

"For us?" he asks.

"For you," I say.

They finally ask for letters from doctors and stuff about me I'd like them to read, and I give them the doctor's letter about my terrible hay fever and asthma. They are relieved to declare me a "physical reject."

Talking to Sun Tzu

To win one hundred victories in one hundred battles is not the acme of military skill. To subdue the enemy without fighting is the acme of military skill.

On the Greyhound out of Georgia, there are only five or six of us. No women. Everyone has a row of seats to himself. I stretch out and curl up somewhere in the middle of the bus, and am falling out and away, drifting over the road asleep, when I sit up to a finger poking me in the chest. I look up and see a young soldier, just out of basic training. No stripes on his sleeves. No hash marks. "Are you an American Indian?" he asks.

"Yeah, man," I say, and turn to curl up again when he sticks his right hand over the back of the seat.

"So am I," he says, shaking my hand.

When you are ignorant of the enemy but know yourself, your chances of winning or losing are equal.

17 April 1961. 1,400 U.S.-financed Cuban exiles attempt to invade Cuba at the Bay of Pigs.

If ignorant both of your enemy and of yourself, in every battle you are certain to be in peril.

October 1962: The Cuban Missile Crisis.

Frank Chin

Between the Western nations and China is no common psycho-logical speech. Their thought processes are radically dissimilar. There is no intimate vocabulary. The Western mind penetrates the Chinese mind but a short distance when it finds itself in a fathomless maze. The Chinese mind penetrates the Western mind an equally short distance when it fetches up against a blank, incomprehensible wall. It is all a matter of language. There is no way to communicate Western ideas to the Chinese mind. . . . The Chinese mind cannot thrill to short Saxon words; nor can the English-speaking mind thrill to hieroglyphics. The fabrics of their minds are woven from totally different stuffs. They are mental aliens.

> Jack London
> THE CHINAGO
> 1914

BEN FEE

His hometown, Chinatown San Francisco, has forgotten the name of Ben Fee and the man he was, for its own good. In New York he's what he was in Frisco, but more so, a word-of-

Confessions of a Chinatown Cowboy

mouth legend, a bare-knuckled unmasked man, a Chinaman loner out of the old West, a character out of Chinese sword-slingers, a fighter. The kind of Chinaman we've been taught to ignore and forget if we don't want America to drive Chinatown out of town.

Ben Fee looks like a scaled-down Edward G. Robinson, a slightly shorter version of a short tough guy. An open, boyish smile on his face all the time and a Tiparillo in the right side of his mouth, all on top of a loose, careless, swaggering tough chubbiness that stops for nothing, not for moving cars, traffic jams, falling safes, nothing but the touch of Chinatown ladies, members of the International Ladies Garment Workers Union in the daytime, members of his English classes Friday nights, his friends all the time, who can't talk to him without touching his arm or hand, ". . . to see if I'm real," he says.

He's sixty-three years old, nearsighted, and on the move. I say that about him without any extra heart for an old man still going strong at sixty-three. He's from Chinatown. In Chinatown the old aren't expected to stop until they drop. What makes him a special old man is that he's not afraid of America, doesn't hate Chinese America, and likes himself enough to talk about a past that runs from China to San Francisco to New York. Unlike most of his generation, he hasn't given up memory and pride as the price for life in this country.

I looked to meet him researching "Chinaman's Chance—a Portrait of Changing Chinese America," a documentary I did with Ene Riisna for WNET-TV. Ene Riisna, a tall, six-foot, skinny blonde braless filmmaker, wore a shrunken pullover sweater that reached to her waist with a stretch of the imagination and a skirt that hung around her hips. She tried to pull herself together, keep her navel covered, and look straight, responsible, objective, not knowing what to expect, and expecting the worst as we were over an hour late for our appointment with Fee. My hair was long, parted in the mid-

Frank Chin

dle. My beard was long and as effective as a beard as needles are at making cactus look hairy, but it was me then, a kind of topping for me all in black: black cowboy boots, black denims, black leather belt with a tough, but not flashy, two-fanged buckle instead of the standard one-prong job, black western shirt with phoney pearl snaps, a silver vest, a toothpick in my mouth, and a Chinese wiseass beard making me solid affectation. Alice in Wonderland growing out of her clothes and a Chinaman dressed for a barn dance were on the scene. But we shared an attaché case.

Shirtsleeves rolled halfway up his forearms, tie loose, collar unbuttoned, waving his Tiparillo, he appeared out of too many old movies, a mobster ordering a hit, a cynical news-hawk stopping the presses, a labor organizer, sauntering, looking something like a teddy bear, and broadcasting all the instant charisma of a man wearing nothing but dynamite sticks, there he was, unmistakably nobody else but Ben Fee, wondering who the hell we were. Everything about him shifted into a "Who the hell are you?" when, suspecting this was Ben Fee, I said, "Ben Fee?"

He shifted his weight to the leg farthest from us, while appearing to stop slightly forward, coming out of the Chinese movies now and westerns at the Palace, put the Tiparillo in his mouth, passed a quick look over us, and took it out again. A sheathed sword in the right hand is a sign of trust. You can't draw your sword when it's sheathed in your fighting hand. Shifting it to your left hand is a warning. You can't shake hands with a burning cigar in you right hand. It's all a matter of language. He smiled, snapshot a quick album of us, then put the cigar back in his mouth, freeing his hand for a shake. Chinatown, Frisco all the way. He was from home. There was a moment of Chinatown manhood, not a kingdom of style, but a moment, at least a Frisco moment I had to come to New York to discover.

Confessions of a Chinatown Cowboy

Now that we were home, I wondered how much home would get in our way.

In the code of Chinatown, only fools and finks took the English language, or the Chinese language, or words, written words, spoken words, seriously as language. Language as it was known in the world was emasculating, sissy stuff. That's how we compensated for the humiliation of all the time being heard talking in language lessons by Chinese folks and American people who never heard any sense from us when we opened up. Instead of real talk, we memorized phrases that worked, kept a stock of clichés we could string up in combos for any occasion and say nothing at all, no more. Polite, sort, and out. Out without being corrected, an "I'm fine, thank you," and swoop free. We'd pulled one on the *fan gwai* white man.

There were two kinds of talkers among us, two kinds of clowns, for only clowns talked. Talking made you a clown. On the street, if you kept your hands loose, not so down and tight as to look a chicken, but loose enough not to be mistaken for action, and kept everybody laughing, you wouldn't get beat up. "I'm going to beat the shit out of you," a big guy with a gang says. "Well, you better hurry up, man, cuz I gotta get to Chinese school," you say, making it a joke, making them busy with some fun. That was practical language skills of the here-and-now school.

There was something of a man in that clown act, but not the one where you talk college white. That college white in your mouth was the sound of shame on us, the sound of teachers calling us stupid, and you talking like a teacher grading papers meant you were too good for Chinatown and Chinamen. It meant if you weren't thinking of graduating the town for whiteness, you'd better. Hungry, all the time hungry, every sense was out whiffing for something rightly ours, chameleons looking for color, trying on tongues and clothes and hairdos, taking everyone else's, with none of our own,

Frank Chin

and no habitat, our manhood just never came home. Everything was copycat. Hunger and copycat. We had a lot of stutterers, thumb suckers. The sound of whiteness inevitably crept into our tongue, became the sound of good grades and making good, and Chinatown didn't want us anymore. The language I wrote (which Thom Gunn, the first real poet I ever met, and writer Phillip Roth told me wasn't English, making me go "huh?"), the sounds out of my mouth (which a black migrant worker giving me a lift in Florida told me were "pretty good language for a Chinese person"), is just good enough to turn off many in Chinatown. What they hear in the way I talk is a message white schools put in the sound, a message I don't mean—that I've turned my back on Chinatown and become white, worse than white. To become white, you shit in your blood, hate yourself and all your kind. For *juk sing* to become "Chinese" (pass for *juk kok*) means the same thing, a treatment, a session between electrodes, called an education.

Ben Fee and me, both from home, a generation between us, out of the town, working in white businesses that have done Chinese America bad in the past. The labor movement in California was formed to exclude Chinese labor and drive us out of the country. It led lynchings and made outlaws and scabs of every one of us who drove a truck, tended a bar, or worked at hundreds of other jobs until the fifties. My China brother was the first Chinaman to crack the bartender's union. I was the first Chinaman brakeman on the Southern Pacific Railroad. If I wasn't prejudiced against a Chinaman being into the union movement, I was at least suspected. Every Chinaman who ever wrote, came on proud of his education and English language, wrote a combination tour guide and cookbook—a clown act, showing Chinamen off as "Chinese American" fools. Educational TV served up a formula for being Chinese American: "I'm Chinese because I like chow mein, and I'm American because I like spaghetti," the "Chi-

Confessions of a Chinatown Cowboy

nese American" writer/reporter said on a program aired special to grades 3–6 in Frisco last year. Fee looked at me, Mr. TV in black and silver, wearing boots, from Oakland really, and an old Oakland at that—Oakland was never quite Frisco—affecting Oakland for TV, come to do a job on New York's Chinatown for TV, come to talk. Talk what? Talk how? We'd show in the talk whether we had anything to say to each other, other than "whiter than thou," "more Chinese than thou," "more assimilated than thou."

Between us was our awareness of our history, white racism's success with our people, and the new wave of writing calling white racism's success our success, off the pens of Tom Wolfe, explaining "why there is no National Association for the Advancement of Chinese Americans" ("Most Chinese who get college educations and good jobs leave Chinatown and the village life forever. But the Chinese heritage, the Chinese 'pride,' does mean that it is impossible for the Chinese in America, poor or rich, to picture themselves as a weak and helpless minority, hopelessly adrift in the tides of circumstances"), Kenneth LaMott, explaining "The Awakening of Chinatown" ("A central point at issue is that, whereas the blacks see the dominant white society as their chief enemy, the Chinese activists are primarily in rebellion against the older generation of their own people. . . . Perhaps it is an over-simplification, but I don't think it is far wrong to say these young men are more in rebellion against Confucius than they are against Mister Charley"), and others writing in *Esquire* (Tom Wolfe), *Atlantic* (Mary Ellen Leary), *New York* (Tom Wolfe), *West* (Kenneth LaMott), the *New Yorker, U.S. News and World Report, Time,* on Chinatown Frisco standing against busing, on our preservation of culture, our assimilation, our "outwhiting the whites"—all of it penning love for us racistly. All of it making us look good at the expense of the blacks, all

Frank Chin

of it full of disturbing echoes of the Nazi anti-Semitist argument, all of it cunningly white.

Thanks to our lives in America I could call Ben "Chinese" and insult him. I could call him "American" and insult him. I could call him "black" and insult him. I could call him "Japanese" and insult him. Between Ben and me it was all a matter of language, whether or not we talked, because we were Chinamen in America—and the most suspicious kind of Chinamen. Each of us in his own way was something of a star or a pet in a bit of the white world, doing a white thing. He stepped forward, up close to me, grinned, and said, "Welcome, Chinatown Cowboy," and I was finally glad to see him. Thanks, Ben. Ride with this Chinatown cowboy a bit while I run off to rustle strange words and maverick up a language to write this mess in. Remember Burt Lancaster in *Vera Cruz,* a grinning gunfighter in black, always talking about some "Hannah" fellow who taught him everything he knew, a kind of foster father–priest of the badass good-time way of life, like the master in the Chinese movies, the old teacher? I come from your school. (It's an older school than you know.) My right hand is free. Tom Wolfe, I'm talking to you almost in your own language. And it hurts. We can only be wishy-washy in your mouth and untrue.

RACIST LOVE

White racist is the baddest word in the language today, not *motherfucker, cocksucker, sonofabitching cocksucking motherfucker,* but *white racist* isn't a word we're expected to use, speaking for ourselves. It's impossible for us to be taken seriously as victims of white racism by whites who are convinced that, no matter what, we are sustained by Chinese culture and that "the Chinese heritage, the Chinese 'pride,' does mean that it is impossible for the Chinese in America, poor or rich, to picture themselves as a weak and helpless minority." Blacks agree with you. They don't see us as a weak and helpless minority; they see us as a strong and helpful one, a race of agents for Mr. Charley whose "Chinese culture" is a white racist institution. Both despise us with racist love.

David Hilliard of the Black Panthers, interviewed in *U.S. News and World Report*, called us "the Uncle Toms of the non-white people in the U.S." In Richard Wright's autobiography *Black Boy* is a famous scene involving Shorty, an elevator operator in the South. He makes quarters off white men by letting them kick him in the ass. They kick him in the ass, and he laughs, wriggles his butt, picks up their quarters with his teeth, and thanks them. "You're all right, Shorty, you sonofabitch," the white men say. And he is a good sonofabitch. He's assimilated into white Southern culture without violence. He's entertaining but not obnoxious to whites. What Betty Lee Sung said of us in her 1967 *Mountain of Gold: The Story of the Chinese in America* holds true for Shorty: "Much to their credit the Chinese view prejudice with a very healthy attitude. They were never overly bitter. They have gone into occupations which command respect and which lessen conflict from competition."

In 1876, George D. Roberts, the president of a company that had used Chinese labor to reclaim thirty to forty thousand acres of California tule land in the Sacramento Delta, spoke to Congress, in fore-echoes of Mrs. Sung, giving us the roots of a "Chinese American" psychology. "To the general prosperity of the country," he said, "I think they are a great advantage. I think they fill a place that white labor would fill very reluctantly. . . . I think the wealth they produce stimulates prosperity to such an extent that it gives white men higher positions." We went into occupations that commanded

Frank Chin

respect and lessened conflict, doing a job that's been forgotten by whites and by Chinese America because the story of the job, though nice in numbers, was not a story the Chinese wanted to tell their children. "In my opinion," Roberts said, "the aggregate product of the wealth produced by the Chinamen in this state is equal to the mines, including the mines of Nevada and Dakota. Probably they produce sixty, eighty, ninety millions a year in wealth."

The Chinese laborers Roberts was talking about came from Chinatown, San Francisco, like the Chinese laborers who built the railroads. The railroads created a detention camp and called it "Chinatown." The details of that creation have been conveniently forgotten or euphemized into a state of sweet confusion. The men who lived through the creation are dying out, unheard and ignored. When they die, no one will know it was not us who created a game preserve for Chinese and called it "Chinatown."

Betty Lee Sung, a Christian, goes on to prove that being a Christian Chinese is like being a Nazi Jew; it cannot be done. The Nazi craves the death of the Jew, the Christian the extinction of the Chinese: "The Chinese are not concentrated entirely in one section of the country. More dispersion away from the vortexes of San Francisco and New York should be encouraged. This ought to be a long range goal of the Chinese because distribution reduces the degree of visibility."

"Murder without blood," said Warner Oland, Charlie Chan the First. ". . . like Amos without Andy," in *Charlie Chan at the Racetrack*. I asked Mrs. Sung why not being overly bitter was a healthy attitude toward prejudice, and she answered, "If you make yourself obnoxious . . . that is a hindrance to acceptance." Shorty doesn't make himself obnoxious to anyone except his fellow blacks. He is accepted in the South. And the Chinese Americans are accepted coast to coast as a showcase

Confessions of a Chinatown Cowboy

minority. "At a time when Americans are awash in worry over the plight of racial minorities," says *U.S. News and World Report* (26 December 1966), "one such minority, the nation's 300,000 Chinese Americans, is winning wealth and respect by dint of its own hard work."

"I'm going north one of these days," Shorty would say. We would all laugh, knowing that Shorty would never leave, that he depended too much upon the whites for the food he ate.

"What would you do up north?" I would ask Shorty.

"I'd pass for Chinese," Shorty would say.

The *U.S. News and World Report* story "Success Story of One Minority Group in U.S." makes it clear that Shorty wouldn't make it up North, not because letting whites kick your ass for a quarter is looked down on, but because the success of the Chinese American minority is based on their being mightily, sincerely, definitely not black: "Still being taught in Chinatown is the old idea that people should depend on their own efforts—not a welfare check—in order to reach America's 'promised land.'"

David Hilliard and Richard Wright are correct—coldly and painfully so. We are the Uncle Toms of the nonwhite peoples of America, the despicable Shortys, a race of yellow white supremacists, yellow white racists. We're hated by the blacks because the whites love us for being everything the blacks are not. Blacks are a problem: badass. Chinese Americans are not a problem: kissass. Tom Wolfe suggested in his December 1969 *Esquire* article that kissass was Chinese and that badass Chinamen boys was the result of school integration:

The Chinese teen-agers who ended up at Gompers, many of them immigrants from Hong Kong, found that Chinese culture— obedience, filial piety, hard work, self-respect—didn't mean a damn thing at Gompers. Being a cool and bad-ass cat, that was

Frank Chin

*all that mattered. The gangs ran the show at Gompers, the bloods
and the Mexicans, but mainly the bloods. They were loud, violent,
sexually aggressive—stuff that really stunned most Chinese. But
if it was the bloods who ran the show, maybe the thing to do was
to get in on their thing. . . . That was when one really started seeing some exotic sights in Chinatown. Here came the Chinese kids
who really had the gait, man, down pat, the cooooool rolling gait,
with the hips and the shoulders turning over like the wheels on a
railroad engine.*

Ah, Tom, writing of the great American haps the way Stan-
ley Kramer makes movies, you roused the Chinatown establishment coast to kissass coast; the English-language mouthpiece of the Chinese Six Companies, the Chinese American
Citizen Alliance (the Chinese NAACP you said doesn't exist),
felt betrayed. They protested your piece with a description of
Chinese culture out of a white fantasy of Charlie Chan. "Chinese culture—obedience, filial piety, hard work, self-respect.
. . . " *Esquire* didn't publish their letter. The San Francisco
East West Journal, a Christian English-language newspaper,
did: "The Chinese remember that no people in our country
have suffered discrimination as we have. But we have proved
to our own satisfaction that from the personal efforts of our
parents and of ourselves, we have won the respect and esteem
of the non-Chinese community, and at no time have we ever
had to resort to violence to achieve the status we now enjoy."

Not true. Life is war to the Chinese. The personal form of
the Confucian mandate of heaven is the Confucian ethic of
private revenge. There is no justice without revenge to Confucius. The Golden Rule is, You mess with me, I mess with
you. Both you and the CACA saw it but were blinded by
Christian white racist love, as the CACA said: "Of course we
have had problems with young immigrants from Hong Kong,
handicapped as they are by language problems and a lack of

Confessions of a Chinatown Cowboy

marketable skills. Too, they have acquired some of the less desirable mannerisms of other youngsters in this city similarly handicapped by lack of marketable skills."

It was you, Tom Wolfe, who made Chinatown openly, publicly, turn against school integration, you who said the white image of Chinese culture was being blacked out in Chinese schools and made it a national issue. You didn't have to say whites hated blacks, that turning black meant white disapproval; we already knew that was part of being "American." Then *Newsweek* springs Min S. Yee, a literate, educated journalist, obviously making good in the white world—a choice example of the assimilated Chinese American—right in the middle of the Chinese New Year's celebration. Instead of chickening the seasonal bagaw for bucks to come home to Chinatown, he said Chinatown "has some of the worst conditions in the country" and sounded black to the CACA, a bad way for a Chinese American to blow, and then blew apart the image of Chinese culture and assimilation with: "But there is no question in my mind that our people must have the same social, economic and educational rights as the other citizens. I never had such problems—but then, I was white-washed."

Chinatown went nuts! The sky was falling. The white press was betraying the loyal nonblack Charlie Chan mascot people they had spent over a hundred years of imagination to create. That race of good Chinks hopped up on the Confucian ethic, stooping high into acceptance and approval by keeping their place preserving Chinese culture with its emphasis on industry, honesty, frugality, intellect, and patience, winning more attention and recognition than could be expected of such an amazingly small minority—that is a racist cartoon, a creation of white male science fiction, Christian missionaries envisioning us as sheep "characteristically timid and docile," hack writers and the Celestial Empire (under American guns) and later

Frank Chin

the Nationalist Chinese government working through the recognized unofficial Chinatown establishment, known variously as the Chinese Six Companies, the Chinese Consolidated Benevolent Association, the Choong (or Chung) Wah Benevolent Association, by any name the same outfit, unregistered agents of a foreign power, fronting for the Chinese Nationalist Party, allowed by the U.S. government to carry on running Chinatown as if it were a foreign colony, a bit of China, a city within a city.

In San Francisco and New York the president of the local chapter of the Chinese Benevolent Association is traditionally called "the mayor of Chinatown" by the press and the president of the United States. In the honorary title is recognition of an understanding between the press and the Six that they are the exclusive source of Chinatown news, an understanding between the U.S. and Nationalist Chinese governments that was being violated. A secret meeting of the "mayors" of all the Chinatowns in the United States and Canada was held in San Francisco soon after Min Yee's *Newsweek* article. The word from that meeting was, Lock up the town. No news is good news, and from now on it's good news only. They knew you'd take the Chinatown boycott of busing as good news, Tom. And you rose to the bait in *New York* magazine's special issue "China in America." They knew, I mean, they really knew you were white, white, white. Owwooooo! Hear that wolf?

THE WRONG MOVIE

I learned of that meeting from a friend, an American-born Chinese American grocer with stories Chinese America must forget to preserve Charlie Chan.

I was collecting oral history on tape. It was like a movie, a gangster flick, complete with the "I can't talk on the phone" line, and "come alone," and to come clean, no recorder, not

Confessions of a Chinatown Cowboy

that the words would have become guns to his head, or mine, no, just the end of his business. I walked into his store, alone, clean, feeling strangely all them "but this is America but this is America but . . . ," wanting to wave my arms. My friend, born here, the American dream come true, a little business, last year's Pontiac, talks that fine English, sounds like Chicago on the phone, no pigtail and no walk, part Okie sashay, part black strut, the walk of the chameleon Chinaman, the most typical Chinaman born in the most typical Chinatown, a town that's nothing but a state of mind in a multiracial ghetto . . . usually near railroad tracks . . . a chameleon Chinaman who was born to and never gets used to the Negroes and Mexican people, most of the people of his childhood, his world . . . Fresno, Seattle, Sacramento, my old Oakland . . . looking at him, looking at me, as if our . . . as if we and our families didn't live here, never lived here. Later we learn we're loved by whites, creatures from planet White who suit up and ship across the concrete universe to teach us and treat us better, making treacherous sense of the looks we live with from the people who surround our homes. He finished up a customer, asking about the family, smiling, tying string. He led her to the door, opened it for her, locked it after her. We were in the wrong movie. All I wanted to talk about was his life, a few stories about this town, nothing necessarily scandalous.

"Not here," he said, and deeper into the wrong movie, to the back room and closed curtains, just to say, "I can't talk to you. I'm telling you this because we're friends." Then the news of the meeting. He'd been asked not to tell, but since we were friends . . . all the wrong movie. How'd we come to this? That only among ourselves, even as grown men, only in secret, among ourselves and selected friends, we're not "Chinese." ("If you make yourself obnoxious . . . that is a hindrance to acceptance.") I recall what George Takei (the Japanese American actor who played Mr. Sulu on "Star Trek," the

Frank Chin

ARVN officer in John Wayne's *The Green Berets,* Richard Burton's Chinese houseboy in the *Ice Palace,* a Chinese miner in an episode of "Death Valley Days," and the offscreen enemy of NBC's impending revival of Charlie Chan) said, talking about some Asian American actors being so conditioned into playing the role of the stereotype that they had what he called a "Pavlovian" reaction to lights and cameras, how men who walked upright and talked straight carried hidden in their every muscle the strong right hand of white racist imagery, how the son the great white father sacrificed to planet Chinatown, Charlie Chan, to teach us to live righteously in his image takes over the bodies and voices of many Asian American actors. ("The only thing that stands out in the mind when you're playing an Oriental of *education* is that, number one: his manners are very good. . . . So you do a lot of bowing.") In front of the cameras they crumpled up into that Charlie Chan fetal position, screwed up their faces, and talked buck-buck bagaw. It was always the wrong movie.

Keeping us foreign, semi-assimilated aliens with our hearts and souls in China and our labor in America was a matter of government policy, an unwritten under-the-table gun-at-the-head understanding between China and the United States. America put pressure on the Chinese government to discourage yellow immigration to this country for the purpose of settling. Still we came, with eyes to settle here. All who had the money brought their families (until women were outlawed, first by California, later by U.S. law), bought property (until owning property was outlawed), went to the Supreme Court of the state of California or the United States against repressive laws and practices at least once every year between 1850 and 1906 (until prejudice against Oriental became a national hysteria after the Japanese sank the Russian navy and, with the power of the mightiest navy on the seas, outraged America by threatening to go to war unless Japanese children were admit-

Confessions of a Chinatown Cowboy

ted into San Francisco's public schools). The laborers who'd come without their families regularly returned home, when they could afford to, to say hello, make children, then returned to America, saying, "Me longtime Californ" to the immigration officials, telling them they were coming home, "Me heap sahbay."

We did not make life bearable here with idealized notions of Chinese culture and a dream of going home rich until an honorable life in America was made possible. We were fishermen, farmers, shoemakers, cigarmakers, laundrymen, miners, all over the West wherever we could go, until we saw that America, not just San Francisco and California, was determined to wipe us out. The California laws against the entry of Chinese women had been struck down in court because the Constitution didn't allow states to mess with immigration; that was for Congress to do, and in 1924, Congress did.

The law warred against our women to deny us our manhood, to drive us out of the country, to kill us. Our American-born women lost their American citizenship if they went to China. They lost their citizenship if they married a Chinese citizen. And to become an American citizen, you had to be born here. Twenty to thirty men for every woman, a woman who would not, could not marry any Chinaman not born here. Those who could afford it carried on long-distance family life, trans-Pacific commutes between years of work and months of family, coming home "longtime Californ." Others of us would never get to China, except as bones and ashes, never have families; our future was simply a matter of growing old and dying. Out of our despair, we took to burning our letters from home, burning the pages of our diaries and journals as we wrote them, burning tickets, receipts, bills, burning everything with our names, everything written in our hand, and throwing the ashes into the sea, in the hope that at least

Frank Chin

that much of us would get home to China. America had taught us, finally, that China was our home and inspired the invention of this little Chinese American ceremony.

HONG KONG DREAM GIRL

Meantime, America picked up the charleston, big bands, and ragtime jazz, and put to music the agony of our old men doomed here without women or a hope of returning to China, and danced to it. The songs of the old forty-niners about "John John Chinaman" were updated and civilized in New York's Tin Pan Alley to become "Little Chinky Butter-fly," "China Girl," "Chinese Lullabye," and a song that must have been sung a lot around the piano, for I've heard bits of it sung by Chinese Americans, mothers of grammar school friends who sang it in their school days in talent shows—I found the sheet music and remembered hearing it, a song featured by Fred Schmitt and his Rialto Orchestra called "Hong Kong Dream Girl":

China boy is very said because he went away,
From his little China maiden,
China boy feel very sad and only yesterday
He wrote a note to her to say:
My little Hong Kong Dream Girl
In every dream you seem, girl,
Two almond eyes are smiling,
And my poor heart is whirling like a big sail round by pigtail
I dream of you till dawning,
But early in the morning
Oriental dream is gone,
China boy is so forlorn,
Hong Kong Dream Girl good-bye.

Confessions of a Chinatown Cowboy

I understand why we of all the immigrant minorities have left no folk or literary legacy, why I don't know my great-grandfather's name, my grandfather's name. But I keep looking. My mother says her father had an imagination like mine, that he made up stories when she saw him, that he was gone all the time working in the steward service of the Southern Pacific. He collected railroad watches. There's a picture of him sitting with the family. And a watch with a train engraved on the watch.

THE MYTH OF THE CHINESE SOJOURNER: A WESTERN MOVIE

The Chinese swordslinger begins with a master of martial arts, a young protégé, and a crime against the protégé's family that sends him on a mission of revenge, away from the school for a distant mountain where the invincible enemy waits. The crime against the family always involves death. I took my grandfather's watch and worked on the Southern Pacific. I rode in the engines up front. I rode in the cabooses where no Chinaman had even ridden before. I was hired with the first batch of blacks to go braking for the SP, in the sixties when the fair employment legislation went into effect. (Ride with me, Grandpa; at least it's not the steward service. You get home more often now.) Life for the Chinese in America was over. There wasn't a Chinaman in the country, man, woman, or child, who didn't feel extinction happening.

We had been forced out of our fisheries, laundries, cigar factories, forced out of our women, forced out of American sight, mind, and culture, by blatant exclusion laws, laws designed to protect fish, secure fire safety, protect public health and morality against us.

The few Chinatowns around the ports of entry and exit grew large, attracting us like elephants' graveyards. The only possibilities we had left were death and China. Those of us

Frank Chin

who stayed prepared against America closing the last loophole in its plan to stamp us out by preparing ourselves to become Chinese. Deportation wasn't a fear among us; it was a dead certainty.

In 1934 Jimmy Ginn sent his father back to China to be done with it. "At that time," Jimmy says, "he didn't want to go. He wanted me to go first and marry, you see. He wanted me to go home. Get married. Have a family. I think then he figured I'm more apt to tie with the home and the family, with my country, than the United States, but mainly he wanted me to go back because of the fact—and if he told me once, he told me about five hundred times—that this is a white man's country. 'You go back to China when you make your money. That is where you belong. If you stay here, the white man will kill you.'" Here is the root source of our culture, our sense of being Chinese American, our self-effacing presence on the American scene, our so-called Chinese culture—"obedience, filial piety, hard work, and self-respect." The white version roots our psychology in China, not white racism, because it's prettier and far away. Thus the substance of Jimmy Ginn's conversation with his father has become the white myth of the Chinese Sojourner and Chinese pride, what Tom Wolfe calls the "Aramco psychology":

Most Chinese who have come to the United States since 1850 have looked upon their experience in America as an interlude in their careers in China. It is the same state of mind an American has when he goes to work for Aramco in the Near East. He may run into all sorts of religious and even stature laws that bar him from Arab life. Yet it would never occur to him to think of it as "discrimination." . . . Weird cockamamie foreigners, nothing more. . . . That is because his psyche still resides in Portland, Oregon or Noman, Oklahoma. . . . The Near East is just an interlude in his career in America.

Confessions of a Chinatown Cowboy

The logic of the myth of the Chinese Sojourner duplicates the logic the Nazis used to justify anti-Semitism in Europe. We came to America without our women (a sign we had no intention of settling here), refused to assimilate, were alien and incapable of accommodating the democratic, individualistic, manly ideals that throbbed in the guts of every American word, breath, and deed, established our own clannish social structures in defiance of the laws of the land, robbed America of her wealth, and took it home to China and our women; therefore, we deserved the exclusion laws, the anti-Chinese riots, the lynchings, to stop the drain of America's wealth.

Miraculously our attitude changed at the outbreak of World War II. We woke up one morning transformed from despised "Chinamen" into "loyal Chinese American citizens." The "conquest of affection by which the Californian Chinese transformed themselves from our race adversaries to our dear, subject people," envisioned by a white writer in 1908, was complete in 1943, when the publishers of Pardee Lowe's *Father and Glorious Descendent* touted his book as "a timely document at a moment when America must learn how to assimilate its loyal minorities and noted that "Pardee Lowe . . . enlisted in the U.S. Army shortly after delivering the manuscript of this book."

The most authoritative, complete, influential, and scholarly expression of the myth of the Chinese Sojourner as Jew of the Orient is *Bitter Strength,* by Gunther Barth of the University of California, Berkeley, History Department. Born as he was in Germany in 1925, the Nazi anti-Semitic logic of his time had his mind and his body, until Allied troops captured his body in World War II. Gunther Barth's high flying white supremacist vision of my history has directly influenced everything written by anybody about Chinese America and been given a Chinese American signature in Betty Lee Sung's *Mountain of*

Gold. This book by a former writer for the Voice of America, now teaching Asian American studies at the City College of New York, has gone through two printings of seventy-five hundred copies each since its 1967 release and in 1971 hit the streets in paper. Out of the five serious literary efforts ever published by American-born Chinese Americans, it's the only book still in print.

As she told me in "Chinaman's Chance," the statistics show more Chinese left the country than entered up until World War II, when trans-Pacific travel stopped. The numbers seem to support the myth of the Chinese Sojourner. But they didn't start counting until late in the game, and when they started twenty to thirty years after we started coming, the numbers didn't show that the bones of our dead traveled as paying passengers and were included in the numbers. They didn't show the number of American-born women returning from China who'd been turned back because their visit to China had cost them their citizenship—so on the books they exited twice and never entered. They didn't show the number of illegal entries who came to settle, the families who landed and got out of California quick for parts of the country that did not outlaw Chinese women and children.

But the most original restatement of the myth of the Chinese Sojourner has to be Tom Wolfe's "Aramco psychology." Because our psyches still resided in China and America was just an interlude in our career, those of us who came over since 1850 didn't look on the repressive laws as discrimination: "If things should become absolutely repressive, he might pack up and go home." (". . . and if he told me once, he told me about five hundred times—that this is a white man's country. 'You go back to China when you make your money. That is where you belong. If you stay here, the white man will kill you.'")

Confessions of a Chinatown Cowboy

In 1915, a young Ben Fee left Canton, China, for the Golden Mountain. His right hand was full. The sword was sheathed. His grandmother was the second Chinese woman to be born in America. Ben was a long time coming to the Golden Mountain to meet the Invincible Enemy. He came to stay.

"I can't get a haircut outside Chinatown, no matter how far away from Chinatown. I can't get a meal outside Chinatown. . . . Course I can't live outside Chinatown."

". . . But he would not be likely to waste many hours thinking about organizing a protest movement."

"So all these racism developed . . . sit-down, and sit-in . . . we going through that as a kid. And we are way ahead of the civil rights movement, in San Francisco!"

In the twenties, Fee developed his skills as a labor organizer integrating San Francisco. He used the laws to build up the bucks to pay his way out.

"San Francisco had a law, when you pay a deposit down, if the landlord welshes on his promise, he has to pay double the deposit. We raised forty dollars, and we get the two American kids and two Chinese. The Americans, they go in and look for apartment and pay down ten-dollar deposit. The next day, we would go, all four together look over the apartment. And the landlady say, 'Hey hey hey hey! . . . What is these things here?'. . . In eight weeks we make that forty dollars be four hundred dollars! Just by collecting deposits."

He leaned back in his chair, and deliberately put his closed right hand on the table, and drew on his Tiparillo, grinning like a fox.

"And we fight from block [down comes his fist, thunk] to block [again his fist, thunk], push from Stockton [thunk] to Powell [thunk], from Powell to Mason, from Mason to Jones and Taylor [his fist up and down, taking him along]. It's just

Frank Chin

like fighting a war! That we keep on pushing [thunk] and pushing [thunk]. And on Geary Street and Van Ness Avenue, there's a restaurant called Almond Blossom. Now, that's a typical name," Fee says, laughing.

"We went there," he says, and is suddenly in the character of the waitress, talking the movie about him.

"'Nope!' the waitress said. I said, 'Well, how dare you call Almond Blossom and don't serve Chinese!'

"'Oh,' the waitress said, 'I have no prejudice against Chinese, but the manager . . .' So the manager come out. 'I have no prejudice against Chinese, but the customer objects. Sorry.' So we left.

"So one day . . . we'd counted how many seat there at the counter. There're ten of them. And the most expensive item on the menu those days is the Porterhouse steak! Three dollars. We get ten American kids. And the three of us—one Filipino, one Japan', and one Chinese—we went to the Almond Blossom. [His fist thunks the desk.] And the ten kid went there first, and they order, all of them Porterhouse steak! A thirty dollar o'steak there. Oh! The manager so happy! He never had such a good day. And he begin to fry it [thunk]. . . . And when we smell that pretty good steak flavor, we come in [thunk thunk thunk], sit down. We went through the same routine again," he says, rushing now.

"[Thunk.] The waitress say [thunk thunk], 'You come in again, gentlemen?'" in the waitress' voice, his laughter showing how long ago that was, how little times have changed.

"'You know I have no prejudice against you.'. . . And then get the manager. And the manager begin to say the same thing [thunk]. Then I raise my voice. I asked these kids, I say, 'Hey, gentlemen!'"

("Morning, Mr. Clanton." Thunk. "The only thing that stands out in the mind when you're playing an Oriental of education is that, number one: his manners are very good.")

Confessions of a Chinatown Cowboy

"'We have never met. I have never crossed your path before.'"

("He's very simple and very courteous. That's about it. So you do a lot of bowing.")

"'I never did you any wrong. Why do you object to us to eat?'"

(". . . I deliberately kept my hands at my side. I very rarely used any gestures, unless they were absolutely important.")

"'Why do you object?'

"And the kid say, 'Who object?' [thunk].

"I say, 'The manager say you object to us eating here.' [Fast fists now, thunk thunk thunk thunk. The Fox and the Tiger strategy.]

"They say, 'On the contrary! If they don't serve you, we object!' So they all line up and walk out. . . . Oh, you ought to see this manager! . . . Run out and watch those ten walking down the block, and then come back and look at those ten steaks. . . . He finally, he submit. He let us eat."

There were others like Ben who left meat burning on the griddle, walked out of barbershops with half a shave, half a haircut, breaking out of the Chinatown game preserve. But what they were doing scared Chinatown. Chinatown knew the whites would be antagonized, that white park rangers would sweep in, and thought it better for all to ignore and dissociate from men like Ben Fee, lay low, and stall the day of the big deportation.

BETTY LEE SUNG

There came a day when the worst thing a Chinese American parent could say to a child, or a Chinaman to another Chinaman, was, "You act like a *hok gwai*"—a black. In trade for appearing in the documentary I was doing, Betty Lee Sung asked me to speak to the three classes in Asian American stud-

Frank Chin

ies she was teaching at City College. Afterward, jumping from parked car to parked car down the street, keeping my feet out of the moving living tide of dog shit devouring New York, toward a coffee shop, I heard her say something I can't get out of my mind. We'd been talking about her classes, about teaching, being a Chinese American, and the special Chinatown issue of *New York* that had hit the streets the day before. Nothing by a Chinese American in it, I said; the same racist love by Tom Wolfe, going to an imaginary China to tell us who we are. "You take it too personally," Betty Lee Sung said.

"I take being a Chinaman pretty personally," I said. "Don't you?"

"No, I don't. I can't. If I did, I'd be miserable all the time. . . . You know, Frank, you're really very black. You talk like a black," said today's most respected and influential Chinese American teacher/scholar/writer.

"Why can't you boys, you Negroes and Mexicans," the visiting cop said, all creases, jingling metals, and hair on his knuckles, setting every Chinaman boy of us up for an afternoon of fights, "stay out of trouble like the Chinese? Mind your folks? Study hard? Obey the laws?" And there we Chinamen were, in Lincoln Elementary School, Oakland, California, in a world where manliness counts for everything, surrounded by bad blacks and bad Mexican kids who were still into writing their names into their skin with nails dipped in ink. They had a walk, a way of wearing their pants on the brink of disaster, a tongue, a kingdom of manly style everyone respected. Everyone knew what they called you behind your back because you had to, to survive in the yard. There we were. There I was, hair held up high and back with Tuxedo wax, edges of hair by my ears turned down and shaped into fake sideburns and spit curls, toothpick in my mouth, pants low, belt buckle on my hip, and black-and-white basketball shoes, suddenly stripped and shaved bare by this cop, exposed

Confessions of a Chinatown Cowboy

for copping another man's flash, imitating this from the blacks, that from the Mexicans, something from the whites, with no manly style of my own, unless it was Charlie Chan swish Fu Manchu. There was Chinatown where I lived, but nothing Chinese in my life as real to me as the clothes people told me were foreign, "American" things.

Nobody knew what Chinamen called anybody behind their backs, and nobody cared. I was saving up for shades to hide my Chinese eyes, like the Lone Ranger, and going out into the sun to make me darker because I hated being hated by the rogues I admired for doing things. They were like the gangs of tough swordsmen in the Chinese movies I saw with my grandmother in Frisco. But the going image of Chinese manhood wasn't swordsman. It was a sissy servant, Charlie Chan and his fuck-up sons.

Chinese from China, whose experience told them they were Chinese just as everything about our experience tells us we are not Chinese, were secure in their Chinese manhood and capable of choosing to hate themselves, be converted to Christianity, become "Americanized," be assimilated. For them the concept of the dual identity, being foul Chinese and righteous American, is real. The Americanization of Chinese Christians Lin Yutang (*Moment in Peking, A Chinatown Family*), C. Y. Lee (*Flower Drum Song*), Chiang Yee (*The Silent Traveler* series), Frank Ching of the *New York Times,* and Simon Li ("one part of town the Chinese mission from Red China are almost sure to visit is Chinatown," New York) has invariably meant their absorption and acceptance of white Americanism—not just the stereotype of all of Chinese America being obliged to be definably Chinese and American, but the white male racist overtones of that stereotype. With the aid of a Social Science Research Council grant, Francis L. K. Hsu disguised as a sociologist became a yellow propagandist for white male supremacy, pushing the concept of the dual personality

Frank Chin

and not too subtly reminding us American-born *juk sing* that we're not really Chinese but must, if we're going to live here, learn to be Charlie Chan, that we're all of us, born here or not, obliged to please white racist prejudice:

The Chinese in America, in common with other minority groups, will have a continuing problem of double identity. But the effective way of dealing with it is not to deny its existence but to face it squarely. The first step is to realize that the double identity of a minority group is not dissimilar to that of the professional woman. She is a woman and a professional. Some American professional women have tended to forget about their sex identity but most have kept some sort of balance between it and their profession. In the latter case, their sex identity sometimes becomes an advantage rather than a disability.

To achieve this balance, the Chinese in America will do best if he knows Chinese as a second language or at least will take the trouble to familiarize himself with aspects of Chinese history and culture.

Although Hsu's book, *The Challenge of the American Dream: The Chinese in the United States,* could have been written by Jack London in the nineteenth century, it is fresh on the market this year, down in the skid-row twenty-four-hour dustless dens of paperbacks, college outline series, and hometown papers; better yet, it's in colleges and universities that have adopted it as a sociology text. To these Chinese writers, Chinatown is fake China, and we *juk sing* are contemptible for being incapable of being authentically Chinese in anything but yellow skin and black hair.

Chinatown is my home. All of America is Chinatown. I'm real here, and it's real in me—no fake China. The Chinese cannot see that we *juk sing* are neither Chinese nor American- or does Simon Li expect the delegation from Senegal to cab it up to Harlem for a breath of home, too?

Confessions of a Chinatown Cowboy

With rare exceptions, all that has been published in this country by "Asian Americans" writing about themselves has been white racist propaganda, quietly and subtly stated like Hsu's, but propaganda nonetheless. The use of the word *propaganda* implies a plot—control and censorship of Asian American publishing. Acting on a firm belief in the stereotype of us being foreign, though born here, precludes the need for a conscious plot against us.

John Okada, author of the first and only Japanese American novel, *No-No Boy,* was born in Seattle, an ocean and a generation away from Japan, spoke Japanese, but grew up with English as the language of his soul, a tongue developed in front of the class telling movies, telling radio shows on rainy days. He wrote a book on it, about a Japanese American who does two years in prison for refusing the draft in World War II and comes home to a world where all the men, especially the Nisei, seem to be vets. The novel was rejected by several publishers because of "language"—some objected to the cuss words, others to his fluency with the English language. Strange for a man who made his living as an advertising copywriter. His novel was rejected by every publishing house in the country. Finally Charles Tuttle, a Japanese company, published the book in 1957.

The 1941 publication date of Toshio Mori's collection of short stories *Yokohama, California* was delayed until 1949. The very first sentence of William Saroyan's introduction led you to believe that, contrary to fact, Mori was foreign born and not native to English and gave the reader to understand that he was reading, not a book of stories, but a series of English papers: "Of the thousands of unpublished writers in America there are probably no more than three who cannot write better English than Toshio Mori."

Frank Chin

Rose Hum Lee, whose *The Chinese in the United States of America* is considered the definitive work on Chinese American history and sociology, could not find a publisher in this country. She published it at her own expense in Hong Kong.

In light of the publication of C. Y. Lee's eight novels, Francis L. K. Hsu's two books, the big printings of Betty Lee Sung's work, with another book under contract, the publishers' arguments about readers and lack of interest in Asian America fail to convince me. It's not a matter of, "It doesn't pay to write about Asian America," as it is, "It doesn't pay to challenge Charlie Chan."

America doesn't want us as a visible native minority. They want us to keep our place as Americanized foreigners ruled by immigrant loyalty. But never having been anything else but born here, I've never been foreign and resent having foreigners telling me my place in America and America telling me I'm foreign. There's no denial or rejection of Chinese culture going here, just the recognition of the fact that Americanized Chinese are not Chinese Americans and that Chinese America cannot be understood in the terms of either Chinese or American culture, or some "chow mein/spaghetti" formula of Chinese and American cultures, or anything else you've seen and loved in Charlie Chan. A Chinese can take being told he speaks English pretty good and that he's pretty "Americanized and aggressive" as compliments, as English and being American are for him the results of conscious effort. The same things said to a Chinaman are insults. It's putting him in his place, not in the Chinatown a Chinese could see today, but in the Chinatown that's in the blood of all *juk sing*, the death camp Chinatown, Chinatown where the missionaries erected forty churches and church agencies and opened "Chinese schools" to teach us to be Chinese, the way NASA teaches Americans to be citizens of the moon playing on our fear of deportation by perpetuating, if not the fact, then the psychol-

Confessions of a Chinatown Cowboy

ogy of the Chinaman facing certain extinction by death or deportation. That Chinatown is our language. It's in our silence.

MOVIES IN CHINATOWN

Like the languages the Chinese brought over 120 years ago that developed into an instrument of a Chinese American intelligence, making sense of a mess of weirdness and happenings that didn't happen in China, and the kung fu that became high-class dirty street fighting, the Chinese movies that I grew up with, that grew me up to figure in the myths of a teacher, a quest, a gang, and bloody death, were only academically Chinese. As parts of my life and the lives of maybe 200,000 like me, second, third, fourth, fifth, sixth, seventh generation, born here, bred here, home here, the Chinese movies are not foreign entertainments, nor is the meaning we take from them particularly Chinese.

The most popular Chinese movie is the swordslinger, a form comparable to the American western that serves the same popular function of articulating the culture's fantasy of ballsy individuality. The a-man-has-got-to-do-what-a-man-has-got-to-do ethic of gunslinger balls that says the individual rides alone, fights alone, and duels man-to-man is exercised only by fools and the bad guy in Chinese movies. The bad guy, a man invincible in individual combat, goes down under the gang swords of a hero, who's stepped out into life to learn that the lessons of the master's school were right, that a man invincible in individual combat will go down in gang action, that the individual needs friends. The balls the Chinese movie celebrated in Chinatown was gang balls and didn't really clash with John Wayne, who was an extension of the master in *Red River* and *Flying Tigers* and fit right in with street gangs. When Frankenheimer's *The Young Savages* hit the streets, Chi-

Frank Chin

natown had been ready a long time with gangs. His movie just gave us names for our gangs. We discovered names. Names were big. From the dap-down-inspired badass Puerto Rican gang in *The Young Savages,* one Chinatown gang took the name of the Horseman and was home! That was a good movie. Most were and are fatal doses of white supremacy.

The movies were teachers. In no uncertain terms they taught America that we were lovable for being a race of sissies, cowed by women, and not black with all our hearts, living to accommodate the white men. Unlike the white stereotype of the evil black stud, Indian rapist, Mexican macho, the evil of the evil Dr. Fu Manchu was not sexual but homosexual. The sexual "evil" offered by Fu Manchu to the white race is nothing less than satisfaction of the white male fantasy of white balls being irresistible. Instead of threatening white goddess blond big tits with sexual assault, Dr. Fu swishes in to threaten the All-Joe American with his beautiful nymphomaniac daughter.

The differences between the evil Dr. Fu Manchu and the good detective Charlie Chan of the Honolulu Police Department are superficial. (Except for one. Manchu asserts his will. He uses the first-person pronoun *I.* He doesn't keep his place. Charlie Chan never uses the first-person pronouns *I* or *we* but speaks in the passive voice and prefaces all his remarks with apologies—"So sorry to disagree. . . ," "Excuse, please . . . may make one small observation? . . . ") But Fu Manchu and Chan are visions of the same mythic being, brewed up in the subconscious regions of the white Christian's racial wet dream.

Devil and angel, the Chinese is a sexual joke glorifying white power. Dr. Fu, a man wearing a long dress, batting his eyelashes, surrounded by muscular black servants in loincloths, and with his bad habit of caressingly touching white men on the leg, wrist, and face with his long fingernails, is not

Confessions of a Chinatown Cowboy

so much a threat as he is a frivolous offense to white manhood. Chan's gestures are the same, except he doesn't touch and, instead of being graceful like Fu in flowing robes, he is awkward in a baggy suit and clumsy. His sexuality is the source of a joke running through all the forty-seven Chan films. The large family of the bovine detective is the product of, not sex, but animal husbandry. Hollywood on high sacrificed three white men, gave us their sons Warner Oland, Sidney Toler, and Roland Winters, Charlie Chan the First, Second, and Third, cast in the image of the most perfect Chinese so that we might liken ourselves unto him and be guided along the true path toward assimilation.

THE LAST WHITE MAN TO PLAY CHARLIE CHAN

Chan did not smoke, drink, or womanize, says Roland Winters, the last surviving Charlie Chan of the movies. He was Charlie Chan in six of the forty-seven Chan features, and like Warner Oland and Sidney Toler, he's out there, someplace, an invisible charge vibrating in the air, mainlining to the brains of America from TV and midnight festivals of pop art, driving America crazy. Chan has been with us since 1926 and will live forever, teaching us our place, Chinese culture, Confucius says, how to move. "The only Orientals I've ever dealt with," says Roland Winters, "I've found very reserved of gesture. They don't wave their arms around like Italians or Frenchmen. They're very, very contained people."

"The only thing that stands out in the mind when you're playing an Oriental of *education* is that, number one: his manners are very good. He's very simple, and very courteous. That's about it. So you do a lot of bowing," he said, "rather that saying, 'Right on!' you know, 'Yeah,' or something. And I deliberately kept my hands at my side. I very rarely used any gestures, unless they were absolutely important."

Frank Chin

I asked, "How would Charlie Chan react to a physical threat?"

"Oh, he was the bravest of the brave! Nothing ruffled him, you know; he was a very courageous man. As I recall, when we started this series, I said to them, 'If you want to do any physical stuff with the character, I'll be glad to do it.' I was forty-one or -two or -three then when I started these things and in fairly good shape in those days. And I told them that I was fairly proficient at judo and jujitsu, which I had studied. And they said, 'Oh, no! No! Chan never does anything like that! He never gets into violent things.'"

"Well, let's say you were confronted by a young Chinese American who was bitter about Chan," I asked. "How would you talk to him?"

"I hope it never happens to me," Winters said. An elderly man who describes himself as being "older than God," still recognizable as the last Charlie Chan, knew the lessons he'd been teaching; even when he'd been the guest of honor at Chinatown banquets, he knew the clean fun of the Chan films wasn't so clean and, for some, not much fun.

"The dice would be loaded against me," he said, "because everything he said would be more or less true. You know, you can say, 'Well, those were different times, and people thought differently.' And he'd say, 'Well, that's just what I'm talking about,' you know. 'We were looked on as a minority, and laughed at, and made fun of. And you didn't do anything to help.' As I said earlier, you asked me if I'd ever had any adverse comment from Chinese. And I said, 'No, I never had, but I'm sure that it was around.' I'm sure that any intelligent and proud Chinese would more or less resent the whole idea of Chan. Not so much Chan, because he wasn't too bad, but his silly kids that did stupid things."

The Chinese American actors who played Chan's kids, Keye Luke, Benson Fong, and Victor Sen Yung, thought they

Confessions of a Chinatown Cowboy

were doing good for Chinese America. Being "the silly kids that did stupid things" countered the Dr. Fu Manchu image of the Chinese, they believed, and presented a more realistic image of the assimilated Chinese American, speaking good English, wearing natty clothes and two-tone shoes. The language and clothes might have been elements of a more realistic characterization of the Chinese American, but they were also what made Chan's sons comical. Chan's sons were lovable, respectable fools, funny because they didn't have sense enough to know they weren't white and wouldn't stop trying. Lovable and respectable because they implicitly knew their place. Birmingham (Mantan Moreland), the Chan's black chauffeur, like Fu Manchu's Nubian slaves, places the Charlie Chan (serving the white men with his hands at his sides) and the Chinese American. Honorable sons (laudably trying to "outwhite the whites" to win acceptance) in proper racist perspective. The Fu Manchu/Charlie Chan movies were parables of racial order. In the cockeyed logic of that order, the greatest insult to Chinese America in these films, the casting of a white man in the role of Charlie Chan, was and still is no insult at all but part of the charm of the films and visual proof of our acceptance and assimilation by whites. They just eat us up.

ANOTHER CHARLIE CHAN

NBC and Universal Studios, out to tap the continued popularity of the Chan movies, planned to revive Chan, bring him out in color, and make a prime-time television series of him and one of his honorable numbered sons. According to UPI, David Tebet, vice president for talent of NBC-TV, was asked to "Find us a Charlie Chan." Tebet went around the world trying to sniff out "an Oriental actor who spoke English that would be understandable in the U.S." He failed. Ross Martin was cast in the role of Chan. It was all a matter of language.

Frank Chin

But deep down, in the cultural subconscious, there's a link between tongue and balls that makes us sick. Roland Winters, in an unguarded moment, explained the logic of casting a white man in the role of Charlie Chan this way: "The only thing I can think of is, if you want to cast a homosexual in a show, and you get a homosexual, it'll be awful. It won't be funny . . . and maybe there's something there. . . . " It's all there, the complete message in easy-to-decipher code. Somehow from Charlie Chan and his sons, from television, from school, from just like in America, we all get the message.

THE MESSAGE

Wing Tek Lum, a young Chinese American poet, a winner of the New York Poetry Center award, got the message and recited it from life in a poem, "Grateful Here":

> *When walking with a Caucasian girl*
> *holding hands, I would pass by teenage hangouts*
> *overhearing insults. They would always pick on the girl*
> *as though she were a lesbian. . . .*

Meaning the Chinese American male holding that girl's hand was seen as no man at all but as some kind of perverse woman. The stereotype of us being a race without manhood has been so thoroughly and subtly suffused throughout American culture for so long that it's become a comfortable past of the American subconscious. White America is as securely indifferent about us as men as plantation owners were about their loyal house niggers. House niggers is what America has made of us, admiring us for being patient, submissive, aesthetic, passive, accommodating, essentially feminine in character—what whites call "Confuciusist," dreaming us up a goofy version of Chinese culture to preserve in becoming the white male's dream minority. Our white-dream identity being feminine, the

Confessions of a Chinatown Cowboy

carriers of our strength, the power of the race belongs to our women. The dream women of this dream minority naturally prefer white men to their own. This dream is fulfilled in the movies, in life where the girls laugh your strut away as a cop of another man's flash, easily pinning you for a fake, and kicking you in the head with the news that real men want them.

In our literature, too, Chinese American women have been used to legitimize the white stereotypes of us. Four of the five American-born Chinese Americans to publish serious literary efforts are women. Of these four, Jade Snow Wong, author of the famous *Fifth Chinese Daughter*, the daughter of a Christian convert, was asked to write her book by a white friend and aided by a white teacher; Virginia Lee, author of *The House That Tai Ming Built*, writes of a beautiful Chinese American girl, gaga over a handsome blond "American"; Betty Lee Sung was recruited to write about the Chinese in America for the Voice of America, which inspired her to write *Mountain of Gold*, a direct descendant of Gunther Barth's *Bitter Strength;* Diana Chang, author of *The Frontiers of Love*, the finest book produced by a Chinese American to date, and three other novels. Whether or not the individual works were authored by women or confirmed the white male supremacist stereotype of us wouldn't matter if only they—including Pardee Lowe's *Father and Glorious Descendent*—did not constitute all, I mean all, the sum, the total body, the best, worst, and only Chinese American literature as I write this in 1972.

Beyond these five serious literary efforts, all we've been able to publish in America has been a series of "Inside Chinatown" hardcover softheaded tour guides and cookbooks. America has locked the whole race into the same housewife stereotype women are running out of town. Our lack of manliness and all that manliness means in this culture—aggressiveness, creativity, individuality, just being taken seriously—is subtly but visibly confirmed in the movies and life imitating

Frank Chin

the dark art. Chinese America was rigged to be a race of males going extinct without women. We've always been ridiculous with men and still outnumber our women, but in Hollywood we as men count for nothing.

FAKE MEN, REAL WOMEN

The roles of Asian principals—Fu Manchu, Charlie Chan, General Yang, Mr. Moto, the heavy Asian males from Griffith's *Broken Blossoms* to *55 Days at Peking,* full circle to the 1971 *Fourth Coming of Charlie Chan*—have been played by white men, while the Asian female rarely, rarely has not been played by the real thing. *The World of Suzy Wong, A Girl Named Tamiko, I Was a Japanese War Bride, House of Bamboo, Love Is a Many Splendored Thing, Sayonara, Man in the Middle* (movies of the Asian boom of the late fifties early sixties using Asians as metaphors for blacks by cautious Hollywood), *Alice's Restaurant,* and a TV commercial hawking cheap wine featured authentic Oriental lovelies mixing it up with real white men, a Command hair spray commercial. . . . You had to be a Chinaman to look on the preponderance of white male–yellow female couples dreamed up by Hollywood as another movement in white America's effort to drive us into extinction. What few women we had the whites were taking—that's what we read, and that's what was and is happening. There's more interracial dating and marriage between Asian American women and white men than Asian American men and white women. To our women, we neither act nor look like "men," as a Chinese American girl, a student of mine, wrote: "Chinese guys are not attractive to me because they are not the so-called 'Mr. American' type of people. First of all, most of all, most of them are not muscular and romantic. . . ."

As black skin meant "ugly" in America, so our small size means "sissy." We don't have a surplus of men; we have a sur-

Confessions of a Chinatown Cowboy

plus of sissies in a culture that loathes sissies. To become an acceptable sissy, all America asks of us is to become "Chinese" or "Japanese" aesthetes, foreign, exotic, artistic, shy, what James Shigeta was in those few films that mixed a yellow man and white woman, a kind of male ingenue tomboy, the passive, reluctant lover, virgin, an Oriental art object aggressively collected by Carol Baker in *Bridge to the Sun* and Victoria Shaw in Samuel Fuller's *The Crimson Kimono.*

Every stereotype is based on a grain of truth, I'm told by friends, not really telling me that sissiness is a Chinese cultural trait that has somehow survived six generations of Chinese America, but honestly suggesting that my "heritage" is responsible for the notable lack of Chinese American presence in American culture. We have a fine popular reputation but no popularly known works or political, literary, or artistic spokesmen.

What we are really as Chinese Americans is explained in terms of what was done to us here, what we were made to be, in the same way that the passive, subtly anti-American character of American prisoners of war home from the Korean conflict is explained in terms of what was done to them, what three years of controlled environment made them be. We haven't been here undergoing brainwashing for a mere three years but for six generations. After all, the Chinese learned brainwashing from a century of Christian missionaries during the Opium Wars.

CHINESE SCHOOL

In the late nineteenth century, after the railroads had made San Francisco an elephants' graveyard for Chinaman, Christian missionaries and a California state law outlawing Chinese from all schools but "Chinese schools" confirmed our worst fears and contrived to help us out of America by creating the

Frank Chin

"Chinese schools" of Chinatown, the same schools Chinatown parents against busing look to for the preservation of what they've come to believe to be "Chinese culture." White missionaries and the Chinese Benevolent Association still run most of these schools in San Francisco and Chinatowns all over the country and Canada. Some of us are convinced the schools and the concept of being Chinese American taught in these schools are ours. And the whites love us for it. Luckily— I think, luckily—for me different lessons were taught at my Chinese school.

From five to seven at night, after "American" school, I went to Wah Kue Chinese School, under Chinese Nationalist Party headquarters in Oakland. My mother had gone to this Chinese school and my aunts and uncles. The wood of this old building smelled of them. The building smelled old of a lot of people. And we smelled, too—of hot feet in high-topped rubber-soled black-and-white basketball shoes and the sweat of the quick two hours on the court between schools.

One day the teacher who lived upstairs behind Party headquarters was late. We didn't hear his step working down the old stairs. But people were walking up there. Then they came down. Two men. One, a real smiler, standing on the teacher's platform, told us Mr. Wong was dead. The girls sighed, and the boys . . . for us it was good news. The old man used to beat us. He had a ruler with the measures marked off with brass tacks. One end of the ruler had the Chinese word for *big* carved in it. I used to think he hit us with that thing because we were born here. I still have a scar. The other man was our new teacher, Mr. Mah, a skinny. He wore his blue suit the way lunch wears a paper sack.

Mr. Mah taught math and engineering at a university, the name of which he wouldn't mention, during the day; then he would drive his white Chevy down to the town to teach us Chinese.

Confessions of a Chinatown Cowboy

One day he stomped in with a newspaper and shouted at us, in real Chinatown buck-buck bagaw, an angry quick-tripping tongue promiscuously roaming all the languages we knew, raping them of sense. He said he'd been on the way to school when he saw the headline "JOE," and said to himself, "Joe Stalin alive?" and stopped the car, and bought the paper. "And you know what it said?" He opened up the paper and showed us. "JOE DIMAGGIO MARRIES MARILYN MONROE!" And he was off into how crappy American journalism was, who the *Tribune*'s publisher, Senator William Knowland, was, the China lobby, Mme Claire Chennault, pounding his way to sense the way we told big movies up in front of class on rainy days when we couldn't go to the yard at recess or PE period. There we are, kids. I was ten, eleven, maybe twelve. And he's talking about Chinatown and Chou En-lai, the Long March, and how the Chinese in American have done nothing but keep their place, preserving a Chinese culture white men invented for them to preserve. He named names, raged against the Chinese Americans who were horrified at the sound of the words *Chinatown* and *Chinaman*.

"Who made Chinaman ashamed to be called Chinaman?" he asked. "Not the Chinamen who came over as Chinamen, who were called Chinamen all the time, answered to Chinamen, worked hard and died as Chinamen. Not the Chinamen, but the whites, the 'Americans' the 'Chinese Americans' work so hard to please."

The Chinamen were our ancestors, he said. The price we were paying for getting along here, for being accepted, was our pride. "Give up your father, forget the Chinamen, and talk about Chinese art!"

I used to keep him talking and screaming a show for us the whole two hours to get out of doing my Chinese lessons. I'd go to the library and read books on China, go through the papers for stuff on Korea, the French in Indo-China, Joe

Frank Chin

McCarthy, what was being said about Chinatown, and next day, when we're opening up our books, casually ask something like, "Who was Joe Stilwell?"

Then I began to hear around the town that people thought he talked like a Commie.

The kids told their parents, and they talked, and I felt it was my fault. McCarthy was going then. Mr. Mah was dumping on McCarthy, too, and the whole Red Scare, while the Chinese Nationalists through the Chinese Benevolent Association were forming a new Chinatown organization, the Anti-Communist League, a group that, not surprisingly, loved Chiang and hated Mao. I'm ten. Commies are bad. And to get out of my lessons, and just for fun, I've been making this man talk like a Commie.

He used to drive me home to the restaurant, and we'd talk in the car. I'd invite him to dinner in the kitchen, but he never came; even when I said he could eat in front he never came. I told him I was sorry, that I didn't want to get him in trouble, but there was talk about him being a Commie, and that's why kids were dropping out of the school. There was a new school down the street, a free one, but that wasn't why the kids were being pulled out in the middle of the semester. I told him I'd been making him jump and scream to get out of doing my Chinese lessons. He hissed, turned his head around this way and that, pounded the steering wheel. "I hate the Communists!" he said. He'd welcomed them at first, thought there would be more freedom under them, enough for him to start a school.

He started a school and was kicked out of the country. But he was glad to see China in the hands of the Chinese for a change. Did I know they were producing steel? Yes, he'd told us. There was that pride, for he was still Chinese and would always be, in the same way he hoped we would be "Chinamen."

Confessions of a Chinatown Cowboy

He told me he'd started a school on Taiwan and the Nationalists kicked him out. "I'm not a Nationalist. I am not a Communist! I am Chinese. I am a teacher," he said. He said he wanted us to know there was no shame in being born here, that it was all right not to be a Chinese from China, that it was all right not to be a white American. Those "Chinamen," those yellow men who worked on the railroad, the people whites collapsed mines on, paved over, and built towns on, called names on, made laws against, and made their children want to forget, they, the Chinamen, were good men. They'd fought.

There'd been brave men who stood out among them. Their fights and their brave men had been forgotten in favor of remembering white champions standing up for Chinese (these champs had been bought and trained by the Chinese Benevolent Association, hip to the fact that whites didn't like Chinese to be so aggressive and obnoxious as to speak for themselves but would listen to another white man) and perpetuating the myth of timid, meek, passive Chinamen. He said their children's children, if not their children, should be proud of those Chinamen. And I was one of the children's children. I didn't know what he was talking about. All I knew was that I'd done it again. I'd triggered nerves in this man and made him cry and angry.

The Joe McCarthy thing caught Mr. Mah when the university came out with loyalty oaths. I learned this later. Much later, looking for the man years later. He wasn't an American citizen. He couldn't in good conscience sign an oath of loyalty to America.

The school closed with a party. There were now five students left. A slow change had been working in Mr. Mah the past few weeks. One day he asked us all what we wanted to be. I said "artist or writer." Bill wanted to write sports. Calvin some kind of science. He told us all to go into engineering,

Frank Chin

and we knew something was wrong because before he was saying we should grow up and make Chinese America *appear!* And becoming an engineer was to disappear.

We all brought goodies to the party. Calvin's sister made a cake. She's married, a mother and a schoolteacher now. Calvin became an engineer, gave it up, and is now an orthopedic surgeon. Bill Wong is a staff writer for the *Wall Street Journal.* We had a party eating off the Ping-Pong tables, the five of us—the fifth changes sheets and sweeps rooms in a large motel near where the school used to be—and Mr. Mah. He gave things from the school. The school bell, Ping-Pong sets, swords, martial arts paraphernalia, and Mr. Wong's studded ruler went, and nobody seemed to want anything else. He asked me what I did when I was on my own, what I did for fun. I told him I went to the library, read books on China, newspapers, Edgar Allen Poe, Sherlock Holmes. He asked Calvin, my best friend, what he did for fun. Calvin said he listened to baseball on the radio. And the skinny Mr. Mah, rattling around in his blue suit, pointed at me and told me to stop. "Stop!" he shouted, and hit the top of the table with his hand. "Stop reading! Go home and listen to baseball on the radio!"

McCarthy only helped. It was the five of us, like the characters in those old Chinese swordslingers we watched and mixed up with westerns to make a Chinatown soul, we the master's loyal protégés of *I Shot Jesse James,* who brought down his school and him toppling. We'd done what the Communists, the Nationalists, the Sino-Japanese War, World War II, the Revolution, Korea, the whole world, and Joe McCarthy alone couldn't do. He, Mr. Mah, was the Invincible Enemy on Golden Mountain, and now he was bowed. We made him stop being obnoxious, set him on the path to a healthy attitude toward prejudice, an acceptance of the Aramco psychology," assimilation into America without violence. He was the best teacher we'd ever had and the bravest. Now he was the

Confessions of a Chinatown Cowboy

most broken man we'd ever seen in our lives. He looked like everything he hated, at last and finally a "Chinese American." As with most of Chinese America and dutiful housewives, the price of acceptance was his soul, but he didn't pay it up. We had to take it from him.

The myth of the Chinese Sojourner, the stereotype of the gutless, passive, effeminate Chinaman has become too precious a part of the American white male legend for America to give it up easily. Virtually everything being written about us today reveals our true racist value to America as a race of white right hands to hit the blacks and "less assimilated" races in the head with. We're numerous enough to showcase as a minority but don't count enough to take up America's media time and space speaking for ourselves.

THE MOVIE ABOUT ME

Meantime, in the Hollywood Old West, we're dreamed up again as passive Chinks sucking up to the white man and blowing opium in Robert Altman's fine *McCabe and Mrs. Miller* and Frank Perry's awful *Doc*—the only version of the ok Corral showdown to epitaph us that way. ("Morning, Mr. Clanton. . . . Which one of you killed Virgil?") In the Hollywood movie about me, I'm a sissy. In the making of *Another Train to Rob*, a 1970 production recently aired network coast to coast as a Saturday night movie, Guy Lee, a Chinese American actor, was given a history lesson by veteran western director Andrew McLaglen. McLaglen kept cutting the shooting of one scene. Finally he told the Asian actors what was wrong. They were moving forward and lifting their picks and shovels threateningly when the white stranger (George Peppard) rode into the mining works. According to Guy Lee, who holds a shovel in the scene, McLaglen said Chinese in the early West would back off and keep their hands down at their sides at the

Frank Chin

approach of an unfamiliar white man, so he wanted the Chinese to back off and keep their hands down. Not the kind of ancestors a kid would go looking for or want to be known by, but the kind of people loved and celebrated in the new movies and the new writing about us.

This vision of our history that blows a racist fantasy of Confucianist, hands-down sissies backing off, bowing, kowtowing Chinese pride, has turned off too many generations of us, off to exploring our American past. There's very little of it left. Each new word on us creeping off the pens of America's righteous white is an epitaph to our sensibility, another word, another man, another generation away from the truth—one truth being that we were never passive, we had to be beaten down, that the Jimmy Gins, Ben Fees, Mr. Mahs, come from a Chinaman tradition. They come from the Deer Creek Chinaman recalled in James Ladd Delkin's *The Diary of a '49er:* "The miners on Deer Creek below the town turned out last week and drove all the Chinamen off that stream. The heathen had got to be impudent and aggressive, taking up claims the same as white men and appropriating water without asking leave. They cut one of the miner's dams and, when he attempted to repair it, chased him away, brandishing their shovels and making a great hullaballoo."

My sword is sheathed, but in my left hand now. Tom Wolfe, Kenneth LaMott, Mary Ellen Leary, Gunther Barth, Stuart Miller, Gerald Haslam, you're white racists. I was asked to end on a positive note, show a sign of hope. Name-calling is nothing, but it's all I can do where there's not a hope, not a prayer, not a Chinaman's chance in hell of being heard above the snores of America's established writers Hollywooding us to our rightful place as the children of Charlie Chan in the American dream.

Confessions of a Chinatown Cowboy

BULLETPROOF BUDDHISTS

"THEY LIKE TO CARRY THE NINE-MILLIMETER HANDGUN"

Roy Moody

"They like to carry the nine-millimeter handgun," Officer
Roy Moody says. He's talking about Lao and Cambodian
gang kids. "And, of course, they do like the semiautomatic
rifles like AK-47s. They like AK-47s, even though we haven't
seen an AK-47 in a while. But definitely the nine-millimeter
handgun. They like 'em. They like 'em! They absolutely like
'em."

He looks like a big kid, I mean an enlarged, robust four- or
five-year-old kid ready for some fun. He looks like Bob the
Big Boy in front of Bob's Big Boy coffeeshop with a flattop.
He goes out of his way, a long way out of his way, to make
you feel he's not as big and dangerous as he really is. He talks
in the tone of voice and rhythm of a dog handler talking a
strange ugly dog out of a corner.

"You know, we get threats on police officers. Some definitely wouldn't hesitate shooting anybody, *anybody* now. So
it's definitely changed.

Bulletproof Buddhists

"The things that have happened to these communities didn't have to happen. You know, it's just, I think, in the seventies, early eighties, our whole system just wasn't prepared for that mass influx of refugees. And the police department definitely didn't know how to deal with them."

I don't want to be mistaken for a dangerous dog. I glance around the framed photos and citations on the wall of his office, learn his father is a retired San Diego cop. He's thirty-five. He's married. "As a matter of fact I'm married to a Southeast Asian lady. I was not in the service. As soon as I turned twenty-one I became a police officer."

He answers every question in even and complete sentences, in words you know he's deliberated over before letting me hear them. He also weighs me in a glance, and measures me, and gives me a complete physical, frisks me for weapons, and knows more about me than I know about him.

So what does he know about Southeast Asian gangs in San Diego? I ask, amazed at how San Diego cops have this way of being great big guys trying to look like teeny little guys, and failing miserably, like the Three Tenors singing "My Way" to Frank Sinatra. One great tenor was overkill. Three was the end of the world. San Diego cops come on nice and slow, big men singing the songs of little men and working hard at making it look easy. And it's never easy. There's always the guns. Among the Polaroids of guns confiscated off gang kids is a nasty little Mac 11. From the back end of the receiver to the end of the muzzle, it's only eleven inches long.

"Well basically for Southeast Asian gangs I started in 1989. I was working a beat that had a very large Lao population on it. So through a period of 1989 to approximately 1992: patrol. And then over here as Indo-Chinese community relations officer.

"Cambodian gangs tend to copy the Hispanics in dress and tattoos.

Frank Chin

"The Lao gangs are a little bit more upscale. They like to get dressed up a little bit more. They've been known to wear jacket and tie, yes.

"When I first started working with Southeast Asian gang members, I'd pull them over. I was very polite. They did exactly, Yes sir, No sir, did exactly what you wanted 'em to do, and you go away feeling, What a nice kid! But, you know, this guy could have been the worst kid in the world. And so they play that game.

"You know, they try to come across—especially if as a policeman you don't know—they'll come across as, 'Well, I stay at home. I'm a hard-working student.' When, in fact, he hasn't been in school in two years. A lot of times you can't identify them by their dress. You've got to know this person is a gang member by being out there all the time.

"There's a lot of problems in these communities, so you gotta know the difference between—most people don't know the difference between an immigrant and a refugee.

"An immigrant was mentally prepared to come to this country, where a refugee didn't have any choice. And a lot of these refugees that came—and more so in the Lao and the Cambodian community—didn't think that they would be making the United States a permanent home. They were always thinking they were going to go back. But the reality is there's not much to go back to now. So the reality is that most of them are here for good."

SOUTHEAST ASIAN GANGS: THE BEGINNING

"Basically, Southeast Asian gangs were first documented in the early eighties. Basically, the violence didn't really get started until about 1989. And it had an explosion of violence between Lao and Cambodian gang members. The shootings started—that's when they started getting all the attention."

Bulletproof Buddhists

Shootings attract attention.

"The shooting between the Lao and the Cambodian gang members happened in the beach area. And prior to 1989 they were pretty much fronts because they could identify with each other.

"Maybe I should go back to the very, very beginning. What happened was when they first came over here, they were put in lower economic neighborhoods where there were already established gangs. African American and Hispanic gangs. And so as they're going to school, because they were different they were constantly being teased and picked on. And with Cambodian gang members, more so than the Lao, back in the early eighties they started doing that new wave style.

"I don't know if you remember the hair and whatnot. And so they were teased even more. And they were picked on at school, after school. And so basically what they did is they came together. And they found that by coming together they were stronger. And then they started fighting."

"Who did they fight?"

"Well, just pretty much everybody."

Yeah, that's Asian, I think.

"When they were at school, you know, they were Asian; they identified with each other. There wasn't a lot of problems amongst themselves. And so they started coming together to protect themselves.

"Oh, they went to Crawford, Horace Mann, Gompers, Lincoln, Kearney High School, Linda Vista.

"We're talking about three main areas in the early eighties. And recently we're talking about a fourth area. In the early eighties we're talking City Heights, Southeast Division in San Diego. And the Linda Vista.

"And then they slowly emerged into a criminal group or a street gang.

Frank Chin

"And then lately Mira Mesa has been getting a lot of Asian gang activity.

"And basically when they came together, they found that they were stronger. And so they would band together to protect themselves. But one of the things that occurred was, Well, let's go look for so-and-so because he used to pick on us. And so they'd go out like after school or on the weekend, and then a lot of these guys, they were already gang members, and all of a sudden they're starting to get shot at. And they're thinking, 'Oh, man! We'd better get guns to protect *our*selves.' And so, as you can see, there was a slow progression.

"School officials did what they could. Police did what they could. But actually, because of a lack of communications, a very serious lack of communications, they were pretty much—you know, there weren't a lot of resources—and they were pretty much just left alone.

"And back in 1989 what happened was, down at the beach, between Cambodian and Lao gang members. They were at the beach. They were partying like they did every week. And some gang members came down from Long Beach. These were Cambodian gang members. And they were friends with the Cambodians that were there. And evidently what they tried to do was pick up on one of the Lao's girlfriends. There was a fight. And before you know it they were shooting at each other, which ended up as a double homicide, in the Sports Arena area.

"And then there were several homicides after that.

"About a year later some Lao gang members they did a drive-by shooting where a fifteen-year-old girl was shot and killed. She was sitting in the backseat of the car. And it was just a bullet, a stray bullet that went through the car. Hit her in the back of the head. And she was Long Beach also. They were having a party there.

Bulletproof Buddhists

"I would say that because you have never had such a mobile group of kids as you do with Southeast Asian kids. You could be talking to 'em, in the daytime here, and then eight hours later they're in San Francisco, or they're in Long Beach, or they're in Fresno, or they're in Las Vegas, or they're in Texas. So they're very, very mobile. A couple of years back, I stopped a thirteen-year-old girl. And she was a runaway from San Diego. She'd come back to San Diego. But in the course of a year, she had gang pictures of gang members from Florida, Boston, New York, Chicago, and Michigan. And this was a thirteen-year-old girl. And there's kind of like a built-in circuit. And they make the rounds.

"You've gotta remember, for Southeast Asian gangs, this is new. This is something that's only been around for thirteen, fourteen years at the most. In San Diego they weren't fully fledged gang members till six or seven years ago, when they actually became a gang under the attorney general's guidelines.

"The attorney general's guidelines say you have got to have two or more members who associate on a regular basis, who claim an area, who are engaged in criminal activity. And that, they claim, is a gang.

"We don't have like . . . it's anybody's guess what's going to happen next. We don't have a history to go by like we do with the other, more traditional gangs.

"What we have is we're starting to see kids as young as ten years old saying that they're OKB or OBS. Up to the early twenties.

"What we have is they get gang members that come in from Boston to San Diego for a week. If they commit a crime, they're back in Boston. It's so difficult to solve these crimes."

Frank Chin

Are we talking about real crime or kid stuff?

"Crime," Roy Moody says, and gets specific. "Well, mainly for Lao and Cambodian it's auto thefts. Auto thefts are their bread and butter."

Do the thieves have a favorite car?

"Honda Preludes," Roy Moody says with a nod. "They love their Honda Preludes and Toyota Supras. Definitely! Absolutely! Back when I was in patrol, almost once a week I was arresting 'em for stolen cars. Kids. Southeast Asian gang members. For stolen cars. And almost every time it was a Honda Prelude or a Toyota Supra.

"Stolen car parts. Stereos. You know, for the Vietnamese you can get into more of the organized crime–type aspect. They haven't really reached [the level] of organized crime as we know it. But yet they're, you know, between street gangs and organized crime.

"You used to get down with the Lao gang members down in southeast San Diego, or as they call it District Four now. In Southeast Division, there used to be a pool hall down there. And then we heard stories about older Vietnamese males going into the Lao pool hall there, saying, 'I need a. . . .'" Instead of naming a specific auto part, he makes a little face and says, ". . . placing his order. And the first one that gets it gets $200 or $300. And so there's definitely a correlation between . . ."

He doesn't say the words *gangs, auto theft, and Asian fix-it shops.* He's a cop used to talking to people and the press.

"And then from a period of 1989–1992, we definitely easily say Southeast Asian gang membership grew 300–400 percent. Tremendous growth."

"Numbers?"

"Unfortunately, I'm not allowed to give out those numbers.

Bulletproof Buddhists

But it's tremendous. Just to give you an example, and I won't identify which group, but one group of Southeast Asians have a hundred something kids, just a little over a hundred something kids. Two are in college or universities. Yet their gang membership is over two hundred citywide.

"They come from all different types of families. You know, it's real popular to say, because we're so quick we say, Why are these kids gang members? Well, they must come from dysfunctional families.

"But a lot of these kids come from very, very good families. And some of these families are very well educated. You know, I think it's a combination of a lack of communication on the parents' part—whether that be because they don't speak English too well—and geography, where these kids grew up. One of the things that we see is that geography plays a very important role.

"If these kids grow up where the gang members are, you know, there's a better chance of them becoming gang members. But not all the kids that grew up in those particular neighborhoods became gang members. So there's other reasons for it."

Bounhong Khommarath

Bounhong Khommarath agrees. The gang kids' favorite crime? "Auto theft is their number one. They say that Toyota is a lot easier to get in, so any sport looking Toyota and late model, that's their preference. For joyriding they just take any car that is available, from A to B. And then if there's no gas, they just use the vehicle as an escape tool."

Bounhong Khommarath is the project director of the UPAC (Union of Pan-Asian Communities) Pan-Asian Youth Project.

Frank Chin

UPAC is a storefront office, a long walk on University Avenue from the Storefront Office of the San Diego Police Department. The shops in the Chinatowns of San Francisco, Oakland, Seattle, Portland, are connected by a few steps, a side door, and narrow alleys and streets. In San Diego one Chinese, one Asian shop is connected to another by long walks, long drives, long wide streets.

Bounhong Khommarath continues the list of the favorite crimes of Lao and Cambodian gangs.

"Then the next would be home burglary. They keep on watching almost a week before they break in. The other type of break-in, let's say that I have a kind of kid that's acting up. And then he knows your son, your daughter that's also gangs. And then they rob their own parents when the parents are not home. But this one is kind of minimal.

"The armed robbery. The kids from Orange County come in here and know a couple of gang kids in here that used to run away, and they associate, and they just go over and rip armed robbery, but this is less number.

"For the home burglary, like relative. Burglary, armed robbery, these, they target their own people. Their own Asian people. We have heard that especially the family that's on welfare, they know that the family do not keep the money to the bank, they're just hiding it at home. So these do pop up news here and there. And again, if they're on welfare, they tend not to report to the authorities."

Middle-class Asians?

"That probably be the Filipinos and Vietnamese. For the Vietnamese, they're the ones that came in here in '75, '76, '77, those are the ones that are the elite group that escaped right at the fall, and then relative leaves. So we could see here lots of doctors, lots of physicians, the store owners. And then residential areas would be in the Rancho Penasquito, those areas.

Bulletproof Buddhists

The lower ones, the late arrivals, the new arrival here, tend to live in the lower social economic areas mixed with the other so-called poor."

THE LEGEND OF ITH

A French philosopher said, in the absence of myth, people will create myth. On the street, even in the Storefront, where no stories of heroes of your own kind were told to you, you will create stories of heroes to tell your blood and kin. Though he tries to neutralize the heroic effect of the story of the founder of the Lao gang by avoiding using his name, the good officer's omission is a form of respect and deepens the legend and mystery of Ith Chernivase, the first Oriental Killer Boy.

"One thing you gotta remember is that these were kids that started this," Roy Moody says. "There was very little adult influence when they started these gangs. Take the Lao. They used to call themselves the 48th Street Crips. Most of the neighborhoods that they came into the African American gangs were Crips sets. Crips sets were supposedly the biggest and supposed to be the meanest.

"There was a kid that was a couple a years older than most of the other kids. And he was in high school. And he came along and said, Okay, no more. Nobody's gonna protect you anymore. The school's not going to protect you. The police aren't going to help you. I'm going to help you. And anybody who said anything bad about them or picked on them, he would attack 'em. He would physically attack them. He was big. He was very aggressive. And so, all the kids, they loved him.

"And he's the one that formed the main Lao gang here in San Diego.

"So these kids said, Well, we're a Crip set too. So the Lao in the Southeast Division used to call themselves the 40th

Street Crips. But then the leader, when he was arrested the first time, he went to jail. He was eighteen, came out at the end of 1988, and he told everybody, We're no longer the 40th Crips. So something happened in jail for him. He didn't want to have any association with Crips. And he said, We are now the Oriental Killer Boys.

"And they would idolize this guy. They would do anything for him. They would break into cars. They'd break into homes. They would even do shootings for the guy. Because here was somebody that finally would stick up for them when they saw that nobody else would. And this person incidentally was shot and killed in a gang-related shooting in 1990. And the kids definitely see it as, Hey, nobody's going to stick up for me.

"Ith [pronounced "it"] was one of the first nine of the OKBs.

"Ith made everyone feel like they were his best friend. Some boys remember Ith told them not to hang out with him, to stay in school and stay home. Ith forbid his sister to go out with gangsters and kept gangsters away from her. He made sure she stayed in school. He took care of her," Roy Moody says. "She loved her brother very much, and it devastated her when he was shot dead by a rival gang. Just devastated her. Young men cry when they speak of Ith's death. If he were still alive, the OKBs would have continued to grow instead of splitting and fragmenting."

The story of Ith, Roy Moody tells me, is told by girls as a bedtime story to their children—the only story they know.

"I actually believe what kept everybody together were personalities, individuals who said, This is it! And of course, these kids growing up, most of them live in lower economic neighborhoods. And they see that maybe the gang member's driving a nice Honda Prelude, with all these stolen parts on it. A nice car. And he might have a few dollars in his pocket. Some girls are attracted to that element. And so they see the pretty girl on his arm. And so these young kids growing up think that's success. Their center, even though they're used to traveling to other cities and whatnot. They go from one Lao community or Cambodian community right into another. And so they're very limited in knowing what opportunities are out there for them. So they see that as success. It's very hard for them to picture themselves as a doctor, as a lawyer, as a police officer."

THE UNION OF PAN-ASIAN COMMUNITIES (UPAC)

Bounhong Khommarath

"UPAC started in 1973. And this program started 1991," he says.

He counsels Cambodian and Lao kids and thinks up ways to keep them out of gangs.

"Just recently, like four weeks ago, at another high school in the San Carlos area, during a PE period, a African American student kind of bumped intentionally the Lao kid, and then after that a verbal exchange, but the Lao kid do not do anything.

"Then over lunch period, the Lao kid tell his friends, and it seemed some of them also get bumped by that same person, so they get together and jumped to that group, and then two of the first students and then the two groups fight. Yeah, so they would wait to get the retaliation. They do not come back right away.

"And after the fight the teacher come and investigate—nobody say who start first, not anything. After the fight, everybody just run. And again, I think, next day again, or maybe after school. Another fight."

Frank Chin

It sounds familiar. In the early eighties I was in Portland high schools, telling Chinese and Japanese stories in the morning, and loaning out bilingual Chinese fairy tales and comic book novels of the heroic tradition, overnight, at noon from two milk baskets. Every day, in every high school, Asian immigrant kids took all my books at noon and brought them back at nine the next morning.

I was surprised to learn most of these kids had reached high school and were ready to graduate without ever having been told a kid story while they were kids. Not just the Asian kids, the Chinese and Vietnamese and Lao and Cambodian and Thai children of boat people. The big black kids in their letter jackets, punching each other for fun, the squirrelly white kids with more hair on one side of their heads than the other, didn't know "Rumpelstiltskin," "Sleeping Beauty," "The Tar Baby." So I told them their own stories before I told them stories from China and Japan. And another surprise. All these angry kids listened. They were kids again. Their childhoods had been on hold.

I was the marketplace storyteller. In one school, an Asian kid walked up to me, smiled, opened his jacket, and showed me a gun—because everybody liked the storyteller. A gun! A revolver. .38 caliber. I looked him in the eye, smiled, and told him to get out of here, be a good boy, go home, and don't come to school with that thing, and saw him out one of the big front doors. Whew! The power of the story.

In another school the teachers told me a couple of white kids jumped a couple of Asian kids talking their Asian language to each other at their lockers. The next day, before school, five or six Asian kids jumped the white kids and beat them up. At lunchtime, the Asian kids jumped the white kids and beat them up. After school the yellows in numbers beat up the two white boys. It went on for weeks. They wanted to know why.

"Because these kids are small and speak a language that's funny nonsense to young white American ears, the white boys think the yellows are easy pickings," I told them. "These kids were born in countries that have been in a continuous state of war for four hundred years. To get here, they had to escape war, the Communists, pirates, small boats, and gang warfare in the detention camps in Hong Kong. They have seen or been a part of real war and murder while these kids were doing kindergarten. To these kids life is war. Unless you are willing to kill them, don't mess with them. Beating up bullies is the easy part."

But that was back in the eighties. San Diego is another time. Another story. Here the Lao and Cambodian kids of today's gangs never saw the war. They remember TV, not boats and camps. They are the children of the children who escaped Pol Pot, the Pathet Lao, the Khmer Rouge, the Cultural Revolution.

Roy Moody

"You see, with these kids," Roy Moody says, "they were very, very young when the wars were on in their countries. And you know, Cambodians suffer very high posttraumatic stress. But you don't see the violence attributed to posttraumatic stress in the adults. You see it in the kids that aren't suffering from the posttraumatic stress.

"Why they tend to be so violent at times is because of their physical size. Somebody insults them. You know Asians tend to be smaller than Occidentals, or Hispanics, or African Americans. And so what they do is they always take one more step of violence. They're not going to go toe to toe with some-

Frank Chin

body. They might pick up a chair and hit the guy, but they're not going to trade punches with somebody that's physically bigger. Except there . . . there are a few that are exceptions to that rule. But they always take that step further. If a gang member they know is a gang member throws something at their car, they're not going to get out of the car and confront them. They'll go home get the gun and come back and do the shooting."

Bounhong Khommarath

How many Lao and Cambodian people are we talking about in San Diego? Where do the kids of gang action in town come from?

Bounhong Khommarath says, "Yeah, for the Lao, easily count fifteen thousand. But lots of people may say eighteen, twenty, depending on who you talk to. But I agree, fifteen is an easy count for Lao people.

"And Cambodian, about five to eight thousand. But mostly they have the big community in Long Beach. They coming down to the gang kid, children go to school, make friends, learning the American way of life, many times they learn the bad side, they do not learn the good side—of course, a thousand kids go to school, maybe 100–120 learn the bad behavior. And that's the number people really see.

"These the wanna-bes, the associates, or the hard core, this kind of start from anywhere age nine, ten, and so on, that they misbehave in classrooms and express themselves with antisocial behavior, talk back to the teacher, disrupt the class. When the teacher wants to finish, maybe send them home for two, three days home suspension, now kids enjoy freedom and get more acting out at home. So parents don't know what to do. This is how the problem started. The bad kids just band together with the bad kids. And of course they do not choose to fight with anybody. So they always have fights with the other ethnic group that already band together as a gang. So that's why we seen that no matter when we look at Hispanic, or African American, or Lao, or Cambodian. They just fight among so-called gang type. But they just do not go after any normal blacks or any normal Hispanic to treat to the fight. But they just choose to fight with the gangs."

"Are you saying that Lao gangs will fight with black gangs?"

"With the attitude of the gangs. There's the same thing with African American gangs. They just do not go around and beat all the Lao kids. But they just have with the eyes contact. That triggers the conflict. And if you are gangs, the chance of fighting would be like 90 percent. But if you are decent black student and a decent Lao student, you could make friends easily. This is in the pattern of the service I provided this community for many, many years. So trouble keep tend to have problem with other trouble kids. We see rarely that innocent either black or Lao have fight with another innocent.

"Yes, definitely with drug and alcohol prevention. Our community, the parents do not see. Because it is invisible for them. But gang kids, runaways, truancy, misbehave, or acting up and do not obey parents, that's a very visible problem for the parents. That's how they refer their children to us.

"The kids that are referred here by police or probation to do community work, to do counseling, have some kind of activity and linkage among themselves, but speaking about the numbers, of kids in gangs, the police they take record, they take pictures, they probably have a better sense of the numbers. But for us, when we talk to a kid, he says, No, no no! I not belong to a gang! But he knows friends that commit shooting or commit burglaries, auto theft, and so on. So why you come here? Oh, I just joyride with my friends, you know."

Frank Chin

STOREFRONT POLICE STATION

Roy Moody

"This is a very mixed neighborhood. City Heights. But this Storefront Office, even though we're located in City Heights, would be citywide services. It's just that this is more the center of the city.

"The Storefront was established in 1987 because the San Diego Police Department knew that there was crimes being committed in the Asian community but the crimes weren't being reported. And so it was designed to be away from the traditional image of police stations so we could get more people in.

"We have our community service officers that come from the community here in San Diego. We go to all the events. All the activities. We've gone out and built a relationship between the community and the police department. And people come here, they can report crimes. This acts pretty much as a central referral system for the Southeast Asian community. They can go to a phone book if they don't read and speak English. If they need help, they come here, and we'll find the answer for them. We don't turn anybody away. We try to find the answer for 'em. It might not always be the answer that they want to hear, but we'll get 'em an answer.

"Problems with their kids. Husband-wife problems. Everything. It could be problems with the landlord. Crime. They ask us to mediate neighborhood disputes. It could be a host of anything. There's a lot of fraud in the community, so when they get ripped off, they come in and say, Hey, what happened?

"Oh, you got ripped off. Fraud between Asians, right. You got real estate frauds that are going on. You have new arrivals, so they're saying, Look, you put the house in our name because you can collect AFDC or some other help, or put in

Bulletproof Buddhists

our name and we'll share it with you. And they give them an extra four months like a quick claim deed. And so these people are basically being ripped off all the time.

"Or the cars. All the time we get people coming in here that buy cars. And they're thinking they're legitimate in buying a car. And the person that sold it to them then reports it stolen. And because they don't really know the system, about pink slips and registration, then, of course, you've got a problem here.

"Cuz all the transactions are in cash. So there's no paper trail. Usually the person gets the car back after getting the cash. And it's very difficult to prove otherwise. So this Storefront is pretty much a catchall for anything and everything that can go wrong in the community. So currently we have nine community service officers. We're budgeted for thirteen. We're in the process of hiring. And the breakdown will be five Vietnamese, three Cambodian, two Lao, two Hmong, and one Ethiopian, which serves the Ethiopian community out of here.

"Back in the early eighties we had extortion here. A lot of communities were afraid. But the last few times that we had extortion groups that came into San Diego, we were notified. The police department was notified. They were set upon. They were arrested. And they were convicted. So San Diego's gotten a very good reputation in Asian communities across the United States that San Diego's the place not to come to try to set up an extortion ring.

"Most of the extortion that occurs now with the shopkeepers is the under $5.00 type of extortion. You have a gang member who walks in who says, 'Hey, I don't have any money. I just want a pack of cigarettes. I'll pay you back next week.'

"'Well, you didn't pay me back for the last twenty packs of cigarettes.'

"'Well, yeah, I know, but I'll pay ya back. And besides, it's

Frank Chin

better that you lose a pack of cigarettes today than to pay $500 for that broken glass window tonight.'

"And the shop owner's thinking to himself, If I call the police on the two dollar pack of cigarettes, first of all will the police really arrest this guy?

"Yes, we will arrest him.

"But he's also thinking about, My window's gonna get broken by his friends. That's $500 that I gotta pay out right away. And if I have this guy arrested, I'm going to have to spend a whole day in court, probably several days in court. Who's going to take my place here in the store?

"So, you know, before they call us, it's gotta be something that's worth their while to call. It's very difficult to get them to call on shoplifts. Most of the extortions are under $5.00.

"One time we had some Cambodian gang members that were doing door-to-door extortion: Hi, so-and-so. Do you have $5.00 I can borrow? Oh, it's better to lose $5.00 now than for somebody to break out your car windows.

"You even have cases of kids extorting their parents. We had a thirteen-year-old gang member kid who admitted to his mom, Yeah, I need money for rock cocaine. And she told him no. He wanted eight bucks, and he broke all the windows in the house. He was arrested.

"Our residential robberies have gone way, way down. We've been very aggressive here attacking the Asian gang problem. We have our detectives who know who the players are. This Storefront has definitely opened the doors of communication between the Asian groups. So the communication's going back and forth both ways. Asian gang members can no longer operate in San Diego like they did in the past, without being identified. We know who they are. And if they commit a crime, we will arrest them.

"When I do patrol. You know, I say, Hey, you know, Yeah, I am policeman. Yes, if I catch you doing something wrong, I will arrest you. But, you know, in the meantime, I'll go out of my way to do what I can to help you. And so, it's like I was always honest with them. And when I caught 'em doing something wrong. A stolen car or whatever. You know, I never belittled them. You know, it was like yes, they always knew where they stood with me. And sometimes I had some of these Asian gang members who said, Officer Moody, I know I'm wanted. And I want you to arrest me. I don't want any other policeman to arrest me.

"One time they actually ran out into the street, and stopped my car, and said, Hey, I know I'm wanted. Go ahead and take me in.

"Of course those moments are rare."

THERAVADA BUDDHISM: BIG WHEEL–LITTLE WHEEL

Roy Moody

"You gotta understand Theravada Buddhism. Let's just take the small country of Laos, where conflict is something that's to be avoided at all times."

Does the righteous Buddhist repugnance for conflict explain why a relative handful of aggressive, cruel Pathet Laos could take over the entire country of Laos? No, Officer Roy doesn't want to go that far, sounding very diplomatic, or very Lao. He is saying that because of that attitude of avoiding conflict at any cost, some Lao and Cambodian parents are at a loss dealing with their children raised in the American soup of conflict.

"Here in America there's always conflict. Everybody's in conflict, it seems like. And they don't know how to deal with the kids who aren't minding because, where they come from, there are no street gangs.

"When the parents sent kids to school, they went to school.

Frank Chin

You know, they learned! But here, kids go to school, but they don't learn. They ditch. They . . . you know, they do what they want to. And their parents are having a very hard time coping with that.

"This thing with the gangs is they see a transference of power between parents and the kids. Parents who might not speak English, who can't read English, they have to depend on their kids to get 'em through everyday life here in America. Read bills, read anything that comes through. So there's a shift of power. All of a sudden these young kids have all this power. And pretty soon it's like, I'm going to do what I want to do, you know, because you don't know."

Bounhong Khommarath

Bounhong Khommarath sees the Buddhist avoidance of conflict as a strategy instead of as inhibiting dogma, as an advantage and not a handicap that has helped the Lao and Cambodians settle in San Diego. "Because that's the way guide me to respect other people, no matter what they believe, and accept another way of life. Also I have the sense of, because I have these kids, that's why they give me reward that my kids doing well, so that urge me to help more people in my line of work. America is the land of opportunity, and is a materialized world and a lots of TV, automobile, and this. And then if I don't have the sense of Buddhism to refrain me, I would maybe try to get a Mercedes or BMW, or whatever. So if people have that, that's the opportunity, that's what they should get. So I just happy what I have here.

"I think the young couple that maintains traditional ways, and then try to also adopt the new ways, would be manageable to continue their lifestyle here. So the traditional way have a lot to play in their lives. They cannot be American totally. They cannot be Asian totally. But maybe have a sense of awareness of both worlds and then try to guide them through."

It sounds like Monkey leading the pilgrims west through strange countries, strange people, strange ways, to India to recover Buddhist scripture.

A STORY GRANDMA TOLD ME

Bounhong Khommarath

"Personally, I'm forty-six, going to be forty-seven. I'm a refugee from Laos, came to this country in '78, June '78, and with the agency ten years—in and out—shuffled from project to project, depending on the funding and the program design.

"My grandma. Father's mother. I recall my grandma. I have less interact with my mom and dad. They're real busy. Grandma is always there at home. She's just like—not baby-sit, but also give nurturing and guidance.

"Mostly the story that she told us is like the Bible story is in the Buddhist Bible let's say. The good manners is always the winner, but at first the bad, the evil win first. But at the end the good manner is the one that the winner. Teach us about how to behave. Teach us about to pay the gratitude. Respect the elderly, respect the teacher, respect to the boss to feel proud of your job, or whatever you have. Do not jealousy other people have more that what you got. So that I think that's applied to my life now.

"I know that. Because my family is not that in the upper level. We are in the upper level of the low class. Let's say, we were not even the lower level of the middle class.

"Father. He is a office clerk in the government office. Mother. She buy foodstuff and cook, just like the fast food, and precook and sell at the market. So every brother and sister help in put in the ingredient and help prepare, and when

Frank Chin

it's cooked, she go to the market. And then when people get off from work, they just buy this already-cooked food to go home.

"Eight in the family. Four boys, four girls.

"Mom's always mad and talk when children misbehave. Dad come and then give the punishment. My father give the punishment. Even he don't talk much he would tell one time, if you do not remember, you got the stick [a spanking]. Sometimes he use a stick, and he hang the stick on the wall. And then, even he's not there, Mom says, You watch out for the stick! So that's why the American, the English word for ruler, really translate if you do not follow the rule, that's the ruler." He laughs. He enjoyed his childhood.

"In Laos, after high school, I have two years in economics, which is more like a business school. And I even do not finish four years college there, but there's an opening, so I quit school and start working. By the time my colleagues graduate they find no job. So I just grab a job first and work my way up with the American firm to do the international transportation, to do packing, crating, shipping, both by sea and air. So at the time at the height of the Indo-Chinese War, so many serviceman from the U.S. and the other free world countries coming out of Laos. That's our line of work with those clientele. And sometimes you have to ship bodies of GIs in bags to Thailand and to have an airplane transport it back to the U.S.

"The company itself have a lots of involvement with Air America, but we are our own entity. It's called Rent Service World Wide. We have the alliance with Rent Pax, that's a big company here in the U.S. And Air America, when they have a shipment come for their own delivery to the home, that's our job. They just do the transport. Also with the Marines or the military attaché people want to move in or out, we do the packing, and then we put the crate into the Air America, and that's their job to fly out.

Bulletproof Buddhists

"Laos was under the royal government, involved with the Vietnam War against the Communist invade to South Vietnam, but they crossed to Laos for the Ho Chi Minh Trail, so that sucked Laos into the war without any way to avoid it.

"When Saigon fall, Phnom Penh fall two weeks later. The high ranking, they escaped. So leave the country very tricky. And the Communist force just take over Laos easily. At first I said, I'm not going. But when there is no high ranking, they take middle-class ranking out for the reeducation camps.

"They take the head of the household. If your wife is a teacher, they take her to a female camp. If you're a merchant, they say that you're capitalist, you're making money on somebody else, they take you to the reeducate. In some case, let's say you are the principal of the school, they say, Okay, we have new doctrine. You ought to learn the new doctrine. So once you graduate you come back to your same position. Some people volunteer to go. Some reluctant to go, they come and get you at night.

"Reeducation means not just only you educate on the new doctrine, on the new propaganda. It's also a hard labor camp. You have to cut the wood yourself, among your group, to build a hut, to build a house. You have to build a pigpen. You have to raise cattle. So for someone who's been teaching all of his life, that's very difficult to transfer to be a farmer right away. When you get sick, there's no medicine available. They only give very sparse food, just like prisoner of war. That's in '75–'80.

"If you're taken away, the children is leave at home, so have to depend on other relatives who've not been taken. That's why many family, when they take the husband away, the wife take the children, escape to Thailand.

"They take the merchant, then start taking teacher, the policemen that direct the traffic, then, I said, Well, if I'm not leaving because of my background working with the Ameri-

Frank Chin

can firm, it would be my turn! So I took my family and escaped. Because Cambodia, Vietnam is already on the Communist. And now Laos on the Communist. The king signed a paper that give up the throne, and the Communist Lao establish their government.

"So I escaped to Thailand with my family.

"At that time I had four children. Now I have five. The fifth one born in France. So I escaped to Thailand, and the camp is so boring. And children and adult get sick constantly. Then I ask the dispensary run by the Red Cross, said I'm not from the medical field, but I like to help.

"So they give me okay, line up people, you weigh the baby, which is okay. And then people get sick, give the numbers so the doctor could call you this way, see what kind of illness, so give the chart to the doctor or medical team. By doing that— at that time they change from Ford to Carter, in the U.S. No refugee admission.

"Okay. Carter has to do his job first, and then they freeze the program for refugees. Well, in the camp life is so difficult, hardship, and you have depend on the food rationing. And then kid get no education. But in France they still take applications. So by volunteer in the camp, they have allocation. When people work so long for the camp, they say, Okay, give the credit to apply. And I was lucky to be on the list and apply to France. Even though my line of work all the time was with the American firm. Let's get out of camp first, so we have a chance to admit to France. For three days that I was in the receiving home, I run to the U.S. embassy in Paris, submit my application, along with other Eastern bloc colleagues, the Ukrainian, the Jewish, the German want to come the U.S. for reunification that the immigration have a few numbers for immigration quota. So I tell them, Look, I worked for American firm. I shipped GI dead body and so on, and now I want to come to U.S.

Bulletproof Buddhists

"Well, there is no quota for East European refugees. So he sneak me in with the number of East European refugees fourteen months later. And we could get grant to come to the U.S. as refugees.

"The youngest one at that time, three months. The older ones, I believe, was six years. I have three boys, two girls. And the youngest now is the 11th grade. One work full-time. Three work half-time and then go to school.

"Luckily, luckily, very luckily none were involved in gangs.

"We live in the neighborhood that are local gangs already there, and kids tend to acting out, like among ducks want to be a duck. And also because working with this agency I see a lot of what happened, and then my job also to go out and teach all the parent, so I'm equipped with a material resource to teach my own kids. That's why I say lucky. If I'm working in let's say in auto mechanic field or sales, I'd probably look at money money money, and I'd have no time to interact with my own family.

"Everywhere that I have time to mingling with the group that my staff bring here, I told them a story."

"Tell me a story."

"There's a boy that's in the poor family, and mom and dad just go out gathering the food. Just like a version of the Jack and the Giant? And the same kind of story. Very parallel. Family very poor. Mom and dad try to get rid of him. But he managed to stick with the family. But somehow parent finally manage to leave him in the woods.

"Later on parents kind of becoming stable economically and want to get the boy back. When they reach to the jungle now, the boy all grow hair, becoming like the monkey or something. The story end that way. The boy is a monkey. And they say that because the parents have sinned in the previous life, and then they're so poor, and after that they teach kid to

Frank Chin

behave well. So when you have your own child he will not become like a monkey in the jungle.

"So, when you're a kid, just preparing yourself, and you become a parent yourself. And at the same time, we tell kids, because your parents probably do good in the previous life, they could raise you, becoming stronger in yourself, and you'll get older, just go back and take care of them. If you do not take care of them, your next life will become having poor parents and then your kids will be in the jungle.

"Those are the sort of stories that we were taught."

"IT'S KIND OF A CATCH-22 SITUATION FOR THESE PARENTS"

Roy Moody

"We had a meeting here at our Storefront with Cambodian gang members; then we had a meeting of the Lao gang members at the Lao temple. First they say that they came together for self-protection. But the biggest thing they say is, Hey, it's fun! I'm having fun! I'm having a good time. I like the freedom. I like excitement. I'm having a good time.

"You know, a lot of kids don't ever associate with gang members. They stay at home. They go to school. Nobody comes along and forces you to join a gang.

"You know, we've heard stories that people are pressured. Like we had one where a father's oldest—and I think he had four or five kids—and his oldest son, who was about thirteen or fourteen, was claiming a Cambodian gang. And what happened was his father told him not to, and he still was. And one day he saw him hanging out with the boys and came home. And the father said, 'Why? Why're you doing this?'

"And he goes, 'Well, if I don't hang out with them, they'll beat me up.'

"And so for this Cambodian father, what he's thinking is, Are you going to be more afraid of them? Or are you going to be more afraid of me? And so the father beat him, and beat him real bad. And CPS [Child Protective Services] came, and they took all the kids out, and the father wasn't beating this poor child, you know, because he liked it. He saw that as his only option to save his son. Because we're getting calls all the time from parents who ask, What can I do to get my kids to quit hanging out with gangs?

"And the reality is, there aren't any systems set up to help parents in this situation. We gotta wait for the kids to break the law to get 'em in the criminal justice system. Or if you beat 'em up, then we can have CPS come in and take the kids away. There's nothing in between to force these kids into counseling. There's nothing to force these kids into any type of program that will help 'em. So it's kind of a Catch-22 situation for these parents."

THE SNAKE AND THE MONGOOSE

Vitou Reat

Vitou Reat and his older brother saw their father taken, thrown to the ground in front of them, and tied up. He was eleven and his older brother twelve. The Khmer Rouge wanted to kill the boys, but they were too young. Their father was taken away and killed. Vitou is twenty-six now, working as a Cambodian counselor at the Southeast Asian Project. Occasionally he works at the Old Temple Cambodian language school as a substitute teacher. He thumbs through a book of Cambodian folktales, points to the pictures, and tells me his favorite, "The Snake and the Mongoose."

"The crane lives near the snake, and every time the crane has children, the snake eats the children. So the cranes get

Frank Chin

together and have a meeting, and one of the cranes has an idea. I know the mongoose. The mongoose can eat the snake. The problem is how to bring him here to eat the snake. One of the cranes says, Just leave a trail of fish leading to the snake's den. The cranes drop a trail of fish, and the mongoose comes along eating the fish, finds the snake, and eats the snake, and sees the baby cranes, and eats them too!"

He's a kid again and laughs, sees I don't quite get it, and explains the story.

"They like to warn the children that if you thinking, you have to think all the way. Like what's going to happen next? The cranes didn't think what the mongoose would do after it ate the snake. They want the children to think long, not short.

"My English is so young. I hardly able to tell you the story. From Cambodia. No just me. I got married. A chemist San Diego State. I speak Russian. In Moscow. Six years in Moscow. I just go to college there. I don't English before I came here." He's been here a year and a half.

"When Pol Pot there, nobody left the country. The border closed.

"My father, Pol Pot killed, just like that. My mother in Cambodia still. One younger sister, and one older sister, and one brother older than me.

"Yeah, Pol Pot kill my—just like come to the house, and tied him up with his arms behind him, right in front of us, and take him just like that.

"So we can't do anything. I don't want to talk about that story."

He turns away, holds back tears. But more of the story comes. "They want to kill all the men, you know. That was their plan, but I was too young. Eleven years old.

"After my dad run away I run after them, and they want to take us too, and they have gun on us and everything, so we just run away."

Bulletproof Buddhists

Cambodian grammars are hard to find because Pol Pot killed all the teachers and burned all the books.

Outside, Pematokyryrasmey Chuun, a community service officer at the Storefront office of the San Diego Police Department, offers me a can of soda pop. The women who come to the temple with food for the monks got soda for us. It's Saturday morning, and children from six to eighteen years old come into the temple yard for Cambodian school. The boys wear white shirts and khaki pants. The girls wear white blouses and blue skirts. The morning is cold and rainy. No one complains when the kids show up with all kinds and colors of sweaters and jackets over their uniforms.

"I am not a psychologist," Chuun says. "I do not know psychology. But the psychologists say the kids go into gangs and shoot and violence because they saw nothing but violence and murder escape from Pol Pot. Look at these kids here. They are all born in America. What do they remember from Pol Pot? The oldest ones, they are two-, three-, four-year-old babies when they escape. What do they remember?"

"I remember," Chuun says. "I am not doing violence. I am not gang. I hate them gangs."

This guy hurts. All the Cambodians twenty-five and over hurt bad. They all have bad memories that won't let them go. Memories about Pol pot the dictator taking daddy away and shooting him dead.

Chuun's father was a congressman. King Sihanouk began giving chunks of Cambodia away in the hope of not being drawn into war and enraged the intellectuals and middle class. They cranked the mandate of heaven, dumped the king and the monarchy, and established democracy in Cambodia in 1970. And Chuun's father was elected to congress.

Chuun looks at the children hunched over their books, pencils in hand, and the memories come back to get him. Pol Pot burned books. The monster killed all the teachers, all the

Frank Chin

writers, all the artists and intellectuals and lawyers and college educated, and with them effectively destroyed the culture, the very language of Cambodia.

In San Diego, at this Old Temple, for these girls in blue skirts and white blouses and boys in khaki pants and white shirts and odd sweaters and jackets—the death of all the teachers and artists, writers, intellectuals, and college educated, means the books of grammar, the books of folktales, the books of proverbs, the books of manners and history, all were written here, in San Diego, from memory, by hand, and photocopied, hundreds of times, by those who had the memory and the hands.

"We escape Pol Pot, we cross the minefields, cross the mortar, we cross the river, come to America to save the children, and still we lose them. They become Americanized and go with the gangs. The violence, the gangs are American, not Cambodian. The psychologists are American. I don't care what they say. The psychologists don't know."

The first grade has a mix of little kids and not so little pubescent girls and boys. They take their seats under a plastic awning. The first grade seems to be meeting in an open carport. And the second grade is meeting in a garage, with the garage door open.

The kid teaching the first grade looks thirteen. He's nineteen and a half. His name is Sophea Ross. He uses the nickname Tommy. He says the police regularly stop him and refuse to believe he's not thirteen and too young to drive his car. Escaped Cambodia at two. In a camp in Thailand for four and a half years. Ten years in the United States. Three younger brothers. Two younger sisters. He learned Cambodian here, in this school, with these homemade books. He was a monk here at the Old Temple for six months in 1990. Shaved all his hair, his eyebrows, and wore the robes. He's in San Diego Community College now and is the editor-writer of

Bulletproof Buddhists

Cambodian Now, a Cambodian-language monthly magazine with a print run of two thousand. They print five thousand for the month of Cambodian New Year. Tommy Ross's friend Woody Mean is the publisher of *Cambodian Now;* he's also the printer and owns the print shop. Tommy hates gangs, has never been a part of gangs. But he dresses like gangs. "Style," he says. It's style, not content.

The enrollment at the weekend language school is increasing. Parents and the teachers and the temple are talking of expanding, building another building for more classrooms. For some of the young, the adventure of rescuing Cambodian civilization, language, and literature from the ravages of the Cultural Revolution and Pol Pot out of the memories of old learned men in America and Xerox machines is more attractive than drugs, gangs, and guns.

Bounhong Khommarath

"UPAC is the umbrella organization. UPAC stands for the Union of Pan-Asian Communities. UPAC is the umbrella organization that serves the pan-Asian, the Korean, Japanese, Chinese Lao, Vietnamese, Cambodian, Filipino, and Hmong. And all the ethnic groups from the pan-Asian community.

"This program I'm in charge of, High Risk Youth, got funded from the county of San Diego, from the Alcohol and Drug Prevention Services. And we focus to serve children nine to thirteen, and their family members, for drug and alcohol education and prevention, in the community of Cambodian, Lao, Vietnamese, Filipino, and Hmong.

"And the focus of the services is targeted in the schools in this area. Of course, for the Filipinos it's in National City and Chula Vista. We organize a after-school program, recruit students from the schools, and we talk to the counselor, district

Frank Chin

counselors, and principal so they open a classroom for us, for kids to come in with the parents' authorization to participate in the twelve-week session for controlled competency training curriculum, include the students to learn about their own home culture. So students would have a better understanding of their parents' culture. And in addition to that we teach them about life skills, like communication skills, problem solving, anger management, and include a big piece of alcohol and drug education. What they should be aware of and what they should know. So when they grow up, they should be equipped with these knowledges."

The English he speaks is original and strange to my ears. A strange mash of baby-talk vocabulary, shipping expediter verbs, and bureaucratic gibberish that works on me. The grammar is a mystery to me, but it always was. Understanding what he just said sometimes comes as a delayed reaction. There's a lot of impressionist art in the way he makes himself understood in English. I wonder what the French thought of his French?

"To me as the counselor or somebody that provide advice, they do not identify themselves: I am here from the Dragons, or Crips, or whatever. They don't indicate those numbers or identify themselves as gang members here."

Numbers of gang kids—up or down?

"It's kind of grow up and rising. Then six months ago stable. And three months now, I do not hear anything that increase, seems to be a quiet moment. But kids are kids, and always they are just like a time bomb. If something clicks, they would gather friends, and then another fight, another shooting occur. But for the time being, for the last three months, it's kind of going down a little bit. Six months ago: stable. But nine months before this, it's kind of really high.

"This is the fourth year of the program now, and we serve close to one thousand kids. And we do not count the family members, dad, mom, and maybe sometimes sisters and brothers, but just individual kid that we register, and we open the case file for them.

"Mixed gender in prevention work. Intervention, kids referred by police and probation, 90 percent boys. Less than five girls. Runaways, referred by probation, that associate with joyriding, auto stealing."

Cambodian gangs fight Lao gangs, he says.

"I have working with some Cambodian kid, he said, 'I don't hate Lao kid. I only hate Lao gangs.' For the Lao also, you see Cambodian walking by, doing the same thing they are doing.

"And I have one time another gang, Linda Vista area, dress red. Red cap. Red shoelaces. Red T-shirt. And another one we do an interview here, and another one come in for counseling. Blue, and he's from this area.

"Oh, they look at each other just like about to grab the neck. I said, Oh, no no no, I cannot place the one from Linda Vista to work here, while the other one already works here. I have to tell the mom, 'Okay, you have to look another agency, for the community work.'

"But other than that, if a Cambodian gang's in here and they see Lao kids come in and out, no problem. The same thing if a Lao gang's in here and they seeing Cambodian walk in and out, talking in Cambodian, they just do not bother each other."

Did this Lao-Cambodian rivalry exist in Asia?

"No, No. Just happened here. In 1980–82, they're still good friends. But somehow with the girls coming in, and treat the violence, and afterward retaliation come forth and back, forth and back. Even exploding to the level of drive-by shooting.

"Even now, the original first guy is already been away, but still the younger one have still continue the quarrel."

Frank Chin

CAR TOUR

Roy Moody

Roy Moody drives with his nice Smith and Wesson tucked into his belt and his walkie-talkie by his side. Blocks of slab-sided stucco boxes with little yards. "The Laos refer to it as the Market Street Area. It's in Southeast Division. You can see it's not too far from where we came from; City Heights is just a couple of miles."

We rubber past a group of boys slouching home from school.

"Market Street gang members. They're Hispanics," Roy Moody says.

"Do they mess with Asian gangs?" I ask.

"Every once in a while there's some conflict between the two. But it has more to do with machismo for Hispanics; machismo for Asians is saving face. You know, words are exchanged.

"See the Neighborhood Watch signs?

"So the main gang in this area is Lao." He points to graffiti spray painted on a garage door. "'OKB,' 'Oriental Killer Boys,'" he reads off the doors as we pass. We are driving the streets of OKB turf, looking for gang kids hanging out and kicking back after school, and the streets are bare.

"We might be out just a little bit early," Roy Moody says. "And it's a little bit cold.

"See the Neighborhood Watch signs? I'm very proud of it. In the Lao community we've got sixteen Lao Neighborhood Watch groups. And I was told that this would be impossible to do, given the history of setting up Neighborhood Watches in the community. It doesn't sound like a big deal. You gotta understand, with the Southeast Asian countries, when their countries fell to Communism, they set up a series of neigh-

Bulletproof Buddhists

borhood watches, but the purpose of those neighborhood watches was to report political indiscretions. So just the mere idea of that kind of system here, of course, they're going to be resistant to it.

"We meet, we try to set up two meetings a month. To try to get across the city. Then we have a Lao advisory board to the Storefront. We meet once a month to discuss neighborhood issues and problems with kids.

"We definitely stress that what the kids do, it will come back to haunt the parents. That's why it's so important to know what their kids are doing at all times.

"As a parent, you feel your kids are doing something wrong? You have a right to go into your kid's room. You have the right to go into the cars and look for illegal things. As a parent, not only do you have the right, you have the responsibility to do that. And we've gotten, in our Storefront, in a year, a year and half or so, we've gotten about twenty-eight firearms turned in. And they range from .22s to nine-millimeter handguns to shotguns. We tell parents where to look. Look in the vents. Look in the fenders of the cars. Look under the engine. Look behind the heaters. Look under the beds. They find 'em. They call us, and they turn 'em in.

"As a matter of fact, today, this morning, we had a Cambodian father find . . . he found a .22 hidden in the backyard, and he brought it in this morning."

We drive by a high school. Girls are on the field for cheerleading practice.

"There's been an increase in reporting, and there's been an increase in the willingness to become involved with the police. It's very, very difficult. It took me over five years before I could get 'em started," Roy Moody says, searching for kids hanging out in baggy clothes.

"You know that's one of the things—that is, people come

Frank Chin

in, they say, Oh, we're going to do this, and we're going to do that. And then they disappear. And so, because I worked in this neighborhood for such a long time, I've got a little bit of credibility.

"And it's working. Crime only flourishes where it's tolerated. Somebody on the Neighborhood Watch reported Lao gang members were putting a stolen car into one of the garages, and so we went out there. I called for units, and units went out there. And the car was, in fact, stolen. Nobody was around the car. But at least we have 'em watching. And so I think the community is getting the idea that if they don't tolerate it, it won't happen.

"This area here is Gompers Park. At two o'clock this should start filling up. But it's cold right now, so it's going to be hard to find just people hanging out.

"You know, it's very hard to convince them that—" He nods toward a row of garage doors and reads the graffiti. "See, 'OKB Jr.' 'LOK' means 'Little Oriental Killer Boys.' 'Laos Pride.' And then the rest of this stuff is just tags. Tag. Tag.

"And then you have your Market Street gangs. These alleys, they keep 'em pretty clean. You know, they don't get a lot of city services back here. 'LOK,' 'Little Oriental Killer.' 'Gekko,' 'Rascal,' 'Bull.' Nicknames. Lao. Someone wrote 'OBS' and crossed it out.

"'12 15 11.' The twelfth, fifteenth, and eleventh letters of the alphabet. L-O-K.

"They crossed them out. 'OKB Jr.' 'L-O-K.' 'Remember Little Oriental Killer Boy.' 'OKB Jr.' 'OKB.' 'Laos Pride.' 'Oakland Crips.' Same thing. 'Oakland Crips.' 'OKB.' 'Oakland Crips.' 'OKB.' 'LOK.' 'Laos Pride.' 'Fuck all them.' 'OBS.' Crossed out. 'OKB.' 'OKB Jr.' 'Laos Pride.' 'OKB.' 'Laos Oriental Killer.' Now see you got 'TOC,' 'Tiny Oriental Crips,' which is from the Linda Vista area. 'TOC #1.' Now,

Bulletproof Buddhists

see, a lot of 'TOC' and 'OKB,'—they're relatives from Linda Vista and Chollas View Area. So— 'OKB.' 'Penguin Jr.' 'Lorrie.' 'Blue.' 'T-Fu Jr.' 'T-Dog.' 'LOK.' 'OKB.' 'LOK.' 'TOC.' 'OKB Jr.' 'TOC.' 'OKB.' 'OMC,' 'Oriental Mob Crip.'

"LOK is not really a big—Technically they're just smaller OKB. 'OB' crossed out. 'Oriental Boys.' Crossed out. '187' in its place. 187 is the penal code for homicide.

"You had OBS come in here one night, back in 1990, and they wrote OBS, which took a lot of guts for them to come down and do that in these alleys back here.

"See you got Orange Seals. 'Orange C.' 'TOC.' "

Interesting. War is waged on garage doors.

"'Asian Pride.' Man, there's all sorts of different—They're all white! 'OKB.' 'Penguin Jr.' 'Dog.' 'OSD.' I don't know what 'OSD' is. 'BM.' 'Barrio Market,' for Barrio Logan Heights. 'OKB.' 'OKB Jr.'

"Yeah, that's real new. It wasn't there a couple weeks ago. Or even last week. Back in 1989, I had this beat, I was the only officer up here. Me and a partner. One patrol car."

STREET SCENE

It looks like a fight and doesn't look like a fight. People of all ages and roughly the same height watch on the sidewalk in front of their yards. Family groups watch the blur of bare arms and baggy pants from their doorways. Officer Moody stops the car. He talks to the fighters, who've stopped fighting. I walk down the street and talk to a sixteen-year-old Lao kid in baggy shirt and baggy pants.

"Whaddaya wanta know?" Drippy asks with his hands in his pockets.

"You in a gang?" I ask.

"No," Drippy says. "I used to. I used to be in OKB for

about like a year and a half. Get like hang around for a long time. So they just jump me in."

"So everyone gathered around and beat on you."

"Yeah," he says with a shy smile, like I've guessed the name of his girlfriend.

"Did you get to fight back?"

"Yeah. I get to fight back. But now, I just goin' to school. Stop all that stuff."

"Did you enjoy being in the gang? Was it fun?"

"Yeah, it was fun, a little while."

I turn to Stout Kid, a couple of years younger and a few inches shorter than Drippy. "How about you, young man, are you in a gang?" I ask.

"Naw."

"Naw?"

"Naw."

"Sure?"

"Yeah."

"Wanna be?"

"Naw."

"Why not?"

"It's not cool."

"You dress like a gang kid."

"Yeah, but, I'm like—I jusssss. I used to play with them, but not no more. So I play with him." Nods to Drippy.

"You go to school?"

"Yeah, Gompers."

"How old are you?"

"I'm thirteen."

"What grade are you in?"

"Seventh."

"How old are you, Drippy?"

"I'm sixteen. I'm in tenth grade."

"So, how do you get out of the gangs?"

"Stop playing with them. Stay home. Go to school. That's it. When you see them, we just talk to them and just go home."

Down the street, people, Lao and Mexican, recognize Roy Moody. He's taller than anyone here and is the only man I've seen in San Diego with hair this color of red. Short, short hair, like a dry, well-mown lawn. The color and texture of his hair and his eyebrows make Roy Moody's face look like a furry, cuddly toy. He keeps himself on a short leash and works hard to consider everything he says and communicate respect for his listeners when he says it. Everybody knows he has a nice Smith and Wesson nine millimeter tucked under his belt. But everybody on this block, at least, likes talking to the big guy being gentle and patient and polite.

"They don't beat you up before letting you leave the gang?" I ask Drippy, with an eye to the action around Moody.

"No, they never do that," Drippy says.

"So is it hard to stay out of the gang?"

"It's not hard; just walk away."

"Then do they diss you when you walk away?"

"No, they don't diss me."

"You got brothers and sisters?"

"Yeah, I got three sisters."

"They hang out with gang kids?"

"No!"

"How old are your sisters?"

"Oh, one is juvie for being a gang. And one graduate already, preparing for college."

"How old is your sister in juvie?"

"Fourteen."

"And you're sixteen. Did you talk to her about being in a gang?"

Frank Chin

"Yeah. I told her. I told her a lot of things. Why do you want to join a gang? Just going dying or going to jail."

"And what did she say?"

"She just go and play outside, you know. Hang around with the wrong crowd."

"So, how'd she get arrested?"

"I don't know. I didn't ask my parents that."

"Your parents work?"

"Yeah. My dad's a security, and my mom makes clothes."

"What do you want to do?"

"Go to school, graduate. Be somebody."

"How old is your girlfriend?"

"Sixteen."

"She in a gang?"

"No."

"Do these gangs have bosses? Leaders?"

"Not no more. The leader died."

"Who was the leader?"

"Ith. Yeah."

"How old was he when he died?"

"Eighteen. Nineteen."

"How'd he die?"

"I don't know. From some friends shooting him or something. They have some fights a long time ago. It stopped all that when he died. He was the big leader. A little guy."

Back in the car, Roy Moody completes the unavoidable legend of Ith with a name.

"Ith Chenevisai," Moody says. "He got shot and killed up in Colina Park, by another Lao gang member from Anaheim. But you know, the funny thing is, they knew each other from a long time ago.

"He was the one that formed, actually *formed* OKB. He was the one that would stick up for all the Lao kids against anybody. And so they loved him! And they would just do anything in the world for him.

"Did you see the girl I was talking to out there? Now see, she's a pretty good student. She graduated; she's never been involved. You were talking to her brother, who was involved. There's even a little sister who's been nothing but problems.

"Drippy said she was in juvie now."

"I think her sister said something about drugs. Fourteen years old. Run away numerous times. She's definitely got— But see the contrasts? You've got the oldest, who's not that old. What, she's eighteen at the oldest right now. Her parents are good parents. Both parents work. The oldest has turned out great. The middle one is right on that borderline. He can go either way. And the youngest one is totally out of control. You know, that's not a dysfunctional family.

THE TIGER AND THE MONK

Vitou finds the story of "The Tiger and the Monk Who Lives in the Forest" in the homemade Xerox book. I ask him to tell it to me.

"The monk finds a tiger dead on top of the den of a big snake. The monk has the power to make somebody dead to be alive. The tiger wakes, and gets angry at the monk, and says, 'I was sleeping, and you woke me up, and I don't get enough sleep. So I have to eat you because you woke me up.' The monk tries to explain, 'You were sleeping on a hole where a snake lives,' and the tiger didn't believe him. The monk says, 'That's not right.' 'Ask any animal,' the tiger says. The monk ask the wolf if it's right for the tiger to eat the monk. The wolf thinks that every day of his life he lives off the leftovers of the tiger's skill, so he doesn't want to make the tiger angry, so it's right for the tiger to eat the monk. So they ask the buffalo. The buffalo says, 'People are no good, people make the buf-

Frank Chin

falo work and then eat them,' so it's okay for the tiger to eat the monk. So they go to the elephant—the people are bad because they make the elephant work all day. So people are bad. Eat the monk. So they go to the rabbit, and the rabbit says, 'I cannot say anything. I have to see what happened where it happened.' So they walk back to the hole, and the tiger lays down over the hole as if to sleep, and the snake comes out and bites the tiger, and the tiger dies again, and the rabbit says, 'Don't make him alive again.'"

Vitou laughs. With this book in his hand, he's a kid again. Some of his childhood had been on hold till now. He grins as he thumbs through the book of Xeroxed pages.

"I enjoy this. I read this a lot."

Same thing. Alligator lives in the lake. The lake dries up, and the alligator's stuck. One day the farmer comes and frees the alligator and takes the alligator to water. Once in the water and feeling himself again, the alligator wants to eat the farmer. That's not right. The elephant says it's fair; the horse says it's only right. And the rabbit wants to return to where the alligator and the farmer met.

"In the Cambodian story, the rabbit is good," Vitou says. "The alligator and the wolf and the tiger are bad people."

BULLETPROOF BUDDHISTS

Roy Moody

"With the Lao and the Cambodian gangs, most of them are Buddhist. Theravada Buddhism. Your destiny's mapped out. And if something happens, it happened, it was mapped out, there's nothing you can do to change it. With Theravada Buddhism, what you do in this life determines what you're going to be in your next life. And so even though they are gang members, they're very loyal to each other. And most of the older ones are very loyal to their families. And they're more than willing to share. I've seen them share money. I've heard about how like one gamer will get a lot of money and they'll more than gladly pass it out among the other gang members."

So the kids are good, nonviolent practitioners of Theravada Buddhism? No, Roy Moody is not saying that.

"The only thing that—See, these kids tend to believe to take parts in what they want to believe."

He picks his words carefully, even as they flow. Sometimes a bit of a conversation with himself about the words he's picking flows out.

"I mean, we do have our drive-bys also, but we have so many that are willing to walk up because their Buddha will protect them."

Asian kids doing drive-bys. I make a note and listen on.

"One of the things that is definitely an important factor is the role of their religion. Buddhism. They definitely feel that Buddha will protect them. That's why we've had so many fatal homicides with Southeast Asians is that they will walk right up to their adversary.

"And in a group of other gang members, you know there might be ten or fifteen other ones there, but they will walk up, vastly outnumbered, and shoot point-blank range.

"See, they hear stories that their fathers and their uncles back in Laos, Cambodia, Vietnam, you know, Aw, I was shot, but nothing happened. The bullet bounced off of me. Or, the bullet went right in and right out because Buddha protected me.

"We all know that different things happen in war. Maybe he was shot, maybe the bullet did pass through him and didn't hit any vital parts. But they hear enough of these stories that actually, especially some of the original gang members in their late teens, early twenties actually do believe that their Buddha

Frank Chin

will protect. So you definitely have to look at the religion aspect of it."

SHADES OF THE BOXERS OF THE BOXER REBELLION

The Chinese insurrectionists known as Boxers of the Boxer Rebellion, out to oust the whites from China, said they were protected by Kwan Kung, the god of war and hero of the popular *Romance of the Three Kingdoms,* by Lo Kuanchong. Kwan Kung was such a powerful exemplar of personal integrity among the folk that the Buddhists made him the Buddha who defends the realm and the Taoists made him the guardian of borders. Heavy kung-fu training and fanatical belief in Kwan Kung supposedly made the Boxers bulletproof. The only thing religion is good for to Asians is making them bulletproof. Ironically, folklore has it, Kwan Kung as the god of war destroys all magic. Ghosts of the dead disappear, the human disguises of spirits dissolve, and all magic spells crash in the presence of any image, an actor wearing Kwan Kung's face on the stage, the sound of his name in a dark room. Sun Tzu the strategist knew religion didn't work and said to ban all religious practices and superstition in the ranks when waging war. But sometimes, and in some places, it's good tactics to wear the tattoos of nuts and unpredictable fanatics.

The 108 heroes of the *Outlaws of the Water Margin* are wrongfully outlawed in the latter Song dynasty, a period when traitors occupy the throne and bandits, the exiled, and the condemned who wear the tattoo of the criminal are China's only defense against the invaders from the north. Ngawk Fay (Yue Fei), the great exemplar of loyalty, was trained in the martial arts by the teacher of one of the heros of the *Water Margin*. He's legendary because his mother proclaimed her son's loyalty by tattooing it on his back, and Ngawk Fay and

Bulletproof Buddhists

his son became the Batman and Robin of the Song after the *Water Margin*. As the Song gave up chunks of China to the tribes who would become the Mongols and Manchus in the north, Ngawk Fay and his son fought to get them back.

Corrupt officials trick him into approaching the emperor in his private sanctum with sword in hand, and, even with his loving mother's tattoos on his back, Ngawk Fay is condemned for attempting to assassinate the Son of Heaven. Legend has it corrupt officials bribed the family who supplied food to the jail to poison Ngawk Fay. At his tomb, destroyed during, then restored after the Cultural Revolution in China, in Hangzhou City, next to West Lake, there are statues of a kneeling couple representing the man and wife who killed Ngawk Fay. People visiting Ngawk Fay's tomb spit on the statues.

ASIAN FAGIN

Wolf

The survivors of the trauma of the war suffer or enjoy the stress of the postwar years differently. At least one old soldier who escaped Pol Pot made the violence and thievery of gang kids work for him. He was a warrant officer in the Cambodian army. Here he became a Fagin to the Cambodian kids of the OBS, the Oriental Boy Soldiers.

I sit on an old couch in what looks like a garage from the street. The place isn't a garage. Garages aren't carpeted. The place is another world, another time. This may have been a driveway at one time. The walls and the roof are made of what looks like gray driftwood, and scraps of lumber, and pieces, very small pieces of razed crack houses carried back here in a shopping cart and tied together into boards, into beams, into joists, into walls and a pitch roof, with insulated wire, and wire, and string of all kinds. The floor is lumpy. Layers of car-

Frank Chin

pet smooth over lumps of what nobody asks and nobody says. This is the shady place. There are a couch and a few chairs. Bamboo shades give a little light and a lot of prickly shade behind the couch. Just behind the couch in the real world of this place is a pond where the Wolf raises fighting fish.

Pematokyryrasmey Chuun from the Storefront stands apart and looks disgusted. He uses subtle movements to direct my attention to the letters "OBS" scribed on the arms and legs of all the tables and chairs.

Wolf tells me the sad story of his life in a drowsy, wheedling whimper. He holds his little son on his lap, and his second wife, and mother-in-law, and two children by his wife's last successful marriage, all sit or stand out here, not so much watching me talking to Wolf as posing for a family portrait for my eyes and hiding from the old man throwing a fit of the delirium tremens inside the house. While things go smash inside, the Fagin, in his sleepy ooze of a voice, says he was gangs. He was bad. But now he's good. Yeah, sure.

"Just out of jail. No names," he says softly, sweetly.

"I'll call you Wolf."

"My wife. She's deaf. She's a second wife. I have ex-wife in San Diego.

"I used to be a machinist, work at General Dynamics for thirteen years. I lost my job. Been laid off. I been on drugs. True story," he chants in a voice meant to please, ease me into a drowse. "All kinds of drugs. Marijuana. Cocaine. True story. Not lies. If you want a story, I give you story. I lost my family good," he smiles. Bashful of the seven dwarves doing his cute dwarf act. But he's not bashful. He's hustling me, fingering me for buttons to push. This is the "We are all victims" button.

"My life is sad. Before is all right. Before I came, I really enjoy with the American. I went to school a month and a half. And I find a job. I don't know how to speak English."

"How old were you when you came over?"

"About twenty-nine. 13 July 1976. Twenty-eight, twenty-nine, I can't remember."

"You came over with . . ."

"Only me and my wife and my daughter. Only three people."

So he came over, then he went to school for a month and a half?

"Month and a half. Then I find a job because I couldn't got enough money from welfare to support the family. So I look for a job. And later on I got a better job. I went to training machine shop. After that I got a job better and better. Then 1990 I been lay off. So far it's been four years. I been lost my family about four and a half years so far.

"I mean they kick me out because I'm been do the bad things, you know. I been have friend. Hang out with friends. Forget the family. Bad things. I mean go around at nighttime," and he whimpers into a laugh and a leer.

"Bad things?" I ask. Can I get him to tell me about the boys he flatters and the runaway thirteen-year-old girls they bring him without loading the question with young runaway girls? "Hurt people?" I ask. "Guns and knives?"

"Do something wrong. No, not hurt people. Been on drugs," he says, with a little threat in his lean forward and voice and on the last words, "That clear?" CIA-, Green Beret-trained command voice. He knows how to use it.

Of course he's quit drugs. Yeah, sure.

"So far, so good. I been quit for a little while. The time I miss them, I need something to forget. Only drugs can forget my family. When I have drugs in my body, I forget about it. Say, Fuck it!

"It's fun because drugs. Okay. People don't give up about drugs. You gonna have fun. After fun you gonna have sad.

Frank Chin

You lost your job. You lost your family. And the last one, your life. If people give up. You good. Many time I gave up, but give up not too good. Because I don't have family. Start grow up the family.

"Now I give up, I say, No, I not going to say fuck it! I give up for good. Because I start a new life. I got one son. This is Wolf Jr. And my baby girl. So I'm growing up. I give up good.

"I live on welfare. Welfare supports me because the kids still young. I can't go nowhere.

"I have no friends no more. I don't hang around with anybody. Just with the family right there. This my stepmother. This my stepbrother, stepsister, you know. And my dad been sick in the house."

He means mother-in-law, brother-in-law, sister-in-law, father-in-law.

"I hope when my kids grow up, I'm going to start a job the same experience I have before. I have experience from machinist. Sixteen years in the United States. I'm forty-seven.

"I been in jail for three times. I got out of jail. I got probation. In a prison for seven months. Not too long. That's why I learn. Some people got to be learn. How to know, how the jail look like. How you do with bad thing, you know. You do it wrong. You got to go to jail. You do time. If you do it right. You never been to do time. Some people don't know what kind a jail look like. So I already know what's going on in there. Now, I don't want to go back. That's the truth!

"I don't like because, especially after soldier. I been at war for five years from '70 to '75. So I got a lot of enemies back Cambodia." The United States created this monster to service its secret war, made him an officer, a leader of men, an example to his people.

"I love to be here. I wouldn't go back to my country," he says, living in America, the way Americans taught him to live in Cambodia. Wolf is what they mean when they say, "The chickens are coming home to roost."

"Now, I have family. Nobody can lie me about drugs. What kind? Oh, this good, this good. Bullshit. Just stay away. I don't hang around. I don't got friend no more. Before I got a lot of friend because I got money. I got job. Got a nice family. Now I live like, you know, you see how look like. Just like that. I don't care. I don't be used to be live like that. But I have to learn. I got a lot of friends, like 90 percent in San Diego. They respect me. I'm their brother, uncle, you know. I go everywhere with my family, they respect, you know. 'Come on, please sit down.' Now, they won't let me. I ask them, they won't answer me. I call them, they won't turn around, you know. I'm down the hill. That's why I say I don't need friends. I try to give up by myself. Hey, nobody can tell me, Hey, stop doing this, doing that. Don't have to. Do by myself.

"Do this, do that, you know. Cut garden. Help mom, dad, you know. Because they gotten old. After a while, maybe can't help them. Especially my two kids right there, too little. And my wife, she's deaf. She don't speak any English. Only Cambodian. But she has to read your voice. Sometime you talk one side, she answer through another side. I look to my two kids right there, what's why I give up good. But I still miss my ex-family. They still live close here. But I got no time go to see. When I see, might be, my heart go crazy or something. My daughter go went to college. Another two kids in high school. They grow big. Boy and girl, twin children. They good kids. They follow the Morman. My daughter the big one is a counselor of the Morman. And my wife the same thing, she translator to a Cambodian by the Morman."

Is he a Morman?

"Last time I went to church, and later on I lost my family, I don't believe no more, because I'm a Buddhist. I got tattoo.

Frank Chin

I believe Buddha. I believe my master, you know. About the church and something, I don't believe because is not show. I been at war. I believe my master, you know, in my body, you know tattoos sound like that. You can get away with a gun."

"Get away with a gun. He means bulletproof," Chuun says. He can't stand this guy. And Wolf knows it and plays it.

"One time I carried a gun. That's why I been in jail for thirty days. That gun I picked from the dumpster at a new year."

Ah, the famous "Merry Christmas-Happy New Year Gun in the Dumpster Story." I could listen to him all day long. I *am* listening to him all day long.

"Yeah, I carry. Go into store and walk out. And the customer, he see I have gun. And that owner that store they know me, and they know I have gun. They say, Just play gun, you know. It can't be shoot. But I just play around because nothing I can do. Just like I scare people, you know, you on drug. I been on drug. Lost mind. Cocaine."

Yeah, nothing Wolf could do. Chuun stomps the carpet softly and turns his head.

What was Wolf doing looking in a dumpster? He's an environmentalist, a recycler, an entrepreneur.

"Nighttime you pick up the can, you know," Wolf says. "I got no place to go. I pick up the cans at nighttime. In the morning I sell. Then I have breakfast. I know a lot of people in San Diego, but I'm not going to ask, Hey, give me breakfast, eat something. Not me. I do my way. I go around dumpsters nighttime, pick up the cans. Big bag. In the morning I take to sell. I got four or five dollars. Better than you steal, you know. A lot of friends they call me, ask me give them the money. I say, No, thanks."

Chuun looks like he has to pee. Wolf likes that and shyly presses on with his sad story.

Bulletproof Buddhists

"See, I'm lucky. If that gun kill people, I be do time forever. And the police took that gun away from me. I do time for thirty days."

He no longer goes out looking into dumpsters. He's not looking for school or any retraining for a job.

"I got my kids, my wife. I got take care of them because the kids, they're young. I got no time. I spend time, all day, all night. Sometime I sleep two hour, three hour at night because of the kid. My wife can't hear the kid cry. So you understand what I'm talking about. The kid cry, I'm the one up. The time I up, I gotta change diapers, feed them, something like that."

So he does the cooking in the family?

"No, not really. I'm lazy right now. I make she cook. I baby-sit. I do it that way. You gotta share, you know. Got to be fair."

"WHY DON'T YOU TELL HIM ABOUT YOU USED TO HANG OUT WITH OBS GUYS?"

"Why don't you tell him about you used to hang out with OBS guys?" Chuun mutters across the room, almost too low to hear.

"I never hang out OBS," Wolf snarls. The bashful song is gone with the twang.

"I'm not a gangster.

"The kids just come around like this, like that, ask me, How're you doing? something like that. But I'm not go with the kids. You know, the kids come around with me. So nothing, I can't say, Hey, man, stay away from me. But I'm not go out with them. I stay home. They can come. They can tell me OBS, too, you know. I got their case, OBS, you know. The gang, too. But what can I say? If you say I'm a gang, I'm not

Frank Chin

a gang, you know. Maybe someday, I be a gang. If you push me, I be a gang, too. I can't go because my age forty-seven years old. I can't hang around with a ten, eleven years old, you know, something like that. But if you push me, you know. I say I'm not, you say, Yeah you are! I gotta go, you know what I mean? Nothing I can say because I'm Cambodian. Police officer Cambodian, too. Is he OBS, too? Ha ha ha.

"See, everybody Cambodian have to be OBS. Not police. They put me like that. Nothing I can say. I say, No, I'm not a OBS. They put OBS. And I look at my kid in prison, I think, God damn! I'm OBS! What the OBS, man? Then I say, Oh, Oriental Boy Soldiers. I say, Oh, no, man. I don't believe that.

"I don't think nothing. I don't know what look like. But they say like that. Before I don't know what the color blue, red, white, whatever. I just like blue. Red, whatever I wear, together, you know."

So the red T-shirt he's wearing doesn't mean a thing.

"I don't care! Just for protect my body. The time I working at General Dynamics, I used to have a parade blue. A shirt that's blue. And jeans that's blue, too, you know. And my car is SR-5 truck, you know, big tire, is blue, too. I like blue. But I don't know the gangs. But the colors. I just know in 1992. Oh, this color is Crips, and this is Bloods, whatever. But I not a gang, you know. And police, they see my tattoo, they say, You're a gangster."

What about the tattoos around his neck?

"Just protect for the gun, that's all. I'm a soldier. Gun protection."

Chuun speaks up. "In Cambodia, during the war, the people that have tattoos on, they believe in a superstition. They said that it's bulletproof. It's like no modern equipment like bulletproof vests. In Cambodian army when they go to the battlefield, they have tattoos on them. The letters are Indian,

Bulletproof Buddhists

Hinduism, but they have nothing to do with Buddhism."

Wolf says, "Yeah some people say it's bullshit. But I don't care what they say, you know. "

The first time in jail, he didn't mind jail.

"The first time, yeah. The second time, I learn not to because I got into fight in jail. Dirty and, you know, boring. No freedom. You need to see your family. For some people it's honor to do time in jail."

Life is better here than in Cambodia?

"Oh, yeah. But I hate just a little bit. Everything's all right. I hate drugs. In my country nobody go crazy this way, like here. This is crazy drugs. You know make kids go out and get killed, steal, robbery, whatever, because of drugs."

What about his kids?

"Yeah, they have to go school when they grow up. I don't know, when they grow up, they go to school, I die already. I'm forty-seven, maybe I live another three years. Maybe I make it fifty. You know, disease, whatever. Or somebody hate you, you get killed from somebody, I don't know. Sometime, any minute, later on after you talk, you walk in there, you follow, pass out, you know. Nobody knows the life. Sometimes you walk on the street at the curb, run fast, bang! Gone! I better quit doing kids no more." He laughs. He wants to be buddies.

Who wrote all the OBS stuff all over the furniture? On the bench over here? All over?

"The kid come to play around, six, seven years old."

Is he saying six- and seven-year-old kids wrote this stuff?

"Oh, yeah. They already know. From six years old. Because the big one train already. They know, all right. They going to stick together."

What if his kids start hanging with the OBS, is he going to move? First he says no, then he says yes, fishing for what I want to hear.

Frank Chin

"I'm not going to move. I'm going to teach him. When he understand, you know the talk. You know, he's Jr. If I'm a gang, he's supposed to be OG, you know. Old Gang. But I'm not so. This is for temporary, you know, around here. When I got a little money, you know, I'm go somewhere, quiet area."

When in doubt, keep hitting the pity-me button.

"My stepfather about fifty-five, fifty-six years old. Young man. I call him Dad. I'm supposed to call him Uncle or Brother, but you know. I got no, no family in the United States; after my wife kicked me out I got nobody. He picked me on the street. He say, You used to work nice job, good money. Why you hang around on the street for nothing? Come to live in my house."

Oh, yeah?

"He call me come. So I can sleep. Better than homeless, you know. My mom support me. Buy cigarettes. Give me food, whatever. So I respect them. I do whatever they have, you know, need help. Everything. The roof, everything. I build everything. I build this."

The *this* he's talking about is this building of scrap tied and wired together with scrap. The beams tying the walls together and holding up the roof are made of bits of short scrap tied together several times until they are just the right length.

What about the skull-and-crossbones ring on his finger?

"On, no. Just pick from the street. I'm not wear a ring like this. That's something, I don't know. Just this morning. I take Mom to the store buy cook—"

Sirens. A paramedic wagon. Fire department. What's going on? Wolf called 911, said an old man was throwing a fit. The paramedics come out of the house with an old man strapped to a gurney who doesn't look that old. DTs. The paramedics are disgusted. Only twelve teams are up for the whole city, and right now all of them are screaming. Busy all day. The paramedics are fried, fast, efficient. Wolf and his family watch from another world, another time. Whatever they did to get the old man out of the house seems to have worked.

YOUR HAND IS YOUR FRIEND

Vitou Reat

Vitou grins at a section on the meaning of dreams in Cambodian folklore.

If you dream you lose a tooth and it is clean, not bloody, it means someone close to you is dead.

If you dream you lose a tooth and the tooth is bloody, it means a relative is dead.

If you dream you are fat, it is a bad omen.

He shows me a picture of a boy showing his hands to a boy across the table, whose hands are on the table.

"One student lazy. One student not," Vitou says.

"This not a story, but just like a article to teach the children not to leave the food out or the flies can come. And flies not good cuz the legs carry disease. It's just like Chinese.

"This talk about your hands. It say your hand is your friend. Like you say, your hand help you to understand. I make my hand so you can better understand, and you do everything with your hands. He say that he gets smart because his hands help him. He write a lot with the hand. So this one [he points to the boy not using his hands] doesn't know how to write. So it say your hand is your friend, use it, don't keep it lazy. So you learn to read it, and the idea is good, too.

"My teacher used to say that, too. Use your eyes, you know, read! Don't be sorry for you eyes; use it all the time."

Frank Chin

Rabbit and Baboon

Rabbit is a twenty-one-year-old baby with maybe a ninth-grade education and two kids. She's small. She looks thirteen, maybe fifteen. She was born in Cambodia, came to the United States when she was seven, doesn't remember Cambodia. She speaks and reads three languages—English, Lao, and Cambodian. In none of these languages does she have the words to say the father of her kids is doing life for murder. He killed a boy.

Bunny was a father and a murderer at nineteen. Rabbit didn't think much of it then. But now, Bunny Jr. is about to start school. She tells him not to join a gang. And she tells him stories. The only stories of the only history she knows are stories of Bunny Jr.'s father, a Cambodian gang banger since fourteen. These are the myths and fairy tales the child who never had a childhood tells her kid. She doesn't want Bunny Jr. to be jumped into a gang. But what else does the kid of the gang kids know but gang kids?

"Are you a gang kid?" I ask her.

"Well, I hang around with them," she says. "It's just that when I was young, I was fourteen, I ran away, and then I have nowhere to go, so I hang around with them cuz they stay up all night."

Wow, the ultimate in American free expression of self, the great rebellion of the spirit is to stay up all night. Her life changed forever at fourteen because she wanted to stay up all night.

"When I was a kid, I didn't even think my mother loved me. I mean, because I have a stepdad. And she pays more attention to her other kids than to me. They're on welfare. My dad's on SSI.

Bulletproof Buddhists

"I ran away, and I live with a friend. She was on welfare, but then she used to know me when I was real young, and she saw me, and she took me in. She's on welfare, too."

"*Hanging out* means?"

"You kick back at the beach, drink, do whatever. . . . Sometimes the girls have money. And sometimes it's the guys. I never have money, though. I never have money. But the guys have the money for us, and they take us out. . . ."

Where do they go when the boys take them out?

"Not Red Lobster," Baboon says, and the girls laugh. I can't tell if she thinks the Red Lobster is high class, or trash, or white, or what, to make them laugh. Did something happen at a Red Lobster?

Rabbit likes them to take her out to "any Chinese restaurant." "Every time I go I always eat noodles," Rabbit says.

"Noodle soup? *Pho?*" Baboon asks.

"Yeah, the *pho*," Rabbit says. "They have beef and, you know, those meatballs. And that long white thing in the *pho*. It comes out from the cow. Kind of crunchy. Tripe! Fried rice. And the fried noodles."

She's talking about a good time, now.

"Either we go to like Family Fun or the Yellow Brick Road, it's a place where there are video games. I don't game. I just hang out and have some fun. You know, like just talk to them. Say, You have any homegirls? Come on, pick us up! You know, like that."

Yeah, *like that*. It's not hard to see how fights get started.

"Then I would like call my friends up and everything, and take them with us, and we went and have fun. Anyway, come back to where we kick back."

No furniture. There's a mattress on the floor. An old motel couch she must have found dumped on the street.

"Like the last time I ran away we kick back at Four Seven, you know that Four Seven place?" She says "Four Seven," not

Frank Chin

"Forty-seventh." "Four Seven" for Forty-seventh Street. "Five Oh" for Fiftieth Street.

"Do you know them? The Four Seven OBS. That's where I hang with them that time. And every time we hang out with them, we come back to that place. They'll be smoking and everything. They ask me to, but then I don't want to get involved in it. But they would like, if they're temper, you know, some of them would be having guns. They have a place for the guns. And if there's trouble, they bring it out. Last time, I was at Four Seven, you know? They were in some kind of trouble, right? With some other gang? And some other gang drive-by, and everybody was in each corner! They were hiding in back of the wall; there was some up a tree just ready to shoot 'em. And instead, it didn't happen. The cops came. And they took everybody. They got almost all the guns. When I seen it, a lot of guns. More than ten. Not more than twenty. Between ten and twenty. And they pass it to each of the gang-ster, so they can get ready for—But it didn't happen that day, right, they got caught that day. And the next day, the gang that they have a problem with came by and shot one of their friends. And that's when they weren't ready. That friend was hurt bad. Really. It's my cousin, too. He was walking, and they came by and shot him. I mean, he was bleeding everywhere.

"That time, I think the gangsters went out, they were going out, and like some of them, they don't want to go, so they hang out right there, wait for them to come back. And like only two people were there. See one of the guys who knows that it was them, so he ducks. He yelled out for my cousin to duck, but then my cousin, he didn't— They just shot him before he could duck. Now my cousin's twenty-two. This happened about six years ago."

On the couch, under the long front window, the fifteen-year-old girl nicknamed Baboon boasts of running away at eleven and belonging to a gang, the Asian Crips. The gray, milky light of a cold afternoon, threatening rain, intrudes through the window. There's a triptych with an Asian theme in red on the wall. Something else junked from an old motel. That's it. The rest is a few battery-run electronic gadgets, a boom box. There's nothing in the next room. Nothing on the walls. Nothing over the windows. Nothing on the floor. Nothing. A nothing kitchen. A nothing bathroom. I plug my tape recorder into the wall. No electricity.

"How long have you been living here?" I ask.

"Five months now."

"At first when I got my place, I get to stay there for only a month. Because the gangsters, you know, they got me in trouble. Well, they were making noise and everything. The neighbors complained, and then they would be cussing at my neighbors. And then my neighbors would tell my landlord, you know. There was nothing I could do."

"So you were kicked out of that place," I say.

"Yeah, and then I moved in at Forty-ninth," she says, "and I get to stay there for like three months. And they raided the place, I think for drugs, and people they were looking for, and everything. Well, they find some runaways, you know. I tell them not to come, but still they come. Then, you know, they took 'em away, that's all. And some was on drugs; they took 'em in. And some that was on probation—took 'em in. I never got into that kind of trouble."

What kind of trouble is that? She's never been arrested.

"Well, they got me into a lot of trouble, and I have one kid at that time. And I have nowhere to go. I mean, they won't accept me. The other one was at Auburn Drive, right there. And I get to stay there for like a year because the landlord knows my dad. He said, Whatever happens, you know, like blame it on him, he'll take care of it. For like a whole year nothing happened. But then after like about to move out, there was trouble, you know like SWAT team came over and everything. I don't know why! I was walking out of the house, and the SWAT team came; I mean they were carrying guns. A big one, too! I got scared! I say, 'What is this?'

"I—I've seen it. Like jump people, you know. And they drive-by. I've been in a car when they drive-by. Yeah. I don't know. A lot of things they do is bad. I see a lot. That time it doesn't scare me because it doesn't happen to me. Now, I know.

"But that time when I was with them? The people that they were hurting, I didn't feel sorry for them at all. Yeah, I know the people they were hurting. To me, when I hang around with them, it's not my business, you know? I just keep out. But then, you know, when I hang out with them, I can't disagree, you know, because they won't like me.

"They would like let me alone, you know; wherever they go, they wouldn't take me around anymore. They think that, you know, that I don't like what they do. That's why I don't like to tell them anything they were doing was bad. They would diss me. They do gang rape, but they didn't do me. I was just one of, I mean . . .

"Drive-by is no fun.

"I don't go out with them now," she says. "Now, it's like they would just wave hi. Yeah, we're still friends, but now we don't get along that well because I have my own family. And I don't want to get involved in it. I don't want to get involved in anything because if I have them here, they're just like bringing problems to my family. But I'm still friends with them.

"My first boyfriend that was in OBS was Bunny. Ever since then I haven't gone out with them, and I have his kid.

"And you know, it's like they give respect to Bunny. You know, they see me, they say hi, they just give a smile or wave. They at least have respect for Bunny.

Bulletproof Buddhists

"Bunny told me, he said that they won't ever diss me or ever say anything bad. If they see me, they'll just say hi or whatever. He even told them to keep an eye on us."

"So you feel protected by them?" I say.

"Umm, no. Uh uh." Bunny shakes her head. "He told them, and they say yes, but I'm pretty sure they aren't, you know . . ."

"What do you want to do in the next ten years?"

Baboon can't think ten minutes down the block. Ten years makes her show her tattoo. A Janus. The masks of comedy and tragedy. Under the masks, "Laugh now. Cry later."

"I want to have a family," Rabbit says. "You know, someone who's going to care about me and my kids. And settle down and everything, which I *am*, but then it's not that good. I want to start working. I want to get my kids to go to school. All of them go to school because I can't trust other people. I mean, if my mom watch my kids, I would start going to school. Adult school? I know my mom, I mean, she would watch them, but I know that inside her, she would have something else to do, too, but she just don't want to say it. I know how she feels, but I just didn't let her watch my kids. I'm going to wait until they're five years old, and both of them go to school, and then start to go to school."

"You ran away from home and are still friends with your mother?" I ask.

"Yeah, I used to think that she never loved me. But now I know if anything happens, there's always my mom."

"Are you a good mom?" I ask.

"I don't think so."

"What can you do better?"

"Nothing, right now. I can take care of my kids, give them a bath every day. Make sure they eat."

"Do you tell them stories?"

"No. . . . Well, I tell them about their dad. He asked me

Frank Chin

about his dad. And I said, Your daddy's in jail. And he goes, My daddy's in jail? Yeah. I ask him if he miss his daddy, he says yeah. He says, When is he coming out? I say, I don't know."

"What's he in jail for?"

"For the trouble that he made." She can't say he shot somebody. She finally says, "Drug possession," senses I'm not buying it, and says, "He violated his parole."

"Oh," I say.

"Well, he just go in and out of juvenile, but then after that he go to jail, and we have kids, and he starts going to jail, the adult one? It's harder for me to see him. Right now, he's twenty-one."

"OBS territory?" I ask.

"It's separated. It's not together," Baboon says. "This side is all Five Oh, and that side is all Forty Seventh. I don't get along with OBS. I don't know OBS; I hang out with OKB.

"My problems started ever since I was born!

"You know rebelling? Stopped going to school four years ago."

She's fifteen now. She was eleven when she faded from the school system.

"HOW DO YOU SURVIVE? DO YOU WALK THE STREETS? HOOK? WHAT?"

"How do you survive? Do you walk the streets? Hook? What?" I see I've struck a nerve.

"She just, you know," Rabbit says, instinctively rising to protect her friend, whoever she is. "No, she just come stay at, like either my house, or one of—"

"No, no, no, no!" Baboon says.

"She stay at my house or, you know, one of, you know. . . ."

"I don't hook or anything. I just sell dope and stuff. But I don't *hook!* or anything."

Bulletproof Buddhists

"Would the boys like you to hook?" I ask.

"Umm-mmmm!" Baboon shakes her head emphatically, pursed lips and all. "In our gangs, we don't sell, like, you know . . . like that."

"Just drugs, not flesh."

"Yeah."

"Do you have a special boyfriend in the gang?"

"I used to go out with a few of 'em. But . . ." She tilts her head to the side to complete her thought.

"Hmmm," I say, as if I understand what she said.

"So what do *you* want?" I ask Baboon. "What's your future?" Whoops! She's not ready for that question. "Or do you think about it?" There's a wordless whimper. Wrong question again. This is worse than asking if she hooks. "Is there anybody in the gangs you'd like to take with you? No? What would you like?. . . You obviously like the gangs. What do you like about them?"

"I don't! I don't like them," Rabbit says. "Now, I don't! Before I do. But now I don't like them. Well, before, they took care of me. They, like, they don't let me get in trouble or anything. They watch out for me; just because I was going out with one of the homeboys, they watch out for me. And, you know, I go on out wherever they go. But now, when I think back, I think back, now that I have my own kids, I know how it feel like for a mother. Now, I know how it feels like for my mother, for me doing that to my mother. I mean, I know how she feels now."

"Do you feel the same way, Baboon?"

"She hasn't been through it yet," Rabbit says.

"I'm not involved or anything, but my mom don't care about me," Baboon says proudly.

"Oh, she does," Rabbit says.

"She knows I go and sell out there to make money and

Frank Chin

stuff," Baboon says. "She didn't help me all through that time; she knows what I was going through. She didn't help. So I don't care."

"What's your mom do? Does she work? She on welfare, too?"

"Hmmm," she ways, fading fast.

"I'm a boy. How would I get into a gang?" I ask.

"Okay," Rabbit says. "They jump you in."

"Huh?"

"They jump you in!" Baboon says, as if I'm stupid.

"What's that mean?" I ask, stupid to the end.

"You gotta have your juts and see how down you are," Baboon says. "You can't be anybody like, . . . Let's say I just meet you off the street. And all of a sudden you want to be jumped in. We gotta see how you are for a while, to see how down you are. . . . Whenever there's trouble, you're there. . . . Yeah! You know. . . . But if you're someone that's weak and stuff, that don't even wanna, you know, fight or anything, then . . . who wants you?"

"*To jump me in* means I can't just join? I gotta hang out with them a while?"

"Umm hmmm." Baboon shakes her head, emphatically, no.

"And then I gotta get shot at a few times?"

"No," Baboon says.

Rabbit laughs.

"What? I gotta go out and get in a few fights?"

"No, there's not all the time in a gang you go out and look for trouble!" Baboon says, defending some sense of gang ethics and moral proportion.

"If you want to get jumped," Rabbit says, taking over, covering for her friend. "If you want to be in a gang, right. All the gang it, like. . . . One wants to be in OBS, right? All the OBS gonna jump on him."

"And beat him up," I say, filling in her fade.

"Uh huh," she nods. "Do anything, no matter what. They don't know what they're going to do to him, but it's all of them. Fifty or something, they'll do it. And if they rejump each other, like all of them just hit anybody! All of them hit anybody!"

"And if you want to get out of the set," Baboon says, "you gotta be jumped out."

"Yeah," Rabbit nods.

"You just can't walk out," Baboon says, then reconsiders. "It depends if you want to walk out or not."

"I gotta fight my way in. I gotta fight my way out," I say. Rabbit nods. "Yeah," she says.

"And you've seen this?" I say.

"Um hmm!" Rabbit and Baboon both nod.

"And you say there are fifty?"

"Oh! Once they jumped each other down at the beach!" Rabbit gushes. "That one Cambodian beach? They were full of them! Full! in that place. And I was standing right there watching them jump each other in. But some, you know, they can tell, you know, if he's down or not because some would act like they're already hurt!" She laughs at the silliness of the crybabies.

"Some would act like they're really hurt already, and they would stop. And then one would say, Oh, man! You need more! You need more! And one would go, Aw, come on, man he got enough, come on! Attack! But they'll know! They'll know who's weak and everything."

"So *weak* means the guy who stops fighting first?" I say. They nod. "So how many people are in the gangs?" I ask.

"More than anybody can count," Baboon says. "Because they're from different states, not just San Diego."

"Yeah," Rabbit says.

Frank Chin

"They live all over the place."

"And they all come here. . . ," I say.

They nod. I nod.

Rabbit says, "I don't want my son to be in a gang. I'm not proud of it either. I'm not proud that my boyfriend's in a gang. A lot of things he do I'm not proud of."

"But you still love him."

"No, not anymore."

"Do you have a boyfriend now?"

"Yeah. Not a gangster this time."

"Does he have a job?"

"No, but he try to get anything for me, you know. Anything I want, he'll get it. He helps me out. I mean, he don't do bad things for it, you know. If he has to go to his mom and dad, he goes to his mom and dad. Right now, I don't care about those gangsters and all that."

"But they still come over," I say.

"Not anymore! Uh uh." She shakes her head. "The last time was two weeks ago. And I think we misunderstood each other; everybody's, you know, banging on each other. Saying this and that, you know. I don't let them come over no more cuz they disrespect my house. They were being noisy, and I didn't want them to make that much noise. But then, I understand everybody was down with drinking, you know, like, okay, some were smoking weed, but I understand that. Not in my house. I don't mind if they come and don't do it, you know. I don't mind if they do it and then come over here after, you know. I don't mind."

Officer Moody comes by to pick me up. He glances into the open doorway and asks if she has any food in the house. No. He fishes ten bucks out of his wallet and hands it to her. About an hour later we see her and her two kids and her fifteen-year-old runaway friend walking back from a restaurant.

Bulletproof Buddhists

"I'm glad she really went out and got some food," Roy Moody says.

The next day Rabbit comes into the Storefront. It's a step. Roy Moody calls her caseworker and gives her leads on help finding Rabbit money for food, day care for her kids, and three schools that might accept her. She may think it's too late, but five years from now, she'll wish she had started something five years ago, and five years after that, she'll wish she had started school five years ago," Moody says.

"A lot of these older gang members have definitely said that they had wished that five years ago they had listened to what I said about staying in school, cuz they have no future, there's nothing for them. You know, they're not going to be picked up, like in the movies, by some Chinese—" And whoops, I knock over the styrofoam cup of machine-made coffee, and the good Officer Moody never finishes saying that, after watching too many subtitled Hong Kong videos, the Lao and Cambodian gang kids dream of joining the Wah Ching or a criminal triad, the Chinese M. M for Mafia.

The Wah Ching used to be what the police called Chinatown gangs of kids from Hong Kong in the seventies. Now *Wah Ching* means organized crime from Hong Kong. The triads are centered in Taiwan. For years, both have been using nice restaurants in American Chinatowns as their Swiss banks, places to stash the cash they'll need to fulfill their dream of all their children in nice American universities, a condo in LA, an apartment in New York, a new nympho ego-licking wife in her early twenties. From restaurants owned by a brother, to jointly owned farms in California, and Texas, and maybe New Jersey, the triads have nice legit, big-money business to wash and dry dirty money from Asia.

They all used to be kid gangs and gang kids. They used to be called *tongs* in the nineteenth and early twentieth centuries.

Frank Chin

Kenji Ima—twenty years on the sociology faculty at San Diego State University—is a paper activist, "not a street person," out to turn kids away from gangs. Dead kids get to him. He writes the grant applications for UPAC. He connects with the San Diego Police Department on Asian gangs.

"The Black Jacket Boys used to dominate Madison High. Chinese Viet. Low profile and retired," Kenji Ima says. The bad boys grew up and entered the middle class. He feels funny about that because "they were involved in an unsolved homicide. It was done inside a restaurant on Convoy Street, which is a very busy street. People knew who did it. But no one was able to come up with the goods on them. The police are kind of frustrated over it because no one would testify. They killed somebody, and because nobody would appear to testify against them, nothing was done about it. I feel that you did it, you should . . . but for them, life just goes on. The gang retired, and they have jobs now and are just living their lives.

"You know, it's water under the bridge to them. As one kid told me, 'Well, they really didn't mean to kill him. It just happened.'

"That caught your attention, huh?"

"It sounds very Chinese."

"Those who lived through the Cultural Revolution and survived and came over here affect many people over here as —ruthless. Do you know the word *schnorr*? A schnorr is someone you don't invite to your wedding but who shows up and eats up all your food."

He says he has been pushing the cops for years to put the lid on the homicides. What homicides?

"You had a Marine, he was Hmong, Hoa Lee was his name," Roy Moody says, "who had just come back from Operation Desert Storm. He was at a party. Six OBS gang members thought it was a rival gang's party, but it was not a gang party. He was standing out in front. This kid was definitely not a gang member. And they just came up and just blasted the front of the house, and he got shot and killed. It definitely made an impact. You know it bothered everybody.

"And we just took six of those guys off on that. In December, just before the new year, we arrested six hardcore OBS guys, original. When I say 'we,' I mean the DA's office and the homicide, and they went out, and they finally cracked the case.

"That happened back in '91, and, you know, it took about three years." He sighs. In a kid's life, in a murder case, three years is a long time.

"Well, when I got this job, Kenji Ima came in to pretty much meet me," Roy Moody remembers. "I'm not really sure if he was . . . I think he was a little hesitant about me when he first met me. But I think I addressed all those fears. And of course a lot of people say, Why is this white guy? What's this white guy doing here? But I definitely know that doors have opened for me, more so than most. Even some Southeast Asians don't have so many doors open for them as for me in those communities."

IT WOULDN'T HURT THE GOOD SOCIOLOGIST TO READ A FEW COMIC BOOKS

Kenji Ima believes there's something in the culture. He finds a certain ruthlessness common among Asians from the continent.

He doesn't know the source. It wouldn't hurt the good sociologist to read a few comic books. The culture comes to the kids in the stories that shaped their childhood. He doesn't know Sun Tzu, the strategist, or the comic-book versions of *The Book of Thirty-Six Stratagems,* published in Korea, Singa-

Frank Chin

pore, and Hong Kong, or *Romance of the Three Kingdoms,* or *The Water Margin.* The Chinese and Vietnamese gang kids do.

Back in the depths of the Cultural Revolution in China, and the Vietnam War, and the Great Society, George Woo, a photographer for *Sunset* magazine, became the Big Brother of the dreaded gangs of Hong Kong kids known as Wah Ching by telling people there were people who looked on him as the reincarnation of Kwan Kung, the second brother of the oath of the garden, and a hero of the *Romance of the Three Kingdoms,* and god of war, plunder, and literature. Just the right god to tolerate no magic or other bullshit in his presence. He reminded one and all that all Chinese organizations, the associations for men from specific counties of Kwangtung Province, the wooey goon, the tongs, all were simply gangs once, and all were modeled on the oath the three men from three different walks of life took to become blood brothers in the peach garden from *Three Kingdoms.*

Nobody else in Chinatown looked as much like Kwan Kung as George Woo. And nobody messed with him. He had the ruddy complexion, the beard, the eyebrows like black caterpillars, the deep, dark, frying eyes, the voice like thunder rumbling down the mountain, and turned the Black Panthers on to Mao's Little Red Book being a book of military strategy based on Sun Tzu's *The Art of War.* George Woo tried to tell the patronizing American-born Chinese Americans running for office and running the Great Society and War on Poverty programs in Chinatown that Sun Tzu was a shortcut to understanding the way the immigrants, the gangs of Wah Ching, the Chinese born and raised in a Chinese childhood, see the world.

The Black Panthers listened and made a bundle selling copies of the Little Red Book just outside the student union building in Berkeley. The Chinese Americans full of sociology and contempt for anything Chinese didn't listen, and the kids scammed up the grant money and scholarships, and broke the Chinese Americans' hearts, and killed a few.

A gang kid in New York introduced me to the *Outlaws of the Water Margin* by pointing to a poster of the 108 outlaw chiefs standing on the Golden Shores of Mount Liangshan on the wall over his bed. "Recognize them?" he asked.

It was a test, and I'd flunked. The kid was surprised, and offended, that I didn't know what every kid knew.

Mao Tse-tung tells the world through Han Suyin that his favorite books are *Three Kingdoms, Water Margin, Journey to the West (The Monkey King)*, Sun Tzu, not to impose his will on the masses, but to identify himself as one of the people.

These are the works that have dominated the Asian childhood and Asian folk art and opera since the Ming. All the works of the heroic tradition, including the fictionalized legend of Ngawk Fay, the tattooed general, feature Kwan Kung, the god of war, or a fictional descendant of Kwan Kung as a blood brother.

Three Kingdoms is comparable to the *Iliad*. *Water Margin* to *Robin Hood*. *Journey to the West* to the *Odyssey*. How deep and how common is this stuff among the Chinese?

The tongs were once gangs. Some tongs were for legitimate businessmen. Some were for criminal business. When the tong wars between criminal tongs threatened to bring the National Guard in to end Chinese control of Chinatown, the good tongs banded together and formed the Choong Wah Wooey Goon to drive the criminal tongs out of Chinatown, like the 108 outlaw chiefs and their gangs banded together in their marshland stronghold to resist the corrupt Song court. The Choong Wah Wooey Goon and its member organizations are now the establishment in Chinatowns from Panama to Alaska. They own land. They own businesses on the land. They own banks. They recruit members. They attract members by appealing to a common culture and common values: folk lit.

The tong historian, writing in a recruiting pamphlet from the fifties, sounds like gangs sound today:

From China, one of the oldest of civilizations, beginning in 1848 there came to America an outpouring of Chinese who sought to better their personal fortunes, as men everywhere seek to do. Their first port of entry was San Francisco, which eventually became the capital city of Chinese America. The Gold Rush and then the building of the transcontinental railroad swelled the Chinese population. By 1851, with a Chinese population of 12,000 in the city, a need was felt for some type of social organization for mutual help and protection, and thus was born the formal Chinese association.

The connection with childhood lit is not subtle or hidden:

A Concise History of Lung King and the Genealogical Origin of the Four Families

One of the most stirring periods of the Chinese people—a time of brave men, brutal warfare, and court intrigue—woven in the tapestry of Chinese history as the era of the Three Kingdoms is preserved for posterity by the Long Kong Associations.

Kong is a confraternity of the members of the Four Families of the surnames Lew, Quan Chang and Chew. Among the Chinese people this tale, told countless thousands upon thousands of times, is stories of historic facts of four men whose spirit, sense of sacrifice for the people and their bravery made them bigger than life, and therefore legendary.

The elders of the Four Families erected a Lung Kong Temple at Brooklyn Alley, off Sacramento Street, traditionally known by the Chinese themselves as The Street of the Men of Tang. This was the 1876 during the reign of Emperor Kwong Shui.

Spiritually it duplicated the original Dragon Hill temple, for here too were consecrated statues of the Four Ancestors of the Four Families.

While serving the ritual and spiritual needs of the members of the Four Families, the Lung Kong temple in the United States functioned also as a fraternal organization. As did the others already created by other groups, Lung Kong fulfilled the social welfare needs of its people. From this period through World War II, the Chinese in America were subject to highly unreasonable legal restrictions, social pressures, an absence of civil rights and unequal employment opportunities. In the oppressive atmosphere of those times they had to turn to themselves. They had to care for themselves. These conditions foster the social associations.

These associations, like the Four Families, cared for their own sick, fed and housed their own unfortunate, buried their own dead.

They banded to fight discriminatory legislation against the Chinese. They arbitrated in legal questions. All of these organizations, in spirit and practice, were akin to the pattern of the Four Families, blood brothers in helping each other and the Chinese people.

How organized, how legit can a gang get in a hundred years? The bylaws of the association are in the California attorney general's office. And what do the bylaws say about culture and the god of war?

The Bylaws of the Lung Kong Tin Yee Association

1. The name of the Association shall be Lung Kong Tin Yee Association of the Americas.

2. The Association shall abide by the spirit of the "Confraternity of the Peach Garden" and the "Old City Meeting" of the Four Ancestors of Lew, Quan, Chang and Chew; and by the "Rules of Conducts" bequeathed by Emperor Lew Pei such as loyalty, righteous, fraternity, charity, sincerity, solidarity, cooperation, mutual assistance, and a unified effort for the promotion of the general welfare.

Frank Chin

The criminal tongs are back. They're now properly known as triads and also known among the gang kids as the Chinese Mafia. America is their Swiss bank. America is their laundry. The triads send their dirty dollars to farms in Texas, to Chinese restaurants supplied by these farms, to Chinese games played at casinos on Indian reservations, to be washed, fluff dried, and folded. Gang kids dream of taking the oath of a triad before Kwan Kung, the god of war, and sipping a tea of the blood of the brothers, and becoming a legend.

How does a gang become so organized and legit or criminal? It's happening now. Money. In the family association, or the district association, or the tong, a brother says, "Brothers, I have $6,000 here I'm willing to loan out. What am I bid?" And Joe, who wants to start a laundry, and Jake, who wants to buy a car, and Jimmy, who wants who knows what, and any brother who wants the money bid on it. "1 percent." "3 percent." Making the loan is an oath. Your word is your bond.

Bounhong Khommarath nods. "This still happen in Lao community," he says. "But very small scale among brother and sister, among relative, uncle, but it's not on a large scale because of the issue of trust. If somebody got money and run away. . . . But among brothers, uncles, aunts, and grandma, close-knit relatives, yes. Especially want to help out a young couple to buy a car or something.

"We have like original association, like the people from this province get together, try to support each other. Especially when somebody dies. Everybody pitch in to help. Because we are now, after five, ten years, we're still in survival stage. So we're not really that sophisticated.

"The loan money would only be in the family, brother, sister, blood family."

Bulletproof Buddhists

Why should people trying to stamp out the gangs or modulate the gangs into normal and still enjoyable childhoods know the childhood stuff of Asian culture? Why should fully grown adults dip into the myth, lit, operas, and comic books of "Life is war. All behavior is tactics and strategy. All relationships are martial. Love is two warriors back to back fighting off the universe"?

One might learn that there is a sense of honor and nobility in these kids that can be appealed to. One might devise a way to tell the kids the gangs are bad strategy. One might quote Sun Tzu and Br'er Rabbit: "The acme of military skill is in winning without taking a life or losing a life and taking the state intact." You want all the money in the bank. A strategy to get it without getting shot, getting arrested, getting wanted by the law, might be better than sticking it up. And that might strike a chord. One might find a way of saying there are better, less lethal, less offensive, still very thrilling and macho ways for boys to show off for girls, make an intimidating presence, compete with the strong, get money, and still be a good soldier, be heroic, make history.

I can't remember when I've seen a cop want to respect the culture of the Asians he was policing. Or, for that matter, a city. In New York, respecting the gang's culture meant social workers charged with turning the kids to the sunny side of the street went out shoplifting with the kids, to show they understood. They burned out fast. Roy Moody is the first cop, and San Diego the first city, to show enough respect for the Lao and Cambodian cultures to study them. Is he embarrassed when people tell him he's not like other white men but a member of the family? The sad thing is there are, in too many cities, too many Asian American cops no Asian immigrant or refugee would treat like a member of the family.

Frank Chin

"I went and I talked to the temple," Officer Roy says, "and I told 'em that one of the things we've learned is that the kids, that are teenagers, when they're more accepting of their own culture, they do better in school. They do better everywhere. And those kids that might not necessarily speak their own languages too well, or write, we're going to very much encourage them to do so."

It's just like the detective novels. The good cops have cultural mobility. Uptown to Harlem for some jazz. Down to Chinatown for some late-night noodles. The locals at home or in the store let him and call him by his first name.

THOSE WEDDING BELLS ARE BREAKING UP THAT OLD GANG OF MINE

Roy Moody

"They don't really want to continue on with crime, but they have no options at all. The thing about it, with these gangs, a lot of gang members they want to get out. But a lot of their cousins are gang members, or their brothers might be gang members. The thing is they try to get out but they're sucked right back in. Especially when they can't find a job, they get sucked right back into the gang. And they go through that gang cycle.

"One of the things that we've seen with a lot of Asian gang members is that they do tend to get married at an early age. And that seems to take them out. The sense of responsibility. A lot of things that we see with Asian gang members, too, is that sense of family. Especially with the original Southeast Asian gang members. They seem to be more accepting of their cultures than the twelve- and thirteen-year-olds that we have today."

Bulletproof Buddhists

"And a few kid that been shot dead at age fifteen and sixteen. Yeah. And one is paralyzed, and that gives us a lot of leverage to deliver the message: Either you end like that one still in a wheelchair and blind. Or the other two that died.

"I been to both funeral. So and then kids know the story, because San Diego is a large city, but not big enough to hide the secrets.

"Some of them who's overwhelmed with problems, their parents ship them out. We tell parents, Look, father, if you do not do something, your son will end up in jail, or paralyzed, or been shot dead. So once we know that there is no other way to, we ask them to ship them out or move out. And then when he's coming back, he's already eighteen, he changes.

"They know that when they reach eighteen, the law is not treat them as easy as when they were fourteen years old. I see many kids that get out of the gangs get married and have two jobs. One full-time and one part-time job.

"So I seen it's very productive work that we outreach to the ones that wanna be gangs or acting out, somebody that work with them, give them guidance."

YOUTH CLUB

Roy Moody calls. He's upbeat, hopeful, enthusiastic.

Parents have been turning in guns to the Storefront, no questions asked, since December.

"In exchange for guns—the first thirty-five didn't get anything since they didn't have any incentive, but now, drop into the Storefront, and turn in a gun, and get free medical services at Paradise Valley Hospital, or a U.S. savings bond from San Diego First National Bank, or a month of free cable TV from Cox and free pay-per-view movies."

Frank Chin

He's got a major project going. "We started a youth program." First meeting—thirty kids from Southeast to Southcrest Park Mira Mesa. Junior high to high school. Mixed races. The Lao have their schools for the Lao. And the Cambodian their temple school for their kids. And the Vietnamese their schools. This is mixed races. All kinds of Asians. Even two Filipino kids have been coming to the meetings.

Second meeting—sixty-three kids. Third meeting tomorrow. He expects a hundred kids. Storefront, 1:00 P.M. "I'll be there," I say.

Tomorrow comes, and the air is full of the bullets of the Kurosawa rain from *Seven Samurai*. Every drop hits my windshield with the sound of meat. A million cars splash through the rain like hysterical villagers and galloping bandits. The road to San Diego is sloppy with rain. Panic at seventy miles an hour, then bumper-to-bumper clenched teeth listening to leprechauns clog dance on the roof of the car and identifying the roadkill that floats by. The outside lanes of I-5 are flooding.

The rain hits the streets of San Diego so hard they seem to spark flames.

The girls arrive first, in pairs and small groups, dropped off by their parents. Some keep their jackets on. Most shuck their coats for baggy T-shirts and baggy jeans of many colors. Some wear baggy overalls. Then the boys in cars of their own. Baseball hats, jackets. Kids drift into the Storefront for about an hour. The girls take up most of the seats around the big conference table. The boys sit in groups against the window and the wall. A few boy-girl couples sit at the back, on unused desks, and wave and do eyejazz to their friends. It's not the hundred kids Roy Moody had expected, but eighty is a lot of kids. No teacher would want eighty kids from thirteen to nineteen years old for two hours in a classroom.

"We probably would have had a lot more if it wasn't for the heavy rain," Roy Moody says. He wants more kids.

"Part of the problem was discovered in going out and talking with Lao and Cambodian and Hmong and Vietnamese parents, who said they were very afraid of letting their kids out of sight. You know, you've got your bad kids that go out and do awful. And you've got your good kids that do what mom and dad want 'em to do. But even the good kids need something to do. They just can't stay home, go to school, stay home, go to school. They need some sort of outlet.

"A lot of times those kids that are on the borderline could be pushed because their parents are so strict. And so what we're looking at is: We have this Asian Youth Organization. And the parents were really afraid to let their kids go anywhere. They were afraid to let their kids go somewhere on the weekend or maybe in the early evening. But one of the things that we found when we went out and talked to these neighborhoods, these communities, is the parents said they would trust some sort of Asian youth organization that was involved with the San Diego Police Department because then the parents feel safer.

"And I got this idea from the Oakland Police Department.

"I've traveled all over the United States. And everywhere I go I always look to see what their police departments are doing, what kind of programs they have serving Southeast Asians. And the Oakland Police Department had what I thought was the most successful Asian youth program that I've ever seen.

"And their organization is called the Asian Youth Services Committee. And it's definitely 100 percent supported by the

Frank Chin

Oakland Police Department. And, like here in San Diego, we have our different Asian advisory committees, they have their Asian Advisory Committee on Crime. They've only got one."

The Oakland Asian Advisory Committee on Crime conducts its meetings in English, and the Asian Americans who sit on it are from the establishment, the elite. In San Diego, the Lao and Cambodian and different Asian advisory committees conduct business in English and their own languages, and members are from all walks of life. Some are prominent in groups in their own communities, and some walk in from off the street.

"That makes our advisory committees unique," Roy Moody says.

Robert Sayaphupha, community service division, Asian liaison officer, is Roy Moody's opposite number in the Oakland police department.

"Robert Sayaphupha does a lot of fund-raising," Roy Moody says. He likes the young Chinese Cambodian Oakland cop, but doesn't like the idea of cops fund-raising.

"They do things a little bit differently there. In our police department, I'm prohibited from going out and doing any fund-raising on my own. That's why I have to rely on the Asian advisory committees. I can understand why we can't do it. Just the mere thought—I personally just would never walk into—I just couldn't do it—into an Asian restaurant. A policeman asking for money to support a good cause. People are going to give it to me whether they want to or not, just out of the mere fear. There's no way I could do that. There's no way you can take advantage of that.

"And the basis of it was—It was open to Asian youth between thirteen and twenty-one years of age. And the whole idea was, first, to have positive interaction with Asian youth and the police department. Cuz out on the street there's very,

very little interaction. And second is to give them something to do.

"What I really liked about this was that the kids, they pretty much do everything. They decide what activities they're going to do. They come up with their own budget. They run their meetings. They run their own committees. And, of course, it's just adult supervision over the top.

"The money's going to have to come from the kids. I've already told the kids we don't have any money. They're going to have to do their own fund-raising. As you saw, there was an overwhelming response. They understand that. And a number of kids are going to be working at the Lao and the Cambodian car wash. They'll raise their own money. And in the meantime we'll look for what grants we can apply for. There are several people who've already expressed interest in donating money. There's a lot of different associations that have said this is a great idea, and they'd be willing to help out any way that they can. This is just getting off the ground. We'll find the money.

"The parents. A lot of their expression is in terms of fear. How is this going to hurt me? How is this going to hurt my family? And they're very, very concerned about their kids. And this was also a way of preventing some violence that's been occurring between different Southeast Asian groups. And because, like I was saying before, a lot of Southeast Asian kids, they only interact in their own communities. And so you don't have Cambodian kids from Mira Mesa interacting with Lao kids from Chollas View area and the Vietnamese kids from City Heights. There's no interaction.

"This is a way of bringing the kids together so that they can say, Hey! You know, these guys aren't any different than I am. They're maybe from a different culture. But they're the same. So some violence prevention is going on.

Frank Chin

"I think the hardest part's been accomplished: getting a cross section of the kids. Probably the largest group here was Cambodian. The second largest group was Vietnamese and Lao. And we had a couple of Hmong. A very good mix.

"The mix very much reflected in the elections we just had. For president it was a Cambodian. For vice president was Lao. Secretary it was Vietnamese. Treasurer it was Vietnamese. And for sergeant at arms it was Vietnamese. There was only one person that wanted to be sergeant at arms.

"What's really interesting, though, wasn't so much one ethnic group stood out more, but it was definitely females that wanted to be more involved with the group. So on the youth executive board we've got four females and one male. So the females were definitely a lot more aggressive.

"We're going to have to work on the Hmong community cuz they view this as, Why should my kids participate in this? Because my kids aren't bad kids. And we've got to get the idea to them that this isn't just for bad kids; this is just for kids period! And for those kids who are right on the borderline, that can either go with the gangs or stay out of the gangs, we're hoping by creating something like this, it'll pull in these kids to stay out of gangs and finish school."

The races of Asian kids are gathering at the Storefront around Officer Roy Moody, San Diego Police, just as the 108 gangs of wrongfully outlawed men from all parts of China gathered at the stronghold on Mount Liangshan around the humble clerk known as "the Timely Rain."

It's a strange thing to say about a white man.

Two weeks later, on a sunny day, at the next meeting I see Roy Moody has taught the youth organization's officers enough *Robert's Rules of Order* to run the meeting. The kids talk about raising $500 at a car wash in Mira Mesa, and selling food from a booth at a Cambodian and Lao New Year's festi-

Bulletproof Buddhists

val at Colina Park, and starting a basketball league. They decide on a design for their emblem, their logo, using elements from many of the designs offered by the kids.

People from other agencies and community service organizations have shown up with their own kids to see if these kids can keep it together. Do they have the discipline? Can they keep their word? I don't see Rabbit or Baboon here. Rabbit's too old, maybe too far gone. A kid who had to take a course on how to heat up a bottle to feed her kid, it's too late for Rabbit to have a childhood. And Baboon is laugh now–cry later. Happy face–sad face.

Two little boys, one just a bit younger and one just a bit older than my Sam. They fold paper gliders out of flyers announcing the gun exchange and fly them in the little hallway between offices in the back of the Storefront.

A twelve-year-old girl and the nineteen-year-old kid who teaches first grade at the Old Temple school, and gets stopped by the cops for looking thirteen behind the wheel of his car, hear that I write for the mighty *San Diego Reader.*

The twelve-year-old girl is twenty-one, and the San Diego police have just hired her as a Cambodian community service officer. She writes, too, she says. She wants to be a writer. She's written several stories she'd like to publish.

"What kind of stories?" I ask.

"I write fairy tales," she says.

Sophea "Tommy" Ross gives me a copy of his magazine, *Cambodian Now.* I ask him if someone told him stories when he was a kid. Oh, yes. They both remember the fairy tales. I ask them if they've heard of the story of the parents who purposely take their little boy into the jungle and lose him and, when they want him back, are forced to leave the jungle alone and live in sadness for the rest of their lives.

Yes, they've heard that story. Do I like that story? Why do I like that story?

Frank Chin

"I have come to San Diego with lots of money in my pocket. I will pay $1 million for each and every Cambodian and Lao and Hmong kid from newborn to eighteen years old," I say.

"My parents love me too much to sell me," they say.

"$3 million each. You've got five brothers and sisters. Plus you. That's $3 million times six. Your folks will have the good life. And if they won't sell, I'll raise my offer. And five years from now, I'm coming back with more money in my pockets to buy more Cambodian and Lao and Hmong and Vietnamese kids. And five years after that. And five years after that. What's going to happen to the Cambodians and the Lao and the Hmong and the Vietnamese in San Diego?"

They look at me. Do they remember Pol Pot? Pol Pot in Cambodia, the Gang of Four in China, and gangs in San Diego rewrote the story. Here it's not, "Parents, please don't sell your children to monsters for the good life." Instead it's, "Kids, do not sell your parents for the life of laugh now–cry later." The result is the same. "There will be no more. Not a soul, not a story, not a kid." I think they understand the story better than I do.

Officer Roy is on the detective's list. He hopes to be assigned to Asian gangs and be stationed at the Storefront. "But there are no guarantees." What happens in one's life may well all be written, but the good officer has not read it yet.

He's also on the sergeant's list. The engines of gang prevention and control he's built, the Neighborhood Watch groups, the advisory councils, the gun exchange, and now the Asian Youth Organization, are not self-maintaining, though he says they are. Everything in the Southeast Asian communities works by personal example. If Roy Moody is promoted out of the Storefront and away from the Southeast Asian communities, what he built over the last six years might sputter out. It's a delicate time. Summer's coming. But right now

Bulletproof Buddhists

it's spring. It's Saturday morning. The sun is out. The Marines fly pairs of pretty, twin-tailed F-18s out over the road, loop around over the blue water, and sleek back the way they came. People drive their Miatas topless. The sixteen Neighborhood Watch groups are working. Gang leaders are off the street and gang activity down. Sophea's teaching first grade at the Old Temple this morning, then writing for the special New Year's issue of his magazine. Twenty kids actually show up ready to wash cars at $3.00 a pop. Officer Roy tells the girl holding the money to button her pocket and towels off a wet Jeep. They make a little more than their $500 goal. About $3.00 more. I have my car washed and drive into downtown San Diego to show it off.

Frank Chin

LOWE HOY AND THE STRANGE THREE-LEGGED TOAD

The world is just putting on the new Year of the Dog, and I discover I don't know anything anymore. I'm stupid. There are more Chinamen under the sun than are dreamt of in my navel and mediocrity. It's a good time for this Chinaman boy to dive into the unknown Chinatowns, find out if I know anything at all, and fill my well. Down by the Mexican border, down below sea level, in the Imperial Valley, I hear there was an all-black town where the leaders of Chinatown were Afro-American and the Chinese learned American citizenship from blacks. An American dream under a dried-up sea. I'm ready to go. I notice toads in Chinatown.

Check out your Chinatown shops for three-legged toads, folks. Don't be shy. I'm not making this up. Some are reddish, made of fishbone, and feel like plastic trying to be ivory. Some are carved jade on a jade pedestal. They come in all sizes. The small ones hold one coin in their mouths. The larger ones hold six coins. The largest ones are studded with fake jewels in the bumps along the back and in the eyes. The claws on the

The Three-Legged Toad

three legs are like chicken claws, maybe buzzard claws. Some are very well crafted. Some are clumsily done. With or without jewels, they're all of them ugly.

A three-legged toad? What's a three-legged toad supposed to mean in Chinese street culture? "Money's coming," the people selling the ugly things in their curio shops tell me. "Lucky."

"Why does it mean that?" I ask.

They know a little, but not enough to make sense. "Look at the coin in the *gop nah*'s mouth," is all they can say, and shrug. "Special to the Chinese people." They remember the ugly three-legged toad meaning money is coming their way since they were children. People always had three-legged toads in their homes. Yeah, sure. Except during the Cultural Revolution, of course, that dark period when all Chinese culture was banned. The fairy tales, the heroic adventures, the operas and the toys and the shrines and the knickknacks inspired by these stories, all were banned in the hope of stamping out, once and for all, what these stories teach: Life is war.

The war is waged by the world against your personal integrity. We are all born soldiers. All behavior is tactics and strategy. All relationships are martial. Love is two warriors back to back fighting off the universe. *Nah Jah, the Boy Born from a Lotus; The Fox and the Tiger Strategy; The Wolf of Shandong; The Dragon and the Phoenix* (the Chinese wedding ceremony)—these are some tough fairy tales. Read these fairy tales and you'll understand "Kingdoms rise and fall, nations come and go," the Confucian mandate of heaven. *Heaven* is a euphemism for *the will of the people*. The mandate of heaven is why the Chinese people cannot be conquered. No matter how many times China has been taken over by foreigners—the Mongols, the Manchus, the Japanese, the corrupt Nationalists, the Communists—the Chinese people stayed Chinese and

Frank Chin

did not become Mongolians, or Manchurians, or Japanese, or Christians, or Marxists.

The mandate of heaven is why Chinese individuals aren't victims. Chinese aren't born sinners. Chinese are born soldiers. Whatever else they might become or learn to be—doctors, lawyers—they are fighters. For the Chinese there is no Original Sin, or social contract, or Marxist-Leninist dialectical thinking. All that presumes a higher moral authority than the individual, and, in Chinese thought, there is none. To give up your power of personal revenge to the state for the benefits of a stable society is self-contempt and betrayal. If the society or the state is unstable, move on—get out or get rid of it. You don't need the state to be you. The idea of a perpetual state in Chinese thought is immoral and perverse.

The mandate of heaven says rulers of all kingdoms and nations sooner or later go bad, fail the people, and the people naturally form alliances and become armies to bring the kingdom down, choose a new ruler or rulers, and the mandate of heaven is cranked for another turn. The Cultural Revolution was out to erase all Chinese history and culture and rewrite the minds of a new generation of Chinese fit to accept the social contract and the perpetual state.

Banning Chinese culture and breaking up families, exiling the parents, and separating the children seems to have worked. The students at Tienanmen Square in 1989 were the children of the children of the Cultural Revolution. Second-generation no Chinese culture. They were at the right place for the enactment of the mandate of heaven: the Gate of Heaven Square, where emperors rise and fall. But they didn't declare the state dead, null, and void, as the Chinese expected. To their horror and grief the students asked for "reform." They failed because they no longer knew the mandate of heaven. They were no longer Chinese. They were mascots of Western civilization. All

The Three-Legged Toad

the Chinese who knew the mandate of heaven had left China. They were in Malaysia, Singapore, Hong Kong, Taiwan, Japan, and over here, in the Americas. (Of course, you knew the world capital of Cantonese opera is Vancouver–Seattle–San Francisco.)

Over here *Americanization* meant the sparsely populated American-born generations of Chinese were force-fed the Christian stereotype of the only good Chinaman being a Christian Chinese American. As the bachelors died and became pariahs, Pearl Buck and the Chinese American Christian autobiography taught the young American-born Chinese that they were so much more misogynistic and morally perverse than whites that their civilization, their culture, their race, didn't deserve to survive. Several generations of American-born Chinese Americans huffing hyphens sponged up Charlie Chan–Fu Manchu at the Bijou, never heard of the mandate of heaven, and don't want to now because it's Chinese and sounds icky. I belong to one of those generations of the American Cultural Revolution born and raised in the United States between 1925 and 1966.

In 1925 they made the Chinese Exclusion Law of 1882 perfect. No Chinese women allowed. Those Chinamen too stupid to go back to China will die without reproducing. Between 1925 and 1966 the American-born, "Americanized" Chinese American became the majority of Chinese in America, as the laws, World War II, and the immigration quota allowing only 103 Chinese a year into the country stoppered up Chinese immigration and the Chinaman men—the bachelor society that built the railroads, worked the mines, built the Chinatowns, built Mexicali—died. The bachelor society. The Chinamen who came here as boys and died without the society or company of women are today despised as misogynists and abusers of women in Chinese American Christian autobi-

Frank Chin

ographies and in the movies, back home again with Charlie Chan–Fu Manchu.

I'm one of the thousands of Chinese Americans who reputedly cringe at the word *Chinaman,* and understand spoken Chinese to hear it but can't and won't speak it, and hear and understand Chinamen telling everyone in the Chinese-speaking world what kind of stupid, American-born fool I am in the slang of four villages and a northern dialect.

But I don't mind bumbling as much Chinese as I can get out of my mouth and take them by surprise. Sun Tzu would give me points. And they give me a second look and a second listen when I tell them the Chinese fairy tales and adventure stories in English. They know enough English to hear the shape is right and begin talking to me as if English is a variant of Say Yup Cantonese.

The mandate of heaven. I don't have to talk about it with the Chinese in the restaurants and shops. It's in the figures and little statues and geegaws they sell. The statues of Kwan Kung, and Kwan Yin, and Monkey, and Nah Jah with his three heads and six arms. The shopkeepers and clerks know these stories. The dealers in Chinese art goods know the stories that go with everything they sell. But what has the mandate of heaven to do with the three-legged toad meaning money and luck?

They don't know the story behind it.

"You don't know the story behind it?" I ask.

No, they don't know the story behind the three-legged toad meaning imminent money.

"I do," I say, and catch another degree of their attention. "I know the story, but I don't quite understand it."

"What's the story?"

"'Lowe Hoy and the Strange Three-Legged Toad,'" I say. I see them relax a bit, become kids again, as I tell the story in

English, making it easier to understand how I can know and tell the Chinese story and not understand it.

A village in old China. All the water for this village comes from one well. All the water they use to drink and bathe and water their plants and crops comes from this one well.

One day the people discover a strange three-legged toad at the bottom of the well. It has strange, sad eyes. It smells bad. It fouls the water of the well.

People who drink water from the well all get sick, and some die. The plants watered with water from this well wither, their leaves turn black, and they die.

"How can we get this horrible toad out of our well without making the water unfit to drink?" the other smart people ask.

Lowe Hoy, a petty official and student of Taoist magic and an odd sort himself, steps forward and looks down into the well at the three-legged toad. He looks and dresses and acts like a little boy. The top of his head is shaved. His fringe of hair hangs down like a boy's. His clothes are open, and his belly shows. He's bare legged. He doesn't look like an official at all.

"Whew! Does that ever smell bad!" he says.

"Can you get the toad out of the well without killing it?" the people ask.

Lowe Hoy laughs, reaches into his pocket, pulls out a gold coin, and flips it into the well.

The three-legged toad jumps at the gold coin, catches it with its tongue, and gulps it down. "Ooooh," the people say. "Did you see that?"

A few people smile and toss a coin or two down the well. The toad snatches every one and gulps it down.

"My friends," Lowe Hoy says smiling, "let us not forget what it is we want. We want water that does not kill our plants. We want water we can drink without getting sick and dying. The problem is not entertaining ourselves throwing our money away at the strange three-legged toad."

Frank Chin

Lowe Hoy takes out a long string with a large knot at the end. The string runs through the square hole stamped in the coins. He drops coins down the string, and they clink, and, with each clink, he jerks on the string. The large knot stops the coins from falling off the string.

Every time Lowe Hoy jerks on the string, the toad jumps at the coins, higher and higher, and jumps so high it lands outside the well, and Lowe Hoy steps on the toad.

"Please, don't kill me! Give me money! I'll give you money!"

Lowe Hoy steps a little harder on the toad.

"Ah, I see you can't be bought," the toad says. "For you, I have something money can't buy."

"What's that, Toad?" Lowe Hoy asks.

"World travel," the toad says.

"World travel?"

"Touch me, with your foot, your hand. Touch me, and think of a place, anyplace in the world, and you will be there."

The strange three-legged toad speaks the truth. When Lowe Hoy touches the toad with his foot and thinks of peaches in the summertime in his childhood, he finds himself transported to the very spot of his thoughts.

He lingers awhile in his childhood, then thinks of China at the time of the Great Sage and is there, in a China near the beginning of time. He hears what Confucius has to say with his own ears.

Lowe Hoy touches the three-legged toad with his foot and thinks of the Monkey King leading the pilgrims to India to collect Buddhist texts and is just where he wants to be when he sees them, in the distance, all headed west.

Then he touches the toad and thinks himself back to when and where he has come from. It is as if he and the toad haven't been away.

Even the three-legged toad enjoyed the trip. Lowe Hoy

The Three-Legged Toad

agrees he and the toad seem to bring out the best in each other.

Lowe Hoy uses the strange three-legged toad to travel. Everywhere he travels he collects knowledge. He uses his knowledge and becomes a famous master of statecraft and a minister of state.

Now and then the strange three-legged toad hops away and disappears down a well or a pond. The people always become anxious about their water smelling like the toad and turning poisonous. Lowe Hoy always catches the toad with his string of coins before it fouls the air with its stink and poisons the water. And the people are always relieved.

"Give me money! Money! Money! Money!" the toad sings, snuggling up to Lowe Hoy's foot.

THE SHOPKEEPERS SMILE

They smile. They like the story. They understand it. They can't explain it. The toad means lucky money.

I know the story but don't understand it. Why is the toad a symbol of luck, money, and happiness? I can buy the toad without understanding the story.

I don't have to understand the story to get along with the shopkeepers in Chinatown. I don't even have to speak their language, or they mine. We can stay private in our own languages and cultures and get along with each other and do business with each other on the street in English. And we do.

American English is a language of trade between traders. It is the language of the rendezvous. We are not all one. We are all traders.

Everyone came to America as a migrant and has been moving on, sometimes forced to move on, but moving on ever since. American culture is not a fixed culture. There is no one American culture. What we call American culture, like Amer-

Frank Chin

ican English, is a pidgin marketplace culture. That's the mandate of heaven. But much of America wants a dictated, strictly Judeo-Christian culture and is deaf, dumb, and blind to reality. They're freaked with the fascist myth of the Tower of Babel, afraid of languages they don't speak and cultures like the Chinese that do very well without religion, or organized superstition.

In the real world, the model of civility, of civilization, is the marketplace, not the court, not the church, not the cross, but the crossroads.

Toshio Mori, the Nisei fictioneer, wrote up a vision of America as the house of "The Woman Who Makes Swell Doughnuts," and he called her house "a depot." In this world, through this depot, "everyone was moving." This modern Nisei story published in the forties was written as a reminiscence of childhood. The story affects Japanese who read English more deeply than the reader who grew up without the stories of a Japanese childhood. "The Woman Who Makes Swell Doughnuts" is deeper, richer, more eloquent for being modeled on the traditional Japanese story "The Old Woman and Her Dumpling."

"The Old Woman and Her Dumpling" is a folk vision of marketplace crossroads civilization. The old woman makes and sells dumplings at a crossroads marketplace. One of her dumplings drops and rolls. She chases it as it rolls into a hole and into another world. A stone Jizo, the god of travelers and children who died in miscarriages, tries to hide the old woman from the demons known as *Oni*. The *Oni* find her, take her across their river, give her a magic rice paddle that fills an empty pot with rice merely by stirring, and make her their cook. She steals the rice paddle and a boat to escape home to her world. Halfway across the river the *Oni* come down to the river and start drinking it up to beach her boat and walk out and capture her again. While the *Oni* drink all the water out

The Three-Legged Toad

of the river, the old woman stands in the boat and makes faces and tells jokes, and the *Oni* laugh, and they laugh gushes of water they've drunk. The more they laugh, the more water gushes out of them, and they drown in the waters of their laughter. The old woman gets to the other side of the river, returns home to the crossroads marketplace, and makes rice as well as dumplings.

This crossroads civility was not a story but a reality in the Imperial Valley and along the Mexican border. It turned out to be a bubble that burst for the Japanese. The Japanese came to the Imperial Valley and successfully farmed cantaloupe and other melons, in spite of the state alien land laws, which made it impossible for them to own land. A spate of popular racist novels in the thirties damning them for being too Japanese and damning their American-born children for being too American argued for alien land laws banning not only long-term but also short-term leases to the Japanese, withdrawing citizenship of the American born, and sending them all back to Japan. The Japanese grew their melons and prospered. Come Pearl Harbor and World War II, and the American dream was gone. The Japanese of the Imperial Valley were sent to concentration camps in other deserts where they weren't wanted. Phil McGee was a baby at the time but remembers his father had a Japanese friend in El Centro, in the center of the Imperial Valley.

ELIZABETH AND PHIL MCGEE

"Did you tell the Mr. Moto story?" Phil McGee asks his mother. She's a little slip of a woman now. If I breathe on her, she might blow away.

"Well, you mean during the war? What was his name?"

"Moto?" Phil says, and thinks again. It is not good for the dean of the College of Ethnic Studies at San Francisco State

Frank Chin

University and the general manager of Walter Hawkins and the Hawkins Family Singers of Oakland to muff the names of people of other colors. "Momita," he says.

Elizabeth McGee says, "He had this pharmacy, drug store, restaurant sort of thing. He tried very hard to turn it over to some black pharmacist. And the people that could do that were reluctant to leave the Los Angeles area. But we were very close friends. The people on the corner, Mr. Woo . . . Young Yee. His name was Yee, but everybody called him Mr. Young. He had a large family. And most of those kids went into dentistry. I don't know why, but almost all of them went to dental school."

As with the story of the toad and its symbolic meaning, I'm not sure if the story Elizabeth McGee just told is finished or how it is the story of Mr. Momita. Phil doesn't know for sure.

He asks, "Did you finish the story about Daddy, you all taking over the running of the pharmacy, the store? So did Young run it for a while?"

"Oh, DuBois was probably doing the business," she says. "We didn't run it."

The blacks got along with the Japanese. The McGees, though, were a unique family. The patriarch was a school principal. The McGees were educated, musical, and close-knit. They not only got along with the Japanese-, Chinese-, Punjabi-speaking immigrants and the Mexicans living on the east side of the tracks in El Centro, they "Americanized" them in school.

The whites hated the Japanese. The old movie *Bad Day at Black Rock* was set in the valley. One night Robert Ryan leads all the men of Black Rock out of town and kills a Japanese farmer, and buries him in the desert, and keeps it a secret through World War II, till Spencer Tracy comes back from the war with one arm and a medal for the father of the Japanese American soldier who'd died saving his life in Italy.

The Three-Legged Toad

The Chinese let the Japanese take the heat and seemed to disappear under the rocks. The Chinese were there in World War II. They've been there since the time they are said to have dug tunnels under the border from Mexicali to Calexico to traffic in men. There's talk of a "Chino Mountain" where Chinese dumped in Sonora died in the mountains trying to make it to Mexicali.

The McGees talk of the Chinese as friends, but they never had supper in their houses, nor the Chinese in theirs, because, while they were all men of the same family, they were all men and boys. A family without women. The McGees are full of clues about a trove of the last of the bachelors of the bachelor society, the last of the sons of paper sons, their friends in El Centro, I hear later transcribing the tapes. And all the men and boys are of the same family. Whatever their paper names, they are Mahs. All men were brothers in the Imperial Valley.

Mah, sometimes *Mar,* is horse in Chinese.

William A. Payne was the principal of the school where blacks, Mexicans, and Chinese sent their children. His daughters tutored Chinese children. His third child still lives in El Centro. I spoke with her and her son Phil in Phil's home in Oakland.

Elizabeth McGee says, "I was born in Pasadena. My parents—William A. Payne, my father, and Zenobia—came out here in 1907.

"My father was an educated man. He graduated from Dennison. Well, he had gone to Pasadena because he had hoped to teach in Pasadena or Los Angeles, but when he got there, he found that if you were black, you were not hired, and those kids in Pasadena in those years, 1908, when they finished high school, that was it. And he began to . . . wherever he went, he was always preaching education. So he encouraged a number of the young people to go on to school.

"My mother had gone to normal school. In fact she taught

Frank Chin

in El Centro for oh I guess twenty-seven years after the kids got old enough to be left.

"There were eight of us. Three older girls were born in Pasadena. The oldest girl was Octavia. And Ethel was next. And I was next. I was the third child.

"And then I had a brother William Jr. And John. And Ruth. And Virginia. And Sarah. The last two girls, Sarah and Virginia, were born in El Centro. Jean was born at home with a midwife *and* a doctor. And Sarah was born in Los Angeles because that's where we were for the summer.

"Then we moved to San Joaquin Valley. My father and a retired chaplain, Colonel Allensworth, established an all-black town in Allensworth, California. And we lived there for ten years. And they built a school. It was a two-room school my father was the principal of. And they taught everything from first grade through high school. I think the young people, as I remember, went to Cochran for their last year, to finish up. Cochran was another small town. The school was well built. Wooden. And it's still standing today. They had a post office. There were about a hundred families. Many of them had come from Fort Huachuca because that was where Colonel Allensworth was chaplain. They had a constable and a justice of the peace. And so during those first years they were quite prosperous because there was plenty of water. And then we had artesian wells then. The water table dropped, and it was no longer possible to farm the area. But they had been sold water rights by this Pacific Land and Development Company. They gave them a bad time. A bad deal. And they were in lawsuits almost from the beginning of the community starting.

"The town of Allensworth has been made into a state park. And it's about twenty miles from Tulare and forty miles from Bakersfield. They have redone it, preserved some of those early homes. Colonel Allensworth's home is still there.

"So my dad came to El Centro in 1920.

The Three-Legged Toad

"In El Centro. When we first went, we rented, and I think we had one of the two houses with indoor plumbing and a bathtub. The McGees had the other. Mr. McGee was a plumber, so it was no trouble for him [to put in some plumbing]. But mostly everybody had outdoor plumbing for many years.

"We [cooked on a] kerosene stove. And wood. And, in fact, it was 1929 before we had streetlights. We had electricity in the homes, but no streetlights. After dark it was pitch black. It took years for them to pave the streets and get sidewalks. When it would rain, in our part of town, it was just—The soil is adobe. Slippery. We couldn't make it to school. We had what we called mud holidays, and you turned on the radio to listen and see if there would be school. And many days there would not be. Of course, we weren't too sad about a mud holiday. But after it rained and rained, which didn't happen too often, and it didn't dry up, it got to be tiresome [being] shut up in the house."

What about the man she would marry? "DuBois McGee, the plumber's son, and I were the two youngest kids in the sixth grade. We mostly would play jacks.

"Most of the black families had come to pick cotton and work in the fields, so that they didn't start school until, oh, maybe November, early December of every year. So that it took a while to get through eighth grade.

"I begged and begged my parents to let me go out. And I worked three days. I made three dollars and eighteen cents. And the man that gave us transportation charged me three dollars to get to the fields. So I had a net profit of eighteen cents. So I sort of lost any desire I had ever had to pick cotton. Oh, I was eight or nine or ten, I guess. It was just a matter of being with other kids. And I wanted to see what it was like. But I remember we did more playing up and down the rows than actually working.

Frank Chin

"And DuBois was a very bright kid and didn't work in the field. And so when he was ten, some of those kids were teenagers, and you know how kids are, there was this big age difference, and so then we went through high school and junior college together and both went to UCLA. The families paid the way. There were very few scholarships being given. In fact, most of the African American kids did not go to high school because when they finished eighth grade, they felt they had accomplished a great deal, and then they went into the fields. Watermelon. All the crops that were growing then. And there were a number of farmers. Until they started the cotton pickers—you know, the automatic cotton picker—they needed lots of people to chop cotton and pick it.

"Well, we sort of set a lot of precedents. I mean our family. Most of the people only went to town when they had to shop and had to go to the courthouse for business. If you lived east of the railroad tracks, you mostly stayed on that side of town. And, once a year, the white Elks had a big outdoor Christmas tree, and they gave every kid in town who went down there a sack of candy and oranges, so that was one day a year when kids went uptown in large numbers. But we used to go to the show. And we wouldn't see any other black kids in the show—until they saw that we were going. And because we were a big family, they sort of, you know, what we did they followed along.

"There was a Palace Theatre. And few years later a Valley Theatre. Because of the prejudice, we always had to sit in the balcony—until we became rebellious teenagers, and I remember that we decided to sit downstairs on one occasion. And they finally called the police and ushered us out.

"My oldest sister was ready for high school. And she was little, about five feet tall, just a scrap of a little girl, and when she went over to enroll in the high school, they almost had a riot. The kids were out in the hall, and they were screaming, just making a nuisance of themselves. Although El Centro was the only town that was that prejudiced, because there were a few kids that went to school in Brawley and a large number in Imperial. Well, Imperial I guess was the first town that was organized. In fact they considered themselves the county seat. But because there were more people in El Centro, there was political shenanigans, and they made El Centro the county seat. So Imperial and El Centro are not too friendly to this day. Well, there is a certain amount of hostility among the people.

"Anyway, because they were so hostile, my dad picked up a baseball bat, and the principal at Central said, 'Oh, Mr. Payne, I don't think that will be necessary.'

"And he said, 'I'm going to protect my child.'

"And so she didn't enroll that day. She went home, planning that he'd take her back the next day. But when he told my mother what had happened, she said, 'Oh, no. I'm not going to let my little girl go over there,' because she would be hurt.

"So he said, 'What will we do?'

"And she said, 'We'll have to teach her at home.' Because he did have his high school credential. So he started teaching her at home, which got tiresome. And then she started going to school, and he would give her classes and recesses and noon hour, after school. And then the next year, when several children graduated from the eighth grade, then their parents asked him if they could take classes. And the next year they had built a new school for him. Because the year we went there, we were in school, right in the heart of the red-light district. There were gamblers, pimps, prostitutes, all in that area. And these thugs would hang on the fence, you know, when the girls came out, you know, cuz they were quite mature. And so when my dad went there, he was determined to bring the school up to standard. And it's interesting to read the minutes from the

Frank Chin

trustee board to hear some of the things he said, which were not very complimentary about the whole situation.

"But anyway, there was an extra room at the elementary school. So that was where the high school kids had a room to themselves at the elementary school. And then people from all over the valley began sending their children there, getting permission for them. . . .

"And my dad was a kind of an educator that was far ahead of his time. So he would assign a tutor to each youngster—if they couldn't speak English, then they would have their own tutor, plus attending classes. So they learned very fast. And my sisters who taught remember, Oh, yeah I taught, I tutored so-and-so . . . kids around the community."

And Elizabeth McGee taught and tutored as a girl, also.

"I taught Bobby, and I taught Phil," she remembers.

Phil says, "I can remember she used to tell us stories about the origins of songs. How the slaves used to have to put their head under a bucket to sing, or how 'Steal Away, Steal Away to Jesus' meant that the slaves were getting ready to escape."

"Or 'There's a Meeting Here Tonight,'" his mother says.

"Yeah, 'There's a Meeting Here Tonight,' 'The Old Campground,' they were actually Negro-oriented stories about the ancestors. And so we had storytelling time and those specific radio programs that came on at night, like "The Shadow," and "Mr. Valentine," and stuff like that.

"She raised us to believe and to understand. You know, you come home, 'Mommy! Someone called me a nigger!'

"And she say, 'Well, what's wrong with you? Why are you upset? You're not a nigger.'

"She'd take me to the dictionary, show me the word *nigger*, tell me to read it. I'd read what it says, and she'd ask, 'Now is that you?'

"'No. Sniff. Sniff.'

"'So what are you so upset about?'"

The Three-Legged Toad

"Rednecks?" he says. "Yeah. We really didn't come into real contact, social contact with them until high school. And then it was through sports, and it was through scholastics. The town was really separated, except there were a few mavericks —a few very rich mavericks, I think. If you're down there— Brock Farms is a big establishment down there. And his son, Don Brock, was a good friend of mine. In fact, my aunt worked for him, for their family. And so after school I'd go by there and just be there, you know, like kids go by school. Well, that was a very rare occurrence in the community for a white kid and a black kid to get together like that. But he had kind of a different family. Otherwise it was sports. It was band. And it was California Scholarship Federation kind of things—at least for me it was.

"We just would not accept the Western way of looking. We just would not. And did not. And we did not have as much to draw from—like China and Japan—as easily. Because the African dynasties and all that stuff had not really been uncovered yet. And so we were simply riding on the energy of the W.E.B. Du Boises, the Frederick Douglasses, and the Harriet Tubmans. . . ."

"And also," his mother interjects, "your own great-grandfather!" She turns to me. "My grandfather wrote *The History of the Jones Family.*"

"Oh, yeah."

"And had it published at his own expense and sent it around to all of us. I guess that was in 1928. And he goes back to—"

"1754," Phil says.

"Yeah," his mother agrees, "And—"

"Coming over here," Phil says, nodding and gesturing emphasis.

"Coming over here as a slave?" I ask.

"Yeah," Phil says.

Frank Chin

Mother and son nod.

"My father's father was born a slave. He never knew who his parents were. He says he just woke up one morning and knew he was Robert Frank Payne. And that was all he knew. He would laugh. He would always tell us stories about the plantation and Old Man Barnett. The rest of the family took the name Barnett. He kept Payne—I don't know why. He said the people around in the area, they didn't know whether Old Man Barnett owned the master or the master owned Old Man Barnett cuz Uncle Nelson Barnett was blind. But he was the overseer of this plantation, and I mean everything by him. And he would tell us those stories. And some of them were funny. And some of them were interesting. But the people were always on top. This was all you knew."

"So Alex Haley wasn't the first."

"No. We just never thought it was a big deal," Phil says.

"El Centro was quite a segregated community because most of the Anglo-Americans had come from the South and they were accustomed to separating themselves by races. So the dividing line in El Centro was the railroad tracks. Many of the people—Hindus, and Pakistanis (whatever they called themselves—various names), and Portuguese, and Mexicans, mostly lived on the east side of town where the blacks lived.

"And the Chinese were scattered around the community because they began in the twenties to build grocery stores. Hong Chong Store was started in 1920. It had been owned by a black man, and when he got too old to maintain the store, he sold it to Hong Chong. So there were two Chinese stores in my area. And my husband in the thirties and forties was very close to the Chinese people because they were suspicious of lawyers and so on and the banks were rather slow about lending them money. So they would get together and pool their money. And DuBois because of his—my husband because of his background in economics was sort of their official accountant and even lawyer, even though he wasn't a lawyer, and they would meet when they were having disputes, and he would sort of be the arbitrator. Then as they became more prosperous and began to farm and make money, they started sending for younger Chinese people. Well, then mostly boys of course. And when they came to El Centro, mostly they didn't speak any English.

"When the Chinese youngsters came over, then the Chinese merchants who had children sent them to Washington School—the school where my father taught—cuz they were just treated better and there was no prejudice in those early years. I mean, people got along. I think the Hindus and Portuguese intermarried with black, more than other races.

"But in researching the history of the black Americans, we find that there were some who came to the valley in 1904. And some of them were . . . some of them came by covered wagon. And there are still people, middle-aged men, who as children remember crossing the desert from Arizona in covered wagons and camping out all night.

"And the Chinese people—well, many of them came into the valley from Calexico because it was easy to cross the border and sort of lose themselves in Calexico.

"In '29 they built a real high school. When they were in the elementary school, they had a number of bungalows they pulled onto the grounds. So they had home economics in one bungalow. And they had—well, manual training they called it then. And the chemistry lab was in this long building. And they got some very fine teachers from all over the United States because so many people wanted to come to California and teach. And the rule was you could be a substitute teacher if you were black but you could never get permanent employment until you had spent a year in a regular school. Well, if they wouldn't hire you, you could never get permanent employment. But they would come to El Centro and teach for

Frank Chin

a year, sometimes three years or more. And then when they went to Los Angeles with their credentials, because they had graduated from UCLA and 'SC and all the colleges around there and had had a year's regular employment, they couldn't say no.

"So we had no trouble getting teachers. And they were mostly black for many years. Then we had a Hispanic teacher who later went to Los Angeles, and the last I heard of him, he was a district superintendent. And then they hired some Anglos. It took a while, but gradually it became more integrated.

"My father majored in letters and science, so his knowledge was pretty general. But he was very interested in music. We had an outstanding glee club and choral group. And we had the first school orchestra in the Imperial Valley. But we had to buy our own instruments and pay the teacher out of our pockets. He was an Englishman. And we had the first PTA in El Centro, I know, and probably in the Imperial Valley. So he was very forward-looking and very advanced in his thinking. And he also started—they called it "Americanization"—the woman that taught that was an Anglo, and those were in the first two or three years that we were there. And he had started an adult evening school, and they had a large adult school. I mean people in their seventies were coming there to learn to read.

"We had several churches. When we first moved there, though, I think there were three. Oh, yes, the church and school were quite closely connected. The thing about those years, you had to make your own entertainment. We'd have hayrides and go out to the sand dunes between El Centro and Yuma. They had huge sand dunes, you know, where they ride the dune buggies now, and we would go out there and have wiener roasts. And we had box socials. And a lot of it was church and school together. For example, the school would provide entertainment during the Christmas season, and many of those affairs were given at the churches. And we would go

The Three-Legged Toad

out down in the river bottom and take pictures. Or we'd go to the mountains for picnics. And you did your own planning, which made us better kids, I think then, than youngsters now because there weren't a whole lot of people that had cars. So there wasn't a great deal of cruising. There was plenty of mischief they could get into, [but] it had to be on foot.

"There was a Catholic church. Well, when we first moved to El Centro, there was no Catholic church on the east side. Everybody went to the one sort of in the middle of town. Now they have a quite large Catholic church. They have school. I don't know what they call it.

"It was when they brought in the nuns to teach the children because, of course, the kids they went at Easter and Christmas to mass, but they didn't attend too regularly. So they brought the nuns in, and they would take them away from school and have classes, have instruction in their particular religion. And they were the ones who started separating the Hispanic and black kids. And teaching them not to fraternize. And we had a large YWCA group—all races. And the bishop of San Diego put a restraining order—oh, I don't know if you call it a restraining order—but anyway he sent word that no Hispanic children were to be members of the YWCA."

I ask her about celebrations at home, big Sunday dinners, entertainment at home.

"There was not much of going out for a celebration because we didn't have a whole lot of money. With eight kids in the house, money was very scarce. And so we had a croquet set set up in the lot next door. There was room enough to play ball. And my dad was like a kid when it came to games. So our house was always full of youngsters." And she talks a scene out of F. Scott Fitzgerald or Ingmar Bergman. Young black ladies in white blouses all buttoned up to their throat and long skirts listen to the gramophone and pass the Viewmaster, or stereopticon, and a box of its double photographs for a glimpse of

Frank Chin

the Eiffel Tower in 3-D, with all the doors and windows open to the ninety-degree heat of the below-sea-level desert night. "On our front porch we had a swing, and we played checkers, and we had card games of all sorts. And danced. We always had a Victrola or gramophone—whatever you call it—with lots of jazz records and classical music. And so home was . . . we were very home oriented. And then if there was something going on in Los Angeles, for example, I remember when 'Green Pastures' played the stage show, my dad took us up on the train to Los Angeles to see the show. When they would have the national Baptist convention, he—and I don't know how he afforded it because all of us, well mostly the three older girls, we would go and stay up there with relatives. But anything that was outstanding we got to see. And then Sunday dinner was—we always had extra people there because my mother was a wonderful cook. And she could find the biggest roast, which she would usually get from Hong Chong because we were close friends with Henry Quan.

"In fact DuBois and Henry Quan were—they were really close friends. And the thing that is interesting to me, and just shows the difference in people, when I go into stores, people that knew DuBois, knew my dad, you would think I was the queen of Siam coming in there! I mean they'd come out and just make a big fuss over me. I mean to this day! And I went into a shoe shop just before I left home to come up here and have some shoes repaired. And this woman—I don't even know her name—but she, 'Oh, McGee!' [in Chinese accent]. Yes, and then she's telling this other woman in Chinese, so I don't know what they were saying, but I mean she was explaining who I was and so forth. And they just never forget.

"I can remember when DuBois was living, and I went into a drawer one day looking for something, and it was just stacked full of money and receipts and papers. . . . It scared me so, I called him. I said, "Come here! What is this?"

The Three-Legged Toad

"'Oh, Henry and so-and-so . . . Butch . . . they were getting ready to go into something, and they have me working on it, and I'm keeping their money.'

"Yeah, as I say, he was the lawyer, the arbitrator, and of course, after they had been here a few years they began to get more confidence. Then the banks were [letting them deposit their money]."

I ask Phil about Chinese friends.

Phil says, "The Chinese kids I knew normally had to work in the store after school. They weren't very involved in any of the extracurricular activities at school."

"What's a teenage boy do in El Centro on a Saturday night in the fifties?" I ask.

"On a Saturday night, if there was not a neighborhood— you know, if one of my friends wasn't having a party, we would sit under that famous lamppost and sing. Doo-wap. Or, as we got old enough—you know, after you were fifteen and a half you could drive. So if you were old enough, or you knew somebody with a car, you tried to sneak into Mexicali."

The little old lady with goldfish-bowl glasses knew about paper sons, all-black towns in California. The Chinese bachelors, men of the Mah family, forming a family association, a family bank, a tong around a black man holding the cash and writing the contracts? The Imperial Valley sounds better than Oz!

THURSDAY, 10 FEBRUARY, THE FIRST DAY OF THE YEAR OF THE DOG, THE DAY OF THE CHICKEN

The giant Poon Goo wakes up inside an egg with his ax. It's been eighteen thousand years. He breaks out of the egg with his ax and for the next eighteen thousand years separates the stuff inside the egg into heaven and earth. He dies, and one of his eyes becomes the sun, the other the moon. His hair

Frank Chin

becomes forests and grasses. Other parts of his body become different minerals and geographic features, covering the eggy stuff with soil, mountains, rivers, forests, and plains.

His sister, Nur Waw, comes down to a world that is a garden but has no animal life. On the first day of the new year, Nur Waw, the mother of creation, creates the chicken. The second day, she creates the dog. There are fifteen days in the New Year's celebration. On none of those days did Nur Waw create the toad.

First the giant comes in a boat. The egg is a boat. The Chinese creation myth has no religious significance. Poon Goo is not a sacred name. Poon Goo, who creates heaven and earth, and Nur Waw, the mother of creation, are really a migration myth. Most of the days of the fifteen-day celebration of the Chinese new year I'll be looking around and among the Chinese of the Imperial Valley and Mexicali, where Chinese and other migrants have been settling, passing through, and passing on since before whites settled here.

SATURDAY, 12 FEBRUARY, THE DAY OF THE PIG

Sun Tzu the strategist would tell me not to go to El Centro and Calexico-Mexicali alone, snooping and stupid. Take a friend to take the heat. Get an ally who speaks Chinese. Someone to see I don't fake it.

"Aren't you ashamed to be a man telling us what is and is not Chinese culture?" the fans of Maxine Hong Kingston, David Henry Hwang, Amy Tan ask me. I give what I think is a reasonable answer, saying, "What is and is not Chinese is not a matter of sex, or belief, but Chinese text."

Aha! They say, The Chinese have no texts! as if everybody knew that. And I'm a literary fascist for saying so. They say they know the higher truth of Chinese culture, and there's no way of objectively corroborating what they say unless I want

The Three-Legged Toad

to grab their precious mothers around the throat and beat the truth out of them. Why would I want to do that? None of their mothers are authors or authorities on traditional Chinese stories in any Chinatown or China I know of.

Gracie was born in the Imperial Valley, the daughter of a Chinese father and a Mexican mother. She doesn't speak Chinese, but her father does. Her father also speaks Spanish like a Mexican. She grew up all Mexican and American. She tells me another Chinese-Mexican girlfriend from El Centro who grew up all Mexican and American and zero Chinese bought a copy of Amy Tan's *The Kitchen God's Wife* and recommends it to Gracie to "get in touch with her roots." She sounds so young and sweet. Married. A teacher. Mother of two. I hate to disappoint her.

"You won't get in touch with any Chinese roots. You will get in touch with the stereotype," I say. "All her Chinese culture is fake. She asks why the kitchen god's wife isn't honored. The answer is, She is. The poster of the kitchen god was a double portrait of the kitchen king and kitchen queen. And making the kitchen god a lucky man is like making Jack and his mother in 'Jack and the Beanstalk' rich folks. It makes no sense."

She can't believe American publishers would sell the fake. I laugh. Either they're lying, or I am. I'm not going to teach her twelve years of fairy tales, myths, and heroic adventures in one convincing line over the phone. I'll send her a collection of Asian fairy tales to thank her for hooking me up with her father in Calexico.

In Asian America, I'm the designated Asian male for saying there is no Chinese fairy tale that teaches "the worth of a woman is measured by the loudness of her husband's belch," no matter what *The Joy Luck Club,* the Amy Tan novel or Wayne Wang movie, says. If they insist such a story exists and was as influential as they say, it should be a simple matter for

Frank Chin

them to present the text, to prove it's real, and the toys and art inspired by the story to demonstrate its influence. The stories the Chinese say are the real stories are easily found in Chinese and English and Spanish in every Chinatown I know, along with the toys, children's books, coloring books, comic books, playing cards, art, and criticism the stories inspired.

So when I ask people in the Imperial Valley and Mexicali and Tijuana about the toad, I don't want to be alone. I'll get my friend Pok chi to ask about the toad. The question will sound a lot better in Chinese. Whatever I hear is going on tape. I want a Chinaman camera eye that has seen the contents of a Chinese childhood and has a twenty-four hour bullshit detector.

Will I find the difference between the real and the fake in the valley?

Are the Chinese along the border and the Imperial Valley so "Americanized" they never heard of the three brothers of the oath of the peach garden, *Three Kingdoms,* and Kwan Kung? The thought is shocking to the man I've chosen to be my ally.

Pok chi Lau is a fastidious photographer who can work with the light and the degree and kind of hostility on the scene he happens to find without intruding. He has spent the last few years getting into the houses, apartments, and rooms of Chinese in Chinatowns and Chinese suburbs around the world. He snaps shots of what people put up against and hang on their walls. He photographs them among the contents of their homes in such a way that we seem to be able to read them like a book. He teaches photography at the University of Kansas in Lawrence, Kansas. Click on your best friend the TV set, here comes *The Dark Command;* Walter Pidgeon is Quantrill. His raiders burn Lawrence, Kansas, to the ground. John Wayne shoots back and has a climactic fight scene. 1940. Old movie. That's Lawrence, Kansas. What's a Chinaman doing teaching

The Three-Legged Toad

photography and owning a house in Lawrence, Kansas?

He's been trying to grow his own Chinese vegetables in his backyard. *Bok choy*, the Chinese broccoli called *gai lan*, and *lin ngow*, lily root. He doesn't know why his *lin ngow* turned out small and short and red instead of the pale pink of the lily root. I don't understand why he would choose Lawrence, Kansas, for his experiments in Chinese agriculture. Is this another expression of Chinese self-sufficiency? Everyone is born a soldier? Every soldier is a farmer?

Where we're going is forty-five feet below sea level. Where we're going was largely farmed by the Japanese. The Japanese pioneered the growing of cantaloupes and melons in the valley. In the twenties and thirties a number of novels set in the valley portrayed the Japanese farmers as despoilers of the environment, evil enemy agents, and a secret army awaiting orders from the emperor to drop a secret chemical into the waters of San Diego to eat holes in the bottoms of all the warships harbored there and slowly go from house to house torturing white people to death. These novels screamed for stronger alien land laws against the Japanese. The Charlie Chan movie set in the valley, *Castle in the Desert*, has Sidney Toler, the white man who plays Charlie Chan this time, spout a phony Chinese name of a phony Chinese goddess right in front of Victor Sen Yung, a real Chinese boy from San Francisco who should know better. But Victor's gone Hollywood and is the Chinese of Hollywood fantasy Charlie Chan's honorable Number Three Son.

SUNDAY, 13 FEBRUARY, THE DAY OF THE SHEEP

We stop at the Tien How Goong, the temple of the queen of heaven. Outside, the banners of Kwan Kung hang on the fence. Kwan Kung, being the embodiment of self-sufficiency

Frank Chin

and personal integrity, is regarded by both Taoists and Buddhists as the defender of all borders. It's the fourth day of the new year of the dog.

Well-dressed families, young families, Chinese, Vietnamese, walk in, buy incense, and burn sticks of incense by all the gods, Buddhist and Taoist. Monkey, Kwan Yin, and the god closest to them, the Taoist queen of heaven, Tien How, flanked by her allies, the god of thunder, Gong Gong, and the god of wind. The caretaker of the temple casts the I-Ching and gives each a slip of yellow paper. They read the message and burn it in the flames of the fire burning in an urn by the entrance. There's a lot of smoke from all the smoldering incense. But no blood. No Fu Manchu snake-eyed priest unbuttoning the cheongsam of young sacrificial virgins. There is a roast pig. There is a ceremonial offering of steamed rice, pomelo grapefruit, oranges, and tea. This used to be the Chinese Baptist church. Now it looks like a Chinese building. Yellow walls with red trim. The Chinese Baptist church is in a new, larger building one block north with its own parking lot across the street.

Pok hasn't heard the Tien How story. After a year of listening and reading I think I have it without the frills. Tien How was a strange girl. One day her father and four brothers are out fishing in their boats, and a storm blows up and separates them. Tien How runs down to the beach, goes into a trance, and points out to sea. Each of the four brothers sees a blue light in the shape of a woman appear at the bow of their boat and wave for them to follow. They follow the light out of the storm in sight of home. Tien How's mother is freaked by her daughter's trance and shakes her awake. "Mother, you have done a terrible thing," Tien How says. Her brothers appear, recognize her as the woman in the blue flame, and fall on their knees and kowtow to her for saving their lives. When the father never comes back, Tien How's mother realizes she

The Three-Legged Toad

did a terrible thing. Since then the sailors of Vietnam watch for blue flames on the tops of their masts when lost inside a storm. If the flames stay flaming, they'll make it through the storm. If the blue flames disappear, they're doomed.

Before we cocoon up in the Pontiac with a country music station and take I-5 south, we have fish fillet *juk* in Chinatown. *Hom jin beng*, salty fried bread. It looks like a large gordita, or a fried tortilla as thick and no larger than a large cookie. The restaurant features a large ceramic statue of Kwan Kung watching the door.

Pok chi wants to buy something for his son. We stop at a Chinese department store selling everything from herbs, teas, and dried Chinese fruit to furniture, cookware and cooking utensils, and bowls and plates in real ceramic and durable plastic and of course the stuff of interior decoration, the statues and vases and embroidered hundred birds, drums and cymbals, and lions for the lion dance. There's a foot-tall ceramic statue of a bald-pated boy with his belly showing, Lowe Hoy stepping on a three-legged toad and pouring water from a gourd into its open mouth. A string of coins hangs from his belt. Pok chi's never seen it before. I tell him about the three-legged toads in the curio shops around Chinatown. The toad means money's coming. Why? I tell him the story of Lowe Hoy and the strange three-legged toad.

What kind of Lowe? he asks. The Lowe of Lowe Bay, of the three brothers of the oath in the peach garden. The same Lowe as his name, Lau. All men are brothers.

What kind of Hoy? The Hoy of *hoy*, "the sea." Pok chi grins. He understands the story. He likes the story. But he can't explain what he understands. He's a photographer. He communicates his understanding in photographs. Great.

Pok chi buys a little toy Lowe Hoy playing a string of coins into the mouth of a three-legged toad. He also buys a set of characters from *Monkey's Journey to the West*—Monkey, the

Frank Chin

Tang priest Samsang, the dark-skinned itinerant monk Sandy, with his iron monk's staff, and the purple pig Pigsy, carrying his iron rake.

HEY, TANG PEOPLE!

There are three Seto brothers. They own restaurants in Chula Vista and Tijuana. We stop in Chula Vista to see if the Setos received Pok chi's letter and know we're coming. The restaurant is doing a booming business in the afternoon. Egg rolls and chow mein on every table. Grease. The Seto brothers have learned the secret of American sweet-and-sour. Gooey red stuff. The Seto brother who's in charge of the mailbox is traveling back east. No one has seen the mail in weeks. The Setos were broken up by the Cultural Revolution, and one came over, learned how to cook, saved his money, opened a restaurant, brought his brothers over, opened another restaurant, bought homes in San Diego, and worked both sides of the border. We call the Seto brother at the restaurant in Tijuana. He remembers Pok chi. Good. We're on our way.

We drive over the border into Tijuana and the borderland body-shop bazaar. Pok chi has a lousy memory for streets and directions and a lousy sense of direction. His eye is for details, the meaning of details in a frame. The streets of Tijuana are nothing but details, floods and piles and heaps and layers of details, partials, subtleties, little things on top of each other. He's at home just looking at what's in front of us. We are lost. I tiptoe the Pontiac around the potholes and chunks of pavement on the edges of the holes and stop by a Chinese restaurant. Tijuana has 160 Chinese restaurants. Pok chi jumps out of the car, pokes his head inside the restaurant, and shouts, "Way ah-Tang yun! Hey, Tang people!" Southern Chinese identify with the Tang. Northerners call themselves Han people and identify with the Han. The Tang and the Han were

The Three-Legged Toad

the two great periods of Chinese unification before the Ming. The difference, according to my fellow Tang people, is that the Tang produced the great art and the Han produced the great bureaucracy.

A few minutes later Pok chi comes out with a chain-smoking Chinese, the owner of this particular restaurant, who has offered to lead us to Seto's restaurant on his way to pick up something for his restaurant.

Seto has no time to talk to us. The microphone freaks him. He's friendly and freaked. He says his cook is on vacation for the next two weeks and he has to cook in his place. The cook he hired is from China. $1,200 a month is what a cook from China gets. $280 a month is what a "local," a Mexican or a Chinese too long in America, gets. The young Mexican man cooking with him has been here ten years. He's tried going elsewhere to cook, but he can't make as much anywhere else as he does here.

The fine and serious Chinese chefs don't come to the borderlands. Where could they go if they made a reputation here as the finest Chinese chef in Tijuana? Make your rep in San Francisco, Vancouver, Los Angeles, you can go wherever there's a major international airport. New York. Paris.

Seto encouraged his cashier, Ah-Connie, to learn Spanish and gave her a job. She takes the cash and handles the telephone, taking takeout orders. She tells us we missed the big Chinese New Year's party last Friday, the tenth, the first day of the year of the dog. The party was held in one of the largest Chinese restaurants in Tijuana. Food, the lion dance with drums and gongs. Firecrackers and a beauty pageant and food and two thousand partying Chinese.

Ah-Connie is younger than my thirty-year-old daughter. She and her daughter, with her husband's approval, signed up for a round-the-world tour. Paris, London, Amsterdam, to Mexico City, where she and her daughter faded from the tour three years ago. Her tourist visa is no longer valid. She's an illegal immigrant.

She's worked a series of Chinese restaurants here. Finding work wasn't that hard. There are 160 Chinese restaurants in Tijuana. She did menial kitchen work because she didn't speak Spanish till she came to work for Seto. Seto says to get a job where she can make real money here, she has to learn to read and write Spanish, not merely speak it. And after she's learned Spanish, English won't be that hard.

She's studying Spanish, speaks well enough to carry on restaurant biz, and walks her daughter to Catholic school every day. She lives in an apartment where it leaks when it rains. She and her daughter live a better life here than in China. She doesn't know when she'll see her husband again. I take a look around at what's better than China for her. Even as an illegal staying a few steps ahead of being deported, life is easier here in the squalor and stench of Tijuana than in China. The first day of the Chinese new year there was a party at one of the largest restaurants in Tijuana. There were the drums, and the gongs of the lion dance, and the lions, and firecrackers, and a beauty pageant, and two thousand partying Chinese. "What is freedom if the country's not free?" she asks, as if the individual is always free: it's the mandate of heaven. When the state no longer benefits the people, the people will bring the state down and will choose a new ruler—or leave heaven, or China, or slavery, or disaster, or war, and come to a country that is free. For Ah-Connie this is a vision of a free country. She could have plunked out of that round-the-world tour in Paris —lots of Chinese there—or Amsterdam—nice city with a nice Chinatown. But, no, this was it: Tijuana. She dumped the tour in Mexico City and made for Tijuana. There's just something about this place. People just feel more free to be themselves here. Tijuana?

"What is freedom if the country is not free?" Pok chi trans-

The Three-Legged Toad

lates into English, and tears come to his eyes. I don't think the tears are for the meeting of the Confucian mandate of heaven and Thomas Jefferson's notion of government ruling with the consent of the governed I've just heard.

Pok says he wants to give her daughter a Chinese New Year's present and asks her if she's heard of the three-legged toad. She's not sure. Seto's heard of the three-legged toad. It means money's coming. Does he know the story? No, he only knows what the toad is supposed to mean. You see money in the toad's mouth. That's supposed to mean money's coming.

ARTURO WU

Money's coming is Arturo Wu.

Arturo Wu has the phoenix eyes. Black as intense and dark as the eyes of an eagle. He's a big man. Big chest. Muscles tending toward a taut pudge. He looks good, dresses sharp but not flashy. He sits erect, grinning, friendly, and intimidates everyone at the table into a kind of reverence. In the Cultural Revolution he was separated from his family and sent to the country to live with peasants. He says it was the best preparation in the world for coming to America. He learned how to work like an ox. He learned how to work as a horse. He learned how to cook for himself, how to grow things, how to build things with his hands. The peasants taught him how to work hard.

Arturo married, and his father-in-law in Mexico brought the married couple over to work in his restaurant. After learning to work in the fields of China and live like a peasant, making money in America was easy. From cooking in his father-in-law's restaurant he built an empire and a reputation as a great family man, he says, a great Chinese father. He's so well known as a good Chinese father and family man he gets offers from men to break in their seventeen-year-old virgin daughters and

Frank Chin

dares us to challenge him. Of course he doesn't accept any of these offers, he says. His wife wouldn't approve. There are people around spreading rumors about him that reach his wife because of his money, but as long as he lives squeaky clean and his deals are fair, he never has to lie to his wife. He never lies to his wife. Will I drink to that with him? I sure will.

Good. As long as we drink, I can run the tape recorder. Oh. Okay.

He hands a handful of Mexican bills to the seventeen-year-old Mexican waitress. She puts on her overcoat and goes out into bluish air purpling with the threat of rain and thunder.

Arturo tells us both of his two brothers and a sister now own their own restaurants. Arturo brought them over from China and gave them restaurants. He says he wants nothing in return, not even a say in how they run their business. They are all on their own. And they all depend on Arturo for nerve. Arturo is now opening a new restaurant with his brothers and sister. A big restaurant. He is happy to say he doesn't really work. He spends the day drinking and looking for a friend to drink with him. He likes to eat and drink all day. He'll try anything. He's eaten monkey in Macao. They stick the monkey's head up through a hole in the center of the table. You can see the monkey's eyes. The head is tight in the hole. They slice the top of the skull off, and you eat the brain live out of the skull. It made him sick. He had to leave the table and chuck it up, but he likes food and isn't afraid of trying anything.

Pok chi asks if he's eaten dog. Of course he's eaten dog. Pok chi's eaten dog. It's fat. It's rich. It's sweet.

I say, "I'm known to be such an understanding Chinese father *mothers* offer me their seventeen-year-old virgin daughters and themselves. That's how pure my reputation is. *Nuns* offer themselves to me in prayer. Doing it with me is like doing it with God! But I always refuse."

"Your wife?" Arturo asks knowingly.

The Three-Legged Toad

"I'll drink to that," I say.

He shows off his gold watch. Twenty-four-carat gold on the face. Fourteen-carat watchband. Forty-seven little diamonds around the rim. One for each year of Mao Tse-tung's rule of China. There's a gold profile of Mao at the midnight position on the watch. Why would he want to wear a watch celebrating Mao?

His brother who runs a carpet factory in Shanghai bought two of the watches because they were a limited edition and sure to become collector's items and gave Arturo one as a gift. Arturo likes being a loudmouthed enigma. He won't wear the microphone, and he won't stop talking. He is suspicious and provocative. He doesn't know the story of the three-legged toad and doesn't have the patience to listen to a story unless he has a drink in his hand. He was a kid during the Cultural Revolution, and the Cultural Revolution banned all the Chinese stories, operas, and folk arts. But he's heard about them.

The seventeen-year-old waitress returns in her overcoat with a bag. In the bag is a bottle of some dark and expensive monster tequila Arturo has bought. He plants the bottle on the table, proclaims the quality and deadliness of this stuff, and looks me in the eye and says, "You drink what I drink. I drink what you drink. Drink for drink. And we talk."

Pok chi is fascinated with Arturo's Mao watch. He wants Arturo to hold his wrist up for his camera. Arturo won't lift his hand unless there's a drink in it. When he drinks, I have to drink. Pok chi wants another shot. Great. Arturo holds up his glass and looks me in the eye. I lift my glass and look him in the eye. He drinks, and I drink. The glasses come down to the table, and he pours more tequila. I look at the glasses with terror. Oh no!

He waves his hand. "Igualmente" he says. "As much as you drink, I drink."

Okay, as long as the tape recorder's running.

Frank Chin

Dinner with Seto, and the Chinese help assembles at our table, with Arturo sitting near the head. This is the Chinese America I know. The old men sitting down to dinner of approximately real Chinese food after the restaurant is closed. The Mexican cook, who's been cooking here for ten years, sits down with us. I try offering him a drink of this monster expensive tequila, but Arturo won't allow it. Pok chi says he can't drink, and the Seto who owns this restaurant won't touch the stuff. "This is for you and me," Arturo says. "You drink what I drink. As much as I drink, you drink."

The Mexican waitresses eat off the menu at another table. Pok chi asks them if they'd like some real Chinese food. Their mouths snap shut in tight smiles, and they shake their heads. They like grease. Egg rolls. Fried rice. Chop suey. Barbecued pork. A little roast duck for that grease elite.

Tonight for the Chinese there's a dish with dried bean curd and little wheels of *lin ngow*, lily root. Pok chi asks, "Where did you get the lily root?"

"Oh, it's dried. What else can you get around here?" the young boss says.

Arturo Wu will talk to us again, he says, for only as long as I drink what he drinks and match him drink for drink. I want to hear what he has to say, but I don't want to get stuck drinking any more monster booze. "We'll come back and take you over to the San Diego side for a night of Japanese sushi and sake and beer," I say.

Pok chi repeats what I said in Chinese. But I thought I had spoken in Chinese.

"We'll come back Friday, and take you to San Diego for Japanese sushi, and drink and sushi all night long." Friday's good for Arturo. He would prefer Thursday, but Friday night is good. He lives in San Diego and can go straight home from drinking and sushi with us. He nods and grins. He likes that.

Pok chi gives Ah-Connie the little box containing the little

The Three-Legged Toad

figurines of the Monkey King and the pilgrims from *Journey to the West.*

On the way out of Tijuana, it's dark, and I'm drunk, and I stop the car for Pok chi to take over driving and see we have found the Wah Kiew Hing Wooey, the Overseas Chinese Benevolent Society, above the Café Flor de Loto, the Lotus Flower Café, "Comidas Chinas, Mexicanas, y Americana." We're parked across the street from it. Through the open door we see an old, skinny, tallish Chinese man in shirt and tie, dark jacket, sitting at the front table. This has to be Chon, the old man of Tijuana Chinese. It's late. Arturo has me smashed on I don't know what. Pok chi snaps a couple of shots of the front of the building and the café window. We'll be back to talk to Ah-Chon bok when we come back to drink with Arturo Wu.

"Why Arturo Wu?"

"Both Seto and Arturo Wu. Young boys. Boom! Cultural Revolution snatches them from their families. All the kids are separated from each other. The parents separated. And after years in the boonies learning to work and live like animals in slop they get to America, work and live like animals, invest their money wisely, and reunite their families over here. The Cultural Revolution failed to stamp out their sense of family. Arturo comes on like an amoral hustler, Attila the Hun in an Italian-cut Hong Kong suit and Mao watch. But he really did get his family over. That was a moral act. And not talking to us the first time we meet and stick a tape recorder in his face is the smart thing to do. He's the only one who professes no humble nobility or noble humility we've met. He's the only one who brags about his enemies, throws money around, and challenges us to drink him under the table. You gotta be curious about a guy like that."

Right now, it's time to get to the U.S. side, find Pok chi's friend's house, and crash.

Frank Chin

The cappuccino in the shopping center on Encinitas may be the last cappuccino in the world. Coffee doesn't mean as much to Pok chi as it does to me. I don't expect to find any espresso or anything close to a well-made cappuccino in El Centro or Calexico or Mexicali or Tijuana.

We're in the groove, rolling down I-5 painlessly into a lane of the 805 to I-8, soaring on smooth concrete all the way.

Pok chi tells me the story of Ngawk Fay, the tattooed warrior.

Song dynasty. The emperor is kidnapped and taken hostage by the Mongols. Another Song becomes emperor and under the influence of a corrupt, power-mad prime minister abandons the kidnapped emperor. Ngawk Fay's mother tattoos a declaration of loyalty to the emperor of Song on Ngawk Fay's back, and he sets off to rescue his emperor. Against the wishes of the evil prime minister, Ngawk Fay leads ten campaigns against the Mongols and makes progress every time. He invents heavy armor and armored cavalry tactics. Charges of armored horses chained together. He is finally ordered back and cannot refuse the order. He is arrested and thrown in jail. In jail he is poisoned by food supplied by the couple who sell food to the prison. The couple who poisoned Ngawk Fay is celebrated in the deep-fried double donut called *yow jow gwai,* or demons fried in oil, chopped up in pieces, and floated in hot *juk* for breakfast.

Ngawk Fay, the tattooed warrior, is a model of loyalty, heroism, strategy. But going back to the corrupt court, run by the evil prime minister, to face certain and unnecessary death was simply stupid. The martyrdom doesn't seem worth it, I think.

He's a bird of five virtues. That's his hubris. It's tattooed on his back. He's loyal to the emperor of Song. He cannot disobey an order from the emperor of Song. His word is his

The Three-Legged Toad

law. His word is as good as his name. He cannot go back on his word, especially the word written on his back. There is tragedy in Chinese lit after all. Those of us who take our names and our written word seriously should take warning: don't be a sucker for what's written on your back like Ngawk Fay.

The sky is pouting, threatening to blow out heavy rains all morning, but the drive is beautiful. The wheels smooch along I-8 into a landscape of rock candy piled up by playful giants. I'm glad I'm not driving this road alone. The hills are mounds of big rocks, boulders about the same size and shape as if pooped from the same horse. Grey and red rocks. Giant hard candies in pointy big mounds all around.

"When we get to Calexico, we're hooking up with George Woo. He's big in the Chung Wah there and a part of the Calexico establishment. His daughter by his second wife, a Mexican woman, says she's more Mexican than Chinese and considers herself a Mexican in terms of culture. She also says she used to tell her father weekend visits to Calexico were like long vacations because, after one night there, you feel like you've been there a month."

Pok chi remembers the wife of his cousin, also named Ah-Connie. So Ah-Connie in Tijuana rung a bell.

Pok chi says, "She's about in her mid-thirties now. Very dark, healthy-looking, open Chinese woman who loves to talk and make friends. Very generous. And very cautious at the same time. Very capable of learning new things to survive. When I first met her and her husband, they were selling T-shirts on the streets of Chinatown, New York City. They told me they would begin at about seven in the morning and work until ten at night, sometimes eleven. It depends whether it's a Friday night or a Saturday night. And I think that's how they began making some hard-earned money to buy real estate.

"Later on I found out they were selling bags. They were renting a store, leased it to some of their friends from China who had escaped just like them and needed jobs. I think there is a network of Chinese doing business together, helping each other out. Some of them are dissidents. Some of them are athletes, Ping Pong players, who on a world tour during the early eighties just quit somewhere—when I saw them.

"This network of people, their business at that time was selling fake watches. Fake Guccis and Omegas. And diamond-studded Rolexes. For twenty-five bucks. He said the Latinos and the Europeans just ate them up. They'd buy thirty, a hundred. So Ah-Connie and her husband had been promoted from selling things on the street to selling fake watches. My cousin would supply these street vendors with these watches.

"So one of the Ping Pong guys I met, interestingly enough, he was training his daughter to sing opera. Cantonese opera. And she was born in New York. And he insisted we listen to her tape. He played an instrument. The mother played an instrument. And the daughter sang. And it was a little store with about the floor space of a king-size bed to stamp the name *Omega* on the face of the watch. So this means when these watches came in through customs, from China, through Hong Kong and Macao, the faces were blank. And when they come to New York's Chinatown, they become Omegas, or whatever he wants them to be.

"When I was growing up in Hong Kong, I remember, my neighbors and my distant relatives, in their bedrooms there were just whole mountains of bits and pieces of plastic flowers. And they were assembling them together. And I could never figure out where the hell they would go. I had never seen anyone in Hong Kong having plastic flowers in their houses. They all came to Woolworths. Sears. In the U.S."

Pok chi sees a certain irony in migrant Chinese in detention camps or apartment factories in Hong Kong assembling fake European designer products, trendy goods, watches, electronics, cellular phones, to be wholesaled to Latinos and Mid-

The Three-Legged Toad

dle Easterners, who will hawk them on the streets of large American cities.

"I didn't know they swam to Hong Kong. It wasn't for a few years that they began to tell me. I think my cousin told me the story first. He told me his way to Hong Kong was a lot easier. He told me he got into a boat. A pretty good-sized boat, like a block or two long. For some reason he was hiding inside, and nobody knew about it. He got to where he thought Hong Kong would be, he jumped out of the boat at night, and started floating, and fainted. And a day or so later he was saved by some Hong Kong fishermen. They grabbed him out of the water and began to feed him food, and *mun gum yow* on the back, the front, the forehead, and the throat, and rub him off till the heat comes back. He made it all the way to Hong Kong. So he didn't have too bad of an experience.

"His wife had an entirely different experience. She was able or willing to discuss all these details with me among a lot of her younger relatives."

"Children!" I say.

"All of them at that time were American born. New York born. She began talking about her parents being persecuted during the Chinese Cultural Revolution. They were intellectuals, university educated, from an intellectual family. Their ancestor was a famous poet and government official. He had a reputation as a decent, very good government official, which was rare at that time. His name was Luk Yau. Luk Fong yung is another name. I studied his poetry when I was in high school. So right away that would demand some respect for her and her family. She talked about her parents being separated and jailed and hauled into the streets with signs on their front and back saying people like them were *Ngau gwai siyeh sun*. These are demons, snakes, ghosts, horses, cows, and boars. People on the street would insult them. They would spit on them. So nobody would dare talk to them. Even friends. Of course the children would not be allowed to talk to them. But they need to let their parents know they were doing okay. They don't know when the parents will pass through the street where they're condemned. They know they will not be passing through this neighborhood at the same time.

"And they used the tactic that they used fighting the Japanese. They were told if the broom hangs outside the window upside down, it means that the family's okay. The children are taken care of."

Then we're out of the candyland and down in the desert and going to the bottom of something. The air is different. The air in the air conditioner is different. My ears pop. For a little bit I thought I might have been here before. I was wrong.

"And later they found out from their mother that, indeed, she walked past the house, saw the broom was upside down, and was relieved," Pok says.

If I'd been here before, I'd be crazy to come back, I think. In *The Movie about Me* I stop the car, get out, listen to the air, and freak, tear my clothes off, and run bareassed and barefoot into the desert, and disappear in a mirage of water just short of infinity.

"Ah-Connie was sent to the country to learn from the peasants. And a lot of the farmers, the peasants despised these people because they had never done any physical labor in their lives. And the peasants were already very poor. And the government sends all these inexperienced kids who don't know how to take care of themselves to become a burden on the peasant farmers. Ah-Connie learned to go to the field and do physical things. She remembers having to dig into rice paddies that's eight foot deep. Because the topsoil after a couple of years is exhausted, and they have to recycle topsoil, turn the soil over from underneath as deep as eight feet. So at seventeen or eighteen she's digging trenches in soggy soil. But it

The Three-Legged Toad

turned out to be for her benefit. It made her physically stronger to survive in the water for a couple of days."

The Arturo Wu argument, I think.

"She remembers there was a guy who was extremely handsome who liked her, but she didn't like him. She found out he had all kinds of underground connections and was able to survive very, very well during the Cultural Revolution. He was something of a gang leader. He was a planner who was the architect behind certain gang projects. He never had to dirty his hands. Smuggling. Extortion. They had a childhood friendship. He'd liked her since childhood. So that even though she didn't like him, he agreed to help her out.

"Then another childhood friend she hadn't seen in a long time one day looked her up out of the blue. This guy proposed to escape to Hong Kong with her. She didn't know if this guy was sent to her by the other guy with the connections, who'd promised to help her.

"She asked, 'Why do you choose me?'

"He told her a fortune-teller had advised that he must take another man and two women with him to make this trip. Otherwise he won't make it. The escape must be two men and two women. So he recruited her.

"From the city to swim to Hong Kong is a long distance. That's Poon Yur. The village, Ha Herng, is not too far away from Poon Yur. Her father had a friend who was an accountant. He had to oversee the security of the village so the people could not escape. He took the blame later on. He saw her leaving. He walked with her for a distance. He let her go.

"She walked to the river, met the three others, and boarded a sampan. They get out to sea—by daybreak, before they're out of territorial waters, the coast guard intercepts them. There's no way they can run. The sampan is boarded, and they're physically dragged out of the boat with machine guns at their heads.

Frank Chin

"The captain asks questions. There's an exchange of papers. The captain lets the people go. She suspects her gangster friend has made an arrangement with the captain. After they get back on board the sampan, the coast guard fires toward them, but fires short till they reach Hong Kong waters.

"Then a storm came that afternoon. The sampan fell apart, and they swam to an island. The island is full of corpses. The stench! They were so hungry she said they thought of eating meat off the dead bodies. But they just couldn't do it. They spent the night there because of the sharks around. They spent the night in the cave with the dead bodies.

"In the morning there were fewer sharks. They threw dead bodies out to feed the sharks. Like chum. After a few hours the sharks are all done and gone. No sharks out there. They don't know how far they are from Hong Kong or in which direction it is. The guy rigged up some kind of antenna by using some wire and a piece of tinfoil and a tin can. He received static and swam toward where the static was loudest. The guy took off his pants. They were made with a vinyl coating. So he took his pants off and wrapped them around Ah-Connie's neck to use as flotation. And they swam. And another fifteen or sixteen hours later they made it to the New Territories, the Low Faw Sahn area. When I was growing up, that area was famous for recovering corpses of dead swimmers. But they got there alive. A policeman came by and woke them up and said, 'Since you guys have made it this far, I'm going to let you go.'

"The guy she swam with and Ah-Connie decided to never see each other again. They might be caught and sent back if they were seen together again. Though she didn't like him, she wanted to thank him. After seven months in Hong Kong she saw him working in a barbecue place, chopping pork. She arranged to have a gold necklace sent to him as a sign of her gratitude."

The Three-Legged Toad

In America, and married to Pok chi's cousin now, she and her husband own property in New Jersey and Queens. Happy ending. I couldn't work that hard. I also couldn't get myself to own property in New Jersey or Queens.

Golden Dragon, Yum Yum, China Palace . . . we count six Chinese restaurants driving into Calexico on Imperial Avenue.

GEORGE WOO

George Woo is in the Chung Wah Wooey Goon of Calexico. Every Chinatown of any size has an alliance of the local organizations representing Chinatown businesses called the Chung Wah Wooey Goon, or Chinese Consolidated Benevolent Association, also known as the Chinese Six Companies in San Francisco. He doesn't know the Chung Wah as an international organization with formal ties to the government of the Republic of China. A cabinet post, the minister of overseas Chinese affairs, is devoted to dealing with the Chung Wah around the American continent. John Chiang, the current minister, is the son of Generalissimo Chiang Kai-shek's son, the late Chiang Ching-kuo, and Chiang Ching-kuo's Chinese mistress. The Republic of China subsidizes the annual convention of the Chung Wah.

George wasn't at the convention in Seattle two years ago or last year's convention in Houston. For George Woo, the Chung Wah is a local organization, a Chinese community self-help organization.

What George Woo knows is Calexico, the Imperial Valley.

Back in the sixties, when he owned a grocery store, he says, "The Chinese running grocery stores were so scattered all over the valley, you hardly ever see them." The problem was finding a way to bring the Chinese grocers together.

"In 1966 we chartered what we call the Imperial Valley Grocers' Association, for the independent stores that come

Frank Chin

into the valley, and combine our resources to compete against the chain stores. At that time we had A&P stores, we had Safeway. And we hold, at least, two meetings a month. You know, Hey, uncle! How'ya been? At least we'd get to see those people. Ninety percent of the groceries were Chinese. A few American stores. A few Mexican independent stores. We started about with about thirty-seven, thirty-nine members.

"Henry Quan was part of the Grocers' Association. And Dr. Henry Quan is his son.

"None of the kids are interested in continuing the retail groceries, which is a good business, but then they got their education, they got their own fields of endeavor. They go on their own."

He's in his sixties now, retired from the retail grocery business. Now he stays up late in his office at the De Anza Hotel, working as a regional vice president of Primerica Financial Services. He's Lions Club, Chamber of Commerce, the establishment. Already an old-timer.

"My granddad's a pioneer. In fact. Woo Yin waw, my granddad, was a pioneer in this part of the country, in Mexicali, back in 1916, that area of time. How he came to this country in the first place I never found out. He came directly from China to Mexicali. That part of his history I'm not aware of.

"He started as a farmer. The Mexicali Valley was pioneered by Chinese people. The first inhabitants of Mexicali were Chinese. The Chinese built the first buildings. And then the Mexican people came as a result of it. Mexicali City grew around Chinatown. There's over a million people in Mexicali, Baja California right now.

"Before World War II there were as many as ten thousand Chinese in Mexicali. My granddad was telling me that they still call the center of town the Chinesca. *Chinesca* means "Chinatown." Right in the heart of Mexicali, the Chinesca, all the Chinese merchants, and clothing stores, and restaurants.

The Three-Legged Toad

Laundry was also the main business when Mexicali first started. And they have Chinese opera, *char ngau,* you know, and dim sum. And they had Chinese theater in the early days. So my brother-in-law—the one I told you about running a hotel in Cabo San Lucas—when he was a real young kid, you know, he was running around the street naked in the Chinese restaurant. And they'd call him in Chinese, 'Hey, *how sang!* Come here!' And they'd feed him. So he's just running around naked in the streets.

"So my grandfather, when he was here, they were farming cotton and other Chinese produce and stuff like that. And my grandfather had an accident. They were driving a mule team, with these wheels with the big spokes. His foot got caught in one of those wheels, and the mule team dragged him for two miles. So he broke his leg. So my granddad said, Forget it! No more farming for me. So he went into town and had his own tortilla factory."

Pok chi kicks his feet up and claps his hands. "Chinese got a tortilla factory?"

"It's a tortilla factory that manufactures tortillas on a daily basis. And he starts delivering to restaurants, the Mexican food, Chinese food, whatever the Mexican people wanted. And that's what my granddad did all his life till he retired.

"I was born in Canton. Hoy Yuen. Woo See Lun is my name in Chinese. I was a spoiled brat, they call it. My grandmother, bless her heart, she lived to be 103, I saw her many times since then, but I remember when I first went to kindergarten. My grandmother had to carry me to school because I'd say, Oh, come on! You got to take me to school. My grandmother carried me to my first class in school. She always used to talk about that, you know.

"'Hey, you're going to the United States.'

"'Oh, where's that?'

"'Over there, Gum Sahn, where the Gold Mountain is.

Frank Chin

They pick up gold nuggets by the shovelful, by the bucket.'

"I think it's the opportunity to be somebody in the United States.

"There were emotions, I remember. But you're a little young kid. Your parents say, Go! You go.

"When I came over, there were two young kids came over with me. We were all about the same age. One or two years apart, maybe. And our fathers were in the grocery business in Calexico. So our three fathers were in business together, and we three sons come together in Calexico in 1936.

"We came over on the *President Coolidge,* of American Presidents Line. We came on that boat and had a lot of fun. Chinese food. Most of the passengers were Chinese. In first class were the Americans and the Anglos. If you're not Chinese, hey, you're just a *bok gwai.* We couldn't afford first class. But it was fun. In our cabin we had 450 people. It was like a dormitory. We had a trip mess hall. Everybody eats the same thing. The seas got rough, us three kids were running around the ship, all over the doggone place, you know. People were seasick. We were just going gung ho!

"We stopped at Hawai'i, and then came to LA, and then came this way. San Pedro Harbor. That's what I recall reading when we landed. From there we proceed through the check the documents, and my dad was waiting for me in LA. So we spent a few days there.

"When I get into the States, I was just a young kid. I was eight years old. My father was about twenty-eight or twenty-nine. I didn't know a word of English or Spanish.

"My dad was about average. He was educated. He could read and write Chinese. And he enjoyed music. He played two or three instruments. He played by himself and not with a club. There were not that many Chinese on the American side. The Chinese population in Mexicali and the United States, they were not freely crossing the border.

The Three-Legged Toad

"Even the recent boat people coming through here. Before they hit the Mexicali area, a lot of Chinese died in the desert."

"The recent Chinese boat people died in the desert?" Pok chi asks.

"No," George says. "That's the history of the Chinese crossing the Mexican desert. Back at the turn of the century. The boat people. They just dump 'em off and say, Hey, you guys, just go that way! And point, that's all. I think at that time they were just trying to reach the Mexicali Valley. And they didn't tell 'em how far. They didn't tell them about food and water. And Chino Mountain is where the Chinese died trying to reach the Mexicali Valley. A lot of Chinese died going over the hill.

"Even now the boat people that were caught in Ensenada and San Diego. That's recent history. There were over three hundred people that were caught in Ensenada, brought to Mexicali, and they were there for over three weeks. And the Imperial Valley Chinese community tried to help feed them. They cost about a thousand American dollars a day just to feed those three hundred detained boat people.

"So the Chinese community said, Hey! they don't mind to help out on a part-time basis, but for forever. . . . Three weeks at a thousand dollars a day, there's no end to it. It's like a pit.

"Finally they shipped them from Mexicali back to China."

I'm a little confused, I say. "This is Calexico. Your grandfather came to Calexico?"

"My grandfather's Mexicali, always has been," George Woo says. "My father came directly from China to the United States. Why he picked Calexico of all the cities in the United States, I don't know. My father and his partners started together in the retail grocery business. One of them was Albert Woo. His family's still in the valley. Albert was the one in administrative. And C. Woo was in charge of the meat department. And my dad was Sam Woo, he's the third partner, he

Frank Chin

was over in the grocery department. In those days they were comparable to the chain stores. We had two locations. The first one was on First Street. First and Blair. And that's where we grew up.

"There were three partners in that grocery store. So the three fathers got together, and us three kids came together, so we're the sons of the three partners. They eventually told us we should work our way, You guys are going to be the future owners of the grocery store.

"We didn't enjoy the normal American or Spanish childhood days. We just get out of school, he gives us fifteen minutes to get to the store. There was no after-school parties, or basketball games, or play or stuff like that. Hell, we got fifteen minutes from the school to get to the store, and that was it. My job, what can I do? I haven't learned the language yet. So my job was in the kitchen, learn to start cooking as a young kid.

"We used to have chicken coops in the back of the store. Lot of times, the produce, the trimmings, we feed to chickens and ducks we raised in the back of the store. Regulations those times wasn't the same. Our living quarters were behind the store, yeah, in the same building. Strictly bachelor quarters. The three fathers slept in one room. The three sons slept in one room. We going through a daily routine.

"I came in 1936, we had electricity, adequate plumbing, the comforts of home. We had gas stove. Kerosene heater. The first comfort we had was a *desert cooler*. We didn't have any air-conditioning in those days. We had one of those rotary fans. And this is where the desert cooler thing came in. We were the first to invent that. We used to have gunny sacks, potato sacks soaking wet and put behind the fan and bring a cool breeze into the living quarters. Then came the desert coolers. The desert cooler was the first relief from the heat for the family here. Oh, man, that desert cooler would just . . . in fact, in some of the lower-income homes they still have desert coolers.

"In those days everything was in bulk. The rice, the beans, the flour. We would package those things. We packaged the eggs, too. Everything that comes in bulk we repackaged in one-pound, two-pound, three-pound packages for sale.

"We'd be helping out in the store, too, like stocking shelves. Then as you get older, you get to learning the language and speaking to the people. Spanish was our second language. We were learning Spanish and English at the same time. We learn English language in school; then we come home, and it's a predominantly Spanish neighborhood. That's where I picked up my Spanish.

"And a lot of times I'd go and make the deliveries, and then we'd get to know the people, take the orders, sort the orders, and make deliveries on a COD basis, like that, so I get to know people pretty well.

"And that's how I got my first driver's license. Just by watching them drive, how he'd shift his gears, like that. I remember the first time I took the wheel, instead of going forward, I went backward. I ran into the building. I said, Oh, shit! I got my axe grinded then.

"They used to close on Sunday. Half day. We used to go to El Centro, visit other relatives."

Pok chi asks if George's grandmother and mother ever came to Calexico.

"My grandmother and my mother both stayed behind. At that time women were not allowed to come over," George says.

Yes, the Chinese Exclusion Act of 1882 and the Gentlemen's Agreement of 1925. Pok chi's grown up with a different immediate history than I have and George Woo has. Pok chi is listening for a story of women left behind. George Woo is telling the story of boys growing up with men, without mothers, without sisters, without women; boys growing up to be the fathers of boys growing up without a family, without a grandma to carry him to school, without a storyteller. This is all men living like soldiers on a mission. Men. No families.

"There were very few Chinese families in Calexico. I don't recall having any Chinese families in those early years," George Woo says. "They had a fire accident. And we moved to Second Street. And we were there back in 1938–39. That location, I don't think was larger than fifty-five by fifty.

"I didn't know a word of English or Spanish, so they just look at me and say, Hey, little boy! What's your name? Como te llamas? So I started school here.

"That was one of the outstanding markets. They called it La Voz del Pueblo. The Voice of the Town. In fact, there are people that still remember those days. In those days we had delivery services. People call up their orders. I remember when I got out of school, we'd go deliver till ten in the morning, 4 o'clock in the afternoon. You know, people call in their orders, we do a home delivery service."

"I did that too!" Pok chi enthuses.

Friday nights George would stay up till 11 P.M. with his father's partners' kids and stock shelves and put the stuff from big boxes into smaller lots of smaller bags in preparation for Saturday morning.

Friday was payday. And Saturday people did their shopping for the week. Saturday was a busy day. Somehow he got away to Saturday kiddie matinees.

"One day in the summertime we went down to the canal to go swimming, you know. And I got caught in the rain and came in the store all soaking wet. Man, my dad saw me! We used to have those sticks to get groceries from the top shelf. He grabbed that and just slapped the hell out of me. You three kids supposed to come back from school. The other two

The Three-Legged Toad

come back! How come you don't come back! Broke that stick on me. He was madder'n hell. Right in the store! To show his other partners. There's three fathers in that store. There's no mother to go, Oh, poor baby, like that.

"My teenage years. I didn't have those liberties of going dancing with your friends, and girlfriends, and stuff like that. My life was from the store to the school and from the store to the school, and that was my daily routine. We didn't enjoy the joys of life at home, your mother serving meals to you. Come to that age you kinda take your own attitude toward things. How come the other kids can go to movies and shows and I can't go? So you start questioning your dad and stuff like that. And we were brought up to, when they say, you don't go to movies, you don't go! There ain't no radios or stereos. None of those things, those comforts of home."

I'm shocked. "No 'Lone Ranger'?" I ask.

"Well," George admits, "'The Lone Ranger' is one thing I did listen to, and 'The Shadow.' Well, they had a radio in the store, to play music to please the customers. So I got close enough to that thing while I'm packing groceries, I could listen to it."

"Did your father come to your graduation?" I ask.

"No such animal. They were busy in the store. Like I say, you don't have that, Boy! I'm going to see my son graduate! How proud I am, you know. He just, You graduate? Got your diploma? Get back to the store! Like I say, the relationship, whether it be strictly business or whatever it is, you don't have that feeling, I'm going to take my son fishing or take him to the ball game. . . . You feel that father and son love that way—we didn't have those things. We admire other people doing things like that, but what can you say?"

All the motherly love George Woo had as a kid was a breeze off his desert cooler. The life of the bachelor society was hard.

Frank Chin

"In 1941 Pearl Harbor happened. I was too young to volunteer. I volunteered at the age of nineteen in 1946. I didn't know how to use a knife and fork till I went into the army. So the Japanese saw I was coming, and they gave up. I volunteered in the Eighth Army; I served in Japan with the Occupation forces.

"I came back, and I got out of the army and got my first car. My first car was a 1929 Ford. A two door. Model A.

"See, my generation, most of the guys, as teenagers, they all went back to mainland China because the parents had selected their wives already. They were told to go back and get married. So I can fairly say I was the first guy that broke loose from that chain.

"Like when I met my first wife, it wasn't a date; we just sort of start socializing. Then this Leong family from Mexicali, I was kind of attached to it. I felt a little camaraderie there for that family, father and son. I remember my mom wrote the letter back, she says, Send George to China, I have his wife picked out for him.

"My mother just said, You come home and get married! I've got three girls picked for you.

"Then I said, Hell, no! I don't want to go back there. I'm going to live here. I saw how it was for my grandfather and my dad. Their wives are over there. And they're over here.

"I said, This is the girl I've been going out with and I like, and we're gonna get married. So I got married. So I was disobedient.

"My mother finally gave way, said, Okay, bring your wife home. We'll have the Chinese wedding over here.

"I took my wife back to the village where I was born. It was nineteen years since I'd been back. I was twenty-seven years old. It was very special. Everything looked different. The village came out; all my relatives came out. Banquet. We got off

The Three-Legged Toad

pretty well, and we came back and made our home."

Pok chi is amazed, a little offended George and his father didn't bring his mother over from China.

"My mother was not allowed at that time to come over, no," George says. The quota of Chinese allowed into the continental United States of 103 from all parts of the world wasn't lifted till 1966.

"The other two guys that came over with me, they went back and got married and started Peso."

Peso are two large, obviously Chinese-owned warehouse stores on Imperial Avenue. The Big "PESO" sign is in some awful quasi-Spanish calligraphy in huge letters, and underneath are two obviously Chinese words. One store is just a block from the border, at the beginning of Calexico. The other occupies a huge space between a huge K-Mart and a huge WalMart outside Calexico. The big difference between Peso and the chain discounters is all Peso's signs and labels are in Spanish only. Interesting to see the Chinese defying national biggies K-Mart and WalMart for dominance of an intersection with Imperial Avenue. People seem to come to these places to get away from the desert. Entire families wander around the Peso and the K-Mart like they're on a nature trail in the park.

George Woo says he resents the way he was brought up. What kind of father is he?

"I like my kids to have what I didn't have." He pampered his children. He spoiled his children. He was the kind of father he wished he'd had when he was a kid. "The two daughters by my first marriage, they're married now. In fact I have three daughters and a son. The daughters each has two grandkids now."

His father is buried here. George is sure it was his father's wish to be buried here, in Calexico.

"He lived all his life here in Calexico until he retired and died a few years later. You don't question your dad at those times. He made decisions."

"Your dad ever buy you a present?" I ask.

George thinks a moment and says, "Yeah, he did. A bicycle. A Schwinn."

He's on the phone to the current president of the Imperial Valley Chung Wah. In the flow of a few seconds George uses Spanish and Chinese and tells us this man is the only man to successfully farm lily root in America.

"I want to meet him!" Pok chi yells. "I have to meet him!"

SUN LEE-LOUIE

George takes us to meet Sun Lee-Louie. He is working as a manager of a new Chinese restaurant in a new shopping center built with Hong Kong money. The restaurant seems to be the only occupant in this complex. That's how new it is. Pok chi smiles and asks Sun Lee-Louie why the lily root he grew in Lawrence, Kansas, came out small, short, and red.

Sun Lee-Louie sneers at us and clams up. We are farmers from Kansas come to steal the secret of growing lily root. Right now he is the only grower of lily root in the continental United States. The fresh lily root you find sliced thin and braised or brewed crunchy—the little circular things with the holes in them in a hearty soup—are from Sun Lee-Louie's farm. Others have tried to grow the lily root. Just ask Pok chi Lau, the photographer turned farmer on me. Stop asking for the secrets of growing lily root and snap his picture, Pok chi.

From his father's original forty acres, he has built a farm of two hundred acres. He grows bok choy, the bulbous Chinese green with the dark green in the leaves and white stalks. Other people all over America grow bok choy. Pok chi grows bok choy.

The Three-Legged Toad

Sun Lee-Louie also grows *gai lan*, Chinese broccoli. Lots of people all over America grow *gai lan*. Oh, Pok chi's *gai lan* come out funny looking and skinny.

"Too much rain," Sun Lee-Louie says.

Near the cash register at the reception counter there's a large, reddish fish-bone statuette of a three-legged toad with six coins in its mouth.

"What's this ugly old thing mean?" I ask.

"Oh, that's lucky," Sun Lee-Louie says. "Money's coming."

"Why does it mean that?" I ask.

"Oh, Chinese believe it's lucky."

"Do you know the story?" I ask.

"No," Sun Lee-Louie says, "I don't know the story."

"I know the story, but I don't understand it," I say. "I'll tell you the story." No customers to be seated. No customers with bills to pay. I tell him the story. He smiles. He nods. He understands the story. He knows why the toad is lucky now. He can't explain it. Great.

It's Valentine's Day. They expect a good dinner business. This is a very large restaurant. Three hundred seats easy. Time to run.

On the way back to the De Anza Hotel, George takes us by the Pioneer Park Museum. It was built without government grants. No NEH. No NEA. The past of thirteen ethnic groups is told and displayed in thirteen galleries. The Chinese gallery is the history of the Mah family in the Imperial Valley. Most of the artifacts were donated and collected by the son of Henry Quan, Dr. William Quan. The museum and the idea of celebrating the history of each group in its own space came from the people of the valley themselves. Filipinos, Koreans, Japanese, the Swiss, thirteen ethnic or cultural groups in all maintain their integrity and carry on with each other civilly in this museum without government money. Impressive.

Frank Chin

Pok chi and I have dinner at the De Anza. It's Valentine's Day. There's a nice buzz of couples out to dinner in the booths. The Trio Calafia, stand-up bass, guitar, and requinta wander the aisles plunking and plinking, ready to break into song.

TUESDAY, 15 FEBRUARY, THE DAY OF THE OXEN

Breakfast at the De Anza coffee shop. George Woo gets up early and stays up late. He must live at the De Anza. George has *machaca con huevos*. Pok chi and I have *chorizo con huevos*. When it comes, he asks what it is in a funny tone of voice. I tell him it's what we ordered. That's all he needs to know. He forks that strange food with confidence and anticipation. He likes the spicy sausage.

George introduces us to a young man on the go. Eddie Chun and his super cellular phone sit at our table a while. Born in El Centro. Degree in architecture from California Polytechnical Institute in San Luis Obispo. Now is an architect and contractor-builder in the valley with business as far as Yuma, Arizona. He also does inspections for the state. He says he found tunnels leading from buildings that used to be owned by Chinese to another Chinese business on the other side of the border. These tunnels had to be filled and plugged to save the buildings built above them.

George says these tunnels were built in the twenties, during Prohibition, after the fences were built along the border. The tunnels weren't built to let Chinese into the United States but to allow people from the Calexico side to cross over to Mexicali and drink and gamble where there was no Prohibition. According the brochure, the twenties was when the De Anza Hotel was built and saw its glory, offering a bed and meals on the American side of the border to Americans come

The Three-Legged Toad

to Calexico only to booze and gamble and eat Chinese food in Mexicali.

George leads us out to Lee-Louie's farm, then has to go off to a funeral.

THE PACKING SHED AT SUN LEE-LOUIE'S FARM

A pregnant woman, the wife of the foreman, Sun Lee-Louie's nephew, meets us outside the fence around the house. There's a patch of grass and trees growing on the grass. The plum tree is blooming. There are grapefruit fat on the grapefruit tree. Lemons on the lemon tree. Sun Lee-Louie knows how to make things grow. She leads us to the packing shed, where her husband is weighing the lily root hands bring in from the fields in large plastic crates. They load the crates with lily root, and load the crates in the trunk and on the trunk lid and hoods of their old big-bodied American cars, and bust ass for the packing shed and the scales. They get paid by the pound and make about $120 a day. They want good relations with the workers and no problems with the immigration people, so they like to keep the same workers year to year, and to keep them at this farm, they give them work, even in bad years, like now. They're picking bok choy. The field is a total loss. But they want the same people to come back and work here next year when things might be better.

There is a shrine to Kwan Kung in the packing shed. The candles are electric lights. The fruit is fresh. Someone takes care of this shrine.

Enrique works at a table sorting, cleaning, trimming, and packing lily root. The nicely shaped fat long ones get the tips lopped off to prevent rotting and get packed in wooden crates. The shorter ones and ones with tool cuts and imper- fections get trimmed and packed into cardboard boxes and

Frank Chin

sold for significantly less. I ask Enrique how long he's been working on this farm for the Chinese?

Enrique has worked on this farm for forty years. He has nine kids. Six on the U.S. side of the border and three on the Mexican side. His wife runs a family business. They sell stuff at swap meets. The money he makes packing lily root and bok choy and Chinese broccoli for the Lee-Louie farm buys the stuff they sell.

Pok and Sun's nephew talk the fine points of growing lily root in California.

They spend $70,000 a year on water to leach the salt and chemical fertilizers from the sand and gravel they use. They dig trenches eight feet deep. They grow the lily root in a mix of sand and gravel and topsoil. If you don't plant deep enough and don't have very pure sand and soil, your lily root will come out short, skinny, and red.

Sun Lee-Louie goes back to China every year to study the farming of lily root. The bok choy and the *gai lan* crops of the last couple of years have been total losses because too much rain forced them to bloom early. In dollars that's around $200,000 a year in losses.

Uncle Freddy meets us at Sun Lee-Louie's farm. Everybody knows everybody in the valley. All the Chinese are related to each other. All men are brothers. He is going to introduce us to a real old-timer.

Uncle Freddy takes us to lunch at Mah's Kitchen, a fast-food sit-down Chinese restaurant-café-curio shop where you breathe grease and everything is deep-fried. Uncle Freddy introduces us to the owners. Their hands are wet from washing and cutting up veggies and cleaning and battering up chicken parts and shrimp for the great deep-fry. Uncle Freddy directs us to an empty table and says he'll join us.

In the restaurant, people dressed like the middle class—

nice colors, nice cuts, no flash, no adventure, nobody's name written in hair on anybody's scalp—are lined up against a big window across from the cash register waiting for delivery of their grease. A young, very pretty and working on it teenage Mexican girl flicks and fingers her dyed and permed hair that seems to be droopy layers of curly lightning bolts. She wears designer jeans and a skintight leotard with a scoop neck showing lots of skin, and the edges curl out like flower petals. She takes orders, hands the orders up, and takes the cash in. Two of her girlfriends sit at plates of fried rice and deep-fried stuff and gossip with her between customers.

The only Chinese out in front of the restaurant is the cook. Pok chi points him out behind the counter. A young Chinese man, maybe twenty-five at the most, and maybe just turned twenty. He's all business. The cook. The power of war and peace in all this madness. The cook has the ruddy complexion, the intense angry eyes, the cheekbones like clenched fists of the classic southern rebel of the Chinese heroic tradition. He wears a gold button in his ear. He has a pierced ear. He moves purposefully, with no false steps, no wasted motion, between the cleaver at the chopping block and the stainless steel smoker at the end of the counter. When he opens the smoker, I glimpse inside and see several pork tenderloins and racks of pork ribs being smoked. He handles the knife well, slicing *lop chong*, Chinese pork sausage, into little ovals for his own lunch.

He might be a good cook after all. To find out all I'd have to do is ask him to make me a plate of stir-fried bean sprouts. It's not that I like bean sprouts. I want to test the cook's skill, his speed, accuracy, and proportion. I learned this from a swimmer, one of the Chinese swimming team who'd jumped into the river and swam for Hong Kong rather than be moved to the north. Five made the jump, and three reached Hong Kong. Edmund now owned a restaurant in Seattle. Stir-frying bean sprouts was how he tested his cooks. They have to be cooked hot and fast. Too low a heat means slow cooking, and slow stir-fried bean sprouts come out dark and soggy. They should be white, crisp, and just on the edge of warm, all the way through. Strategy, strategy, everything is strategy.

I don't see a Kwan Kung here. Fook, Look, Sau, the three star gods, yes. They're for sale in the display case. The god of prosperity, meaning happiness and luck, has a black beard, holds a baby. The god of wealth wears the official's cap with wings and a stiff, hoop-like official belt of office around his waist. He has a black beard and holds a jade scepter in his left hand, or against his left shoulder when he holds a boat-shaped gold ingot in his two hands. And the big-domed, bald, hatless, white-bearded god of longevity holds a gnarly wooden staff. All grin like fools. The kid with the knife in his hand slicing the barbecued pork has the eyes of Kwan Kung.

Uncle Freddy sits down with an old Chinaman he introduces as Big Louie and a tray loaded with deep-fried doughy things, barbecued ribs, and a bowl of white rice. Chinese. Southern Chinese. Sam Yup and Say Yup Chinese. When a southerner greets another southerner with the traditional, "*Sick jaw fon may ah?* Have you had rice yet?" *rice* isn't a euphemism for *meal*. They mean rice, white rice. Uncle Freddy is giving us face, treating us like Chinese. Perhaps it's Big Louie Uncle Freddy is giving face. They both reach heartily into the piles of deep-fried doughy things and chomp away.

"Have some shrimp," Big Louie says.

Pok chi and I take a turn breaking one of the deep-fried doughy things from the pile. Chewing on the second one, I realize I'm not chewing on shrimp. It's chicken. Pok chi is still looking at his first doughy thing, undecided after one bite, about it's identity.

"I hope you didn't swallow any of that," I say.

The Three-Legged Toad

A look of pure terror sweeps over Pok chi's face.

"Chicken," I whisper to Pok chi. His mind clicks back on. His brain begins to hum again. I see it in his eyes. "Chicken."

"Yeah, have some chicken," Uncle Freddy says.

THE CHUNG WAH WOOEY GOON

The Chung Wah Wooey Goon building says "Confucius Church" on the outside wall facing the parking lot. On the inside of this wall is the Bing Kung Tong side of the building. The room on this side of the building houses the shrine to Kwan Kung. This wall is bare except for a long brush painting of a horse, all four legs stretched out back and front and neck straining and mouth screaming for the big leap over what seems to be an idealization of the valley. A valley of trees. The horse I take to be a symbol for the Mah-family dominance of the area.

The Chinese school used to be here. The pulp paper textbooks are still here, not so neatly stacked in the room where they play mah jong and gossip late into the night once a month. The seats and tables and chalkboards are still here.

They are four to eight old men, two tables of mah jong, the old men of the Chung Wah Wooey Goon: Uncle Freddy, George Woo, the white-haired Sun Lee-Louie, and Joe Wong, who was a bombardier on board a PBM patrol-flying boat, the reverse gull-winged, twin-engined, twin-tailed Martin Mariner in World War II. I thought the Chinese in the navy never got beyond steward, much less got to fly in World War II.

Uncle Freddy bustles about the Chung Wah building, setting things up for tonight's meeting.

Big Louie sits with us out in the back of the Chung Wah building, in the shade of an awning. He says, "I was born in Toishan. Kwangtung, Toishan bok sop, Ten tiew lee—A Thousand Winters—in 1916. I'm seventy-eight."

Frank Chin

"Where did you get the name *Big?*" I ask.

"In school. In Modesto. I'm a pretty damn big kid. Thirteen and big and fat. I don't know English. They ask what am I? I say, 'I big.' They try name me *Bic* or *Bick*—B-I-C or B-I-C-K. But I write down *B-I-G.* And that's how it is, you know. My name Big Louie." He's not a real Louie. He is a paper Louie.

His family name is Mah. His aunt sold him fake papers with the family name Louie.

I am a paper Chin. How does one come to be a "paper son"? Once upon a time there was a merchant named Chin. He might have dealt in opium, which was legal at the turn of the century. One of the spoils of the Opium Wars for the British seemed to be open markets of opium in Chinatowns around the world. Chin might have dealt in nothing but mail, but for him being a merchant meant he could freely travel back and forth between the United States and China. Every year between 1912 and 1924 he goes to China and comes back claiming to have borne a son. All his sons have the right to enter the United States as the sons of a merchant when they're of an age fit to work.

Merchant Chin goes back to China again, and finds families with boys born between 1912 and 1924, and sells them the paper certifying them as sons of Chin.

My father, a man named Chew, bought the paper that entitled him to enter the country as a resident, as a paper Chin. In Chinatown the real name is the Chinese name. My family association is the Lung Kong Tien Yee Benevolent Association, an alliance of the Lau, Quan, Chang, and Chew families based on the alliance of Lau, Quan, and Chang in the oath of the peach garden that begins the heroic classic *The Romance of the Three Kingdoms.* If I were a real and not a paper Chin, my family association would be the Gee How Oak Tien Benevolent Association, an alliance of the Chan (Chun, Chin,

The Three-Legged Toad

Chon), Woo, and Yuen families, also inspired by the brotherhood of the oath of the peach garden.

Big Louie did not come in as the son of a merchant. He came in as the son of a native citizen. He explains:

"In 1906, the earthquake. All those Chinese people in here, they come in here, as what they call merchants—*sang yee gee*—you know? So after they come in for a while, in 1906 the earthquake; so after the earthquake in San Francisco, they burn all the records. So all those people they want to be changed to citizens, the whores, and the tongs who bring all those womens and opium through Hong Kong—" They all claimed their records were burned in the fire, and were suddenly U.S. citizens, and had had children born here who were citizens. They counted the years and the sons and had their records and birth certificates restored. The paper sons of merchants bought only the right to enter the country and set up residence. The paper of the Chinese of the San Francisco earthquake and fire gave these sons U.S. citizenship.

"You know about *toe gee?* No? See *gee,* the word for *paper,* sounds like *gee,* the word for *cooking, gee fan,* cooking rice kind of *gee.* Sounds alike, right?

"When the opium comes in wrapped in paper, you can tell where the opium is from from the paper. The paper wrapping the opium from Hong Kong is not the same color as the opium coming from Macau. The opium from Hong Kong is better. So the wrapping paper from Hong Kong was called the *ho gee,* the 'good paper.' And that sounds like *toe gee,* meaning 'cooked here,' the slang for kids born on this side. Same sounds, different words."

"I'm a *toe gee* boy," I say. I always thought *toe gee* meant the belly of the pig, *toe* for "stomach" and *gee* for "pig." But it's *gee* for "paper" and *gee* for "cook." It was another play on *gah gee,* the fake papers of paper sons. The fake paper was the bad paper. To be born here, that was the good paper. Or was Big Louie playing language games with us?

All the languages the Chinese down here switched to and from without signaling first are jamming my brain. But Big Louie hasn't even started. He'd heard stories about the Chinese in the gold country. He tells us the story of Lodi.

"You know, like that Lodi? The Chinese peoples they had a laundry over there. And so one day those missionaries come over there and ask him for donations, and she's talking half in Chinese and half in English, see? And he can't get it. Anyway, he's asking for some donations for some kind of charity. He says he's not going to be able to help him very much because, first thing, he doesn't have any money and, another thing, he's getting pretty old and he'll be dying. And he says "getting old" and "die" in Chinese, *lo,* 'old,' and *ay,* 'man.' Old man. And he says, 'Lodi!' I don't know how true that is. But that's the story.

"See, in the old days we are Say Yup people, right? Four Towns. Sun Wooey, Toishan, Hoi Ping, Yuen Ping. The Four Towns. Way back before the war, you *yut chut moon how,* first thing out the door, if you don't speak Four Towns dialect, no one would understand what you were talking.

"The Sam Yup, of the Three Towns, are Chungshan, Poon Yur, Soon Gup.

"During that time everybody asked everybody else what Yup? what Yup you from? And right now, when you go and say *ah chin bock ngun,* nobody knows what you're talking about. In the old days they always used to say *chin bock* for a quarter, twenty-five cents, you know. And *luk yee* for policeman is from Hong Kong because the police there wear green, right? And *fahn gahn,* foreign soap, was that white people's soap powder for washing clothes."

He balks at the idea his aunt sold or he actually bought

The Three-Legged Toad

papers giving him the name Gee. "Actually they not sell it to you because they just more or less get their expenses. During the Depression, in 1930, you know, nobody hardly make any money. Whatever little money they spend, they're just trying to get it back. That's about all. They're not really trying to sell it to you or anything because she's kind of my distant aunt, anyway. Not real close."

He doesn't like the thought of people making a profit off the fake papers. His distant aunt was doing the family a service. There was no work in China. The family decided he should go to America and work and send money back home. He was eleven years old.

"I came over this country in 1930," Big Louie, Uncle Freddy's seventy-eight-year-old hunting and fishing buddy, says. "It was a Japanese line. *Shurn Yun Yerng*—I don't know how to say it Japanese. It took about twenty-four days to get over here to San Francisco. Some friends with me. My uncle, he coming back, and he has three boys with him, his own sons. Another guy, he live in Brawly—he also come, so we have five kids together. So we have a good time.

"So we went to Angel Island. And at Angel Island, I stayed over there two and a half months. Yeah, detained at Angel Island two and a half months. So they, the other kids, get out a little faster than I do. They are what they call a son of a merchant, see. When it's during that time a son of merchant comes in easier, see? And I was what they call a son of a native, a citizen, so they have to check up on me. . . .

"So I'm the one stuck for quite some time.

"During that time, I guess when those Chinese people back there, when they're back home, they don't have good bed anyway. They sleep on a piece of wood, you know, a piece of board, and it's hard. *Yut jeng deck*. A *chong bon*, you know. A bed board. And a lot of them don't even have a mattress on it, you see. But in here, Angel Island, at least they had a little

Frank Chin

mattress. It's a bunk bed. Three or four, five or six of them, all the way up to the ceiling. See, they stacked them so high, you lay in bed up there, you put your foot up there, you see?

"So they have the footprints up on the ceiling. Maybe some five or six beds—stacked 'em up—and they made footprints out all over the ceiling.

"I think after they closed the place, they took all the beds out. They see some footprints up on the ceiling, and those inspectors or whatever it is, they went over there and inspected the place, they says, "Well, those damn Chinese is a pretty smart. They can walk upside down on the ceiling!

"You just stay there and wait and worry. Yeah, worry. You don't know if you get sent back or you'll be able to get out. Sometimes they ask you questions; lotta times they just don't! They just keep delaying, and so you more or less just had to wait. There's so damn many people in there. They got about three or four hundred people at that time.

"I think I got two and half months was a lot better off than a lot of them guys who got there for three or four years. Yeah! Three or four years, then they send them back.

"I got some uncles and cousins in here. They're waiting for me in San Francisco and Modesto.

"When I get out, I went right to Modesto. When I went to Modesto, during that time, it's in May. 19 May 1930. I remember that. So I went to Modesto. I had a cousin who had a laundry over there. It's called Hop Lee Laundry. And I went to the laundry. And over there—of course, I'm just a little kid then, thirteen years old—well, I stayed over there about three or four weeks. I kinda had my setup to learn some English. A little bit here. A little bit there. So I stay in that laundry, and I learned a few words now. I know this *egg* is an egg, see. I know what *E-G-G* means. So, in the laundry, the guys want something for lunch. These Chinese guys all they do is eat *gai don goh* pie, egg pie, see.

The Three-Legged Toad

"They send me out, go over there about a block in town and get some pie. They give me about twenty-five cents. During that time, it was only twenty-five cents a pie. So I took twenty-five cents down to the grocery store. I ask the guy, I say, 'I want egg pie.'

"The guy look at me. I don't understand him. I keep saying, 'Egg pie.'

"So anyway, the guy brings me eight pies. Eight of them. So I thought, 'Well, I must have hit a bargain!' I grabbed the stuff, and turned around, and give him a quarter.

"He says, 'No! No! No! No!'

"I keep saying 'Egg pie.' But really egg pie is what they call custard pie, see.

"So later on I finally went to work with some people when I was out round the front of the Chinese laundry, and I guess, when I was thirteen years old, I was pretty cute. One of the womans came over, one of the customers come over and saw me around the front there, messing around and working, and she thought I was cute. She talked to my cousin, she said, "I want to take that boy home with me so he can stay and work for me."

"Well, during that time, you know, the Chinese didn't have no families, no kids. I'm just a little kid, more or less in the way, so they want to get rid of me—well, I don't think they wanted to get rid of me; anyhow, they wanted me to work. So she said, 'I want to take him home to work for me, and I'll teach him some English.' Her name's Carlson. A. J. Carlson.

"She's a home science teacher in Modesto Junior College. And he's also the district attorney of Modesto. And they don't have no family, see. I'm just a little kid, so I fit right into it. So I went over there and helped her to rake the lawn, water the lawn, cut the grass, and wash the dishes and do some cooking. And she taught me, and after all that I was more or

Frank Chin

less Americanized. And she set the time: 'Six o'clock, you gotta be up.'

"Of course, at first, she was doing the cooking, you know. She showed me how to cook. So after a while you catch on, you're a young kid, you know.

"So six o'clock, be up. And after a while school started in September. So I went to school. I get up at six o'clock in the morning and get the breakfast fixed up, and pretty soon I learned a little more—whatever she wanted, I fixed it up. After breakfast, I have to get over to the dishes, all washed it up, all cleaned it up by 8 o'clock, I take off, go to school. And the afternoon, around three, three thirty you get out, and you come home, work on the lawn, odds and ends, and get ready for dinnertime. And when she comes home, get the dinner ready around six o'clock, you have to eat, and you go back to room and study. I was getting pretty good. She give me $2.50 a week. And when I was there for a while, and her husband says, "You're doing pretty good. I think I'm going to give you $2.50 too." So I get a raise. $5.00 a week, room and board. Pretty good for a kid going to school.

"Every Sunday, the Carlsons, they're both playing golf. Sunday, every Sunday they both take off around six, six thirty to go to play golf, and they won't come back till noon. After they eat I can get the afternoon off. So I can just go down to Chinatown and all those things. Modesto, there were lots of Chinese. During that time I think they had a couple thousand Chinese that were there. I think in the old gold rush days they had a Chinatown. Modesto's right there on the edge of the gold country with Stockton. The Chinese called it *dai hong*, 'big valley.' They called Sacramento *Sing Yee Fow*, 'the Second Town.' Instead of saying *Sacramento*, they say Second Mento, sounds like *Second*. Just like *Marysville* is *Mee Lee Woon*. Bomb Day in Marysville. They still doing it.

The Three-Legged Toad

"In the old days they have some *Tong Yun Miew* over there. Chinese temples. Every year they have *Nien Cho Yoong Pow*, Bomb Day. So they get some what they call *doe yuen—nee gaw pow*—you know, a gun, a mortar."

"Popping firecrackers?" Pok chi asks.

"Naw, naw, naw, naw! They're using a piece of steel. Back in China they use a piece of like a pipe, something like a pipe bomb. They're sitting it on the ground. They put some powder, gunpowder in it, stomp it down. That's all. They put some paper in it on top. And they have a hole in the bottom of it, and light it; then it blows up. The pieces of paper blow up, and the people all go fight for a piece of that stuff. Who is the strongest gets it, and they take it back to the temple to leave it in there for a whole year. They say it's for good luck."

Racial discrimination is no big deal to Big Louie until his teens; then racial discrimination is not American, it's Mexican.

"I know in 1932 lot of people come over from Mexico. There was a *pie wah*. You know, the Mexican, they discriminated—they kill lots of those Chinese back there, so that therefore they gotta sneak a way over here. I know my cousin, he did. There was a *pie wah* over there, and he come over here, and he went to Stockton. And my other cousin, he went back home because he was an old man.

"You know, before there were a lot of them over there farming. They're big farmers. Cotton and all kinds of stuff on the Mexicali side. In 1937 we had to go through what they call a processing. And I get a what they call a 'citizen's crossing card.' But during that time, all the Chinese on this side from that side cannot go over there. So I get to go through all the processing with the immigrations and get a crossing card. 'For the use of resident citizen in the United States Identification Card. Issued by the Immigration and Naturalization Service, United States. . . .' The first one I got, this card, it was a pink color. They don't make this card anymore.

Frank Chin

"I stayed there in Modesto with the Carlsons for four and a half years. 1934. I just about turned eighteen, I think. Then I kinda get homesick. And I went back to China. During that time, going back to China didn't cost a lot of money; I think it was only about $95.00. Special third class. So you get a bunk to sleep on. Six people in one room. For twenty-four days you get room and board from San Francisco to Hong Kong. Twenty-four days. The name of the ship is *President Coolidge*. Yeah.

"I went back to China, and as soon as I landed over there, and go home, and the folks say they're have a wedding. I say, 'What wedding?'

"They say, 'Yours!'

"So I stayed there for a couple months before the wedding ceremony. Then after the wedding I stayed there about a year and a half. Then I come back in 1936. No, no, you can't. They won't let you bring your wife back.

"Well, one thing, I don't have any money. And another thing, they won't let you bring your wife back, anyway, during that time.

"In 1936 I had a friend from here, he's at Central Food Market, he has the name Harry Mah. You know, my wife's uncle. When he went back to China, I told him, I asked him for a job, so he says, 'You want to grocery business, you come over down here. We'll put you to work.'

"So I come down here with him. During that time, 1936, I was working in Stockton then, he come over early one morning looking for me. I was a waiter. And I run into him on my way to work. So he find me, and I quit the job over there and come with him in July. Because he drove a brand-new 1936 Chevrolet, and he said he needed someone to help him drive it all the way down.

"So we come through San Diego way. And we come through San Diego to here; it took us four and a half hours.

The Three-Legged Toad

Highway 80 at that time. The road's pretty bad then.

"I thought, I'll just come down here and visit. I'm still visiting!" He laughs and slaps his knee.

"They don't have many Chinese woman during that time, you know. When I first coming down here, you know how many Chinese woman in this town here? In this valley? Not more than six! In 1936. There were lots of Chinese in here during that time. All single men. About two or three hundred. Only about four Chinese women here. All married.

"The one I worked for, Harry Quan, his wife and his daughter. They were down here. Their market, F. Sang Loong. At Fourth and Orange. You know, right at that Fourth Street they got four Chinese grocery stores there. In just that street. First there was Peoples Food Market. Then F. Sang Loong. Then Quality Food Market. The next one was called Central Food Market. It was out of the city limits. See, out of the city limits was Fourth and Ross. See, we was out of city limits at that time; we supposed to be able to open Sunday. But during that time, they had curfew in the city; you cannot open on Sunday. So we open on Sunday out there."

I ask about a Quan that owned a store called Hong Chong and a kid they called Butch.

"Yeah, and Hong Chong. Butch. His dad owned the place. He was the butcher there, so that's why they call him Butch. That must be Henry Quan.

"Well, during that time's a whorehouses all over, anyway, what's the difference? How about here? Brawley had lots of whorehouse. And Westmoreland had lots of whorehouse. And here, just right across the street, you know, those two storage buildings—that's whorehouse. And here at Fifth Street was a whorehouse. All over.

"About six to eight months later, I get transferred to Central Food Market. I stayed there about four or four and a half years. I would deliveries and all that kind of stuff. Then in

Frank Chin

1939, I think it was '39, there was an earthquake in this valley here. I think September 1939. I think they got about six point something. The whole town was in pretty bad shape. The California Hotel was just around the corner, and the . . . hotel was over here. Very big hotel. After the earthquake they had to tear it down. And right on Main Street a man named Sim Hill, he bought some old buildings, and he remodel and fixing it. He comes to Central Food Market, he sees a guy named Joe Mah—he's a butcher over at Central Food Market—he asks him, 'Hey, Joe. Whaddaya think, I bought the building over there, what do you think I should do with it?'

"He says why don't you use that for a restaurant?

"So, okay, he fixes it. About a couple months later, and he come in there, and he says, 'Okay, it's already fixed. You better open the place up.'

"So we did. So we went over there and try to get the thing all opened up. In 1940, Christmas Eve, we opened the place up, called the Rice Bowl, on Main Street over here. After we opened it up, we had a damned good business. All kinds of business. First we had a restaurant twenty-five by fifty, we called it Rice Bowl. In '41 we opened the bar next door. And after we opened the bar next door, we had dancing and live music. So a year later we opened a liquor store right next door. We had three buildings right next to each other.

"Yeah, the war had started then. And of course, during that time, no more new place open. So we had what they called Camp Dunlap, in Niland. General Patton was down here training them tanks for the desert—And the Camp Seelye. And a lot of peoples, you know, they can't take, and they overflowed in Yuma, so they use a bus to bring here from all over. Lots of soldiers around here. See, they're going to Mexico, you see.

"And finally, the end of 1942, I left here to go to San Francisco to work in Kaiser shipyards. I was shipfitting over there.

The Three-Legged Toad

Liberty ships. Troop carriers. Cargo. I worked for Kaiser Number Two in San Francisco. Stayed there two and half years. Then I get drafted and went to Air Corps.

"End of 1944 I get drafted and went into the service. I took my basic at Shepherd Field, Wichita Falls, Texas. Yeah, nice and hot. There were three boys from here at that time. Yeah, Eddie Wong, and also Ming Woo. But we didn't see each other till the end of basic. After I finish basic, they ship me back to Leupp Field, Arizona. Just outside Phoenix. During the war there were a lot of those Chinese cadets over there. See, they're from Republic of China, Kuomintang. You know they come in there and train. So they ship me over there. They put as what they call interpreter. Hell, they don't need no interpreter because all those guys are college graduates! I stayed there about six months, and decided I was doing nothing, and decided to ship me overseas. So I went out to Truett Field, Wisconsin, near Madison, Wisconsin, for processing to go overseas.

"By the time I get all finished processing, they said, well, they're not going to need the replacements anymore.

"Well, no replacements anymore, so I eat my Thanksgiving dinner over there. It was so cold. I never see it so damn cold in my life. Day before Thanksgiving it snow for three days and three nights. You know, from California, I never seen snow like before before. So you know what they did. They didn't ship me overseas. They shipped me to Florida. Boca Raton, Florida. When I went down there, eat my Christmas dinner and went to the beach to swim. I stayed there about a year. I was a driver for the colonel. I was chauffeur for the colonel. He was the fire marshal for Boca Raton. He was from Los Angeles. Oh, we had a good time. Those guys were very, very nice, you know. When I'm inside the field, he sits in the back. As soon as we get outside the field, he says, 'I'm too damn lonesome in here. I'm going to sit and ride in the front with you.' Yeah, no kidding.

"I wanted to enlist, but the family don't want me to. Of course, during that time my family wasn't over here. My mother want me to go home as soon as I get out. When I come out, I didn't have any money, so I had to come back here and work for one year. I worked here at the Rice Bowl. I get $300 a month; one year I saved $2,700. So I took off, went back, and bring 'em all back. They come under the GI Bill of rights as war brides. My wife and a boy and girl. I was in China when the boy was born. I was here when my daughter was born.

"And when I came in, the wife and the kid had to stay in the immigration detention for nine days. No more Angel Island then. They stayed in what the Chinese called the *hoong jun low,* the red brick building. Nine stories, way up high. She stayed there nine days. The kids too. The kids were eleven and thirteen.

"We stayed in San Francisco three or four weeks to visit and came back to the Rice Bowl again. See, we had the Rice Bowl over here. I was a part owner. I don't like the big city. I love to hunt and fish. A lot of good hunting, a lot of good fishing during that time. I get up at five thirty or six o'clock in the morning, and I go hunting a little bit, until about eight o'clock. And about eight thirty I go back and open the store up.

"You know, during the duck season, we used to have lots of ducks in here. You know, the Chinese people from San Francisco, they formed a Dai Fung company organized to finish the All-American Canal, in 1937. Chinese and Hindus and all the people buy the land in Imperial. They buy at only $5.00 or $6.00 an acre. So those that buy those lands for only about $5.00 an acre—Of course, when you buy the land at $5.00 an acre, you open it up, you fix it up, you cultivate it. So the district give you all the water to leach the land, you know, get the salt out.

"See, this used to be the bottom of the ocean. So they got lot of salt down here. So they leach the salt out so they can grow something. So the salt keeps on going down to the Salton Sea. So they give you all kinds of water for leaching the fields. When they start leaching those fields, lotta ducks come in. Thousands and thousands of ducks. You get ducks early in the morning about this time of year; you get out in the morning, you see the ducks coming from San Diego ways. You know, flock after flock, they're coming in. Thousands of them.

"In 1948, a lot of Chinese women then, they come over. A lot of them come in under war brides and GI Bill of Rights. Just suddenly we get about fifty or sixty Chinese women at that time. So young Chinese women are over here, and after a while they have babies, and so five or six years later they have a school, a Chinese school in here then.

"We had three children born in this valley here. Boy, girl, boy, and girl, boy. *Mooey fah gan juk*. Plum blossoms, then bamboo. They all speak Chinese.

"They come over here to Chinese school. Before, we had a Chinese school here since 1951 or '52. As soon as the war was over, we had a Chung Wah here. We had the Kuomintang.

"See, we still have, but last year we had some teacher from Taiwan. He taught the kids Mandarin. They don't want to learn Mandarin. Now, it's the kids all grown up. No more young ones come in. Now it's just a few old guys like us that stay here.

"You talk about that Eddie Chun. He went to Chinese school in here. During that time we had about thirty or forty of those young kids in Chinese school."

Frank Chin

"I remember the *ho yeah,* you know. The good stuff. You gotta remember the *ho yeah;* you *bai sun,* pay respect to the dead, when you go somewhere you have to buy *ho yeah.* Good stuff. In other words it's a custom. Just like here. Memorial Day we all go to the cemetery. *Hang San.* Walk the mountains. We don't use the *Ching Ming,* Chinese memorial day. We use American Memorial Day, the last day in May. So anyway, we go over there, one time we take some *gee yuke,* roast pork, all the food out there, and spread it all out, and get some incense, and light it all up. So one of the American peoples—I know them, her husband is a principal at the Imperial Valley College—she walk by and saw us over there and all the incense, buns, and offerings of food. . . . Of course she didn't say anything then. She just standing right there and watch us. Then she took off.

"Then when I come back to the store, you know, she lived in Holtville, also, she said, Fred, 'I saw you over, and you had all this food and everything and burning incense. What's the meaning of it?'

"I say, 'Well, really it's not very much meaning. It's the Chinese custom. It's food for the dead.'

"Do you think your ancestors, or your friends, or whoever it is, be able to come in here and eat your food and enjoy it?'

"I say, 'No, I don't think they going to come and enjoy the foods. But that's what we hope they do.' I say, 'What do you do?'

"She say, 'Well, we just take some flowers over there.'

"I say, 'Mrs. Plus, you think your friend be able to come out and smell your flowers?'

"She say, 'No, I don't thinks so.'

"I say, 'Well, it's the same idea.' Then I explain it to her. I says, 'Way back in China. See, they don't bury in a one place.

The Three-Legged Toad

They scatter the tombs all over the place. So you gotta walk from one mountain to the other, see? See, the deal is, back over there, after you're buried three years, they dig you up again. They dig you up again, get all your bones, they put it in a crock, see? They take it somewhere else where the *fung shui sifu* says it's a good luck place. So you're scattered all over those mountains, see what I mean? Sometimes it takes you all day. So you get a whole bunch of people to help you, to carry those things over there from one place to another; then by the time, at the end of it, you eat the food, see? See, it's more or less is like a picnic. Sometime they go all day long!'"

Pok chi says, "I actually watched one of my grandmothers. After three years. You break the coffin that was in there. Bring all the pieces of bones out. And you ask a specialist to have an urn built about this size. And you're to place the bones in such a manner that it will be in position that is lucky. The skull is the last thing you put in there."

"Yes, then you can put it any place you want to," Big Louie nods.

"You can carry it and ask the *fung shui sifu* to look for a location that is good for the family, according to the year she was born and how mixed in the family, what kind of *fung shui* you want. . . . He asks a bunch of questions."

On the way out of the Chung Wah Wooey Goon building, while Uncle Freddy searches for the various light switches around the walls, Big Louie looks up and points out a piece of calligraphy glassed and framed over the doorway to Bing Kung Tong, the Chinese Freemasons, the room where they play mah jong.

"Foong Goh Book Sick, Inspired by Book Sick."

Big Louie says Generalissimo Chiang Kai-shek and his wife, Shoong Mei-ling, supposedly wrote this bit of calligraphy with their own hands as a sign of gratitude to the six towns of the Imperial Valley—El Centro, Calexico, Holtville, Niland, Brawley, Imperial—for giving a large sum of money to the Kuomintang when the Nationalists were fighting the Japanese.

"This is the hand of Chiang Kai-shek?" I ask. The hand is pretty. The calligraphy is good, but not that good.

"Supposed to be," Uncle Freddy says, makes a face, and the old men laugh.

Big Louie explains the meaning of the inscription.

"'Six towns joined together to save the country.' Chiang Kai-shek likened this act to Book Sick, who was a shepherd when Liu Bong, the first emperor of the Han, was uniting the country and wanted money. So this shepherd, Book Sick, gave him money and went off. And the emperor didn't see him again for a long time, and the next time he sees the shepherd, the shepherd asks him, 'Do you need any more money?' And he gives Liu Bong another huge amount of money. This happens two or three times, and Liu Bong says, 'You've given me so much money. Do you want to be a government official?' And Book Sick says, 'No, all I want is peace for my family, my countrymen, no bloodshed.' And he goes back to his sheep.

"Book Sick never joined the army. Chiang Kai-shek is saying, Book Sick was working as a shepherd and saving his money and giving it to the emperor Liu Bong to unite China under the Han, just like these guys in the six towns of the Imperial Valley."

A one-and-half-eyed old man who speaks a strange English, accented with the Say Yup dialect and a little back east from having learned English as an eleven-year-old houseboy in the home of the district attorney of Modesto, California, talking of Chiang Kai-shek and Shoong Mei-ling with such familiar skepticism, and Liu Bong, the first emperor of the Han, and the legendary shepherd with deep pockets, Book Sick, has suddenly cast us into a world where knowledge of Chinese

The Three-Legged Toad

folklore and childhood lit is real knowledge and glows like the granules of quartz in all the sand and all the rocks around here in the long afternoon dusk.

We had clumsily tested Big Louie with unmotivated references to Liu Bay, the last, last emperor of the Han. Here was Chiang Kai-shek, the generalissimo who copped the revolution of Sun Yat-sen and used it as a license to be a Chinese- and Western-style dictator—and whose wife's family to act like Western-style money-grubbing in-laws—who had seen enough American movies to know the smart thing to do was convert to Christianity, play it big in the West, and hush it up to the Chinese, who will be forever remembered for losing China to Mao Tse-tung and the Communists in 1949, then taking over Taiwan, and declaring it the Republic of China, and maintaining it as a police state. What a man! Here he was in the same room as Kwan Kung, Liu Bay's second brother of the oath in the peach garden, and the painting of the horse soaring over wooded geography, talking about Liu Bong, the emperor at the beginning, not the end, of the Han. And Uncle Freddy and Big Louie know it all like a nursery rhyme.

A few years ago in Seattle, Ruby Chow, the first woman to sit on the board of directors of a Chung Wah Wooey Goon, and then the first woman to become the president of a Chung Wah, ordered the girls of her Chung Wah Chinese girls drill team to roll up the windows of their cars when their mothers drove them past me on the street. I had long hair, a long, raggedy mustache, and a long look. The Chinese consul told me not to bother applying for a visa to Taiwan. I said I promised my mother I wouldn't get my hair cut till the generalissimo Chiang Kai-shek stood once again on the shores of mainland China. He didn't believe me. Ruby Chow didn't believe me. My mother didn't believe me. And Chiang Kai-shek didn't believe me either. I got no calligraphy in the mail

Frank Chin

urging me not to cut my hair. I cut my hair. Chiang Kai-shek never again set foot on mainland China.

Uncle Freddy points at the painting of the horse and says a visiting artist was inspired to stroke out a long composition of a horse soaring over a forest with brush and ink. He inscribed the painting *"Ching wan jing serng."* "Ride in the sky," Uncle Freddy translates. This is a tribute to the Mah family, not just the idea of a horse, I'm sure of it.

UNCLE FREDDY AND AUNTIE SUE

Pok chi has a talent for getting into the homes of Chinese and snapping telling pictures. We return Big Louie to Mah's Kitchen, where he'll snack on big doughy things and hot tea till his daughter picks him up. Pok chi rides with Uncle Freddy in his pickup with a camper on the back. I follow close behind as if I know what's happening. Uncle Freddy drives at thirty miles an hour on the freeway and highways. People come up on me fast at freeway speeds and shake their fists at me.

Theirs was an arranged marriage. They never set eyes on each other before they were married. She remembers being carried to the wedding ceremony in a sedan chair. Was it two guys?

"It was four guys carrying you," Uncle Freddy says.

"No, it was two!" she laughs.

It's an arranged marriage that works. He's brought home the leftovers from Mah's Kitchen. They go fishing together in the camper. They tell fish stories. Pok chi wants to see their fishing gear, their tackle boxes, their fishing poles. Uncle Freddy says he has a copy of Sun Tzu's *The Art of War* someplace in the house.

The Three-Legged Toad

Menudo at Tony's Garden, an Italian Mexican restaurant. It's upstairs in a large Quonset hut. I thought they might have a cappuccino here. No. I need something familiar to bury the grease from the big doughy things. Menudo. Pok chi's never seen menudo before. "*Ngau bok yip,*" I say, "Tripe. Lots of chili. Chopped onion. Oregano." This isn't dinner. I want dinner before we go back to the Chung Wah for tonight's meeting. I know it's a dinner meeting; that's why I want dinner first. The dinner at the meeting will probably be Chinese take-out grease. Egg rolls. Fried rice. Chow mein. Let's give our stomachs a chance to be happy the rest of the night.

Dinner at Yum Yum. A soup. Decent edge-of-the-world home cooking.

Steamed fish. Pompano. A little happy-faced fish. Once upon a time frozen, but a nice fish. The sign advertising the fish is in English and Korean. *Gai lan*. I call George Woo and have him share the fish with us.

After the raffle tickets have been accounted for and the business of the meeting and the dinner is over, I meet Henry Quan's son. He's a young-looking man, just about to turn fifty. He could pass for a man in his late thirties. Unlike George Woo, William Quan grew up with a mother.

"My name is William Quan, D.D.S. I was born December 1944. Father: Henry Quan. Also known as Quan Chew Yerng and Mah Toe wah. He was the one they called Butch. When he first came from China from Hang Lung Lee village, southern Canton—He supposedly was a pretty skinny little kid when he got here. He was tall for his age. But he was about thirteen, and his first job was at the, you know, the family-owned grocery store named Hong Chong, in the east side of El Centro. And the way I heard the story, he was such a good worker, they put him as the butcher. And as he trimmed the

Frank Chin

bologna or lunch meat, he'd never seen so much food in his whole life. And all of a sudden he's thrust into this situation where he's the butcher. And he snacked a lot on the lunch meat and stuff. I heard he ballooned to three hundred pounds from a hundred-pound kid. But being a butcher that's how he got the nickname Butch. I'm sure the neighborhood people couldn't remember the Chinese name that he had, right?

"I don't know if I'm a third generation or first generation or what. The situation was my granddad came here first. Then my dad came here second. They were both born in China. I was the first one born on this side. So what does that make me? First generation? Third generation? Or what? My mother was born in the old country, too. So my siblings and myself were the first born on American soil."

William Quan is a good man. I wish he knew more of his father's Chinese language. Names of villages. Names of his grandfathers and grandmothers. He wishes so, too. Like all the Chinese he has a strong sense of history. He says, "I have one foot in the old generation and one foot in the new. I can remember, and I experienced the old days. And I'm sort of a sentimental guy because I took it upon myself, the museum project at the Pioneer Park Museum, as a debt to the old generation. Their story must be told. But as they get older, it's like losing volumes of material, you know—history, valuable stuff that won't be around anymore."

The old Wah Kiew might have things to hide, secrets to keep, and be shy and hostile to my microphone biting a hold on their collars, catching their every breath. But they know that Pok chi and I have arrived as the agents, if not the angels, of history. Our begging the use of microphones and tape recorders and cameras in the name of objectivity is both flattering and threatening. We're not here to nail them to the family scandal, but we're not here to fake it either.

"Now, I'm what they call the proverbial—what banana-

The Three-Legged Toad

type person or what do they call that bamboo thing in the middle? *Juk sing*. Yeah, I'm a *juk sing*."

Chinese old-timers, perhaps Chinese parents used to tell the American-born kids they were useless by calling them *juk sing,* "hollow bamboo." A hollow section of bamboo was useless for carrying water. The Chinese-speaking American born would in turn call the Chinese-born Chinese *juk kock,* "stopped bamboo." A section of bamboo solid at both ends is also useless for carrying water. *Juk sing* I can understand, but why is the good dentist calling himself a banana? Yellow on the outside, white on the inside? Why put himself down?

"Yeah, my dad came through a series of stores. The one that he started at is Hong Chong Market on East Main. That's where all the family came together as they came off the ship in LA. Most of the male relatives of the Mah clan would come into Hong Chong. All my dad's cousins, they come in there and sleep there. They eat there. They work there. You know, where they waited on people was a counter, where all the boss and workers could look at the customers. And they had this string up there, and it'd come from a little loop on the roof, come down to tie packages, and to tie around these boxes to make them a little taller so you could stack more groceries in.

"Wooden floors. And in the butcher shop where my dad used to cut meat, since it was a communal store, they would all sit down after work at this little discarded chopping block, and we'd stand on soda boxes, and we'd eat there. And they had these claw things on the end of a pole and claw these cans up on the shelves. And my brother, he's into antiques and managed to salvage one of these things.

"That was at the first store. Mostly Negro and Mexican. Then at the second store, on the west side of Fourth Street, which was to my dad an improvement, instead of the east side of Fourth Street. It was still Mexican and Negro and a mix of the low end of the Anglo neighborhood.

"I remember playing in the grocery store. The store sold Christmas trees at Christmas time. And they'd stack them up in stacks outside, and I'd be running around. Playing cowboys and Indians between the Christmas trees. One situation I remember, the story's told to me. I craved soda pop. Evidently at age six or seven they refused to give me any more soda pop. I drank too much. Then being the creative-type person that I am, I went out there in the backyard and pooled all these bottles of half-drank soda. You know, put 'em all in one. And I supposedly just walked in the store drinking soda pop like crazy. And they just about kicked my butt. They couldn't believe what I'd done. As a kid, I was thirsty for soda pop. So that's what I got.

"You know I understand we had a Negro woman who was a teacher. I kind of vaguely remember her visually, but I can't put a name to her. She tutored us. She taught us English. I remember this woman, she must have been well traveled; she had one of these Viewmasters, that old 3-D viewer. I must have gotten an interest in the world at large through this thing because television was barely around at that point. I remember we supposedly had one of the first TVs among the Chinese here.

"I think my dad was very progressive for his time. I guess he came from China with nothing. And he wanted to make sure we were taught well. We had the latest things, like air-conditioning, TV, and stuff like that.

"He didn't make me work in the store. That's funny. You know, my dad came up the hard way, right, from China? He had to make his own living, even though he was surrounded by all the family members. Then when it came time for me to work in the store, he didn't make me work. You know what

The Three-Legged Toad

he did? He made me go to the back room in the warehouse—I stacked all these boxes of groceries around. I made myself a desk. And he made me sit at that homemade desk and study.

"So what does that mean? He had an idea that education was a way to improve yourself in this new land, right? So, ever since I can remember, he might have me be the cashier, but he never had me stock groceries, sweep floors, or nothing. He had me study. My sisters. They didn't do anything either. They just stayed home. Now my brother did basically the same thing to the point where, you know, you grow up thinking, 'Oh, gee, I am a good cashier. And I can study well. . . .'

"My first paying job was at another family-owned supermarket called New Star. You were just talking to the fellow there next to me, Eddie Wong. He's the manager now and part owner with my mom. But my first job, when I walked in here, I was age seventeen. I must have had this swollen head or something. You know, we're coming from this background where I didn't really work. I decided I needed a job, get my own money and stuff like that. So I figured I'd walk in as a manager, or at least assistant manager, because my dad owned this store.

"I walked in there, boy was my ego shattered because I expected a desk job and they handed me this stupid broom and told me to go sweep the floor! I told myself, I don't even do this at home! What am I doing, doing this here? But my dad had told me before I went for this job, he said, 'You know, I might own this store, but you have to listen to the boss that is there. You do everything he tells you to do. And you'd better do it, or I'm going to kick your butt when you get back if I hear you didn't do it right.'

"So I reluctantly picked up that broom and cleaned the bathrooms and everything. And I couldn't believe my dad would make me do this kind of stuff.

"But as the years go by," the dentist nods. "My dad was

Frank Chin

crazy like a fox. That was a very good beginning for me because that summer I learned how to work. I learned how to take orders. Because there'll come a time later, in our lives, we'll give the orders, but at first we'd better know how to take orders. So I learned that very well.

"And let's admit it, back in those days, there was prejudice! This town was actually separated. The minorities were on this side of the tracks. And everyone else, the Anglo population, was on the other side of the tracks. Here were the Hispanics, and the Negro people at that point, and here were these FOB Chinese, coming fresh off the boat—you know, they identified with each other. And Mrs. McGee and her family, they were very good friends with my folks, especially my dad. They shopped at the store. He gave them credit and stuff. They kind of developed together.

"I can remember on this main street here called Imperial Avenue, I can remember as a kid in the early fifties, we were told, You can't live on the west side of Imperial. You have to live on the east side of Imperial Avenue. I took that as a challenge, myself. As a kid I remember hearing that, and I go, Who do they think they are to tell us that we can't go that way! I think that's part of the way I developed. And that really bothered me.

"Maybe in school your classmate will say, 'Hey, you Chink. You're a Ching Chong Chinaman sitting on a fence.'. . . All that kind of stuff. I'd whup 'em. I'd get into a lot of fights over that. I wasn't the one to sit back and take it. I was more active. So I didn't like that kind of stuff. There wasn't that much. It wasn't that bad. I really can't say I experienced that much discrimination."

White girls asked him out. He thought about it, he says. His father never told him not to go out with white girls. He says, "If I didn't look in the mirror every day and see I wasn't the blond, blue-eyed kid I thought I was, I might have gone

The Three-Legged Toad

out with them." There were simply more white girls than Chinese girls. A lot more.

"I think my dad and mom was more traditional. The two boys went to college. The daughters, especially the younger daughter, wasn't educated much. The older daughter, my bigger sister, I must admit, I think intelligence-wise, she had more on the ball than I did, but, you know, she didn't go far in her education. She married early and became a businessman along with her husband. And I went to college. And my brother went to college.

"I must have been six or seven when I started Chinese school. But you know, I hated Chinese school. Why did I need Chinese for? I was a *juk sing*. I spent half the time my hand paddled, sitting on the wall, sitting in the corner. I can't remember anything positive about Chinese school. I must have learned something. Because in my predental schooling, I happened to go up to my maternal grandparents' house in the Redondo Beach–Culver City–LA area. I spent a year with them to save costs on schooling. I lived with them. And they didn't speak English. I didn't speak Chinese. I *thought* I didn't speak Chinese. But you go deep at that point, pull something out, and say *something* to your grandparents, right? So, lo and behold, that year I spent up there was very helpful for me. It either jarred my memory, or *I learned Chinese!* And I know enough spoken Cantonese Say Yup dialect that I can get by. I don't understand Taiwan, Hong Kong dialect, but I can get by. I cannot read. I cannot write. But I can speak elementary Cantonese Say Yup dialect."

I ask him if his brothers and sisters had birthday parties and got birthday presents and celebrated Christmas with Christmas presents. He answers nodding his head as if birthday presents and Christmas presents were nothing unusual.

I tell them of all the people I've spoken with, he's the only

Frank Chin

one whose family had birthday parties and Christmas presents for the kids.

"See, my dad, I think, was more progressive than the average Chinese from his village. Just progressive is a good way to describe him. And yet, you know, he never asked for much. You know, when I graduated, I knew there was no strings attached, like I told you. I think I took him out to dinner once before he died. He died a year after I graduated. I know he was proud of me and all. There was no strings attached.

"My dad didn't deal out the punishment. My mother, she was the one dealt out the punishment when you're bad. And I have nickname of Ngun Pay—that means "Thick Skin," you know. Must mean "Independent Kid," that's the way I take it, because my ma would tell me to go left, I'd go right, on purpose! And the teacher in Chinese school would try to teach all this stuff. Hey, I didn't have any use for this!

"Hey, my older sister. She's the one. I don't get along with her to this day! She's the one that always made life miserable for me, and she got me in trouble that day. And my dad stepped in. He didn't know what was happening. I said, 'This is none of your business. This is between me and my sister!' And I decked him. I gave him a black eye. That's unheard of, in Chinese! And my grandmother, this ninety-seven-year-old woman, I remember she's the one that stepped in at that point. She told us all just to cool down, you know. I was *juk sing*. I was Western. My dad was traditional. I was about seventeen at that stage. I figured, after I decked him, I figured he was going to ban me out of the house forever. But see, he swallowed his pride, as I look back now. My mom soothed him down. My grandmother soothed him down. He actually ignored me for the rest of the year because, shit! That was a bad situation. I was really sorry that I did it afterward.

"Yeah, my dad had a lot of balls to swallow his pride and

do that. I don't even know if I would be able to do that with my kids, you know?"

Self-deprecating, sincere, yearning. "My heart is still back there in that grocery store."

He tells me something I never heard of before. Paper women. In the fifties, to get away from the Communists, his grandmother became a paper woman.

Dr. Quan says, "Mah Yee Shurn Toy, my paternal grandmother, she supposedly had a little farm in a little village, and my dad and my granddad would send supposedly gold coins or something to her for her subsidy, right? So she got labeled rich landowner or quote-unquote whatever—and when the Communist Chinese took over, they made her kneel on glass, hung her up by her toes upside down, and whatever they did to torture her, she won't tell us it's so painful. We asked her from time to time, you know. When we think she's in a receptive mood, we go, 'Hey, grandma, what was it like?' Nothing! It was so painful she won't say nothing.

"She experienced the changeover from Nationalist to Communist.

"I think most of the Chinese from the twenties and thirties immigration days, they're more loyal to Chiang Kai-shek. See, I don't know all that stuff."

Sure he does. He's playing the hick country boy just a little too hard. The old Wah Kiew were loyal to Chiang Kai-shek. Chiang's Kuomintang Nationalist China celebrated the Tenth of October, the Tenth Day of the Tenth Month, or Double Ten Day, as the day the Manchu were toppled and dynastic China was no more. The Communists celebrate the First of October as the end of imperial China. The Chinese, especially the Tang people, the southerners who settled in the Americas, see a big, not a subtle, difference between the Nationalists and the Communists. The all-American, Westernized dentist knows the difference.

Frank Chin

"But, you know, it's funny, my father's mother got out on a paper name as our maid. We couldn't bring her over as my grandmother. I heard something like, if you promise someone a job, you can bring 'em over. My dad somehow got her over as the maid to take care of us as we're growing up. In public we were never supposed to call her Grandma, Ah–Paw Paw because someone would find out and ask, Hey, how come you're calling that maid your grandmother?"

"So she came over on *gah gee,* fake papers.

"They actually tried to get her over before my paternal grandfather died. Her husband. That was in 1955. They tried like heck to get her over, but didn't make it. She came over like two months after he passed away. So they never saw each other.

"He had actually left her like maybe twenty or thirty years prior, you know, the typical Chinese experience. Come over here, the males will work like slaves, and they never see their family again. But they got her over as a maid; then somehow she got to stay. And she's still here."

His language. He uses *going* to mean "thinking" or "saying to myself."

"We were one of the first Chinese to get a TV is the way I heard it. In 1955 I started watching TV. I remember all those Howdy Doody–, the Red Ryder–type programs. Whereas my wife, same age and everything, they didn't get their TV for another ten years. She kept listening to the radio, the Green Hornet and all that.

"Seventeen years old. Friday, Saturday night. I'm not that independent. I'd be in the back room studying. My friends, they'd be out cruising the streets. Going out to beer parties, smoking cigarettes. We didn't have anything worse than that back then. Maybe drinking beer. My friends would go, Hey, let's go get drunk! Go find some hookers! This is high school, you know.

The Three-Legged Toad

"I'm going, No, I don't want do any of that kind of stuff. Maybe I wanted to, but I knew I couldn't go anyhow. So why worry about it? I'll just be at the store. Then at the store my friends would come by, and they'd go, Hey, sell us a pack of cigarettes. At that time you couldn't sell cigarettes to underage kids, but peer pressure, you know, I go, Oh, yeah, okay. Don't tell my dad. Here's a couple packs of cigarettes. So there was a way I had of fitting in, but I didn't really do all that extracurricular activities.

"I remember once, I wanted so badly to throw some eggs at something! You know when my friends would drive around, you throw eggs at people's cars—and I'm going, I got all these eggs here, and I don't even know what to do with them. So I took a couple out there, and I threw at the neighbor's car.

"It's not that my dad told me flat out I couldn't go out there and have fun. My thing was to be around the store, even though I didn't work there much, just to be there, I guess. They never told me.

"My wife, she'd go to all the games and all of that. She was very Western, but when she got home, she was very traditional. There are two sides to everything. I thought I was independent. But I stayed home a lot.

"I married a local girl. As a matter of fact, we used to run around this Chinese school together when we were little. Of course, I didn't know who she was at that time because who was interested in girls at that time? But they took this picture of the Chinese school class of 1957 or something, and, lo and behold, I'm sitting there next to her! I always played with her brothers and everyone else. Her dad used to be very prominent in this local El Centro community. He would be in charge of the Chinese Benevolent Association, the principal of the school. He'd actually take it upon himself, the Ten Ten dinner, the New Year's dinner, and he'd have everything pre-

Frank Chin

pared, and everyone would come in and eat and leave, and he'd be there—not only did he prepare it, he had to clean up afterward. And I found that out because after we got married, I was on the cleanup crew, too. And I'm going, I didn't used to do this! What's the deal here?"

Pok chi is out with the old men of the Chung Wah, skimming the pond for gossip. The pictures of two Mahs are on the wall, past presidents of the Chung Wah. The little speaker's stage is backed with the crossed flags of the United States and the Republic of China, portraits of Dr. Sun Yat-sen, Generalissimo Chiang Kai-shek, his successor and coincidentally his son, Chiang Ching kuo, the ruthless police-state tyrant turned benevolent populist, and the current president of the Republic of China (Taiwan), Lee Teng-hui, a Taiwanese, not a Chinese born in China. On the American side of the wall are the portraits of Nixon, Carter, and Reagan. Clinton hasn't entered this time zone yet.

Dr. Quan says, "My father sent me through school. Financially I had nothing to worry about. Tuition-wise, books, everything, room and board was all paid for. I went through the local system here, through junior college, then USC dental school.

"He went to my graduation. And these business cards. I think, in that one year he was still alive after my graduation, he passed out more of my cards than I have in the last twenty-five years.

"Oh yeah, my mom came to my graduation. And she's still alive. She's about seventy-five years old. We try to include her in everything that we do. I know we go out to eat a lot now. As a kid, you know? We never went to eat out. I'm not kidding you. The first time I saw a sandwich in a restaurant—my cousin Lloyd took me out—I didn't know how to eat it! We were used to eating at home, you know. And then one of my dad's first cousins, he took us out to eat breakfast once in LA,

The Three-Legged Toad

you know, when we made a trip. I didn't even know how to eat with a knife and fork! So now we go out and eat a lot.

"I didn't really appreciate how much my dad was forking over for the tuition until just in the last six years because my daughter went into dental school at USC and I realized it wasn't cheap. I had, at one time, three in college at the same time, and then, having experienced that, I go, Man! I don't know how my dad, being a groceryman, sent me!

"And like my dad said to me, I told my kids, because my daughter graduated as a dentist just a couple months ago. She asked me, 'You know, Dad, now that I've graduated, what should I pay you back?' She knew, herself, it was a tremendous burden.

"I told her, 'My dad sent me. My obligation was to send you. And there were no strings attached. You just go out and make me proud of you. That's it.'

"And I hope when it comes her turn to keep the family going, that she will do the same thing for her children."

He went to Chinese school but knows Kwan Kung only as a "figurine they put oranges around." He says his family wasn't religious. Neither was Kwan Kung. His father's store probably had a Kwan Kung on the wall behind the counter, but there's no point in asking him. For all his lack of Chinese knowledge and cliché misconceptions about Chinese culture and Chinese tradition being based in religion like the West, acting and speaking from his gut Henry Quan's first son acts and sounds very Chinese. So why did he come back to the valley?

"I'm a simple guy. I grew up in this environment. I experienced life in the big city. It's okay. I think, being married at the time—My wife and I are both from this area, both sides of the family are in this area, our roots here are deep. So when it came time to find a place to practice, in my mind there was no other place. There was nowhere else in the world I wanted

Frank Chin

to go to. When I got out of dental school, there was no other place I wanted to be except the west side of Imperial Avenue.

"Maybe, through limited experience, or whatever, or respect for the elders because, now they're proud of you, you come back as a doctor, you're from a grocery store family, you know this is your place in life, right here. So I came back. My brother came back. My sisters never left. Their husbands were in the service, and they came back.

"Maybe I ought to give my parents credit. They instilled in us this sense of community. Then I ask myself, What happened to me? My children want to go to LA!"

Now we talk of paper sons and paper names. Fake papers and fake names. And the sons of paper sons living the hush or being kept stupid about dad's real name. What does this mean to your name, son of a paper son?

His father, Henry Quan, was a paper son, a paper Mah. He knows that and is not touchy about it. Other paper sons around the valley have been giving up their paper names and taking back the name Mah. The horse. He doesn't do it because it's too much trouble, or he's lazy, or he doesn't care after all this time. All the Chinese around know he's a Mah.

I understand his problem and lack of a problem. My father was a paper son. He made the real family name, Chew, my middle name, so my name is Frank Chew Chin. It took me a while to figure it out. The explanations about why my Chinese family name was different from my "American" name made no sense. Nobody wanted to confess to being a paper son before 1966 and an amnesty and naturalized citizenship for paper sons who confessed. This is America, the wild west, where names don't matter, where you make a name for yourself and nobody asks questions about the past.

He understands. He says he did the same thing for his sons. Made the family name, Mah, their middle name. Though

The Three-Legged Toad

we're nothing alike, different in our understanding of the Chinese, we seem to have come to the same conclusions about how to reconcile our names with our history.

To all the Chinese here, the old *Wah Kiew,* the Chung Wah Wooey Goon, the connections to the old times and old-timers, the Mah family, the Chinese here are history. They talk like they're extinct already.

The Chinese putting money behind the Peso stores along Imperial Avenue, and shopping centers anticipating the new port of entry, are from Hong Kong, using Chinese restaurants and shopping centers as their Swiss bank. When Hong Kong goes back to the Communists in 1997, their money will be safe till they can catch up with it.

Then there are the Chinese Mexicans who run businesses in Mexicali and own nice homes on the U.S. side of the border in the Imperial Valley. They don't seem to be brooding on extinction.

WEDNESDAY, 16 FEBRUARY, EVERYBODY'S BIRTHDAY, ASH WEDNESDAY

Over a breakfast of *chorizo con huevos* at the De Anza Hotel with George Woo, Carlos Auyon says his father's uncle came over on a Chinese junk, a kind of wide-bodied junk called a cattle boat because it was used to carry cattle. His father married an Indian woman, Florinda Gerrardo, in Chiapas. He managed the brewery. Taught the local Indians how to run the brewery.

He and two others were born in Mexico. He is the only one of those three to return to Mexico. The others are living in Hong Kong. His brother Eduardo was born in China.

The Auyon family has become one of the first families—if not the first family—of the Chinese of Mexicali.

Frank Chin

Carlos was president of the Mexicali Chung Wah Wooey Goon. The Chung Wah building fronts on a street lined with Auyon family and Chinese businesses. Carlos' insurance agency is next door to the office of Dr. Enrique Auyon Tam—his son the doctor. Next door is the gate to the Centro de Investigacion de la Cultura China, the Center for the Study of Chinese Culture. This is the domain of Carlos' youngest brother, Eduardo, or Professor Eduardo Auyon Gerrardo. The baby of the family, born in China, now fifty-nine years old, is a brush-and-ink artist crazy about wild, riderless Chinese horses.

Eduardo is shorter than Carlos, more intense, and looks strangely like the young Tony Curtis playing Ira Hayes, the American Indian U.S. Marine immortalized in Abe Rosenthal's snap of the marines raising the flag on Mount Suribachi, Iwo Jima, in World War II. John Wayne died in the movie *The Sands of Iwo Jima*. I don't remark on the resemblance or the movies. As the Johnny Cash song goes, "Who remembers Ira Hayes?"

He calls himself "El Dragon Celestial." A Chinaman has to have balls to call himself a dragon in the face of other Chinese. A Chinese Mexican mestizo who looks like Tony Curtis and wears his hair like Elvis is plain crazy to put on his black smock with the dragons embroidered all over it and paint horses to a cassette of wind, rain, and thunder playing on a little boom box. Hmmm. Stereo. He opened a kung fu studio. The signs announced he taught Shaolin 5 animals, a little *choy lee fut,* and *chee kung*. He has researched, written, and illustrated a history of the Chinese in Mexicali—*El Dragon en el Desierto: Los Pioneros Chinos en Mexicali*—that toward the end becomes heavy with pictures of the celestial dragon with beauty queens and tall women in tight sequined gowns.

What counts is the opening chapters. The pictures snapped of him talking with the old-timers, the old men that old men

The Three-Legged Toad

across the border have heard about, mean something. He did his homework before he posed in dark glasses with beauty queens.

1902—We can say this year marked the first arrival of the Chinese pioneers of Mexicali.

Mr. Mariano Ma, also known as Ma Lean and Mr. Chang Pei established themselves in Ensenada in 1890. Later they crossed the desert, moved along the coast of San Felipe and finally settled in Mexicali. In an interview, Mr. Mariano Ma said, "The road lasted 26 days approximately, those days were very hard and very heavy on us."

Mariano Ma, yes. The Ma family. The horse has come to triumph in the valley. Uncle Freddy had talked about a Ma Leong. Mariano, also known as Ma Lean, is the same Ma Leong Uncle Freddy knew.

Mariano Ma lived in Algondones, worked for the benefit of the community and they honored him by naming a city street after him. He was well thought of by all the people who called to him, "TaTa Mariano Ma."

Guillermo Andrade transferred a parcel of 90,469 hectareas in the Mexicali Valley at a cost of 60 cents an hectarea, between the Sierra de Cucapá mountains and the Colorado River. The region covered 283,290 hectareas.

Otis and Chandler contracted Chinese to California to farm corn, barley, cotton and alfalfa.

The first group of Chinese laborers arrived in 1903. 22 persons, including Mariano Ma, Ung, Chan Lei and Ramon Lee, contracted by the Colorado River Land Company to level roads and canals. The pay was 50 cents, 25 cents more than the cost of their food. They lived in cabins, tents, or huts built under the trees, the walls were of wood and adobe, sticks, etc. Mariano Ma said:

"In this place were many mosquitos, many died because of the

Frank Chin

various sicknesses caused by the bites of flies and rattlesnakes, by the intense heat of the place."

Carlos' wife is dressed up, done up and made up well, dignified, not trashy, not flashy. When there was an opera and music club in Mexicali, she enjoyed singing. I'm sad to hear the Mexicali music club didn't survive. Yes, when the opera comes to the border, to Mexicali, it is always special. Now she has a karaoke machine at home and sings karaoke.

She met and married Carlos in Macao. They lived in the same building and saw each other in passing. He noticed her. She noticed him. He did not notice her noticing him. She did not notice him noticing her. I've seen this Hong Kong movie before, haven't I? She finally met him at a meeting of his theater group. Oh, Carlos had a theater group in Macao. She came out to audition for the first play he was directing, *Thunderstorm*. Pok chi hasn't heard of *Thunderstorm* and repeats the name in Cantonese without any lights flashing in his head.

Thunderstorm was billed as the first Chinese play written in the Western, naturalistic, Ibsenesque manner. Three acts of turgid, melodramatic elephantiasis from the thirties or forties . . . though it feels like it should be from the teens. The writing has pimples.

Carlos was a teacher, a student of Portuguese, a scoutmaster, a theater director. His wife met him at the theater and likes to sing. Interesting couple.

I ask Carlos about tunnels under the border, and he laughs. "There was no fence or barriers on the border until the thirties. There was no reason to dig any tunnels. One could just walk across the border back and forth without any worries. So why waste your time digging a tunnel? The Chinese did dig holes in the ground, line the walls with wood, put up a roof, and live in holes and caves. It was a way to get away from the heat. When the Chinese first came, there was nothing in Mex-

The Three-Legged Toad

icali. They built it up. Mexicali at first was an all-Chinese town. There's a bit of the first settlement left called the Chinesca."

"I've heard about a place where many Chinese died, called Chino Mountain," I say.

"Yes," Carlos says. "There is a Chino Mountain, but it's not called Chino Mountain. It's La Sierra Cucapá." He turns to a page in his brother's book.

1908—A group of Chinese braceros moving up from the south of Sonora set sail in a small boat piloted by a Japanese. Part of the group came looking for jobs because their contracts were completed where they had been working; the others heard was easy to find work and make a lot of money in Mexicali. So they left Sonora by boat bound for the coast of San Felipe. The people in charge of guiding the group of Chinese braceros, on seeing that it was impossible to take a boat to Mexicali, showed them the road to Mexicali and left them there, a group of Chinese braceros along on the road. After a few days on the road without knowing where they were, and without a compass to guide them, they were lost. Desperate and tired they set out wandering aimlessly; hungry and thirsty with a temperature reaching 125 °F they began to die one by one.

The Sierra Cucapá where the Chinese braceros died is known as "Sierra de los Chinos" or "El Chinero." These facts were confirmed by Mr. Chan Fuk Yau, one of the survivors of this trek from Sonora to Mexicali, who was interviewed at the age of 103.

Carlos' brother's book says Mr. Chan Fuk Yau lived out his last days at the Gee How Oak Tien, an alliance of three families. People with the family names Chan, Woo, and Yuen are members of the Gee How Oak Tien society. We have to meet this brother.

Groups of women in overcoats walk into the De Anza coffee shop. Rain is expected in San Diego, but here it's sunny and already around seventy degrees. Why are all these young

Frank Chin

women wearing overcoats? Do they think it's cold outside?

"Mothers bring their children from Mexicali to school in Calexico. Catholic school. Then they stop by here for coffee," Carlos says.

Ah, I understand. So when they came over earlier this morning with their children, the morning was colder. The De Anza Hotel coffee shop is the Moriesque house where the Old Woman Who Makes Swell Doughnuts lives. This is the depot of folklore.

Carlos is now sixty-three, closer to sixty-four, he says. He's Chinese and Mexican, speaks very good Cantonese for smart people with a Mexican accent, and speaks Spanish like the native Mexican he is. He looks sort of Chinese, Chinese enough to make me happy, but his eyelashes are long. Chinese have short eyelashes. I learned to look at Chinese eyelashes from Frank Capra. When he cast Nils Asther, a white man, to play General Yen in *The Bitter Tea of General Yen,* starring Barbara Stanwyck, Capra had Asther's eyelashes trimmed and messed up the Swedish actor's eyes. Swedes have long eyelashes because they need long eyelashes. Carlos' lushly lashed eyes droop a little, Tallulah Bankhead eyes, panda bear eyes. His cheeks pudge a little. He has a soft, cuddly look. He has a soft, cuddly voice. He speaks with a smile and an ease as if he has all the time in the world, even when he says he has a meeting back on the Mexicali side at 1 P.M. in the afternoon.

His Chinese name is Ngau Yerng Fay. Non-Chinese know him as Carlos Auyon Gerrardo.

"I was born in 1922, in Montocintura, a town near Palanque, in Chiapas, Mexico. There, perhaps when my father was there, there were more Chinese. Now there aren't very many people of any kind. Chinese didn't move out there to build their own coffee plantations. Mostly it was the Germans, people from Germany, who had the large plantations. The Chinese who came came as contract laborers. My father, he

The Three-Legged Toad

was just eleven years old at the time he came, was like the others a contract laborer. He came to Mexico in a junk to pick coffee."

"A junk? A Chinese junk?" I ask. The Chinese junk is a flat boat. It has no keel to keep it steady in the moving sea. It is an okay river boat and okay following coasts, but on the open sea, the junk is not the boat most likely to make it across the Pacific. But the one carrying Manuel Auyon and six other Chinese laborers made it. And apparently so did many others. That's something I never saw in a Charlie Chan movie—Chinese junks, two-masted flat boats with square sails and big rudders, carried the first "coolies" to Chile, and Manzanillo, and Acapulco, and the Sonora. If you lived, you owed the contractor money for the next ten years.

"The coffee plantations in those days were run by *Toe Yun* Indians. Chinese: there were very few staying there and working.

"Back in the old days my father's uncle, when he was a very young man, developed an instinct for doing business. Back there in Moctoxintlan, it was just one little village. He built a distillery, then a brewery, then a soda pop plant, then a sugar refinery, all when he was just a young man. His shops occupied an entire block. My father ran the brewery. Then when he married my mother, Florinda Gerrardo, my mother helped him. He said with the money he had sent back to China, he had saved enough to support us and our families for five generations.

"When I was four, I heard lots of people saying, Gran China! Gran China!—talking up China as the world's greatest civilization, a country where people knew things other people in the world never heard of. When you're a little older, I'll take the whole family to China. He didn't want us to be without a country. He wasn't sure what Mexico would do with the Chinese.

Frank Chin

"Then he took the whole family back to China with him, and after one or two years, then I came back to Mexico to work in the brewery. Then he sold it all, everything, and we went back to China.

"We weren't in China very long when World War II began, so we couldn't return to Mexico. Now we're stranded. My father tells us, 'You came here to this place, now, we have no idea of when we can return, now there are no boats and no planes to take us back to Mexico. So the thing to do is go to school, learn a lot or a little Chinese, and when you go back to Mexico, you'll find it useful.' So all of us enrolled in school.

"At the beginning, my mother had a hard time of it. In China you find very few Mexicans speaking Mexican Spanish. She goes back to China and finds her father-in-law, mother-in-law, our grandparents are all Chinese, so she has no choice but to learn Chinese.

"World War II lasted about ten years in China. Then the Nationalists and the Communists go to war. We were running this way and that.

"My father said we should all finish school before coming back. My father wasn't in business in China; he bought farm-land in Chungshan and leased it. So, when the Communists came, my father was one of the first people they arrested as a big landlord. And he lost it all."

Pok chi is moved to say, "Wow, you've seen hard times."

Carlos Auyon chuckles. Hard times are his meat. "Back then a lot of people were being arrested and having their money confiscated. Chinese were sweeping other Chinese from place to place like dust. China wasn't a very hospitable place for Chinese after it turned Communist. So Chungshan was finished for us. We ran down to Macao. Macao is Portuguese.

"When we fled to Macao, it was very difficult. There was nothing to eat. Macao depended on Chungshan for rice and staples, and there was war in Chungshan. There was nothing. Even if you had money there was nothing to buy. Christian charities kept us fed.

"My father had several thousand dollars in American money saved for us in a Mexican bank. So, should we ever return to Mexico, we had a well.

"When the Communists came, they arrested my mother and made him give them all the money before they would release her and let her out of the country. My mother told them, 'I'm a Mexican woman, not a Chinese. That money was made in Mexico by a Mexican citizen, not in China by a Chinese.'

"The Communists didn't care. They made my father transfer all the money to a Hong Kong bank before they released her and she joined us in Macao.

"I taught school in Macao. I taught Chinese language and culture. I had a law degree from Canton and was qualified to do more than teach, but getting a job teaching grade school was the easy thing to do. Back then there were a lot of Wah Kiew Chinese schools.

"I taught Chinese in several grades and several subjects in the daytime. And at night I studied Portuguese. Every grade had its textbooks and curriculum set by the Department of Education. At first you teach 'up,' 'down,' 'eye,' 'hand,' 'nose.' Everything is regulated. But a teacher is required to teach everything. Language. Literature. History. In secondary school, I even taught physical education. Calisthenics. Soccer. Basketball. Gymnastics. Yeah. When I was in school studying literature I enjoyed gymnastics very much. I learned a few things, so when I was a teacher, I had a few things to teach.

"Then after I was there three or four years, the viceroy of Macao was looking for somebody who was fluent in Chinese language and Portuguese to be his translator. So I showed up for the test with eighteen other candidates, and I got the job.

Frank Chin

"When I got married was around '63, '64. My wife had a brother in Macao, her father and mother and brothers and sisters in Hong Kong, and an older brother and a female relative in San Francisco. And we told her San Francisco and Mexicali are very close. Everybody's always seeing everybody else's face.

"At that time we had three children.

"I lived a good life. I was in a world of black and white. As the viceroy's translator, all the criminals were brought before me, and I translated for them. Out of the lawyer's hearing I would tell them what they should say to get time off and how they should speak in court if they hoped to get off. And in court I would translate for the viceroy and the accused criminal. They were members of triad societies, and they always gave me a lot of face. See me on the street, How are you? Have you eaten rice yet? Join me for tea?

"I remember I had a friend who lost his wallet, or had his pocket picked, or maybe was hit and had his wallet stolen on Cho Dur Street in Macao. I knew which triad controlled this turf. Mr. Lerng Hung. His flower name was Um Say Um Hur, 'If He's Not Dead, Don't Go.'

"I said, 'Hello Mr. Leong. A little matter. I have a friend who lost his wallet on Cho Dur Street. I don't know if he dropped it and lost it or someone hit him and took it. Could you look into it for me?'

"'I'll take care of it in two hours' time,' he said.

"Two hours later he calls me and tells me to ask my friend if he has his wallet back yet. I did, and he had. So the black societies were very nice and gave me a lot of face. We would go out to restaurants, and a bill would never come. We would be invited to their New Year's spring banquets and sit near the head table. They would invite us to the opera and invite us out to drink.

"My mother had Mexican women's society in Macao, and they're always writing letters back to the Mexican government

The Three-Legged Toad

saying, 'We have a lot of boys and girls stranded in China. Circumstances being so uncertain, we want to return to Mexico.'

"The president of Mexico sent two men over to investigate. They could speak Mexican Spanish, but they couldn't speak English very well and couldn't speak Chinese at all.

"The Mexican government offered Mexican people in China *repatriado,* repatriation, to bring them to Mexico via Hong Kong. In Hong Kong they'd catch an airplane. My mother was a Mexican. I was a Mexican. Chinese origin didn't matter. You could be Japanese Mexican, or Chinese Mexican. If you were a Mexican, you could be *repatriado* and all come back together.

"There were a lot of Mexicans living in China who no longer knew how to speak Mexican Spanish. So how are you going to know where you live? So at that time they were looking for people to help, so I offered my help.

"And as these people we've helped get their papers to return to Mexico are boarding the airplane, the Mexican representative asks me, 'Why aren't you going back to Mexico? You're a Mexican.'

"We found everybody else and forgot me.

"Back in the old days my father became a Mexican citizen. And my mother was a Mexican. And all of us children born in Mexico were Mexicans. So they brought us all back in a group to Mexico in 1966. We stayed in Macao more than six years before coming back to Mexico. That's how I came back to this place.

"We came back to nothing in Mexicali. We lived in the Colonia. Sheds. Pigpens. Dirt floor. No indoor plumbing. No sewage system, so if it rained, you couldn't go out in the street. And when we came, there were sandstorms. It was very hard on my wife. She didn't know how to speak or write the language. And when the sandstorms came up, the three kids would get sick."

Frank Chin

Carlos worked for a bank. The Chinese trusted him, and he courted Chinese to deposit their money in the bank rather than keep it in holes dug under the floors of their house, and slowly dug his family out of the house with a dirt floor, and opened a shoe store, and was as tireless as a dragon and as gallant as the horse.

LUNCH WITH SEÑORA AUYON

We meet Carlos' wife back in the coffee shop. She's sitting at the head of a group of the first young Chinese women Pok chi and I have seen in this place. They're well dressed, well groomed. Overcoats. Young mothers. They look almost too young to be young mothers. Where have they been? Will we see them again?

We follow Carlos across the border into Mexicali. It's not the shock to the system Tijuana is. The slums are not up against the border here. We park in front of his brother's Centro de Investigación de la Cultura China. We get out of the car and hear birds in torment. A parrot screams bloody murder across the street. This whole block is Auyon businesses and the Chung Wah Wooey Goon. Across the street with the parrot are two Chinese restaurants. The real neon fantasy sleaze of their signs blues the blue air mumbling promises of rain. A young Chinese kid walks by wearing glasses and a school backpack and looking guilty of something. Pok chi points him out to me. "That's the first Chinese kid we've seen!"

As the kid strides by us with his head lowered, I jerk my head up and ask, "*Way! Ah-kit doy ahh!* Hey, kid!"

The kid stops and turns around with his mouth open.

"*Gwai jie muh?* You been a good boy?" I gruff.

"*Gwai!* Good!" the kid says, turns, and runs.

"I always wanted to do that," I say.

The Three-Legged Toad

Señora Auyon takes us by her son's doctor's office to meet her son the doctor and for a walk around the immediate neighborhood near the border. The Chung Wah Wooey Goon in Mexicali now displays the red flag of the People's Republic of China. Mexico recognizes the PRC and not Taiwan. The Wah Kiew loyal to Taiwan, or the old Chung Wah, or the history of the bachelor society that built Mexicali to the point where it supported twenty-nine family associations and tongs and two Cantonese opera houses in the late twenties, take refuge in the Chungshan Gay Niem Tong, the private Chungshan Benevolent Association, a temple in Eduardo's compound.

Inside the temple are lion drums with the heads of dancing lions sitting on them. The silk, papier-mâché, and bamboo heads are tattered. The drumheads are split and cannot be played. Against a wall, between the lions and drums, stands a portrait of Dr. Sun Yat-sen in a dark military uniform.

On the street she tells us she cried every day when she first came to Mexicali. She wanted to go back to Macao. Three children. No running water. No indoor plumbing. Such dirt and filth all around. She didn't speak or understand Spanish. It was awful. She didn't speak a word for seven years. Then there was nothing else to do but let go and open her mouth and try to speak Spanish.

I turn to find Pok chi stopped in the middle of a decision in the middle of the street. "That woman has a funny black mark between her eyes!" he says low and urgent. "I've been thinking of taking her picture."

"It's Ash Wednesday," I say.

"Ash Wednesday. What's that?"

"It's a Catholic thing they do before Easter," I say. "It's also a real bad movie with Elizabeth Taylor. But it's religious, so don't get too snappy over black marks between the eyes today."

Frank Chin

Señora Auyon leads us around the potholes and cracks in the street in her high heels. She can't wear flat shoes, she says. As we walk, a Mexican woman comes out of her shoe store to give her a hug and a kiss. Her Chinese husband follows with a little girl about five or six. Their grandchild. Señora Auyon is the queen of the street. Shop after shop, these are her people.

We pass a storefront with a large sign, "Wong's," on our way to lunch at the Hong Kong. Señora Auyon tells us the Wongs worked very hard. For all their success and wealth they still work hard. They work so hard they eat their meals standing up. A Wong son was kidnapped, and the Wongs paid the million-dollar ransom. The son was released. The kidnappers, as far as she knows, were never caught. A million dollars for one son. She wonders if one son is worth it. What happened to the Wongs made all Chinese think. All her children are grown and married. They're spread out around Mexico and the United States. There's going to be a taco party to celebrate the birthday of one of her grandchildren tonight; why don't we come along? Pok chi's up for it. He volunteers to take pictures.

Lunch at the Hong Kong. A steamed black bass. A real fish. Nice. Pok chi is very happy. The rest of the lunch is okay, just okay.

PROFESSOR EDUARDO AUYON GERRARDO

The clouds growl overhead. They clench darkness in their teeth, and bump shoulders and chests, and blot up the sunlight. Against the back wall of a building fronting the street the professor's built a little wire-walled room, two feet wide, eight feet long, and eight feet tall, with corrugated fiberglass, roomy enough for his yellow, green, and blue parakeets to fly.

The yakking parakeets sound like hundreds of happy corks squeaking out of hundreds of bottles of sparkling champagne

The Three-Legged Toad

outside Professor Auyon's door and under the branches of a cottonwood he's somehow cajoled and persuaded to pass for a willow tree. The shade it makes is real. A fast-moving cloud drops big gobby raindrops the size of eggs down over Mexicali. They hit the walls and the ground and crack like shots. The air stays hot. The rain never makes it through the leaves of the professor's tree. The cement and the birds under the tree stay dry. The sound of the rain bouncing through the leaves makes standing under the tree watching the professor's parakeets squawk feel like someplace I'd like to live for a while.

The self-made professor who would be a playboy and a hustler of Chinese artsy-fartsy hoochie-koochie is too much the classic Chinese hermit alone driven by his art, his horses, and his knowledge and not greed to be the ruthless, heartless hustler. The handsome artist is going a little to pot. The hustler went to pot and bailed a long time ago. His struggle with his artistic and his hustling self battles in front of us as he tells us his books in Chinese and Spanish on the history of the Chinese in Mexicali *ayer y hoy,* yesterday and today, are $25.00 *may gum,* American gold, then a couple of minutes looking through books later tells us actually the price is $50.00 American. Okay. We'll be hustled because the information in the book is complete with telephone numbers and addresses and looks like the real thing.

I ask him why he's made a specialty of brush painting the horse.

He says the horse is a symbol of the artistic achievement and power of the Tang dynasty to the Tang people. Individual, personal, private power, not state power, not power delegated from the state, but raw personal power: that's the horse. The riderless horse. The horse that has never been saddled. Everybody who's ever picked up a Chinese brush and ink attempts a wild horse, after they get tired of doing bamboo, birds, and shrimp.

Frank Chin

Eduardo clears his desk and announces he will paint a horse for us to commemorate our meeting in Mexicali. He shows us the paper he will use. The smooth side. The rough side. To the naked eye both sides of the white paper look the same. He paints on the rough side. When the ink touches the paper, the paper will immediately begin sponging up the ink, so he must see what he is doing before he does it. He will put on his special smock, clear his head, and paint to Chinese music, and when he hears the rain and the thunder, he will begin painting. He closes and locks the doors. He adjusts the lighting. He stands behind his desk and calls the girl he lets occupy one of the little rooms out back of the temple with her two children. She's a kid herself. He says he's also trying to teach her to read. She's his nominal assistant. He calls her, and she answers, "Si, maestro!" and brings him his black silk smock with golden dragons embroidered on it. She helps him slip it on, and takes his jacket, and stands to the side, and looks on reverentially. There are pictures of his wife in a Chinese jacket, doing it better. But we won't know that's his wife till he tells us she died forty days ago.

He prepares his brushes. He prepares his ink. A little ground inkstick in a little bottled Chinese black ink. A little water. People usually pay a thousand dollars for one of these paintings, but he will do this one for us as a gift. His assistant pops a cassette in the boom box. Rain. Rain. Thunder and rain. Eduardo dips his brush in the water, in the ink, and lays three or four short strokes across the blank paper. He paints.

It's raining when we get back to the car. Real rain. The streets quickly puddle up.

Pok goes to the birthday party for their granddaughter; I stay in Calexico, have a chicken dinner alone, and take a long walk.

Pok chi comes back from the taco party for the Auyon's grandson's birthday. He says they all wore black marks.

The Three-Legged Toad

They're all Catholic. Think of the *pie wahs,* the periods of riots and discrimination against the Chinese Carlos and Big Louie and George Woo talked about. Becoming a Catholic is good strategy for a Chinese in business in Mexico wanting to stay in business in Mexico.

THURSDAY, 17 FEBRUARY, THE DAY OF THE WHEAT

Yut gay pong sun. "One skill next to the body." It loses everything in translation. The pun on *skill* and *whore* can't be duplicated in English. *Gay* in Chinese is skill, and another *gay* is whore. The real laugh comes from inside the tellers and listeners of this joke. Old men who remember the old men who came to America as boys. No Chinese women in America. Uncle Freddy tells me and Pok chi when he came to El Centro in 1936, there were two hundred Chinese men and four Chinese women. They were the wives of merchants. No Chinese whores for the two hundred hardworking and horny Chinese men. Just down the road from El Centro is Calexico, and just the other side of Calexico is Mexicali. More puns. Between Calexico and Mexicali runs the U.S.-Mexican border. In Mexicali is the Instituto de Investigación de Cultura China, the domain of Professor Eduardo Auyon, a passionate, tender, grieving man who seems to aspire toward being a big-time artist hustler but has too much respect for the Chinese culture he studies, defends, and practices in his little re-creation of a Chinese village compound with a pond of goldfish at the base of the pedestal bearing a bust of Dr. Sun Yat-sen or Shurn Chungshan Sin Sang, "the Gentleman from Chungshan," who led the revolution that ended the Manchu dynasty and dynastic China in 1911, a tree, a large open cage of chattering parakeets, behind the walls of the Del Valle Hotel and the Chung Wah Wooey Goon building.

Here it is quiet and a million miles from the potholes, the

Frank Chin

parked cars, and the bustling and busting dusty happening just outside his gate, on the street. The compound centers around the Chungshan Benevolent Association temple, the main building. Smaller buildings once housed the down-and-out, the passersby, the dying old men of Chungshan. Around the entrance and yard and walks are little shrines covered with ash and the sticks of burnt-out incense, to the memory of the pioneers from Chungshan who died here.

Before taking us out to visit the Chinese section of the graveyard, where his wife, who died forty days ago, is buried, he tells us of a man of Chungshan who was seventy-eight years old, had come to the American continent when he was ten, and in all his life had never had a woman. Eduardo, who presents himself as a kind of gentle, ascetic mystic of the four treasures of the scholar—the inkstone, the inkstick, the brush, the paper—paid for a whore for a night for the old man before he died. The old man couldn't get it up. "He couldn't get his little head to rise. He broke down and cried. The whore was kind and tried to help him get it up all night long, but no luck." Eduardo sighs.

"And the whore burst into tears!" Pok chi laughs. I understand all the Chinese and laugh. Listen to the Chinaman artists and keepers of the memories and history laugh at the loneliness of our old men.

In the car he says there was another old Chinaman who died here who had come to Mexico as a boy, and grew up without any experience with women, and was so crazed with horniness when the Cantonese opera came to town and he saw the beautiful *fah dan,* the female lead, flutter about the stage he took his hard-on out of his pants, and jerked off in the theater, and was jerking himself off even as other horny men with more decorum dragged him out of the theater, and he had to be locked up at the temple till he calmed down. We laugh again. Being a Chinaman in the desert was sad.

The Three-Legged Toad

Maria Lau Lopez Auyon was a beauty. At least Eduardo painted her as a beauty several times. They met in Kong Chow. They married in China, and he brought her to Mexicali, Baja California, Mexico. Here he taught art, painted Chinese horses. They had a boy and a girl. The boy now imports used American cars. His Mexican daughter-in-law cooks *foo ngooey hom ha* better than his wife. His wife fell ill and went into a coma for ten days. Eduardo painted himself and Maria Lau Lopez Auyon as a pair of horses. One dark. One white. She revived, and he nursed her back to health. He studied the healing arts and massaged his wife with knowing hands. Years later she's struck down by a heart attack. He is driven to paint another painting of the dark horse and white horse together. She survives. Years pass. She dies for the third time and is gone. It's a beautiful story as he drives out to the cemetery past houses made of spit and mud and through a landscape that stinks of the shiny, odd-colored sludge frosting the waters that trickle down the banks of ravines.

The cemetery is built on landfill. A river of silvery, milky slime runs along the edge. It seems to have seethed its way through the landfill, exposing layers of colored rags and garbage and a mix of dirt and paper and plastic geegaws and leafy stuff that poses as earth. Thousands of slabs and monuments and crosses made of an aggregate fake marble lay sort of level, tipping a little this way and that, about a quarter of a mile to each side of the narrow path we drive down between the Mexican side and the Chinese side of the cemetery. He has done the calligraphy on the Chinese stones of many of the dead. No one else knows how to write a formal textual style. He does it for free. He can't charge people for doing such a thing. He can't hustle them in their grief. Too much heart.

Frank Chin

When I turn away, Eduardo grabs his wife's marker with both of his hands and drops his head. I ask Pok chi later if he got the shot. He says he did and feels terrible about it. That's his job, I tell him. My job is to go home with memories. His job is to drop the shutter and go home and make pictures.

Everybody here, Mexican and Chinese, is buried in holes dug in garbage. At the official entrance to the cemetery, beyond the little bit of pitiful lawn, people seem to be picnicking in the rain. They're on both sides of the seam of slime scratching out the edges of the banks, mining the garbage for a living.

Several of the crosses and monuments on the Chinese graves are tipped over and oddly broken and broken into. Eduardo says an earthquake knocked them down. But earthquakes don't break open little gates, and break out the glass, and tear out the photos of the dead cemented to the stone at the back of the niche. I see a little owl standing in the shade of an overturned monument. Big eyes. The *mau tau ying,* the cat-faced bird. I wish I hadn't seen that bird staring out at me from a Chinese grave.

We leave Mexicali and drive to El Centro and Lee-Louie's farm, buy a box of lily root, and it's raining when we're on I-8 west toward San Diego in search of a dinner of Japanese sushi and the best cappuccino in America. Before we bring Arturo Wu over here for sushi in San Diego, we're going to try it out, see if there is any decent sushi in San Diego.

"Really?" Pok chi the fisherman asks.

"Really," I say. "I'm all peopled out. One more tough-as-nails Chinaman telling me another story of the miserable Cultural Revolution teaching 'em how to eat shit, and coming over in a leaky boat, and crossing the desert barefoot without food or water, and learning the secret of growing lily root, and bringing a hundred members of his family over, and buying each of them a big Chinese restaurant, and I'm going to roll over and throw up. Let's find a motel in San Diego, and go get some good sushi, and come home to middle-class luxury a while."

We're running toward the sunset now and are making long, smooth curves up mountains of rock. I see a palm tree sprouting by the roadside up here. It looks like a joke, a sign of visitors from alien civilizations. Pok chi didn't see it.

FRIDAY, 18 FEBRUARY, THE JADE EMPEROR'S BIRTHDAY

Across the border into Tijuana. I think I'm ready for Arturo Wu. We stop at the Flor de Loto, "Comida China, Mexicana, y Americana," and ask for the *patrón*. Jesus Chon is sleeping. He won't be in till two thirty in the afternoon. We take a few pictures. I have a bottle of Squirt. An old, thin man with white, white hair walks in. He is not the *patrón*, but a friend, an employee. He says he's been here some forty plus years, and my ears perk up. Pok chi introduces him to me, saying, "This is Mr. Hui Kai hing," in Chinese.

"Where is he from?" I ask in English.

"Canton, China," Mr. Hui says in English.

"Nay sick gong Ying Mun ahh!" Pok says, startled, "You speak English!" in Cantonese.

"Any question you want to ask me, I can understand. I can speak Spanish, too," Mr. Hui says.

"What year did you come over? *Nay gay nien gaw lay ahh?*" I'm talking more languages at once than I can understand.

"*Ngaw Yut gow say yow bot nien, chut yurt, lay luh!* I came over in 1948, in July!"

He tells us about the Tarahumanara Indians of Ciudad Cuauhtemor, Chihuahua. "They're taller than six feet. They say they're Mongolians who walked across the land bridge from Siberia to Alaska and down to Mexico. They look Chi-

Frank Chin

nese or Mongolian. They didn't like the Mexicans, and the Mexicans didn't like them. The Mexicans cheated them, sold them rotten goods. The Chinese didn't cheat them. They liked the Chinese. And once there was a Chinese wearing a sombrero. And they stopped him and told him to never wear a sombrero, the Indians might mistake him for a Mexican. In this part of Mexico it was better to be mistaken for Chinese or be a Chinese mistaken for an Indian than a Mexican."

Good story. Pok chi likes the story. I like the story.

We have come to the right place and the right man. Mr. Kai hing, a.k.a. Fernando Hui, a.k.a. Frank Hui, has been everywhere and seen everything and been to every Chinatown and Chinese hangout in Mexico. He and his friend the *patrón,* Jesus Chon, are the only Chinamen left in the world who value Chinese culture and collect the history of the Chinese in Mexico. He has worked in Chinese restaurants and kitchens all over Canada, the United States, and Mexico. He married a Mexican woman and has a son and a daughter. They have a little house on the U.S. side of the border, in San Ysidro. He doesn't want to be a burden on his wife and sleeps over here on the Tijuana side, in a room at the back of the Wah Kiew Hing Wooey, upstairs, above the restaurant. He hangs out in the restaurant, helping out and talking with his friend the *patrón.* And on weekends he sells T-shirts he has bought for $2.00 in the United States for $3.00 in a flea market over here and gives the money to his wife to help the family out.

He asks Pok chi, "*Nay hie Herng Ha, hie bin doe uh?* What part of Herng Hah are you from?"

"Sun Wooey," Pok chi answers.

"I'm from Toishan," Fernando Hui says. "Now I'll talk. In Mexican history, before 1942 there was no problem with citizenship and customs and immigration. Once you're here, nobody knows where you're from. You're a citizen.

"The first Chinese that came here settled in Manzanillo,

The Three-Legged Toad

Mazatlan, Vera Cruz, the port towns, with harbors. They came over in *junco junks* used for carrying cattle. *Ngau goo toong shurn.* They came to Acapulco in 1864. That boat is a monument dedicated to the Chinese in Acapulco. That monument is called La Nau de China.

"The first Chinese were contract laborers. The largest number of Chinese contract laborers went to Mexicali. They first came to Mexicali in 1923 because there was a campaign of discrimination against the Chinese in Torreaon, Chihuahua, Sinaloa, and Sonora. They drove the Chinese out. They said the Chinese had displaced Mexicans and succeeded in businesses that exploited the suffering of the Mexican people. They say the campaign against the Chinese was launched by people who owed the Chinese money.

"Why did so many Chinese come? They were promised land. The land was desert. They open it, work it, cultivate it, it belongs to them. As much as they can plow. How come the Chinese of Mexicali have so much money? They plowed up all that land. Farmed it. Then by 1930–33 Mexicali had thirty thousand people.

"Wong Fung churk. He owned all the businesses in Torrean. The electronics store, the bank, the laundry, the machine shop. He also owned a ranch, Kwangtung Yuen. He had a school for Chinese kids. And this General Plutarco Elías-Calles thought he owned too much and wanted to buy all of Wong's businesses. Wong refused to sell. When Elías-Calles became president, he launched a campaign of discrimination against the Chinese in the state of Coahuila. They all ran to Mexicali.

"Elías-Calles' face is on the one-hundred-peso note.

"In 1934 the president of the Republic was Lanzaro Cárdena. He was good friends with another Wong. Wong Way or Jose Wong."

And he tells another sad story about another Wong.

Frank Chin

Mr. Hui, a.k.a. Fernando Hui, a.k.a. Frank Hui, was nineteen when he crossed the Pacific on the *General Gordon,* the first of the American Presidents Line ships. He was small and looked young for his age. It was 1949, and he was avoiding being drafted by the Communists to fight the Nationalists and avoiding being drafted by Chiang Kai-shek's wobbly Nationalists to fight the Communists.

"I come from Toishan to Canton. Canton to Hong Kong. Hong Kong to Shanghai. Shanghai to Yokohama. Yokohama to Hawai'i. Honolulu to San Francisco. San Francisco change to train to Los Angeles. Los Angeles to El Paso. El Paso, Texas, cross the border to Ciudad Juarez, Mexico. I study English about two years in Canton but cannot make a conversation. Now I speak English because I work almost ten years in the United States. I chose Mexico because I had my father in Torreon.

"Hur Gum Baw. My father didn't have to buy a paper name to come to Mexico. Before 1942 there was no immigration department.

"In Mexico City, there's another Wong. Wong Chung fook. They call him Chocolate Wong. Very rich. Very privileged. He had a house within a three-mile security radius around the president's Pink House. Anybody else with a house in that zone, the government bought your property in the name of national security, but they didn't bother Chocolate Wong. The presidents of Mexico have come and gone. The estate of Chocolate Wong is still there, and his family still lives there.

"He came around 1905, and he died around 1970. I knew him personally in 1964. He made chocolate better than anyone else in Mexico. His chocolate is really very good. It doesn't melt in the heat like other chocolate. His chocolate is called *Chocolate Wong* right on the label, and it's famous all the way into Central America. Oh, yeah, his family's very rich. There's an Edificio Wong in Mexico City."

The Three-Legged Toad

Times haven't changed for the Chinese. They want to come to America. And in America there are Chinese always ready to help Chinese.

Fernando Hui says, "The year before last the Mexican government had a law that allowed Chinese to turn their tourist visas into resident visas. There's never been such a law. This law is especially good to the Chinese because there are Chinese who are willing to pay for good law."

This old man has no intention or dream of going back to China to live out his life. No. His life, his friends, his family, all are over here. He has a son in his thirties working at Home Depot and a daughter at the Broadway department store.

He guides us to Seto's restaurant, where we're to meet Arturo Wu at three. Pok chi gives several nice lily root to Seto and several to Arturo when he arrives.

Arturo throws the lily root into his Buick and leads us out of Tijuana past huge new hotels to a shopping mall where his new restaurant seats six or seven hundred easily.

Arturo asks what we're drinking. I say, "Beer. Cerveza."

"No, you drink what I drink," he says into my eyes.

"I drink what you drink," I say.

A waiter brings up a new quart bottle of Martell's VSOP brandy.

Arturo also imports silk-screened T-shirts. Container loads come over to him. He sells them to big buyers, chain stores, department stores. Money. Making money is easy after learning how to work like the peasants. His son shows up and asks him for money. Arturo Wu introduces us. The kid is unimpressed and uninterested. The kid in baggy clothes and a baseball cap asks for money to catch the bus home. He wants American money, not Mexican money. The good father Arturo peels off a five-dollar bill. The kid palms and pockets the money and is gone without a handshake.

Frank Chin

Arturo and I down another drink. He likes this brandy, he says, and makes a joke about the brandy's effect on the length of his ejaculation that catches Pok chi by surprise.

The food arrives from the kitchen. Arturo doesn't eat. He drinks and nibbles. The lily root with roast duck is so-so. Nothing special. Nice fresh lily root, but nothing special. The salt-and-pepper shrimp is out of the shell and not spicy at all.

The waiter stands next to our table and makes glazed flaming bananas for dessert. Mr. Hui says he knows how to make flaming bananas and describes the process. He asks Arturo about buying a couple dozen T-shirts. Arturo says we're drinking and bullshitting now, it's not the right time to talk business.

Somewhere around two-thirds of the bottle empty, Arturo Wu orders a platter of deep-fried squid on stir-fried bean sprouts. After some squid and another gulp of brandy Arturo tells Pok chi to try the bean sprouts. "The bean sprouts are the best part," he says.

On the way back to the Flor de Loto with Fernando Hui, we tell him to be careful with Arturo Wu. Arturo deals in hundreds of gross of T-shirts, not dozens.

The *patrón* of the Café Flor de Loto, old Chan-bok, notes Pok chi's family name is Lau, the same Lau as Lau, also spelled Low or Lowe for the respectively old and fancy, as Lau Bay (Liu Pei) and my family name was Chew, the same Chew as Chew Gee Lung of the Lau, Kwan, Chang, and Chew family association based on the brotherhood of the oath of the peach garden that opens the heroic classic *Romance of the Three Kingdoms*. Chew, my legendary ancestor, was a kind of foster child of the brothers of the peach garden. Chew was never in the peach garden. I tell the old man of Tijuana's Chinese my mother was a Kwan and I consider myself more a Kwan than a Chew. Kwan Kung, the second brother of the oath, is, in

The Three-Legged Toad

today's folklore, the god of war, plunder, and literature. A plastic vacuform relief portrait of Kwan Kung, his son, Kwan Ping, and his squire, Chow Chong, behind him, hangs on the side of the large stainless steel beer and soda-pop cooler with the glass doors. Kwan Kung was the most popular role model out of the pages of childhood adventure novels and popular culture among the first *Wah Kiew*, the first overseas Chinese who came and settled here before World War II.

Chan-bok, the *patrón* of the Flor de Loto, "Comidas Chinos, Mexicanos y Americana," is so happy to see us tears come into his eyes. He swallows hard and studies our faces again. My face is red from having been drunk under the table by Arturo Wu. And Pok chi's face is white under the pale blue glow of the fluorescents. A prophecy seems to have come true. One day two of the three brothers will come bumbling into Tijuana. Lau will be respectful, gracious, knowing, royal, and humble. Kwan will be a glowering, red-faced drunk. And, lo and behold, we drive up with old man Hui.

He uses an old word Pok chi doesn't understand. He says this word explains the *Wah Kiew's* way of life in Tijuana and America. He fumbles with the Chinese and finally writes the Spanish word for it on a paper napkin. "ESTRATEGIA." All block letters in black marker.

"Strategy!" I say, and point at the word. "There it is, Pok. The Chinese lived by strategy."

"Yes," Jesus Chon agrees. That's exactly what he means. Then these old Chinese who came over as young boys and lived by strategy had to know Sun Tzu's *Art of War*. Yes, he knows Sun Tzu. He goes behind the counter and comes back with a copy of the book translated by Yeng Chen, published by the Confucius Publishing Company, in Chinese and English. Here he was, a Chinaman out of the heroic tradition. A couple of old boys who'd read *The Romance of the Three Kingdoms* and *The Outlaws of the Water Margin* and *Monkey's*

Frank Chin

Journey to the West, and heard about foxes and tigers and toads and wild geese in their childhoods in China, and taught Chinese language and culture upstairs in the Wah Kiew Hip Wooey hall to Chinese children in the fifties, sixties, and seventies till they stopped coming. There's a vacuformed plastic relief of Kwan Kung on the side of his soda-pop cooler. There's the paper napkin with the word *strategy* printed on it and the book of Sun Tzu itself. I have Pok chi ask him what, after all his years living here and watching the passage of the Chinese and their business in Tijuana, he wants remembered about them.

"There isn't anything worth remembering," he says. "They survived, worked hard, married Mexican women, had children, and the children are Mexican, not Chinese. They're not interested in Chinese history, or Chinese language, or how the Chinese survived here. They don't care. They don't want to know. They're useless. Nothing Chinese about them."

I think he's being a little extreme, perhaps scolding his twenty-five-year-old son Rafael in a language he has no ear for and doesn't speak a little unjustly. Rafael seems to have an ear for his father's Cantonese as good as mine. And he seems interested in the Chinese old men and the stories and the books we pull out of his father and his friend Fernando Hui.

In telling us his life story he says, "I was like a toad jumping after money in a well." Pok chi stops and turns to make sure I heard. "This is a very important line," he says. "Ah-Chon bok says in America he was chasing money like a toad jumping in a well."

That's what that story means. We identify with the toad? The toad is the Chinese as world traveler, as migrant, as Rumpelstiltskin. Yuck. The bachelor society. Old man Chon understands, knows the story, looks on himself as the toad, and says doing anything to make money was the Chinese bachelor jumping like toads in a well.

The Three-Legged Toad

Ah-Chan-bok turns to Pok chi and says, "I have this book. *The History of the Chinese in Tijuana.* My sons are useless. They have no Chinese heart. You are a better keeper of this book than me." He gives the book to Pok chi. I can't believe it. I grab Pok chi's camera and move around to snap a few shots of the old man and Pok chi at the table with this book between them as they chat.

Old man Chon traveled around Mexico interviewing old Chinese and researching the history of the Chinese in Mexico before he wrote his book. Old man Hui, who still seems to have itchy feet ready to travel, is the only Chinaman left in Tijuana who cares, who has a sense of history. Old man Chon is a toad. The Flor de Loto is his well. His power to travel in time is his book. In Mexicali, Professor Eduardo Auyon Gerrardo is a toad. And his Centro de Investigacion de Cultura China is his pond. And he has his book. And west of Imperial in El Centro, Dr. William Quan, D.D.S., is an American-born toad. The Chinese gallery in the Pioneer Park Museum is time machine and pond. The books and the museum echo the accomplishment of Confucius. Confucius recovered knowledge that had been lost and ways that had been abandoned. Old men. Alone in their wells with all they know and all their books, wondering who knows, who cares. And I come hopping along.

On the road back to LA Pok chi asks if I believed what Arturo said about the effect of Martell's on his ejaculation. Pok chi takes everything too seriously. What Arturo was doing with his cronies around him, brushing off business, was bullshitting with the guys. It was dirty jokes, gross talk, bragging, lies, and tall tales. Primitive Chinese bonding ceremony, like arm wrestling and pissing outdoors.

Pok chi is skeptical, then asks if I have the book old Chonbok gave him. No. Whoops. One of us toads messed up. Pok says he plans to go back, tow his boat behind him, and do

Frank Chin

some fishing. He'll pick up the book then. He wants to hire old Fernando Hui to show him the old haunts of the Chinese around Mexico for a month.

Yeah, I'm relieved to hear that. We compare notes on the food. We agree about the lily root and shrimp.

"You know, the bean sprouts under the fried squid was really the best thing there."

SATURDAY, 19 FEBRUARY, THE DAY OF THE STONES

Back in LA I pull off the freeway into Chinatown and find all traffic diverted around Chinatown. The Chinese New Year's parade is in progress. It's still daylight. No more night parades since the riots. The parade is led off by Johnny Something or Other, wearing his trademark yachting cap, a smiling old Chinese-American old-timer of the Los Angeles Chinese Historical Society, carrying a bright American flag. The audience is mostly new Chinese immigrants from Vietnam. They have old-timers of their own. They don't know Johnny or the Chinese Chamber of Commerce.

The Chinese Chamber of Commerce is the power of the parade. After them march the real powers of Chinatown, in blue suits, and dark ties, some red ties, with red ribbons on their lapels, the leaders of the wooey goon, the associations, the tongs. The most powerful this year seems to be the Teo Chau Wooey Goon, southern Chinese, Vietnamese ethnic Chinese. Their temple on Broadway occupies what was once a Bank of America branch building. It is a temple to Kwan Kung, the exemplar of righteousness and justice, the god of war, plunder, and literature, the embodiment of personal integrity, the defender of all borders. The Teo Chow are not timid about announcing they are not timid people. They march first.

It's still daylight. I get glimpses of flashy uniforms and flags

The Three-Legged Toad

and the tips of massed batons as I drive the detour and look up the cross streets.

Later that night I meet Pok chi and his friends for great Chinese food in Monterey Park. Lightly poached geoduck as close to raw as they can get it, with a soy, sesame, chili, and green onion dip. Fish lips with sea cucumber. A lamb brisket casserole with dried bean curd. A dish of lily root sautéed with Chinese side pork and green pea pods and orange carrots for color and contrasting crunch. Great food. A big restaurant full of chomping people and noisy kids. A statue of Kwan Kung, the god of war, plunder, and literature, and a distant relative of mine, in a shrine overlooking the cash and door. The memory of all the mediocre and downright awful Chinese food inflicted on us is gone.

The house is different when I get back. The first thing I do is sweep the floor.

I look in the mirror and look a thousand years older than all the Chinamen I've talked to put together. My hair is thinner; I'm more bald than when I left. Most of my hair is white now. When I left a week ago, it was black. My eyes are tired from reading too many road signs in the rain at dusk and at night. The horoscope says everybody dogs it this year. Hard work and tough going for everybody, even people born in the year of the dog. The dog has just begun. I think I'll go down to Chinatown tomorrow and buy a nice toad and drop it in my well. I can use all the luck I can get.

Frank Chin

SINGAPORE TV CALLING

Just before the Chinese new year Singapore TV calls me up on my unlisted number. How did they do that? They're coming to the United States to interview Chinese American writers in August, and they want to interview me. I don't sniff a hinky. I'm too stupid to be surprised at this attention from apparent Asians from Asia. I've never had any before, but it's obvious, I've been around so long and written so much, anyone interested in Chinese American writing is bound to know me. Yeah, sure. I see Sun Tzu the strategist turning away and shaking his head. What's he want me to do? Kill all scouts? Whaddaya mean I've let flattery snuff my bullshit detector? Hey, Sun, come back here; let's talk about this. . . .

Betsy, my daughter, is visiting from back east. "Why does Singapore want to interview you?" she asks me. A very adult and obvious question. Thirty years old already. I didn't tell her any Chinese stories when she was a child. I didn't know any

A Chinaman in Singapore

Chinese stories then. She looks like my mother by a young Modigliani.

"Why does Singapore want to interview you?" Sam, my ten-year-old boy, asks.

"Because I'm a famous Chinese American writer," I say. "They know I am the only one who does not fake it! They know I'm the real thing." I dream out loud.

Singapore TV calls again in late February. Six months later, in August, they phone they're in town and come with a crew of five and a Chinese American guide slouching in an unbuttoned suit. They set up around the condo pool. Lights on light stands. Reflectors on light stands. A Betacam on a monster tripod. The camera-ready producer buttoned up in a crisp dark suit and tie and the short-haired big-breasted production assistant in jeans push their English as more English than mine. "What prompted you to trace your ancestry back nine hundred years?" she asks, to see what my voice does to their needles.

The wireless mikes don't work. They rewire the producer in a suit. Then me. The producer in a suit asks me, "What had prompted you to trace your ancestry back nine hundred years?"

"I haven't traced my ancestry back nine hundred years," I say.

The suit and the girl assistant exchange accusing looks, and he asks me, "What prompted you to write the book *Ancestors?*"

"Nothing. I didn't write the book *Ancestors,*" I say.

"You said you were Frank Chin!" Production Assistant shouts, huffy, offended.

"I am Frank Chin."

"Frank Chin the writer!" she shouts.

The people with earphones on stiffen their backs and go pie eyed.

"I *am* Frank Chin the writer," I say.

Frank Chin

"You said you wrote *Ancestors!*" Production Assistant shouts at me.

"No, I didn't," I say.

They stare at me. Nobody understands my English.

"You came to me," I say. "You called me. My number is an unlisted number. And it's unlisted in my wife's name, not mine. You did not get my number by dialing information and asking for it. If you had asked me if I was the author of *Ancestors*, I would have said no. You didn't ask."

"What do you write?" she sneers, bug-eyed, flopping sweat. In my face.

"You're looking for Frank Ching, a China-born writer who used to work for the *New York Times*. He's been living in Hong Kong or Taiwan the last five or six years now."

Singapore Producer gets himself together and asks a hard-hitting question: "Are you a *published* writer?"

They won't let go. The camera's still rolling. It's gotta be my fault. I tricked Singapore TV into crossing the Pacific to interview me.

"Wait here," I say, and go inside. I tell Betsy and Dana and Sam the truth about Singapore TV coming to interview the famous me. They all laugh and shriek and have trouble swallowing their food. I go back with copies of my books. I lay them out on the aluminum poolside table with a hole in the center for the pole of a beach umbrella. "If you want to look at my books, you're going to have to buy them first. Cash only. I don't make change." Three paperback books. All he has is a fifty-dollar bill. I snatch the bill. "Sold!" I say. "I'll be inside. Let me know if you want to talk to me or not."

They decide to interview me anyway. Gee, thanks.

They hate me. They love Maxine Hong Kingston and Amy Tan. They like the idea of falsifying Chinese culture in the name of art and Westernization. They are admitted and joyous white supremacists. British-influenced education. When

A Chinaman in Singapore

they say "the queen's English," they mean Queen Victoria. Cambridge form exams to graduate high school. The nine-teenth-century raj lives on. They're shocked to hear me say texts do not change. Aha! A flash from the mind of the British white racist yellow colonial: Texts change! That's why Singapore is European, not Asian. Owooooo! Hear that wolf? I tell them Chinese fairy tales. I tell them at a certain age of adulthood we discover we are all like Monkey: born adults, naked, stupid, and totally ignorant. All the world is at war against our individual personal integrity. My friend Sun Tzu the strategist says, "All warfare is based on deception." The acme of military skill is to win without losing a life or taking a life. The first strategy we have to learn is how to make the difference between the real and the fake so that we cannot be tricked and used to work against our own interests.

"The fairy tales and adventures of that tradition, specific texts, are what Kingston and Tan falsify by name. And you don't care? You cheer it on? But if I tell you, as Shakespeare said in *Romeo and Juliet,* 'To be or not to be!'. . ."

"*Hamlet!* Excuse me, you are quote from *Hamlet,* not *Romeo and Juliet!*"

"'Exactly!' the Monkey said. 'You talked yourself right into my trap and make my point. Texts do not change.'"

"That's not the point of Monkey."

"You obviously have not read Monkey," I say, and their silence tells me they obviously have not read Monkey. Why is Monkey leading Samsang and Sandy, the beggar monk, and Pigsy west?" I ask. And I answer, "To collect books of Buddhist scripture and bring them back to China so the Tang emperor *can read the texts.* Text."

The local guide phones me later and tells me the Singapore people said I talked just like an old Chinaman with a classical education. "I'm flattered," I say.

"They didn't mean it as a compliment," he says.

Frank Chin

Singapore calls. Khirpal Singh. A Sikh. Yes. A Sikh. Beard. Turban. Yes, a Sikh. National Arts Council. As part of "Singapore Writers Week," they want Frank Chin to read to assemblies of grade school students and sit on a panel titled "Where Is Home?" Are you sure they want Frank Chin? Yes. Not Frank Ching? "Yes, it's you they want." Sure? Sure! Make sure, Khirpal Singh. Okay, he'll make sure. He calls again. He made sure. Yes, Frank Chin, not Frank Ching. They know the names of my books. That's a good sign. Okay. I'll come to Singapore for their Writers Week.

I book my flight. Business class, Singapore Airlines. Khirpal Singh says they won't go business class. I have to fly economy. If he pays business class for me, all the writers will want it. But if he did it for me, why would he tell the others? I want leg room if I'm going to be sitting in one place for fifteen hours. He, too, needs leg room. He tells me his trick for getting the leg room he needs when he flies economy class. Get to the airport three hours early and ask for an aisle seat by an emergency door. Oh, great. But I want the leg room. Three hours in the dreary totalitarian Gestapo LAX international terminal with its one horrible line 'em up, shove 'em through cafeteria restaurant. I see it again. The clunky cement hole. One line. One cash register. Singapore may not be worth it.

It's like I'm talking to a hand puppet on the phone. The phone is vaguely occupied by the voice of a little girl with a toy British accent calling from Singapore. Will I fax my passport and flight information to them so that someone can process me a visiting artist's visa from the government and meet me and take me to the Inter-Continental Hotel? I already faxed an invoice and itinerary to the organizer of Writers Week. But my travel agent graciously faxes the invoice and itinerary to the National Arts Council.

A Chinaman in Singapore

The same voice calls again. They received my itinerary by mail. Are the times LA time or Singapore time? Departure from LA is LA time. Arrival in Singapore is Singapore time. I am arriving in Singapore at 12:55 A.M. Sunday morning. That's Saturday night, Sunday morning at five minutes to one. Singapore time? Yes, Singapore time. Someone will meet me and take me to the hotel. Great. Wonderful.

Anything they can do for me in Singapore? Yes, I'd like an appointment with the police to learn the history of the Chinese triad societies in Singapore. Not that I'm looking for the deep scoop on criminal triad action in Singapore. Just a skate over the safe ice. Okay? Oh, they'll look into it. Thanks.

Another voice of another little girl. Snow White. Will I fax my travel information, please? I've sent it to you twice. You have it. Oh? To be sure, can I repeat it? Sure. I'm arriving Saturday night, Sunday morning at 12:55 A.M. on Singapore Airlines. Someone will meet me at the airport? "Yes," she says. I begin to worry.

The first voice, the little Wicked Witch, calls. She checked with Singapore Airlines, and I am arriving Monday morning at 12:55 A.M. No, I am not. I am arriving on Sunday morning. Saturday night, Sunday morning. Not Monday morning. No, she has checked with Singapore Airlines, and I am arriving Monday morning, not Sunday morning. Someone will meet me at the airport and take me to the hotel. Sunday! I'm arriving Sunday! I'm leaving LA on Friday, cross the dateline, it's Saturday, long flight later, I land in Singapore a little before one Sunday morning. She corrects me, "Monday morning." The great bureaucracy of Singapore in action.

THE ULTIMATE BORDER TOWN

I land in the dark of Sunday morning. No one meets me at the airport. I wait an hour. I'm not going to wait till Monday. I

Frank Chin

look under hotels in the yellow pages, and there is no Inter-Continental Hotel. Ah, information says there is. They've never heard of me. Never heard of the National Arts Council. Never heard of Singapore Writers Week. I call home to get the number of Khirpal Singh, the Writers Week organizer. He says jump in a cab and go to the hotel. He'll phone ahead and fix everything. After midnight the cab fare is one and a half times daylight fares, the cabbie says. He's never heard of Singapore Writers Week.

It's Sunday. Yes, make a note of that. Sunday. 2:30 in the morning. Singapore is dark. The streets are empty. The dark air is eighty-two degrees Farenheit. Hot. The freeway from the airport is empty. The concrete is blue. All this land was sucked up from the bottom of the sea by a monster mechanical mudsucker, the cabbie tells me.

What have I heard about Singapore? Just what I've heard on TV. The caning of Michael Fahey for spray painting graffiti on cars. What do I think of that? Singapore is not America. He deserved it. I hear that Lee Kuan Yew is the real power in Singapore. I hear economic miracle. And that Brit trader What's his name? who made a rep making fake deals, then betting the money on the Japanese stock market going up, and when the Nikkei fell, down came one of England's oldest banks. Where is he now? Britain won't admit him. Singapore wants him back. Last I heard what's his name and his wife were in Germany? Does Singapore want him back? And the survivors of the Death March want to sue Japan for reparations. What do I think of that? They were British soldiers. They should sue the British, not the enemy. Japan has paid World War II reparations to the British. Britain has never paid reparations to the Malay and the Chinese for the centuries of colonial subjugation and the Opium Wars.

What else do I know about Singapore? Okay, okay. He squeezes the last Singapore factoid rattling around my

A Chinaman in Singapore

thoughts. There's a Maxine Hong Kingston suite at the Raffles Hotel. Who's that?

Murder in the Maxine Hong Kingston Suite, a Charlie Chan mystery. Charlie Chan, the Honolulu Chinese detective, and Jimmy, one of his many numbered sons, are staying at the famous Raffles Hotel in Singapore. "Gee, Pop!" Jimmy says. "Guess who was found dead in the Maxine Hong Kingston suite!"

We drive by what looks like the fenced-in park where all the high-rises of the world come to die. Black. Steely filing cabinets fifty stories high, and steely broken skeletons. All dark. Some shrouded in a dark netting of diffusion screens that reflect heat away from and sop up some of the noise of the building project. All this, the cabbie says, is Suntec, a complex of office buildings and condos built with Hong Kong money.

Oh. There *is* an Inter-Continental Hotel. It's just two blocks away from the Raffles. Do I mind if they give me a room on the thirteenth floor? Why does an American-style mass-produced luxury hotel have a thirteenth floor? What movie is this? Land at an empty airport one hour after local midnight on the equator. Thirteen o'clock. Taxi through the empty freeways and streets of Singapore that used to be bayou, swamp, marshland, bog, and quicksand. Bat country. And you want to put me on the thirteenth floor? They give me a room on the fourteenth floor. Or so they say.

DUDLEY DE SOUZA

Dudley de Souza calls and introduces himself. He'll be taking me out to two schools in the morning.

He would like to meet me before we go out reading in high schools and sitting on the big panel "Where Is Home?" together. He's looking forward to the panel. Why am I read-

Frank Chin

ing to high school students? Have they read anything I've written? No. But Dudley has.

"How about going out to dinner with me tonight?" I say. "It's Sunday. I've been sleeping and air-conditioned all day. I want to go out. I want to eat on the street. Find a nice pepper crab. Sit in a breeze and watch the real Singapore walk by."

Dudley is the color of weak coffee and a teaspoon of milk. Portuguese father. Malay mother. Born in Singapore in the year of the dragon, 1940. He tells me my hotel is on Bugis Street. Bugis Street used to be famous for the transvestites that walked the street here. The government didn't like the sleazy rep and tore down Bugis Street, and the Japanese built this hotel and shopping mall on it. Now the government would like to glamorize the old sleazy rep for transvestites and make Bugis Street transvestite clubs a tourist attraction. But only one club has been allowed to have a transvestite act. And there's a law against a man wearing a dress. So what's a transvestite to wear?

Change. Sex change seems to be a theme running through Singapore.

"Have you heard that Singapore is the sex-change capital of the world?" No, I haven't heard that. "It's true," he says.

Singapore is known for having the very best sex-change operations, the most experienced doctors; the most up-to-date techniques have been developed here in Singapore. Sex-change operations. Cosmetic surgery. As a consequence of being the sex-change capital of the world, Singapore is also the transsexual capital of Asia.

"The government doesn't like to publicize it, but it's true. Upwards of 60 percent of the sex-change operations done in the world are performed in Singapore."

Given the vulnerability of the clientele and the doctors, I'd

A Chinaman in Singapore

expect the triads to run the sex-change biz in Singapore.

"Oh, if you're interested in Chinese triads, you should meet Wilfred Hamilton-Shimmen. A Eurasian writer who was in a triad gang in his teens." Really? Yes, Dudley knows Shimmen. They are—we are all—the same age. Born in 1940, the year of the dragon. Dudley and Shimmen studied Korean hard-style bone-against-bone karate, tae kwon do, together. Have I studied any martial arts? Kung fu? Wu shu? Tai chi?

"No, I've never won a fistfight in my life. If I can't talk my way out of trouble, I'm dead."

Dudley gave up tae kwon do. Too hard. Dudley doesn't have the bones for fighting bone against bone. Wilfred Hamilton-Shimmen became very good and still works out. "He must have big bones," I say.

"Yes, he's big, like you."

I'm taller than Dudley, but my bones are small, like his. He says the three of us seem to have lived parallel lives as non-Asian Asians under white domination in white countries. We seem to be in a similar struggle to define ourselves and our people's cultural sensibility as distinct from Asian Asians and white whites. We all write in English that is our own, and everybody wants to correct it.

Singapore, as a nation, is only thirty years old. In the world Singapore is an economic miracle, not a culture, not a tradition. Not a soul. With five official languages, what is Singapore's culture and literature to be? What is the place of Chinese, or Malay, or Indonesian, or Tamil, or British tradition in Singaporean writing in Chinese, Indonesian, Tamil, or English? Singapore sounds like the *Pequod,* a whaling ship, a ship of business with a multiracial, multilingual, Christian and pagan crew and a visionary captain. In Singapore, as on the *Pequod,* the relationships between the races, religions, and languages do not evolve naturally but are managed, directed, and

Frank Chin

dictated by the law of one man's vision, or one man's vision of the law.

The writers of Dudley de Souza's generation want to be the Melvilles and Thoreaus, the Longfellows and Whitmans of Singapore. They have it in them to write the great Singaporean novel they feel Singapore needs before Singapore's English-language literature will be taken seriously.

Dudley jitters with the itch to write it. Or might if he were free to publish anything he wrote, and he's not. If he writes a novel and publishes it and the government doesn't like it, he's guilty of a crime against the state, even if his novel is published outside Singapore. But he's used to that. He developed his taste for American English at Paul Engle's Christian indoctrination center, the State University of Iowa's International Writers Workshop, at Iowa City. That's something else I have in common with Dudley's generation of English-language writers; I was in the graduate writers workshop at Iowa City. I had nothing to do with the International Writers Workshop. I wasn't interested in being indoctrinated into Christianity and white racism in the guise of internationalizing English. Still, me being not exactly Engle's idea of an American, he held up my fellowship check and called me in for a little talk. He didn't like it that I had visited Cuba last December before coming to Iowa. If he had known, I might not have been given the fellowship. Oh ho ho! Ooh hoo hoo! Paul Engle, the founder and director and Big Daddy of the Iowa Writers Workshop and International Writers Workshop, wore blue denim overalls, was sitting on a desk holding court, and made me feel like I was interrupting by being prompt. "Frank, you've been to Cuba," he says, when I ask about my check. "They don't have a constitution. Castro promised a constitution. Why doesn't Cuba have a constitution?"

"I don't know. Castro doesn't talk to me. I'm not Cuban."

A Chinaman in Singapore

"I know you're not Cuban, Frank. But you were in Cuba."

"It's been only five years since the Cuban Revolution, and, as I recall, the United States didn't have a constitution till 1789, more than ten years after our Revolution."

"Oh, Frank," Paul Engle says, swinging his legs and crossing his arms. "I doubt that very much!"

"You doubt that very much?" Instinctively I understood this was a fight about who controlled my English language, but I laughed because he sounded stupid.

I should not have laughed at the high priest of international English, in his own workshop, in his own language. I should have doubted what I said and been ashamed of offending Paul Engle. Francisco Franco in Spain, Chiang Kai-shek in Taiwan, are still alive. Samuel Fuller's *The Crimson Kimono,* starring Glenn Corbett and James Shigeta as LA detectives in love with the same white woman while investigating a murder in Li'l Tokyo, is in its first run at the State.

What is the place of Chinese, Malay, Indonesian, Tamil, British colonial tradition in the new Singaporean identity? What is the place of a hardtop nonconvertible pagan Chinaman who's been to Cuba in the Iowa Writers Workshop? What is the place of rabbit biology and behavior in Walt Disney's Thumper? In Singapore, as in the Iowa Writers Workshop in Dudley's time, as in Disneyland, instead of the real, they have law. Lots and lots of law. Owooooo! Hear that wolf?

Law or no law, Wilfred Hamilton-Shimmen's self-published *Seasons of Darkness: A Story of Singapore* is a bold attempt at the great Singapore novel in English. He's never been to Iowa. And true to the tradition of authors of the national myth, complete with national angst, Shimmen lives and dresses himself in the third-person prose of the part on the back cover:

Frank Chin

The son of an English colonial and a Malacca-Portuguese mother of Dutch/Portuguese/Malay lineage, "Briton, Wilfred Hamilton-Shimmen was born in British colonial Singapore in 1940, approximately 11 months before Japan threw down her gauntlet in Asia to join Germany in her world war against Europe and the United States, attacking the former Malay island among other colonial outposts in the region.

Raised as a White, with a retinue of servants to care for him, he was interned as an infant with his mother in the dreaded Japanese Sime Road Internment Camp for White civilians on the island during the Japanese Occupation of Singapore. His father, in the meanwhile, was detained, tortured and executed by the infamous Japanese Kempetai Secret Police as a spy.

At war's end he was placed in a White-run British colonial boarding home for White and part-White children, in Singapore and raised as an English child. As his mother had refused to be repatriated to England, at the age of 12, because he was considered too old for the co-ed boarding home, he was transferred to a local-run boarding school for boys.

Becoming part of his mother's Eurasian/Asian society from then, he had to learn to "adjust" to a new set of mores, change his diet, his very English accent as well as throw out the English attitude ingrained since birth (because it upset the "locals"), and discover the native-parts of his island-home which he had never known.

He has worked as a showbiz journalist, a reporter and sub-editor for a newspaper, and as a foreign correspondent. He switched to advertising copyrighting in his early thirties before turning his hand to public relations.

Five paragraphs. Each paragraph is long sentences, chanting a rhythm I can't count, an accent I haven't heard or read before. From front cover to back, the whole book is long,

A Chinaman in Singapore

ugly, un-American sentences like that because Shimmen wrote it all, the text, the jacket copy, the liner notes, the disclaimer. For me, the book is a hard slog through long sentences and funny grammar, but it's worth it. All of Singapore's bloods flow in Wilfred Hamilton-Shimmen's veins, but the only bloods that are passions in the veins of his autobiographical novel's hero, Thomas Siddon, are white and Chinese. And they hate each other. And at the end of the novel, the whites are out, and the Chinese are taking over Singapore, ending Thomas Siddon's dream of a new Singapore smelted out of the melting pot.

In 1978, long after independence from Britain, the Chinese dominant Singapore Government appeared oblivious *of the* feelings of alienation *its move was inducing among the non-Chinese communities who muttered their misgivings among themselves privately, because no one dared utter any protest out loud as a Government-passed law against the bringing of "communal issues," punishable by imprisonment, saw to that effectively. For Siddon it was the* final proof *that the Lee Kuan Yew government had begun its* open phase *into the* sionization of Singapore, *sending a* clear signal *to the* ethnic-Chinese majority (comprising of the China-born and their descendants as well as the straits-born Chinese and the Baba-Nyonya mixed Chinese-Malay community) *that they could make their* presence *on the island* openly felt.

If Albert Camus had actually thought of himself as an Algerian white man instead of being the white racist white man in Algeria he was, his novel about being a despised white man in a quaint colored country might have been *Seasons of Darkness*. To be assimilated by the Algerians or shoot one down like a dog? That is the question of *The Stranger*. To be assimilated by the Chinese or not to be assimilated? is one of Shimmen's questions facing his protagonist, Thomas Siddon.

Frank Chin

On 20th November of that same year, speaking in Mandarin in Parliament, a PAP member, a Dr. Ow Chin Hock, hit back at Chiam stating that he didn't know what Chiam had meant by a "Chinese Singapore." Dr. Ow said that if Chiam felt that the Chinese should not have their own cultural identity (should the cultural identity be Singaporean instead of Chinese? Siddon asked himself), but should, like what Chiam had said in Parliament, be put in a melting-pot together with the other races, then he had confused national loyalty (what nationality? Siddon asked himself) with cultural identity (what culture??). Chinese Singaporeans, Dr. Ow said, had a right to retain their own language, culture, customs and values. This was not chauvinism, this was cultural identity (!). (It was clear that a "strong signal" had been sent that for "Singapore Culture" one should read "Chinese culture" and that the "ethnic-Chinese of Singapore should remain ethnic-Chinese", to Siddon this also meant that inter-marriage was not to be encouraged.)

Take Ralph Ellison's *Invisible Man*, turn Ellison white, and turn all the whites in his America black, and you have something like Shimmen's novel of a white minority adored and despised in whitest and darkest Singapore.

The chickens of five hundred years of British and European white racism come home to roost in the paranoia of Thomas Siddon, Shimmen's Eurasian protagonist with a grandparent from every race in Singapore mixing in his blood, stranded in the new Singapore dominated by the pure Chinese, Chinese loyal not to any nation of China but to the Chinese race:

The phenomenon of the Hoa-Chinese being kicked out of Vietnam, their *land of adoption, and ending up as flotsam on the other shores was an indication to Siddon of what* could happen *to those such as he, should, for some reason or other his* kind *was no longer welcome in Singapore. Those such as* he *would never be regarded as being part of the* greater whole *because Singapore*

A Chinaman in Singapore

*society since the era of the People's Action Party had been seg-
mented into racial blocs, he concluded. Every "achievement" in
education, business or even the arts was classified by race. Officially. The only two choices left to him, he felt, was to either* sub-
limate *his Caucasian origin and identify as an Asian of "dubi-
ous" racial-strain or, if lucky to be born "White-looking" and be
able to "pass", to claim partiality, return to the land of his fore-
fathers, claim his birthright and identify with his White origins.*
What a choice to have to make after a lifetime in Asia!

*As an Eurasian he felt he had been left out of Singapore's soci-
ety which stressed "room only" for the Chinese, the Malay, and the
Indian.*

Yes, the anger and sorrow at knowing, and loving but not
belonging to, "the majority" sounds like the self-pity and we
are all victims boo hoo of every Chinese American autobiography ever written: "Up to 1971 he had always thought of himself as *Singaporean*. . . . He was not only a first-generation
Eurasian through his father being English, he was more than
half-White because his mother was Eurasian as well. That made
him 'three quarters White'. He had always been aware that he
was regarded 'differently' by the *others* despite taking pains
not to 'divulge' his English origins and behaving Singaporean.
And he would not yield to the *tyranny of the majority.*"

In Shimmen's Singapore, the oppressive majority is Chinese, and the tyrant is Lee Kuan Yew:

Lee Kuan Yew had once used the term amalgam *to describe the
multiracial society he had wanted developed on Singapore. The
term itself had always been distasteful to Siddon because it
denoted a* mixing *without the "main ingredients" ever* merging.
But the Eurasian *was a* living blend *that had come about
because of White colonialism that Lee and his ilk had chosen to
ignore, which was ridiculous because in present-day Singapore
ethnic-Chinese girls were choosing to marry Whites and other*

Frank Chin

races, and begetting yet more "mixed bloods", though the ethnic Chinese journalists in the media were choosing to describe these new half-caste offspring from such unions as Chinese-English, Chinese-French *or* Chinese-German, *instead of* Eurasian. And when he had inquired of the journalist concerned his reasons for using such descriptive terms he was informed that in Singapore it was alright! *Siddon had even read in the local press of children of Chinese-Indian, Malay-Indian or Malay-Chinese unions being described as "Eurasian"! What Lee Kuan Yew had succeeded in doing was to make* everybody *conscious of race and the polarisation of the different communities in Singapore so much so that being Singaporean was so much lip-service, Siddon felt. It was part of the hypocrisy inherent in the society. The first thing* anyone *asked someone in Singapore, on meeting for the first time, was what his or her race was!*

Should I be amused or scared to see those long, ugly, unfriendly sentences and all? Change the word *Chinese* to *whites,* and even I might mistake this for something I'd written and written and written about white racist love in America. Hamilton-Shimmen's novel is self-published. He makes me see a Chinaman who doesn't Charlie Chan or Gunga Din, write falsies and Hollywood, is lucky to get published at all. But luckily not that lucky. If getting published were really that outrageously lucky, I might start believing in prayer and maybe even find religion.

He felt he couldn't fight the greater mass or change its attitude, so he would remove *himself by* relinquishing *his Singaporean nationality which was synonymous with being Chinese as far as he was concerned. He had been born on a* multiracial *island governed by the British who had given it to* all *the races who had then professed a kinship with the Malay island because of historical fact. And he would not accept nationality of an island which had* become *Sino by* transition and deceit and pretended

A Chinaman in Singapore

multi-racialism, by hypocrisy. *He had grown aware that as far as the ethnic-Chinese were concerned they felt an affinity to one another, whether they were from Singapore or* from a different part of the world.

Yes, change the word *Chinese* to *whites,* and a line becomes, "He had grown aware that as far as the ethnic-whites were concerned they felt an affinity to one another, whether they were from San Francisco or *from a different part of the world.*"

Siddon's fear and detestation of the Chinese is the law in neighboring Malaysia across the Straits of Johor and Indonesia across the water. In these Muslim theocracies, Chinese culture is banned. Christianity, a relic of white oppression, and Islam are the only legal religions. Chinese claim Christianity as a way of avoiding religion and still being legal. And some tactical Christian Chinese tactfully take Malaysian and Indonesian family names. During national elections the Chinese stay off the streets to avoid anti-Chinese violence. The great Chinese brains of Malaysia and Indonesia are popping coin in America and Australia and Canada and are not waxing nostalgic about the regular anti-Chinese riots, massacres, and nationalization of Chinese property in the old hometown. Singapore wants the Chinese brains they have to stay in Singapore and proliferate into the Silicon Valley of Asia, the banking and service capital of Asia, the biggest port of traffic moving on the sea as ships and flying the air as chips and Boeing 747s. Surrounded by countries that outlaw and despise Chinese, ethnic or not, Singapore offers the Chinese with brains, who don't chew gum, write graffiti on the walls, or spit on the streets, a haven, maybe even a job and subsidized housing.

In Singapore, the culture, melting pot or not, is controlled by the state control of art.

A shorthaired young woman—perhaps my daughter's age, perhaps younger—a Chinese playwright who wears no

Frank Chin

makeup, tells me her satiric play has been banned. In her play Malaysia turns against the Chinese, and all the rich Chinese of Malaysia storm across the Straits into Singapore. Singapore turns out its dinky army and navy to stop them, but the Chinese of Singapore side with the Chinese wanting in, and Oh, no! "Too close to the state's real paranoid nightmares," she says. "A very funny play."

Her play sounds like a play on *The Water Margin,* the Chinese story of 108 wrongfully outlawed and heroes from all parts of China, possessing all the skills necessary to run a state, banding together on a mountain hidden inside the shifting 350 square miles of swamp, bayou, and marshland neither land nor sea known as "the Water Margin." The Water Margin, or Liangshan Marsh, was like Vietnam, like Singapore, like Barataria near New Orleans, not a nation, not a city, but a pirates' roost and marketplace.

Eton, Sandhurst, Oxford. Lee Kuan Yew does not want himself or his sons identified with Chinese pirates taking over an outlaw stronghold in a marsh. He does not want to be identified with Jean and Pierre Lafitte and Singapore with Lafitte's Barataria. If there is anyplace in the world I would not be surprised to learn Chinese fairy tales and the heroic tradition from *The Ballad of Mulan to Monkey's Journey to the West* would be banned, as they are de facto banned in the public schools of the United States of America and officially outlawed in Malaysia and Indonesia, it is Singapore.

If there is anyplace in the world I would expect the Chinese fairy tales and romantic adventures of the heroic tradition to thrive, it is Singapore, which was itself born as a marketplace in that tradition and stood for freedom of the press when as part of the Cultural Revolution the Communists banned Chinese culture, stories, and opera, outlawed its possession, practice, and recital, on pain of separating the family into reeducation camps and worse, from 1966, a year after the founding of the Republic of Singapore, to 1976, the year of the American Bicentennial and the publication of Maxine Hong Kingston's *The Woman Warrior*. During the Cultural Revolution, comic-book novels of *Three Kingdoms, The Ballad of Mulan, Ngawk Fay* (Yue Fei), *Leong Hungyuk* (Liang Hongyu), *The Yang Family Generals, Water Margin, Monkey's Journey to the West*, and *The Dream of the Red Chamber* were printed in Singapore and Hong Kong and smuggled into mainland China.

The writer of satirical plays the government finds too funny to allow in public for a laugh still collects a generous allowance, from the same government, because she's a writer. If she sounds like a writer running a scam to be paid to offend the state and be censored, she's not alone. What bothers me is, whether they're scamming or not, every Singapore writer I meet sounds like a casualty of state-controlled art.

Ong Keng Sen is the artistic director of Theatre Works, the largest theater group in Singapore—with a full-time staff of eight and a 101-seat black-box theater.

Ong is tall, soft fleshed, not quite slender, Chinese. He wears dressed, longish but not long hair, black dark glasses, black turtleneck, black slacks, and carries a black purse and a calendar notebook. He meets me at the Japanese fantasy of a Euro-American luxury hotel and takes me out to lunch at the British colonial fantasy of a white-railed three-story riverboat named after Thomas Stamford Raffles, the British colonial administrator who made Singapore the great trading post of Southeast Asia, the Raffles Hotel. Like Singapore itself, the Raffles has new owners who have restored "the grand old lady of the East" to its white-plaster glory of 1915. The original Raffles was built in 1887 by the Sarkies brothers and run by Tigran Sarkies. Armenian hoteliers. Memories of Hemingway staggering around the Writers Bar in his hunting jacket, bombed out of his mind, and Somerest Maugham sipping tea. Sing-

Frank Chin

apore. And William Holden and Jennifer Jones playing a Eurasian in *Love Is a Many Splendored Thing,* not a bad book by Dr. Han Suyin, but the movie, part of the William Holden–gets–more–yellow–women–than–Jimmy Stewart–Marlon Brando–and–Laurence Harvey–combined cycle of movies. And that song jumping out of the radio, the "Love" in "Love is a many splendored thing . . ." a screaming Tarzan jungle call from Singapore.

A Vegas lounge-act version of American music plays in the famous Writers Bar. That song! It's that song played on fluffy instruments. Everything at the Raffles is famous. Here the famous Hainanese bar captain Ngiam Tong Boon invented the famous Singapore sling.

Yes, I am Monkey journeying through yet another strange land bristling with strange ideas. Careful crossing my chiasmus, my ass vobiscum. There's a suite named for Somerset Maugham, a suite named for Noel Coward. There's an Ava Gardner suite, a Frank Buck suite, suites named for Charlie Chaplin and Maurice Chevalier. The Ernest Hemingway suite has been renamed the Maxine Hong Kingston suite. How about Sabu and Gunga Din? Down the hall and turn to the right. Ong says he expects government censorship to shut down the play now in rehearsal. The play is about young gays at play in Singapore. Gays are not critical of the state. Young Singapore gays want to express themselves as gays. Not that gays are harassed or beaten up on the streets here. They're not. It's just that gays are not who the government wants to lead the new Singapore culture.

Singapore's artists-as-permanent-residents program is a better scam than the U.S. National Endowment for the Arts. The NEA never gave an artist a place to live and a middle-class income for life. More interesting, as Ms. Young Shorthair describes it, government support of the artists, giving them freedom of expression, but no show, no publication, no production without government approval, also more effectively censors art than the NEA.

The shorthaired Chinese playwright who wears no makeup tells me she is married for convenience. Married couples can buy state apartments reasonably cheap. Family values. The state wants more babies. Babies and culture. She says her husband is gay and has one master bedroom and she and her girlfriend sleep in the other master bedroom. Then she says she wants to take me out to the bird park at night when they sing. "Oh, you say that to all the boys," I say.

"Only the ones I'm interested in," she says.

If I were the kind of writer who wrote not to be published, I could live in Singapore.

What Lee Kuan Yew sees, Chinese or not, is that color blindness doesn't work, the melting pot doesn't work, going unconscious of race doesn't work. The marketplace works. He runs a clean marketplace. Singapore is the big store. And Singapore art and culture are window dressing. The marketplace is the real art and culture of Lee's Singapore, and he's the store manager.

Lee has turned Singapore from a quaint colonial doily into the Silicon Valley, Zurich, and Amsterdam of Asia. With the mightiest port in the world, all the money, all the power of Asia passing through Singapore, Lee sees Singapore, not as a part of China, but as the capital of China, the capital of the Pacific. He sees himself doing a very robust British European thing. He has used British education, Western methods, to make Singapore a player in the world of Western-style business. On the range of dollars and deals it may have been the wild west, but Lee Kuan Yew was and is the law. This is not a Chinese marketplace he's built. He's turned Singapore from a dinky little island swamp into a Western nation. And it is a Western culture he wants to create now, not Chinese.

Frank Chin

That's why, though Shimmen dumps mighty dumps on the Chinese of the world, dumps on the Chinese of Singapore, dumps on Chinese culture, dumps on the Chinese race, dumps on Lee Kuan Yew, dumps on Lee Kuan Yew's Chineseness, in this police state run by Lee Kuan Yew, Lee Kuan Yew has not pulled Hamilton-Shimmen's books off the shelves of Singapore bookstores and burned them, or ended his writing career in Singapore, or deported him to parts unknown. Shimmen may be a rebel and a renegade, but he's the establishment's rebel and renegade whether he knows it or not. How else could he be a host and participant in Singapore's National Writers Week, like Dudley de Souza? What's it like to live as a writer in Singapore, on a guaranteed income from the state, never having to publish or produce the text and scripts you write? I wonder. What's it like to live as a writer in Lee Kuan Yew's miracle kingdom?

SINGAPORE IS DISNEYLAND

Nothing about Singapore has shown up as real on my scopes since I walked into Bradley International Terminal at LAX. Not the air, not the food, not the water, not the light. Not the time. Not the place. It's all chaff and flash. Fly Singapore Airlines. "Singapore Girl, you're a wonderful way to fly!" the ads say. On the plane, in cramped economy class, I hear the public address, and all the stewardesses speak Japanese. The American movies are dubbed in Japanese. The Japanese movies have English subtitles. Japanese is not one of the official languages or cultures of Singapore. Business. A stewardess smiles in my face and asks me if I am Japanese, if I speak Japanese. Ah, Singapore Girl, for your sake, I wish I did speak Japanese.

Most of the passengers are Japanese. The American-style semiluxury hotel hosting Writers Week is owned by a Japanese chain. The mall under glass around the hotel is not Singapore

A Chinaman in Singapore

but a self-consciously unreal fantasy Singapore, a smug, phony Singapore, like the determinedly unreal LA city street of Universal City's City Walk and the proudly fake Matterhorn of Disneyland. The fake is better than the real. One can't shop on a real city street in the real LA. Too many real strangers. Their real strangeness affects the atmosphere with real menace. One can't really shop on the real Matterhorn. Too much real snow. One can't really shop in the real Singapore. Too much real unexpected, unknown, unknowing. One doesn't feel safe. One feels safe in the cities of Universal City, the different lands of Disneyland, in the glossy fake worlds of Disneyworld because they are real movie and television studios and, walking the great soundstage of life, we are as coddled by the studios as real actors and extras. Let there be light. And it is good; it is moral; it is good business to play let's pretend and make getting away from it all a brand name, a paying job, a health and retirement plan, a home.

The Walt Disney of Singapore's miracle kingdom, Lee Kuan Yew, is, in some Singaporean eyes, not Singaporean at all but Chinese. Oh, no! Not Chinese! A new Asian nation that wants to invent a new myth of a miracle synthetic nation. A thirty-year-old Asian nation craving European respect, manufacturing a national myth, history, and culture to make money and win European respect. And as Lee Kuan Yew created Singapore in the image of Disneyland, so now Disneyland is creating a fake town in Florida and running it like Lee Kuan Yew runs Singapore, with an iron fist inside an English-speaking hand puppet.

A generation of Chinese Singaporeans, teacher's pets of British colonial schools, is determined to prove they are not Chinese with the English language. Sounds like the suburban kids of Chinatown parents at UCLA. If there is a place that wants yellow writers whose final justification for faking everything Chinese is the style and beauty of their use of the

Frank Chin

English language, the Singapore that is all fakery and invention is that place. "Number One Son, please come home to Singapore," "Pop," Charlie Chan, the Chinese traditionally played by a white man, writes his son, played by a converted Chinese, raised on converted rice. If there is a community of Chinese where all the misogynist Chinese fairy tales that Maxine Hong Kingston and Amy Tan invented are real, are a part of the national myth, I expect it to be Singapore.

Across the street from the Raffles is a five- or six-story building, covering a city block, full of bookstores selling books in all the official languages. There are several different kinds of Chinese-language bookstores in the building that do not mix their wares. Books from Hong Kong. Books from Singapore Chinese-language publishers. Books from the PRC. Books from Taiwan. The Chinese-owned chain of Popular Bookstores carries all Chinese-language books and magazines and translations of Chinese books in English, Malay, Tamil.

I'm looking for the Far Mulan who is tattooed against her will, brutalized, abused, goes to war, and comes home to slaughter and ruin. I'm looking for that fairy tale that teaches, "The worth of a woman is measured by the loudness of her husband's belch."

What happens if, tomorrow, I cross the street from the hotel, walk past the block of empty lots and footprints of leveled buildings, walk into a Chinese bookstore, and find what I'm looking for? Owooooo! Hear that wolf?

BETTE GREENE

Dudley de Souza is a Singapore writer looking for the soul of Singapore. He is very conscious of belonging to a generation of writers who feel charged, if not chosen, to create and express the soul of Singapore in English-language literature. He would like my novel *Donald Duk* to replace Bette Greene's

A Chinaman in Singapore

fine young adult novel *Summer of My German Soldier* in the schools. But he has no power in the schools. And my book is not available in Singapore. I'm surprised he knows my little novel. In Singapore there are Chinese Singaporeans who follow English-language action in Chinese America and those who follow the English-language writing of Chinese Australians, Chinese English.

Bette Greene's novel about a young Jewish girl in World War II Arkansas falling in love with a German soldier escapee from the local POW camp has been in the Singapore school's lit curriculum for years. All the questions of race, loyalty, betrayal, migration, and assimilation facing Singapore are safely and nobly set in Arkansas in this novel.

The jacket copy reads: "While patriotic feelings run high, Patty risks losing family, friends—even her freedom—for this dangerous friendship. It is a risk she has to take and one she will have to pay a price to keep." The jacket quotes a bit of the book that might explain the novel's attraction to a Singapore trying to program the marriage of mutually hostile cultures into their children:

His teeth pressed together, giving new strength to the line of his jaw. "I'm certain you appreciate the seriousness of what you have done, aiding an escaped prisoner of war. I was wondering why you were taking these risks on my behalf. Because of your German ancestry? Perhaps your father is secretly sympathetic to the Nazi cause?"

"That's not true! My father's parents came from Russia and my mother's from Luxembourg."

Anton looked alarmed. "I'm sorry. It's just that Bergen is such a good German name."

"It's also a good Jewish name," I said, pleased by the clean symmetry of my response.

Frank Chin

His mouth came open. "Jewish?" An index finger pointed toward me. "You're Jewish?"

I thought he knew. I guess I thought everybody knew. Does he think I tricked him? My wonderful Anton was going to change to mean. As I nodded Yes, my breathing came to a halt while my eyes clamped shut.

Suddenly, strong baritone laughter flooded the room. Both eyes popped open and I saw him standing there, shaking his head from side to side.

"It's truly extraordinary," he said. "Who would believe it? 'Jewish girl risks all for German solder.' Tell me, Patty Bergen" —his voice became soft, but with a trace of hoarseness—"why are you doing this for me?"

It wasn't complicated. Why didn't he know? There was really only one word for it. A simple little word that in itself is reason enough.

When we meet at breakfast in the American restaurant, Bette Greene talks about growing up a Jew in Arkansas and how her brief childhood conversion to Christianity turned her against her Jewish grandmother. She refused to visit a Jew and a devil. Only years later, years after her grandmother died, did she realize she'd messed up and missed out. What's the word for what she feels about knowing she was a Bible-spouting anti-Semitic brat when she refused to visit her dying Jewish grandmother? Guilt? Shame? Sorrow? She knows the Christian fundamentalism of the American South.

SINGAPORE NIGHT

The Chinese Hungry Ghosts Festival is about over, and the Moon Festival is beginning. Moon cakes are for sale all over Singapore and at a stand just outside the hotel.

A Chinaman in Singapore

We walk out of the hotel, out of the greenhoused theme-park replica of old Singapore buildings, into the hot, wet heat of the street. 7:00 P.M., and eighty-five degrees Farenheit. Singapore is on the equator.

The alley across the street is stuffed with hawkers' stands under little canvas tents. Lots of watches. Rolexes. Yeah, sure. Thousands of Rolexes. Fountain pens. Little statuettes of Chinese gods made out of plastic. Cameras, film. Chicken and pork *satay*. Phone cards. Shirts. Blouses. Belts and wallets. Luggage. A fortune-telling monkey on a leash. Birds in cages. One layer of hawkers' stands presses against the walls of the street. Down the middle of the street two rows of back-to-back hawkers' stands. People drain in between. Pickpocket's paradise!

At the intersection the stands stop. Two men on different legs of the cross street wave at us and shout, "This way! This way!" Tables and chairs are set up in the street. People sit with cold beers in their hands. It is just dark. A faint breeze fades across our faces. I like it here.

A faint but real breeze sweeps slowly down the street. There's a picture of what I want to eat. Pepper crab. Chinese writing. This is where we'll eat. Dudley orders beer. Tiger beer. He has folklore and gossip about this street, this place. The Tiger beer is cold. The smell is Chinese kitchen. Garlic. Ginger. Black beans. White pepper. The ghost of hot oil on hot iron. The sounds are Chinese kitchen. Around the world. Only a wok sounds like a wok. Chopsticks. Rice bowls. This is where I eat.

"Cheers," Dudley says. He's got this look on his face. It's not a smirk. Not a smug upper lip. It's not silly mischief. His look says he knows something I don't know and what he knows is about me. Dudley grins and shakes his head and slaps the table. He's having a great time.

I order in Cantonese, and the waiter understands. Beer.

Frank Chin

Tiger beer. Beer all around. I order. Shark's fin and crab soup. Pepper crab. Crayfish in garlic and black beans. *Mah bo* tofu. *Ho yow gai lan.* And a steamed sea bass. Good fish. Thirty bucks apiece. The waitress understands. The cooks understand. Everybody understands my Cantonese. Dudley the Portuguese Malay understands my Cantonese. If you want to eat in Singapore, you have to speak a little Cantonese. The cooks are all Cantonese. Shark's fin and crab soup. Pepper crab. Sri Lankan crab or local crab? What's the difference? Sri Lankan are big. The locals are small. Sri Lankan. A big Sri Lankan. Oyster sauce *gai lan.* A bland tofu dish. White rice.

Dudley remembers Singapore as a British colony. Singapore when the Japanese turned off the water. Singapore occupied by the Japanese. We are exactly the same age, and where I spent my life, the only soldiers I saw were walking wounded, one-eyed, one-armed, one-legged men in uniform, and whole soldiers and sailors on leave. I was home in the land of the winners. He was a minority in the land of the losers.

Singapore after the war. Singapore as the capital of the Malay states. Singapore had all the money, all the brains and know-how. Malaysia had all the resources and the water. Singapore split. Singapore became a nation. Dudley remembers it all. It all happened in his lifetime. He has a more interesting childhood than mine. Why hasn't he mined it? Can he tell me a Singapore fairy tale? A Singapore children's story? The cultural specificity of universal moral values, the soul, the sensibility, is real and alive in the stories that are told to the children. Is there such a thing as a Singapore story?

Yes, there are opposing views about the teaching of children's stories and which culture's children's stories to teach in the schools in Singapore. There are those who say literature is literature and teach all the children's stories of all the cultures. There are those who want to invent whole cloth, eradicate history and memory, be creative and just make it up. To be

A Chinaman in Singapore

assimilated or not to be assimilated by what? By whom? That
is the question. That's why they have law in Disneyland and
law in Singapore.

ROBERT YEO

Robert Yeo, a Malacca Singaporean poet, hosts a breakfast
with writers in the Malacca room on the hotel mezzanine. He
asks us how we write a sentence, a paragraph. He's serious.
How do we craft a sentence? Ah, slowly, as he explains the
question and asks how we craft a paragraph, what he's trying
to do comes clear.

Singapore was created following the laws of business; he's
trying to fabricate a new literary Singapore English, rule by
rule, sentence by sentence, paragraph by paragraph, chapter
by chapter. A new language created by the rules of industry
and business, or consensus, a language for writers not born to
English, writers who've given up their past, their race, their
history, to be assimilated by the English language and invent
Singapore from scratch—in an English that will be admired
in, if not the envy of, the English-speaking world.

The back-cover copy to Robert Yeo's *A Part of Three:
Poems, 1966–1988,* reads: "About his last collection of poems
And Napalm Does Not Help (1977) the well-known poet Ee
tiang Hong wrote: 'Yeo's poems provide an absorbing study
on how the poet assimilates and accommodates to his culture
. . . and how this adjustment is reflected in the expanding
range of experience and the maturity of outlook and style.'"
It's exactly what he wanted said about his work. It's chilling.
Machiavelli talking about artists as the crazies whose connection with the hearts and minds of their people and charisma
the state pampers and uses to control the opinions of the people. Is it in Robert Yeo's poetry?

Frank Chin

Our national leaders
Community voices
Reviewed the bestial spoil
In grave and urgent tones:
'We shall not say who fed the beast
Who goaded it, who first saw it
Who strewed corpses and cars in its path.
We have long lived together
We do not hate each other
How can we fight ourselves?
A hungrier, larger monster
Snarls to devour us.
We have no choice, together
We must subdue the beast
Once and for all.'
TV, radio, press relayed
These earnest exhortations.
The rest of us believed and knew
The thinking all the time
The feeling some of the time
The reeling never at all.

Dudley and I talk as if there is no censorship, no law.

The problem of Singapore literary identity facing Singapore writers in English is how to observe and elucidate a Singaporean culture that recognizes the integrity of the other official cultures of Singapore without belittling any one of them. No, belittling them is okay. Belittling the Bible is okay. Respect is to make sure you do not misquote the Bible if you're going to belittle it.

For the writer of English and Chinese that should be easy. English and Chinese are the marketplace languages of Singapore and the world. Singapore is a marketplace. English is a pidgin, a language of trade. Singapore's English-based pidgin

A Chinaman in Singapore

has always had to incorporate all the information needed to do business with the British colonial relics, the Chinese, Malay, Indians, the Muslims, Hindus, Buddhists, Christians, everyone who trades in this market. Cultures are bodies of knowledge. Goods for sale are bodies of knowledge. These bodies of knowledge are taught in the Chinese, Tamil, Malay schools. I don't know if they teach Chinese children's lit in the Chinese school. I don't know if the Chinese here know Chinese fairy tales. But I know how to find out. Instead of reading from my work they never heard of and will never read, I'll tell them Chinese stories in English because English is the only common language between all the schools.

What great literary theme might bind the various cultures of Singapore together into one in the English language of Singapore? Dudley asks.

"Migration," I answer. "Singapore is an island. The cultures of ancient Greece, Japan, China, Southeast Asia, were island and seafaring cultures. Boats, orphans in boats, survivors of war and disaster, come by boat—a peach, a lotus, a node of bamboo, a raft of grass, the back of a turtle—to a place where the people have made a deal to sell their children to monsters for the good life.

"I think the similarity between the Greeks and the Chinese and Japanese is due to similar geography, not any prehistoric cultural exchange. The myths of island and seafaring cultures try to cut fine distinctions between the land and the sea, the sea and the sky, the land and the sky, and the finer the differences, the more whimsical the differences become. For the land and sea can exchange places in an instant. The man who makes his living on the sea does not tell time the same as a man who makes his living on the land, yet land and sea exchange places without warning and kill both men. Singapore is making land out of the sea and depends on the sea and the air for

Frank Chin

all its food, all its fuel, all its water, all its money, and ultimately all its people."

"Sounds like the Filipino writer N.V.M. Gonzalez," Dudley says. Ah, he's talked over these same questions with N.V.M. Gonzalez, the dean of Asian American writing. Yes, it does sound like N.V.M. He was born in a village, of an island people in the Philippines. N.V.M. says four hundred years of Spanish and U.S. colonialism has not wiped out the Filipino folktales. He himself tells folktales. N.V.M. calls himself a Filipino writer, not a Filipino American writer. He claims both the Philippines and the United States as home. He writes in English. He's always properly dressed in suit and tie.

N.V.M. Gonzalez told stories with Lawson Inada and me at UCLA. He brought the boat hidden in all the stories we told out into the open. Water. War. Orphans. Boats. Land and sea. Time. Promises kept. Promises broken. Odysseus of Ithaca. Jason. Orpheus of Thrace. Boats. Baby Moses in a reed boat. The gourd twins. The gourd is a boat. The Peach Boy. The peach is a boat. The boy in a lotus. The lotus is a boat. Urashima Taro goes under the sea on the back of a turtle, falls in love with the daughter of the Dragon King, and after three years returns to land to visit his home and say good-bye. He promises to return to the undersea kingdom. He promises never to open the box the dragon king's daughter gives him. Only if the box stays closed will Urashima be able to return to his love under the sea. He opens the box and ages three hundred years, for a year under the sea is a hundred years on land. And he dies.

"What is the box?" I ask N.V.M. Gonzalez.

"Angel Island," the old man says. Angel Island is an island in San Francisco Bay famous for its Immigration Detention Center, where Chinese trying to enter the United States legally were detained.

A Chinaman in Singapore

I frown, not quite understanding. "The box is immigration," N.V.M. says.

"Ah!" I say, as the lightbulb clicks on over my head.

"Do you want to know the secret of long life?" he asks.

"The secret of long life?"

"Raw garlic," N.V.M. Gonzalez whispers. The Filipino secret of long life is raw garlic. But are Filipinos known for being long-lived? N.V.M. is the only old Filipino I know. All the stories we told, Chinese, Japanese, Filipino, seem made for Singapore. What if the writers see that it is not language, or cultural supremacy, or religion that makes them Singaporean but theme and story, the strategy and tactics of the seafaring orphan teaching the parents not to sell their children to monsters, that brought the Chinese and the Tamils and the Malay and the Indonesians and the British and the Japanese, and here come the Bangladeshi, and everybody else to Singapore.

"We're all travelers," I say. I lick sauce off my fingers. "Singapore is a port. It's a depot. A marketplace." The aptness of these children's stories from the Chinese, Japanese, Filipinos, and Greeks to the experience of Singaporeans and Asian Americans is obvious to only a handful of mostly dead Asian American writers (Louis Chu, Wong Sam and associates, John Okada, Toshio Mori), a living Filipino (N.V.M. Gonzalez), and (other than Dr. Han *Love Is a Many Splendored Thing*, Suyin, and Lynn *Sons of the Yellow Emperor* Pan) I don't know how many Chinese Singaporeans.

Dudley listens and smiles and orders more beer. Dudley visits the States regularly. He visited Stanford. Yvor Winters. He stayed at Malamud's house. He knows N.V.M. He's been to more English-speaking countries than I have. Most of them are in Asia, on the Pacific Rim. India, the Philippines, Malaysia, Australia, New Zealand, Indonesia, Canada, the United States. Ah, a man who reads, who travels, who does his homework. Dudley knows a lot more than he shows.

Frank Chin

Singapore morning TV. Big news is Lee Kuan Yew in Suz-chou, China, to sign a big deal with the PRC to build and run an economic zone like Singapore theme park. Lynn Pan is on his staff and in China with Singapore's strongman. Is it my imagination, or Singapore TV, or do I really see his staff is all young women? Like Singapore TV morning is all young women, like the ads for Singapore Air Lines, like the National Arts Council staff. All young women. Mostly Chinese. A couple of token males seem to be trying to act like women in spite of their suits and ties and soft macho trimmings. It's the first anniversary of the morning show, and everybody's here, on-camera and off-camera people. They're trying to do American morning small-talk, beanball, brainless TV Ping Pong. A young woman reporter smiles and forcibly comes on light and silly doing a feature on all the hotels making and selling Chinese moon cakes for Moon Festival. The traditional moon cakes filled with lotus-seed paste with the one, or two, or three, even four hard-cooked egg yolks reddish orange in the center are all over Singapore.

But the big hotels are going experimental gourmet and secret with their moon cakes. One marinades the lotus-seed filling and the egg yolks in cognac. Another has a secret yam filling recipe. The feature ends with the giggling reporter car-rying dozens of designer paper shopping bags full of moon cakes. She couldn't choose, so she bought them all. Low angle up at all the bags. Titter titter. Giggle giggle.

There's an international stamp show going on. The queen's stamp collection is in town with the queen's keeper of the stamps. The feature on the queen's stamp collection goes on and on watching a stiff-upper-lip ancient British white man talk about his favorites and the rarest of the rare stamps in the collection. Instead of looking at the stamps, we stay on the shot of the learned, well-spoken man and watch him try to keep his spit in his mouth. They edit with a shot of the

A Chinaman in Singapore

reporter and the old man looking very interestedly into the glass cases displaying the stamps we can't see. Is this an accurate reflection of how Singaporeans invent their culture and literature?

A CAR IN SINGAPORE

Dudley picks me up at a quarter to nine and takes me out for my first real drive in Singapore. Seventy-five percent of the population lives in subsidized apartments in government housing projects they call "estates" here. It's the only way they can afford to live here. Singapore is very expensive.

Want a car? You have to buy a certificate of eligibility, a permit to buy a car that is about half the cost of the car you want to buy. Average cost of a car and certificate of eligibility is $80,000. Dudley's car: $80,000. A Honda. $30,000 in the United States. So this is the look and sound of $80,000 in Singapore? The only American made on the road I see is a Harley. Want a Harley? $30,000. A $30,000 road bike? Most of the bikes rolling in Singapore are Suzukis. Malaysian laborers buzz them back and forth, in and out of traffic, across the border. Lots of Volvos, BMWs, Lexuses, Porsches, Jaguars. Lots of Hondas and little Japanese trucks no larger than motorcycles with sidecars. Best-selling car: Mercedes. A cool million plus. I see a yellow Lamborghini whisking in and out of traffic, changing lanes, passing on the inside and outside. A Lamborghini! A million for the certificate of eligibility. A million for the car. A Chinaman sits, all smiles, behind the wheel.

Dudley has his car well knickknacked out like a home. The car seats decorated with doilies and pads like living room furniture. A scented air freshener. Air-conditioning. The deejays gulping and barfing out of the car radio have Australian accents.

Frank Chin

Dudley points out the domed Hindu temple painted in blues, neon greens, pinks, to look like the Babylon set of a Hollywood biblical epic. Do I want to stop and go inside for a look? No, thanks, not right now. It doesn't look real. And a Chinese temple, red and gold, and a great gate, with a tile roof bedecked and lit for the last day of the Hungry Ghosts Festival and the beginning of Moon Festival, looks more like Mann's remake of Grauman's Chinese Theatre in LA. A tiled Muslim mosque looks like cloisonné. The oldest Catholic church in Singapore, a shell, a monument on hold. The decaying building is propped up by a scaffolding of lumber thick as railroad ties. Do I want to stop? We have time. The old Indian market. It's going to be torn down and replaced with a highrise. He knows Singapore building by building. He knows the old buildings that have gone down by name and history.

Everybody drives on the wrong side of the road. The racial color mix on the street is dizzyingly unlike anything I've seen. Browns and yellows of all kinds. Turbans of all colors. Indonesian hats. No whites on the streets of the real Singapore. All the whites are in the hotels. Trees grow out of cracks in the frosting of old three-story colonial wedding cakes. The seeds of the jungle have sprouted out of the downspouts, the ledges. Roots of the ancient jungle push the tops of front walls away from the sidewalls at the roofline. Arches and arcades cut into the cake like mouse holes, reveal deep, high rooms full of darkness and emptiness and one old man in undershirt, shorts, and sandals hunkered in front of a stove, or a lamp, or a TV, or staring outside. All these old buildings and old men with trees and mold and moss all over them are condemned to be torn down and replaced with fifty-story funny-shaped postmodern Lego-block buildings with towers, spikes, clocks sticking out the top.

A Chinaman in Singapore

A cement trench with water in it is a storm canal, one of a network that keeps Singapore from flooding during typhoons. Singapore is prone to floods during typhoons. There is no natural waterway through Singapore. All the land Singapore stands on is man-made land, reclaimed swampland. Singapore has no source of freshwater of its own. All its water comes across the straits at Johor. When the Japanese took over Singapore, "the Gibraltar of Asia," all they had to do was turn off the water and wait. If Malaysia stoppers the pipes running across the Straits of Johor, Singapore has maybe ninety days of water stored in new reservoirs. They turned water into the land of a nation without water, and now . . .

ARE THERE PIGEONS IN DISNEYLAND?

We stop at one of the estates with a food court. *Rear Window.* I look across the building faces of dark windows for Grace Kelly and Jimmy Stewart with a broken leg and telephoto lens. Dudley punches his parking coupon. We have bowls of *chiu chow* noodles. I have rice noodles. He has wheat noodles. He has a beer. I have coffee. Mynah birds about the size of jays with yellow beaks and eyes set in yellow lips hop and flock around the flowering trees and the parking lot. A few hop and strut across the cement floor of the food court, avoiding the cats that stalk skinny and trembling through the forest of ankles. A few English sparrows hop, twitch, and blink among the mynahs. I don't see any pigeons. High in the sky, against the burning blue, I see the silhouette of an eagle with stretched wings. "I don't see any pigeons," I say.

"We have pigeons," Dudley says, as if I hurt his feelings. No chewing gum in Singapore. Why not no pigeons? For all their rep as a police state, the cops here don't have nice, sharply creased, Nazi uniforms, and the revolvers they carry look like starter pistols. No big-caliber magnums or sleek steel

Frank Chin

designer automatics on their hips. No gangster dark glasses hanging their big lenses down either side of their noses. No jackboots. No jodhpurs. Black shoes. Maybe that's the point.

The first school is a public secondary school. Comparable to junior high in California. We meet in a lecture room, a small auditorium with raked seating for about a hundred students. The teachers patrol up and down one aisle like squad leaders checking the dress of their lines at parade rest. All the students wear white shirts and blue slacks or skirts. All the boys are on one side of the room, all the girls on the other. They all seem drugged by the heat and humidity. Bored. "Gooood moooorning, Mr. Chin," they say, with a tired lack of enthusiasm and sincerity. The echoes hiss around the high, slick cement walls. Dudley reads a story about a security guard who hits the lottery, from his collection *Lady by the Gatepost*.

The kids don't know me. They haven't read my work. They're more aware of the kids of the opposite sex on the other side of the auditorium than they are of me. They have no reason to listen to what I have to say.

I point to a girl and ask her if her parents would sell her to me for a million dollars. No, she says, and blushes. "Really?" I ask.

After our hour, Dudley takes me by the largest store of the Chinese-owned Popular Book Store chain in Singapore. Books, audio books, computer games, programs, CDs in Chinese. Chinese fairy tales, the classics of the heroic tradition and basic lit in comic books, children's books in English, Tamil, Malay, and English. I buy translations of Chinese comic books of the heroic tradition. Then we have another bowl of noodles in an air-conditioned food court. All the people moving in lines like ants around every shadow, shopping and selling in holes of poured concrete by dim electric light, walk away with their plastic bags and my imagination. I'd just like to hang out and watch. But we have another school.

A Chinaman in Singapore

We drive past a large hillocked campus. "Raffles Institute," Dudley says. This is the prep school of Southeast Asia. Lots of Chinese from Malaysia are sent to this school. This is the school where 100 percent of the grads are accepted into the American universities of their choice. The Chinese of Malaysia send their kids to American universities because Malaysia's version of affirmative action allows only one student of Chinese ancestry into the national university each year, to give the Malay a chance to catch up. These kids have money, nice bicycles, motor scooters, cars. We are not white or Gunga Din enough to read at the Raffles Institute.

We're to read at a private girl's school. A more upscale school than the first school we visited, Dudley says. The lavatories are equipped with flush toilets instead of holes in the floor. The driveway is still under construction. Dudley parks in front of a hole covered with a sawhorse and in back of a big black BMW.

Two girls in uniforms meet us at the top of the great cement staircase into the courtyard of the new cement building. Polite, smiling, bold girls. They both wear glasses. Blue skirts. White blouses. Blue sweaters. White socks. They lead us to where we are to be and who we are to see. All the teachers of the classes assembled to hear us read as part of Singapore Writers Week are women. They all wear glasses. These teachers have done their homework on us. They know Dudley de Souza's collection of short stories. They have my bio and photo in their hands and have read it. Some have even read *Donald Duk*. These teachers are smart. They and their students move and speak with a hearty confidence I haven't seen anywhere else in Singapore. Everyone in Singapore, from the hotel waiters and bellboys to the few shopkeepers I've met eating and buying books outside the hotel and the school this morning, makes me feel like the white colonial oppressor. The students and teachers at this school are different.

Frank Chin

They have a carpeted floor and a microphone, amplifier, and speakers in the room. Fair acoustics. I can hear my voice fill the room. No strain, no pain.

I tell "The Fox and the Tiger." They listen. They laugh. I ask why the Tiger did not eat the Little Fox. They wave their hands for attention and are eager to explain how the Little Fox used the Tiger to fool the animals into thinking the Tiger was his bodyguard and how the Tiger was fooled into thinking the animals were afraid of the Little Fox. I tell them "The Wolf Shandong," "Momotaro," "Nah Jah," and they listen. They move down from the back, and sit closer around me, and listen. I tell the wedding fairy tale "The Dragon and the Phoenix."

They know these stories already. They have just finished studying some of these very stories. They enjoy comparing my telling of stories in my odd, American-accented English to the versions they read in school. Interesting. In Red China, during the Cultural Revolution, these stories were banned in an effort to stamp out Chinese culture. In the United States, these same stories are de facto banned in the public schools to impose Christian versions of Chinese story as misogynistic and immoral on American students. More and more, as my friends grow older, and their sons and daughters grow up, I hear from Chinese American high school students, in California cities, who have asked the English teachers, in their upscale high schools, using Kingston and Tan to teach Chinese American history and lit, if they would be willing to teach translations of the *Ballad of Mulan* to compare to Kingston's paraphrase in *The Woman Warrior* and Chinese fairy tales and kitchen god stories to compare with Tan's misogynist inventions. The English teachers said no, and one answered she was "teaching American culture, not Chinese American lit or multiculturalism." That's not merely an admission of teaching white racism; it's a boast.

A Chinaman in Singapore

Dudley shows me Chinatown, Desker Road, where the whores stand or sit framed in the doorways, and the thieves market, where dealers sit on their haunches by displays of stolen goods arranged on stolen blankets. The Chinese goat restaurant isn't open yet. Looks good. The arms and necks and black hair of men in sleeveless undershirts sitting under fans and high ceilings flicker out of the shadows of little open-air coffee shops, through open arches of two-story buildings, as we pass. "Be careful when you have coffee in these places," Dudley says. "Especially at night. Some gang fight might break out."

Chinatown is car-parts shops, auto repairs, junkyards, one or two big restaurants, and small noodle joints.

"The red lanterns hanging in the front doorways mean there are whores in the back lane. They don't display themselves in the front." The law again. Some shop fronts have red Chinese lanterns. Some don't. It's hot, muggy, and daylight. We look down the lane behind Desker Road. Empty. The girls come out at night. "The government turns a blind eye to this activity," Dudley says. "And confines it to Desker Road."

Dudley is surprised to find the thieves market empty. The thieves market used to cover the sidewalks for blocks around here with glittering stolen goods of all sizes and shapes. Clothes, jewelry, home appliances, art. There used to be crowds of sellers and crowds of buyers. Now it's a couple of wooden benches set up on the sidewalk with ugly plaster junk you might win at a carnival sideshow. No thief would risk crossing Singapore law to steal this stuff. Like Bugis Street and its government-sanctioned transvestite act, this is all the thieves market the government allows and this stuff all the government allows thieves to steal. Government make-believe sleaze for the government's make-believe tourists.

Frank Chin

Back to the hotel for a shower before the reception and forum "Where Is Home?"

There's a fax. Call Snow White at the National Arts Council. The police want me to fax them my questions. I phone the Wicked Witch at the Arts Council. I have only one question for the police: Tell me what you can about the triads. "Oh, they want detailed questions."

"I don't work that way. I want an interview, not a job application."

"Well, the police are professional."

"And I'm a professional writer. I believe I have talked with enough professional police departments to know the difference between the behavior of a professional police force and that of a professional dictatorship. Thanks anyway. Forget it."

I turn on the TV, flop on the big king-size bed, and unpack my booty of comic books. "Yue Fei," the cover reads. "Glory and Tragedy of China's Greatest War Hero." Asiapac Books PTE Ltd. New drawings influenced by Japanese comic book novels and American comic books. Dialogue balloons. Blur, motion, and speed effects in the drawing. Sound effects in the air above the clash of steel.

The color covers, easy-to-read cover design, and old drawings from old comic books of the Canfonian PTE Ltd. Pictorial Series of Chinese Classics display of comic book classics attracted me. I buy several. "Liang Hongyu," the famous story of the girl who beat signals and directions on the battle drum from high ground to her husband's army in the field. Here's a chance for me to get the story straight. Oh, oh! Her father dies, and she has to take a job in a whorehouse playing the drum and singing. Is this the woman warrior as abused, victim, martyr, of Maxine Hong Kingston and Amy Tan's white

A Chinaman in Singapore

racist imagination? No, she studies Sun Tzu's *The Art of War*. She identifies with the Far Mulan of *The Ballad of Mulan*. The women, the men, the China of Kingston, Hwang, and Tan, simply do not exist. Liang Hongyu is no victim.

"The Yang Warriors." At last a version of "Yerng Gah Jerng" ("The Yang Family Generals") in English. It's a comic book, but the comic book is the traditional underground folk form that has saved Chinese culture wherever Chinese culture is banned. In China during the Cultural Revolution. In Indonesia right now.

American connoisseurs of comic book art dismiss Chinese comic books as "Classics Illustrated," but they're more than that. American comic books have not saved American lit, culture, or civilization from extinction. Chinese comic books have. Paul Revere did not risk his life carrying contraband comic book versions of the Declaration of Independence from American patriot to American patriot.

The Chinese comic book began as cheat sheets for marketplace storytellers and opera people. From the drawings one could do the backdrops and costumes for the opera and tell the story. The comic books meant Chinese could go anywhere, anywhere in the world, and take their culture, their values, their civilization encoded in stories, in comic books, with them, leave copies, and move on. And they did, long before American newspapers invented "The Yellow Kid," Sunday funnies, Little Big Books, and comic books.

Two comic-book histories of Chinese folk insurrections against the non-Chinese Manchu Ching dynasty and Christianity using opium to enslave millions of Chinese and Christian arms to murder millions more are especially interesting because they are written in the form and style of the heroic tradition.

"Taiping Heavenly Kingdom" ("Taiping Tien Gawk"), "pictorial stories of the first-ever Christian regime in Chinese history in English & in Chinese," a comic-book documentary history of the man who declared himself the brother of Jesus Christ come to rid China of the foreigners, and "The Boxer Uprising," "pictorial stories of the Chinese peasants' resistance against western powers in contemporary history, in English & Chinese," append photocopies of significant documents.

WILFRED HAMILTON-SHIMMEN

Writers Week kicks off with a reception. I'm introduced to a strange-looking white man with strange blonde hair and a strange blonde moustache, blue blazer, slacks, and tennis shoes.

Wilfred Hamilton-Shimmen says he was a street chief in a triad society in the late fifties and writes about it in his novel *Seasons of Darkness.*

I tell him I'm interested in the triads, as they seem to have come back and dug new roots into the United States.

He says, "When one triad brother greets another . . . ," and gives a slow push of his open hand, back first, toward the soft of my belly just under the rib cage. I lift my left hand slightly and step back and let the slow hit touch. A shot to the liver and pancreas. There's power in the push. He stands screwed into the ground. Hard-style martial arts. Korean tae kwon do. "And you would respond by deflecting the blow to the side, if we are allied. One might greet the other by offering a cigarette," he says, and describes a ceremony with cigarettes. He offers two cigarettes, pulled partway out of the pack. I push them back in, take his pack from his hand, pull two cigarettes out, and give him back the pack. I hand him a cigarette and take out a book of matches. He takes the book of matches from my hands and lights mine and then his.

Oh, this is wonderful stuff. Chinese triad societies, the

A Chinaman in Singapore

"Chinese Mafia" keeping tight and together with secret rites, ceremonies, and signs, but I think that was a long time ago. The FBI says the triads are in Chinatown, New York, Chinatown, San Francisco. They say the Wo Hop To, a Hong Kong triad group, has taken over the major tongs the Hop Sing Tong, the On Leong Tong, the Suey Sing Tong. These were the tongs that had banded together to form the alliance of tongs called the Chung Wah Wooey Goon to drive the criminal tongs and triad groups out of Chinatown and end the tong wars. The state was threatening to bring in the National Guard to take over Chinatown and end the wars. With the National Guard would come government control. No more Chinatown. The wars had to end. The triads had to go. They went. Why are they back?

Membership in the tongs was limited to China-born, southern Chinese, Chinese-speaking men. Their American-born sons couldn't join the tongs. The Chinese Exclusion Act of 1892, the "Gentlemen's Agreement" of 1925, discouraged and limited Chinese immigration, and World War II effectively stopped it. The immigration quota allowed only 105 people of the Chinese race into the country each year until 1966, when the quota was lifted.

The tongs were nothing but old and dying old men. The tongs and the big alliance of tongs, the Chung Wah Wooey Goon, in small Chinatowns outside New York and San Francisco and Los Angeles, changed the rules to survive. In Seattle, Ruby Chow became the first woman, the first American born, the first with no tong affiliation to sit on the Chung Wah board of directors. Since then women have sat on the boards and become president of the Chung Wah in Portland, Chicago, Chinatowns in the South. In Chinatowns where they didn't change the rules, like San Diego, the Chung Wah Wooey Goon died when the tongs died.

Frank Chin

In San Francisco and New York they didn't change the rules. The tongs were nothing but rickety old men, playing mah jong with the color TV on. The China-born, Chinese-speaking, southern Chinese men joining the tongs after the lifting of the quota were gangsters with triad ambitions and triad connections to Hong Kong. They filled the void of fifty years without new members. Too late the old men of the old days and the old rules discovered their nice old tongs had been taken over by the same criminal triad groups they had driven out in the early twentieth century.

The American-born sons and grandsons barred from membership in their fathers' tongs are cops today and making war on the triads, the gangs, and the tongs. It's strange to see these American-born Chinese American boys and girls too American to dirty themselves with Chinese stuff learning the difference between the real and the fake. They're learning the Chinese myth and fairy tales of the Chinese Americans whites love to read are nothing like the Chinese myth and fairy tales of the Chinese texts. And it's turning their stomachs and bending their minds.

Singapore is small. The cops here keep things tightly buttoned and zipped. No garbage, no spit, no dog doo on the streets. Not even a candy wrapper. I'm assuming they keep the triads and organized crime out. But can they? They still control all the hawkers, drugs, and prostitution, Wilfred Hamilton-Shimmen says.

That's the street.

Wilfred Hamilton-Shimmen doesn't know about the triad action in today's Singapore. He slicked out of the triad by getting permission to go to college, covering up his tattoos, and never coming back thirty years ago. But he's back now. How does he get away with it?

The Chinese triad gangsters don't read English-language

A Chinaman in Singapore

books, he says. And he wears long sleeves to cover his faded tattoos.

His self-published 677-page monster autobiographical historical Singapore novel describes a series of do-or-die ceremonies in a cemetery at night to become a triad brother that reconfirms or was cribbed from W. P. Morgan's *Triad Societies in Hong Kong* (Hong Kong: Government Press, 1960).

Hamilton-Shimmen's account of his triad gaining control of the Singapore River is the stuff of Hong Kong movies and, along with his aging, blurring tattoos, convinces me he actually was a kid in a triad street gang.

Erroll said the "talks" being held at the "Southern Cabaret" was crucial to the chap kapa and all the affiliated groups that belonged to it. "Hylam Kopi" had decided to "break cover" and head the triad negotiations personally because it would be the "final show-down" between the "Zero eight Tong" and the "Twenty four Tong" to decide finally which of the two strongest deserved to be "Number One". "Hylam Kopi's" separate tongs would be meeting for the first time, and Thomas then began to understand that he was in a Chinese tong that was part of a massive network of crime under the control of just one criminal mastermind. He listened intently as Erroll outlined his instructions to all the "seniors" present that day.

No gang member was to "recognise" or acknowledge "Hylam Kopi" on the "big day" of the "talks." Everyone was to know who he was but each was to remain within his respective group at the "talks" side. The two "Big Bosses" from the two rival gangs would discuss "terms" at a table in the middle of the "meet" area, which was the main dining room of the cabaret, between their respective "armies." In keeping with "triad law" there would be an upturned cup placed in a saucer, with a porcelain Chinese coffeeshop-spoon on top of it, between the two men. Everyone was to

*keep his eye on the up-turned cup as well as the coffeeshop-spoon,
and to "forget" about trying to overhear what the two "bosses"
were saying to each other. This part was crucial, Erroll said.*

*If "Hylam Kopi" pointed the spoon-handle toward the other,
everyone was to brace himself for the other man's reaction. If he
turned the handle back toward their leader, everyone should be
keyed to respond to one of two reactions from "Hylam Kopi". He
could choose to again swerve the spoon-handle back toward his
rival to "re-consider" or "Hylam Kopi" could dash the cup and
spoon from the table with a sweep of a hand as he simultaneously
attacked his rival.* Red Pole Fighters *as well as "normal" fighters from the rival tongs would then "battle" until only one side
was left. The side that won would assume control of the stakes they
had all gone to the "Southern Cabaret" to "settle" for. The age-
ing* sar, ji, kow *(the 329 tong), had already relinquished its
"authority" to decide who would finally gain control of the
waterway....*

*"Hylam Kopi" sat down at the "meet" table in the center of
the cabaret-hall, at the same time as the leader from the opposite
side. The young teenager's brain boggled! Dispensing with pre-
liminaries, his "Big Boss" simply swiveled the Chinese porcelain
spoon in the direction of the other man, indicating only one
thing as he calmly folded his arms across his chest and gazed
unblinkingly into his rival's eyes. Thomas knew. There was to be
"no talk." His "Big Boss" had indicated that he wouldn't nego-
tiate, and that it was up to the other man.*

*Without taking his eyes off the spoon on the upturned cup in
the middle of the "talk table", Thomas unwrapped his two
parangs and slid each into either hand, holding both long blades
by their handles, at an upward slant at shoulder level. He read-
ied himself to hurl his body at the enemy gang chief. He could
hear his own side bracing itself. To "glory or doom". Chairs were
being scraped as owners manoeuvered for a good take-off posi-*

A Chinaman in Singapore

tion. Paper was being wrenched off concealed weapons all over the place. Thomas found himself breathing hard. He knew he was about to die that day. Before he had even become a man. His lips lifted in a sneer. He would lop-off the head of the opposing bastard gang-chief first before he was gunned down or hacked in half. Mentally counting his steps, he measured the paces he would take to get to the other gang-leader. Five big steps. From the corner of his eye he saw Erroll, Omar Diamond and Hock Seng take out their hand-guns, and draw a bead on the head of the opposing gangster-chief.

With a quiet sigh the rival gang-boss smiled, leaned forward, lifted the porcelain spoon from the up-turned cup, and placed it beside the cup, which he then up righted as well. There would be no gang-clash! They had won. The ji-tse tong *(the 24 tong) had caved in! Hock Seng's light tap on his shoulder brought him out of the self-imposed mind-set he had assumed to keep out any feelings of guilt which would have slowed down his reflexes.*

Wilfred Hamilton-Shimmen knows it was extraordinary for a Eurasian to be made into a triad brother. He knows, because he is not all Chinese, non-Chinese do not rise far in the triads. He was a tough kid. When he was sixteen in Singapore and extorting protection on the hawkers, pimps, and whores on his turf, I was sixteen in Oakland and discovering white girls were girls, too.

In the States, New York, San Francisco, the kids calling themselves triad don't do a lot of ceremonies. Even in Hong Kong I hear the ceremonies are pretty much the stuff of the past and the movies. The rules have changed. The triads in San Francisco and New York do not bar American-born kids from joining. Lieutenant Chong, a New York cop, tells a room full of cops meeting to get the big picture of Asian youth gangs in America he worked three years undercover as a gang member. "I have the tattoos to prove it," he says.

Frank Chin

CHILDREN'S STORIES

Lieutenant David Chong, NYPD

Fourteen years NYPD. Deep undercover in Flying Dragons, three years. Called "Dai Low," Big Brother. Crew of eighteen. Enforcement unit. Weapons specialist. Recruitment unit.

Tattoos. Over the heart a big dragon. On the right arm another flying dragon. His gang was the bad boys of On Leong Tong.

What he doesn't say is more disturbing that what he does. Flying Dragons—the Fay Lung Tong—is a triad society in Hong Kong the Hong Kong police say is into running drugs, whores, "hawker protection," and "the sale of black market theater tickets."

Theater tickets. Who says cold-blooded, hotheaded robbers, thieves, pimps, kidnappers, and murderers don't have culture? Not me. The white, cold-blooded, hotheaded robbers, thieves, pimps, kidnappers, and murderers who came to Asia and took over Singapore were all led by Christian missionaries who could sing and dance and recite Shakespeare.

For years I've been in a sort of denial. There are no triads in Chinatown. I was sure. It made no sense. When the tong wars in San Francisco, Oakland, Sacramento, threatened to bring the National Guard into Chinatown to destroy the political and geographic integrity of Chinatown, the "good tongs" banded together into the Choong Wah Wooey Goon (Chinese Consolidated Benevolent Association) and drove out the criminal triads.

Chinatown tongs were clean. They had charters and bylaws filed with the state. Since then every Chinatown was governed by an alliance of all the powerful organizations with an interest in the local Chinatown. In New York the On Leong Tong sat on the board of the local Choong Wah. The On Leong has

A Chinaman in Singapore

been the most powerful tong on the East Coast for more than a century.

West of the Mississippi, the On Leong are allied with the Bing Kung Tong (Chinese Freemasons). The Bing Kung Tong and the Hop Sing Tong have been rivals for number one on the West Coast for a hundred years. Hop Sing had an edge in numbers and prestige. The prestige was based on gambling and opera. Cantonese opera.

The triads began as bands of Robin Hood–like outlaws dedicated to ousting the foreign Manchu dynasty and restoring the Ming. In the Ming, Chinese, not foreign conquerors, ruled China. The revolution of 1911 that ended dynastic China and created the Republic of China was Chinese enough for the triads, but not only did they continue to exist, they thrived and multiplied, running the port cities from the dark side of the street so completely and so efficiently the Japanese negotiated with the triad societies of Hong Kong before they invaded and occupied it. The Japanese could not have run Hong Kong without the triads. And after the war, as before, neither could the British. Taiwan, the island Republic of China, uses the triads as a branch of its secret police and overseas spies and assassins.

Now, from the high to the low, the Chinese triad societies are on both coasts of the American continent and Houston, Texas. Owooooo? Hear that wolf?

Lieutenant David Chong describes the method of recruiting for his crew. He targets nerds in junior high. Not the stars. Not the champs. Not the tough and confident. He targets the one everyone picks on. He sets his gang on him. They humiliate this kid in front of other kids in front of the junior high for days, weeks, months— Then one day Dai Low, Big Brother, drives by in his nice car full of nice-looking girls, stops, and says, "Stop! I like this guy." Takes him for a ride in his nice car to a nice restaurant, feasts the kid, lets him play with the girls,

Frank Chin

then draws him into the gang. Sounds like pimp talk. It is. Turns the kid into a "killing machine," he says. To do what? Kidnapping, robbery, and murder. Says he runs his crew and keeps them in line with intimidation, brutality, and fear.

I wonder if he knows his description of how he recruits thugs for his crew is almost word for word a strategy described in the work of the ancient strategist Tai Kung, and later Sun Tzu, for recruiting spies, expendable agents.

He has pictures of the victims of triad house-robbery victims. The Chinese triads strike terror in the Chinese. So the victims are Chinese. Torture-maim-murder. Revenge. Loyalty demanded. No outs. Disloyalty demands violent revenge. Duct tape babies to the wall, and duct tape over the baby's eyes. "Do you know what will happen to the skin of that baby's face when I rip off the duct tape?" Lt. Chong asks. "The eyelids come off. The lips. . . ."

But first they go to your fridge, open up the freezer, take out the ice trays, and throw ice cubes at the baby. Duct tape over the mouth. The baby doesn't cry. The screaming parents don't hear the baby. They hear the ice cubes hitting the baby with one sound and breaking against the walls with a different sound.

The gangs are not afraid of cops. They practice facing a cop and snatching his gun out of his holster. One kid wears a cop gun and holster rig. And another kid snatches the cop's gun. How?

A right-handed cop with his nice pistol or revolver tucked into his breakaway holster with the thumb retainer closed on his right hip stops a Chinese gang kid on the street in New York. The kid makes a fast "karate chop–like" move with his left hand down to the cop's holster, flips the thumb retainer off the back of the pistol or revolver, grabs the weapon by the handgrip, and snatches it from the breakaway holster, with the little finger around the trigger, in one move. This places the

A Chinaman in Singapore

weapon upside down and pointed at the cop, chest level. The kid squeezes the trigger with his little finger. So much for kung fu being David Carridine doing ballet exercises in slow motion for doing good.

It's in the movies; it's in the comic books; it's in the heroic adventures. All men are born soldiers. The war is against one's personal integrity. Men meeting each other stand a spear length apart, where they can see the whole man. A cop that allows a stranger inside an arm's reach of his weapon, his body, isn't ready for the Chinese streets.

The good lieutenant seems a little surprised and outraged that the Chinese gang kids tape their weapons to their girl-friends' bodies, not their own. Ah, yes, it's the dragon and the phoenix. You and me, sweetheart. Together, we make one young kill crazy gunfighter. You and me against the universe.

He warns his law enforcement colleagues about girlfriends trained to carry razor blades in their mouths. She can talk, she can kiss, she can eat and drink with this blade in her mouth. And a cop stops her and her gangster boyfriend. While the partner pats down the gangster, the girlfriend tells the cop she wants to tell him something privately. A secret. She smiles with a razor blade invisible, between her teeth. She slices up the cop's face or cuts his throat. Distraction action. Both run.

The girlfriend who takes herself for real is not a sexual tro-phy. She might have attracted her gangster with her looks, or her sex, or her home cooking, or all of that, but she sees her-self as more than a toy, more than an ego massage for the male. Life is war. All behavior is tactics and strategy. All relationships are martial. Love is two warriors back to back fighting off the universe. The girlfriend is her gangster's equal, his ally.

Cop cars are now equipped with airbags. A cop pulls up behind a car of gang kids in Chinatown, New York. The cops stop the car, and the kids suddenly back into the cop cruiser

Frank Chin

fast—pop go the airbags and marshmallow the cops to the backs of their seats. The kids jump out of their car and shoot the cops through the airbags.

Chong advises cops working Asian gangs in the age of the electronic car to carry knives to cut the airbags when they pop or to get rid of them.

What the good lieutenant, the brave and heroic lieutenant, demonstrates are the effects, the dark side of the universe where the individual is defined by, "Life is war," untempered by the Confucian "mandate of heaven."

Chong forced a gang lieutenant, a *dai low* or "big brother," to sponsor him into the Flying Dragons, a twenty-year-old Chinatown gang known to be what used to be called the hatchets and highbinders of the On Leong Tong. In the On Leong Tong are men connected to Chinese triad societies. The Chinese "M." All the little gangsters of Chinatown, of Little Saigon, of the Cambodian and Lao, sparkle their eyes at the dream of being made into the Chinese "M." The triads. The Chinese Mafia.

Chong was called and given a contract on the *dai low* who had recruited him. Chong's *dai low* believes the guy who recruited Chong is a fink. To prove Chong was the real thing, he was expected to kill his best friend in the gangs.

The cops and feds combined to fake the death of Chong's best friend, and the real best friend disappeared into a lifetime of the Witness Protection Program. The Witness Protection Program is like John Frankenheimer's *Seconds*. Police-state reality beyond *The Manchurian Candidate,* and almost as good a movie, shot by James Wong Howe. We are in the point of view of a man who goes through all kinds of cosmetic surgery, gets new papers, an indoctrination into a new identity, and has become Rock Hudson trying to adjust to being Rock Hudson in a world that will kill him if he ever slips from

A Chinaman in Singapore

being Rock Hudson. In the movie, Rock Hudson slips. In the Witness Protection Program, Chong's best friend is another man.

David Chong gave up the undercover gangster life after being given a contract on an assistant district attorney and two New York police officers. The cops were willing to fake their deaths and take a lifetime vacation fishing off the Florida Keys in the Witness Protection Program, but the assistant DA wasn't. So Chong came in from out of the Chinatown cold and put on his blues.

The good news is house robberies are down. The bad news is credit card fraud is up, way up. Fake credit cards, ATMs, gang chiefs, and gang kids—sounds like something that would fit right in with Singapore's economic miracle culture. High-tech crime.

WHERE IS HOME?

This is the second Singapore Writers Week.

The first literary event is a forum; six writers answer the question, Where is home? The forum is chaired by Koh Tai Ann, a tiny little woman—very tight and tidy—dean of the School of Arts of Nanyang University, National Institute of Education. She wears her hair up. She wears a suit. She raises Milton's *Paradise Lost* from out of the mists of college lit and likens Singapore to the Garden of Eden. I haven't heard *Paradise Lost* quoted since the last time I read Bram Stoker's *Dracula*. Why not Singapore as Atlantis? Or Singapore as Troy? Or the Tower of Babel? Or the Water Margin?

The people at the table sit with one elbow on the table and their hands stroking their chins. This is the major ballroom of the marbled and columned hotel. I look up and down the table of waiting speakers and into the audience of Singapore writers, writers from Bangladesh, Taiwan, Canada, Australia.

Frank Chin

Very international. Very hotel. Very *Shanghai Express.* The missionaries. The colonials. The Eurasian with an identity crisis. The Chinese at last played by real Chinese. Or are they? Everybody looks a likely target. The caper here is to take over Singapore English-language literature and rule the school.

Matthew Kneale's name and picture are not in the program. He's a replacement. He flew in on short notice, happy for the free trip. Puppy dog. He says he was so happy to be invited he would have come even if he'd had to pay his own way. He slouches and humbly eats shit and loves it, with charm and manners—the Peter Ustinov of the scene. He lives in London. "Lots of people live in London. Nobody calls London home."

His father was from the Isle of Man, the island famous for cats with no tails and sheep that eat seaweed and taste like fish. Matthew Kneale says he has no love for his Manx past. Matthew's mother was British. He lives in England but threw himself at Japan with five hundred British pounds in his pocket. Got a hotel. Got a job teaching English. Got a room and lived in Japan a while. He wrote a book about it.

Robert Drewe, a born and bred Australian, reads a ten-minute version of a very nice story also set in Japan. A fiftyish white man from Australia watches a strange Japanese TV game show in a Japanese hotel room and reads a book of English translations of letters by kamikaze pilots sealed with clippings of their hair and fingernails before they flew off to die. An earthquake strikes Japan and shakes up his sense of history and identity. Drew writes everything. Novels. Short stories. Plays. Screenplays. Film criticism. Journalism. He teaches writing. He's won awards. His writing and teaching have taken him around the world. He calls Sydney, Australia, his home.

Poet Michael Donaghy was born in the Bronx but trained to be Irish by his Irish mother. He's never been to Ireland. Lives in London and New York. He tells the story of the Irish

Chicago police chief who made cops of musicologists and ordered them to take down the words and music to all the Irish folk songs around town. A true story.

Think of a pagan Chinese dropping in on England on a dare with $500 in his pocket, finding a series of white girl-friends and larking around London, enjoying the wonder of knowing nothing, and writing a novel about not being assimilated by the totalitarian and superstitious English.

Think of an American of Chinese descent becoming chief of the San Francisco Police Department, hiring Chinese cops to collect and record Chinese folktales. Then think of what's actually happened in San Francisco, where Chinese Americans running the schools have made their careers using *The Five Chinese Brothers* and Christian Chinese autobiographies to falsify and ban Chinese children's lit. Between the Chicago Irish Americans and the Frisco Chinese Americans the difference between teaching the real and the fake comes clear. To teach the fake is to teach racial self-contempt.

Where is home? Singapore suddenly flashes me the big picture of English-speaking Chinese around the world. I see all persons of Chinese ancestry, all of them born to speak English in Australia, in New Zealand, in England, in Indonesia, and in Singapore, writing the very same Christian white racist autobiography, the same old Yung Wing, Leong Gor Yun, Pardee Lowe, Jade Snow Wong, Virginia Lee, Maxine Hong Kingston, Amy Tan, Gus Lee, on and on, the same old book about the same old Chinese Christian me me me, wanting to be free of a Chinese culture so misogynistic and morally despicable it doesn't deserve to survive.

Around the world are all these Chinese in England, Australia, Canada, the United States, Singapore, Malaysia, more white than thou, more hip than thou, writing of how they gave up being Chinese to become human in poetic prose right out of Fu Manchu, and blaming it on their mothers. What

Frank Chin

happens if they all happen to meet at a writers conference? What will be the substance of that "affinity" for other Chinese from around the world? Not these Chinese. Aside from their having worked so hard to tell the world how Chinese they are not and never were. All they have in common is snickering at their parents' funny way of mangling English. How many times can they write the same book? How many times can whites stand to read it? Every ten years, here comes another one. Whoops, here comes Charlie Chan again.

When my turn comes to speak, I refuse to write or talk autobiography. I am not white. I am not Christian. One cannot be a Chinese Christian. It's like being a Nazi Jew. It can't be done. All Chinese American writing proves that.

"Home is a kind of childhood sickness," I say. "There's no such place, no such thing as home. I can't speak for all writers, but this writer is like Monkey. At a certain age, I am born an adult, stupid and naked to the world, and have to learn everything. Life is war; all behavior is tactics and strategy. All relationships are martial. Love is two warriors back to back fighting off the universe. Writing is fighting. All warfare is based on deception, Sun Tzu the strategist says. The acme of military skill is to win without taking a life or losing a life, he says. So the first strategy Monkey has to learn is how to make the difference between the real and the fake. So he can't be deceived.

"Once Monkey starts to learn, men try to trick and control him by keeping him deep in the busywork of ignorance. He learns everything men know. The gods try to control him with a fancy title for a stupid job. He learns everything the gods know. The secret of his mastering the knowledge of all men and gods and eventually the Buddha himself: reading. Monkey reads and writes in all languages and learns and masters all strange languages. The Buddha tries to control him with illusions of time and space and unbearable pain through a golden

A Chinaman in Singapore

headband. The book ends with the Buddha naming him a Buddha to try to control him, but the Monkey keeps on learning, beyond nirvana, beyond the bright lights of enlightenment, beyond everything written. And that's where we want to go and write from.

"I don't need America to be an American. I've been there. I'm like Gene Kelly, an American in Paris. Wherever I live, I'm an American. I don't need China to be Chinese. Monkey teaches that all cultures are bodies of knowledge. They can be learned. Chinese, like Monkey, have traveled all over this world, and some of us are living there, in every city, in every town, every wine and suey joint all over this world.

"Once Monkey learns how to learn, the joy of knowledge is his home. He knows too much for the places of the past not to be seen as corrupted by bullshit and stupidity. So he keeps on moving, keeps on learning. Learning is part of writing. My home is here," I say, pointing at my head, "and here," and point at my heart. I look straight down and say, "Anybody can learn my roots. I don't worry about roots. It's not my Chinese or American roots that worry people. It's my seed that worries people. My home is here," I touch my head, "and here," I touch my heart. "My home is my writing. My home is my craft, my art." Less the five minutes.

Dudley de Souza, a Singapore writer, born and raised in Singapore, disagrees with me, and it bothers him. He feels no connection to the home of his ancestors: Portugal.

The ambitious Singapore-born Chinese of Dudley's Singapore are Chinese in name only. His story "Lady by the Gatepost" is about such a Singaporean:

The house drew him first. Leonard Lin loved looking at houses in magazines as well as in real life. He and his wife had recently moved into the estate—small, secluded, with a suburban ambience and delightfully English names like Cornwall Drive or

Hampton Avenue and, surprisingly, only twenty minutes from the city centre. (That was what Sylvia had liked about it—the proximity to Orchard Road where she spent weekends, often to his chagrin, rifling through the range of Versace, Armani, Missoni, Ricchi, Ferre found in the up-market boutiques.) She had expensive tastes—holding her nose up at OG and Trend—not realizing that her husband was only a poor academic just beginning to make his way up the ranks, he had often told her jokingly. He had come from a taxi-driver family in Bukit Ho Swee and, although he had made good by way of scholarships, he always tried to live as frugally as his family used to. . . .

He remembers the Japanese occupation at the same time and age I remember a little two-room house with a little porch and twin-boomed Lockheed P-38s flying overhead in the California mother lode country. He was a Portuguese Malay boy who thought himself Singaporean in a British colony occupied by the Imperial Japanese Army, who patrolled the streets in little tanks. All Dudley's intense memory is invested in Singapore. World War II. There is no Portugal. His home is Singapore. He remembers when Singapore City was small and most of the country was kampongs and jungle.

Wilfred Hamilton-Shimmen shouts from the audience, "That was a long time ago, Dudley!"

Wilfred the Eurasian with the dreads of both worlds in his blood—British colonist and Chinese—and Dudley de Souza take the question, Where is home? very seriously. As born Singaporeans with a Singapore citizenship created late in their lives, they feel the threat of being disenfranchised, dumped as citizens of the new nation-city-state of Singapore. Why do they stay? Where could they go? England won't have them now if it wouldn't have them when they turned the colony back to Malayan people in 1965.

Wilfred and Dudley were committed to writing, were

A Chinaman in Singapore

twenty-five years old in 1965 when the Republic of Singapore was born. They must have felt chosen. They still feel chosen. Thirty years later, they're still asking the same questions, still trying to create a literature for a Singapore that doesn't seem to care.

The only whites in the audience are writers brought here for Singapore Writer's Week. The first question is for me. "If life is war for you, are you prepared to fight and die?"

"The Chinese Americans are a lovingly despised minority in America. I have been despised all my life in the country of my birth. Fear of white racism is a childhood disease. I am no longer a child. I don't write for white acceptance. I don't write to get along with anybody. I write to tell the truth. Writing is fighting. Nations come and go. It's a good day to die. Let the good times roll."

A brown-skinned black-haired Tamil asks, "Is not living in peace better than war? My people believe in peace, a life without conflict and violence."

"I didn't massacre Chinese in Los Angeles, Seattle, Rock Springs. I didn't write Charlie Chan. I didn't start the war against Chinese history and culture. The war is against your personal integrity. The war is against you personally. You want to be a loser, lose. If that doesn't bother you, it doesn't bother me. You lose. I win."

Muscle Shirt with a baseball hat says, "When I listen to you, I hear American American American."

"That I speak American English does not mean I do not also speak Cantonese. Chinese culture is universal. It translates well into any language. Monkey is Monkey in any language. Chinese ideas are Chinese ideas in any language. If they sound like American ideas when I roll them out in everyday language, all the better. It means Americans can understand Chinese ideas."

From the audience Wilfred Hamilton-Shimmen calls out,

Frank Chin

"Home is generally where one finds he is most comfortable."

"I'm really comfortable in the toilet. So I guess my home is the toilet," I say, thinking very Monkey.

ROOM 1410

Seven Singapore writers, including Koh Tai Ann, dean of the School of Arts at the National Institute of Education, follow me up to my room to talk.

Muscle Shirt and Baseball Cap, who listens to me and hears "American, American, American," gives me his card. "E. C. Goh." His card reads, "The Write One—Journalist, Lyricist, Musicologist, Playwright, Poet, Scriptwriter." He speaks in a deep, creamy voice. He says, "I love the way you stir things up."

"Isn't it interesting; you are all Chinese, except Dudley, who probably has some distant Chinese blood in him on his mother's side?" I say, and everyone glances at everyone else. Shimmen, Goh, Koh Tai Ann, Woon Ping, Dudley, Robert Yeo, the woman with short hair, and one who doesn't introduce himself. All Chinese. Yes, we are all Chinese. All men are brothers.

"What are the Chinese to do in countries that despise Chinese culture and language?" Koh Tai Ann asks.

"Writing is fighting. You fight fake knowledge with the real. You call white racists by their right name. Like Sun Tzu, like Monkey, you make the difference between the real and the fake."

Woon Ping, a native of Singapore now on leave from the English Department at Swarthmore to write poetry for a year at home in Singapore, is interested in me because I call famous Asian American writers white racists and fakes and don't seem to be bothered by them dismissing me as a jealous wanna-be.

A Chinaman in Singapore

"Yes, I do. And no, I'm not. I admit it. I have a lousy personality. Making me famous isn't going to make the fakes any less fake or less white racist."

"What do you mean 'they fake it'?" Koh Tai Ann asks.

"Text. Maxine Hong Kingston falsifies Chinese text. There is no *Ballad of Mulan* where Mulan is tattooed, is abused for being a woman, and returns home to her family slaughtered and impoverished." Aha! Everyone in the room takes another look at me when I mention Chinese stuff. "There is no misogyny in *The Ballad of Mulan*. The last lines, 'The he rabbit tucks in his feet to sit. / The she rabbit dims her shiny eyes. / Two rabbits hopping for the grass. / Who can tell which is the he and which is the she?' describes Confucian romantic love as two warriors back to back fighting off the universe.

"You all know the dragon and the phoenix on the back walls of large Chinese restaurants with the double character 'Double Happiness' shaped like a square or a ball between them. 'The Dragon and the Phoenix' is the wedding fairy tale. And the dragon and the phoenix on the wall means that restaurant wants to do your wedding reception."

Woon Ping is not sure she remembers the wedding fairy tale. Ah, I like tests. I tell a Chinese story to Chinese writers in Singapore.

So I tell it. The dragon and the phoenix leave their territories of the Milky Way River to the west and Magic Mountain to the east and bloody themselves chiseling a newfound crystal into their bright pearl. They become human to love each other and take care of their pearl. The queen mother of the Western Paradise steals the pearl. She shows the pearl to the gods at her birthday party. Dragon and Phoenix crash the party, and the pearl falls and rolls off the edge of heaven and crashes into China to become West Lake, in Hangzhou City, a hundred miles or so southwest of Shanghai, and Dragon crashes into China and becomes Dragon Mountain to the

Frank Chin

west, and Phoenix crashes into China and becomes Phoenix Mountain to the east, and there they are, taking care of their pearl and loving each other, to this day.

"They stood back to back fighting off the universe like Far Mulan and her ally in the *Ballad of Mulan*. Then they took human form and had sex, and Far Mulan takes a lover after she and her ally have proved themselves once around the twelve years of the twelve animals, one life cycle of battle. Then and only then does her ally see that Mulan is a girl—sexual awakening! And then and only then does the 'she rabbit dim her shiny eye. The he rabbit sits on his feet. / Two rabbits hop side by side for the grass. Who can tell which is the he, which is the she?' That's poetry! That's a sexy image! There are no tattoos. No abuse of women. No male superiority. No female inferiority. Love is two warriors standing back to back fighting off the universe.

"The woman general is not tattooed, not abused by any man in or out of her family, is not belittled by either the high or the low for being a woman, and her family is not slaughtered, and she does not return home in poverty or shame."

The dean says, "I thought that was Kingston's 'Americanized' version."

"Americanized?" I ask. "She takes a popular child's chant describing Confucian love and tortures and abuses and slaughters the family of Mulan to characterize Chinese culture as being so abusive of women and morally despicable it doesn't deserve to survive."

"That's what I mean when I say she *Americanized* the story," Koh Tai Ann says.

She's amused by me being so American and still treating Chinese literature as real literature with titles that can be read, dated, traced by comparison with other titles.

"Have you ever met Kingston?" Woon Ping, the poet on sabbatical from Swarthmore, asks.

A Chinaman in Singapore

"No, I have no interest in meeting Kingston privately. Meeting her won't make her work less white racist, less fake. Would a Jew want to meet Hitler to resolve their differences of opinion? There's no misunderstanding Hitler or Kingston. They're both white racists. I don't like white racists. My dislike of white racists is not private. I will only meet Kingston in public, and only for a lot of money, because she charges a lot of money to appear in public. But she won't do it because she knows I'll prove her a fraud with one word: *text*."

How does Kingston respond to my charging her with fraud?

"She defends the fake by faking it. She's now saying there are three lost *Chinese Books of Peace*. She was writing the fourth, but the Oakland fire burned it up. So she's now writing *The Fifth Book of Peace*. There is not one lost *Chinese Book of Peace,* and not two, not three. She's faking it."

"How do you know?"

"Every influential text is written about, and criticized, and analyzed, and quoted, and argued, and dramatized, and parodied in the pop culture. That's how literary influence is expressed—in literary reference, citation, and comparison. Literature, by definition, is text and the reading and comparison of text. And in all of Chinese writing there is no mention, no quotation, no reference, no criticism, no analysis, of any Book of Peace. But there is plenty of quotation of form and content of *The Ballad of Mulan*."

Koh Tai Ann asks how I learned all these stories. "Did your parents tell you stories?" No. Not my parents.

"I learned this stuff the way most kids learn it, from comic books, from good translations, from the opera, from the repetition of specific characters, themes, and forms in the culture, art, and literature, Hong Kong movies.

"I learned most of this stuff taking Kingston and company seriously. They're absolutely right in pointing to the fairy tales

Frank Chin

and traditional children's lit as the source of all Chinese values and ethics in the Chinese people. So if they say these traditional Chinese stories their mothers told them are the source of Chinese abuse of women, I have to find them.

"If, as my gut tells me, they're faking it and writing the same old stereotype, the proof will be *The Ballad of Mulan* and the kitchen god in Chinese lit. No problem. The Chinese become Chinese not by reading the complete and unabridged classics right out of the womb. So, even if they never read all of *Three Kingdoms,* they know it. Most have never read, seriously read, *The Dream of the Red Chamber* but would immediately recognize the behaviors described as Chinese and strategic in structure and tactical in behavior.

"The comic books and children's books presented the works of children's lit in an orderly fashion. It is no mystery which stories were told and reprinted and printed underground when censored. The influential works are reprinted in several editions over and over over the centuries.

"I'm still looking. And most of the new stuff in English is from right here, Singapore. Dudley took me to Popular Bookstore between gigs today. Look, here is the famous story of the drummer girl, 'Liang Hongyu.'

"Early in the story, in the comic book, a popular singer in the whorehouse belittles the drummer girl, Liang Hongyu's study of Sun Tzu's *The Art of War.* 'Being girls, what can we do? We can't go to the battle-field to fight against the Jins!'

"And in the next drawing, Miss Liang answers, 'What you say is not totally true. Wasn't Hua Mulan [Far Mulan] of ancient times a girl? She could go to the battle-field to fight the enemy. If I've the chance, I'll join the army and slaughter the Jins mercilessly. I'll never go down on my knees to sue for peace with the enemy, as the present army officers and generals are doing.'

"Aha! Direct references to Sun Tzu and *The Ballad of*

A Chinaman in Singapore

Mulan. The whole form of the story of Liang Hongyu and her husband is *The Ballad of Mulan*. Against the orders of the Song court, they fight the invading Jin again and again, like the dragon and the phoenix bloodying themselves hacking the crystal into their bright pearl, and Mulan and her ally, in twelve years of war together, they are two warriors back to back fighting off the universe.

"In the course of their lone defense of Chinese territory and culture, they become allies with Yue Fei (Ngawk Fei), another rebel hero of the Song, who disobeys the court to fight the Jin. And look, here is the three-volume comic-book novel.

"And here's the two-volume set of 'Yang Warriors' comic book. Also set in the Song. Also about great Chinese heros generals and their wives and the wives' female servants as allies in war who went against the orders of the court to fight the tribes invading from the north. The Jin and the Liao. All these stories are linked by history, quotation of each other, and Far Mulan. Fake one, you fake them all. And here is the same Far Mulan paraphrased in '100 Celebrated Chinese Women' and '100 Chinese Gods,' pictures and descriptions by Lu Yanguang. Lu lives here in Singapore."

Woon Ping, the poet on leave from Swarthmore, picks up the "100 Celebrated Chinese Women." This is one of her favorite books. She likes the drawings especially. What do I think of the drawings?

"The drawings are too much style for style's sake for my taste," I say.

"But the important thing is that writer Cai Zhuozi and illustrator Lu Yanguang's '100 Celebrated Chinese Women' joins the huge pile of books of pop and folk culture that cite the same texts, choose the same heroines as important, describe these heroines in the same way. The number and variety of these books demonstrate that they express common knowledge, not some exclusive, or private, or obscure, or exotic, or cultish fetish.

"We've all been to American colleges. We're all trained to spot themes and patterns in Shakespeare and Milton and have yet to read Chinese childhood lit for theme and pattern. I'm looking for this theme of female inferiority and the morality of abusing women Kingston, Hwang, and Tan and the Asian American studies programs say is dominant and finding nothing like it. And I tell you true, you can break into Chinese children's lit as surely and easily as I can break into your car or your house. If there's misogyny in the Chinese fairy tale, you or I can find it by reading them.

"Kingston's autobiography, her nonfiction *Memoirs of a Girlhood among Ghosts,* is supposedly based on *The Ballad of Mulan.* When she's called on to produce the text and prove the popularity of her victim, her tattooed, her abused, her defeated, her impoverished Far Mulan, she says first, 'The Chinese forgot the texts and, when they recited them, got them all wrong and created these new texts.' So the Chinese come to America and turn what any American would call a 'feminist' childhood chant describing Confucian romantic love as two warriors standing back to fighting off the universe into a white Christian vision of Chinese misogyny? Amazing!"

"What do you mean by text?" Shimmen asks.

"Text is an arrangement of words on a page by an author. So if I don't recognize you as my blood brother when the time comes, you shoot me with five thunderbolts, not six! Right?"

"Right. That's the oath."

"Text! There's a penalty for misquoting the oath or otherwise breaking its law."

"That's quite right!"

A Chinaman in Singapore

"Keep your sleeves all the way down, Wilfred," I say.

"Perhaps Kingston means the *Tao Te Ching* when she says *Book of Peace*," Woon Ping says.

"But the *Tao Te Ching* is the *Tao Te Ching*, has never been called *The Book of Peace*, and is not a lost text, is it?" I answer. "We know the author."

I pull out my *Chinese Immortal Patterns* and jokingly ask Koh Tai Ann if she knows how to read Chinese: *"Sick dook muh?"*

"Siiick!" she says with a smile. Of course she knows how to read!

I open up the book to the kitchen king and kitchen queen and ask her if this is the kitchen god. Yes, she says. I turn to another page of kitchen king and kitchen queen posters. Yes, that is the kitchen god.

"Good," I say. "Either these are fake, or Amy Tan is a fake. Her book depends on her assertion that the kitchen god's wife is not honored and that that proves the kitchen god is a source of Chinese misogyny. These posters show the kitchen god's wife is as honored as the kitchen god. If these posters are real, she invented all the misogyny in her book, not the Chinese story."

Chin Woon Ping, the poet, asks why I criticize Chinese for writing autobiographies.

"Yes," muscle shirt E. C. Goh asks. "Why don't you talk about yourself? People want to know about you."

"I don't do autobiography. The autobiography is not a Chinese form. It's a Christian religious form descended from confession. The first autobiography ever written was Saint Augustine's *Confessions*. The next autobiography Jean-Jacques Rousseau's *Confessions*. Western culture is religious. Chinese culture is not. Chinese are not born sinners. Chinese are born soldiers. No matter what else we might be, doctor, lawyer, Indian chief, we are all born soldiers.

Frank Chin

"The first Chinese autobiography ever written was Yung Wing's *My Life in China and America,* published around 1910. He was a Christian. All systems of Western thought, philosophy, and religion are systems of perfecting the perpetual state through mass conformity. All systems of Chinese thought are systems of perfecting individual personal integrity. The perpetual state in Chinese thought is, by definition, immoral. That's the mandate of heaven. Kingdoms rise and fall. Nations come and go.

"The individual does not give himself up to a higher authority. That would be betrayal of the self. The higher authority is by definition corrupt and will fail. Knowledge of history, all things knowable, and tactics and strategy is the basis of an individual's moral and personal integrity. To the Chinese confession is an act of moral submission, betrayal. Chinese do not confess. Chinese do not submit themselves to judgment. Wilfred Hamilton-Shimmen knows from his experience in the triads that if the Chinese soldier fucks up, the Chinese soldier deals with it. The individual is the law. He punishes himself. I did it. I messed up. I'll take care of it! The Japanese call it hara-kiri."

Shimmen nods and agrees. "The Thirty-six Oaths," he says.

"The first-person pronoun I in Chinese is made of two battle-axes crossed in a coat of arms. A coat of arms is an assertion of law. *I, me,* and *we* in Chinese literally mean 'I am the law.'"

"The Thirty-six Oaths one takes in the initiation ceremony are just that," Shimmen says.

"What are the Thirty-six Oaths?" Woon Ping asks.

"'I must treat the parents and relatives of my blood brothers as my own kin. I shall be killed by five thunderbolts if I do not keep this oath.

"'I shall help my brothers bury their parents and brothers with my money and physical labor. I shall be killed by five thunderbolts if I pretend not to know of their losses.'

A Chinaman in Singapore

"See, the oath is like a contract for something specific. A part of the oath is the specific penalties to be paid for failure to keep the oath. 'I am the law.'"

They look like they've never heard this before. Perhaps if they submitted their questions in writing to the Singapore police.

"I'll show you you know the autobiography is not a Chinese form with a question." I look the poet Chin Woon Ping in the eye. She's sitting next to Dean Koh Tai Ann on the huge hotel bed. "Would Kwan Kung write an autobiography?" I ask. They spit up laughing helplessly, the thought Kwan Kung, the god of war, plunder, and literature, writing an autobiography is so stupid.

"Would Mao Tse-tung write an autobiography?" I ask. More laughter.

"Right, you understand."

"So how does Kwan Kung explore his identity problems?"

"Chinese don't have identity problems. I don't have identity problems. I know who I am. How would Kwan Kung explore his doubts and fears? How would he objectify his behavior and criticize his morals and ethics? He would write poetry on the barroom wall at night, like Soong Gong, and in the morning the wall would be whitewashed and all the poetry erased. The danger of that is the wrong person might read your graffiti at the wrong time, as Soong Gong found out when he was arrested and condemned to death for his 'rebellious poem.' If he's more serious, he recites Sun Tzu's *The Art of War,* or *The Book of Thirty-six Stratagems,* or another book of strategy, and free-associates and compares and criticizes his moves against the verses."

"You know the dragon and the phoenix are symbols in the triads," Wilfred says.

"Yes," I say. "Who mans the rigging? Who poles the boat? Who guards the holds?"

Frank Chin

"The eighteen disciples of Buddha man the rigging. The four great Buddhas pole the boat. The eight Immortals guard the holds."

"How do you know so much about triads?"

"I read a book on triad societies by a subinspector in the Hong Kong police," I say.

Koh Tai Ann says, "Your Cantonese surprises me. It's pretty good."

"Sick teng, um sick gong," I say. "I understand to hear it, but I can't speak it. And I can't read but a few words. I don't speak or read classical Greek either; most American writers don't; but we play with Greek myth, Greek ideas, Greek texts all the time. If we don't trust a given translation, we can test it against others. So because we express our sensibility in English is no reason for Chinese to dump Chinese culture. Why reject knowledge? The Chinese fairy tale, the spoken language I understand to hear and speak awkwardly, raise interesting literary questions of language and writing no one besides the late Louis Chu and the Eurasian Timothy Mo has considered and should. For instance, spoken Chinese is all present tense.

"*Donald Duk* is written in the present tense. Movie scripts are written in the present tense. Is the vigor of the language American or Chinese? What seems most American is that the English of *Donald Duk* is grammatically a Cantonese dialect."

Oh, that's interesting to some part of all of them. For any question of language is a question of moral philosophy. Why do words get along together the way we want them to? Why do people? Those questions are the same. The languages are different. Doing Chinese in English should be a great adventure.

A Chinaman in Singapore

I walk into the American restaurant for breakfast. The American restaurant is an enclosed replica of an outdoor court. A marble fountain trickles water at the entrance. Pink marble walls. Wooden columns. Gipsy Kings on the muzak. Some solo plunkity plickity lifeless muzak flamenco guitar by I don't know who. The fountain in the center of the court is a tower of breakfast food. Rolls and buns, croissants and brioche. Liver sausage. Prosciutto. Sea biscuits. Blue cheese. Cantaloupe. Honeydew. Mango. Orange juice. Yogurt. Muselix. Granola. Against the wall are hot pans of French toast, eggs Benedict, hash-brown potatoes, grilled tomatoes, ham, bacon. A toqued and white-linened chef stands behind three pans ready to whip up an omelette or eggs to order. The head chef, a fifty-ish white man with a scowl and toque bigger than any worn by the tribe of Chinese cooks he chiefs, strides out of the kitchen every now and then and inspects the dining room and buffet, snapping his linen kitchen towel of office. The host and hostess in black suits slither up to the white chef for scowls of approval. Is this a true vision of old colonial Singapore or a parody? Or is it neither and real unto itself?

Bette Greene asks me to join her. She's a handsome old white woman. A Jew from Arkansas.

Actually, she looks like a worn-out old woman with clean hair and a good tint. She's tired. Hasn't slept since she arrived here Sunday. Ah, are you sure you didn't arrive on Monday?

A waiter appears, says, "I'm sorry," with a smile, and asks if I would like coffee or tea. I ask for coffee. He turns over my cup and goes.

Her husband's a doctor. He's just had surgery. Pancreas. Oh. She wanted to make sure he was able to take care of himself before she came to Singapore. He's an ophthalmologist.

Frank Chin

She hasn't slept since she arrived. Her room on the thirteenth floor has no electricity. Oh, the thirteenth floor. She keeps calling down, and the hotel keeps sending up a maintenance man, who apologizes, says the room is wired wrong, turns on the air-conditioning, and leaves. Then the air-conditioning goes off again. The room hates her.

The waiter reappears with a silver coffeepot and says, "I'm sorry," as he pours me a cup of coffee.

She's supposed to be finishing up a book for Hyperion, a publishing house owned by Disney. She's not going to finish it in time. Nothing she can't handle. It's this hotel's fault. She's very conscientious about her obligations. She travels with work. After Singapore she goes to Bangkok for a week.

I feel like billing her at the end of the month.

Disney is also making her book *The Drowning of Stephan Jones* into a movie for the Disney Channel. *Drowning* was inspired by a newspaper article about Christian boys beating up homosexuals on the streets for sport. She says, "*The Drowning of Stephan Jones* has made me the poster girl of the ACLU. They tried to ban this novel in the Arkansas schools, and it went all the way to the U.S. Supreme Court.

"I've been thinking about what you said, and I don't agree with you. Chinese are not a despised minority in America. My husband and I frequent a Chinese restaurant and consider ourselves friends of the owner. I am sure he does not consider himself despised."

Because she is a writer, an American Jew from the South, a childhood victim of Christian anti-Semitism and Christian moral exclusivity, I foolishly believe she will understand when I say, "The proof that Chinese are despised is the popularity of the patently white racist rabidly Christian writing of Maxine Hong Kingston, David Henry Hwang, Amy Tan, which are taught in the public schools as the real thing while the Chinese

A Chinaman in Singapore

fairy tales they fake are banned. Not one of the champions of Kingston and Tan have done step one of literary criticism. They have not checked Kingston and Tan against the texts Kingston and Tan claim inspired their insight into Chinese morality and history. If they were Jews faking Jewish text, they would have never been published by the houses that publish them. Their fakery and white racist intent is that obvious."

As if I didn't understand her the first time, she tells me, patiently, that she and her husband, a doctor, often go out to eat at this one particular Chinese restaurant in Boston and consider themselves friends of the owners now. She gets no sense that they think of themselves as a despised minority.

"The customer is always right," I say. "White racist love. They tell you they think of themselves as a cherished minority. Until the United States stops fighting the racist Opium Wars on the side of Christianity against China in the schools with Kingston and Tan, they have no right to mention human rights. I predict Kingston and Tan are making the world safe for two crimes against humanity, Pearl Buck, Charlie Chan to make a comeback."

Joan London, an Australian poet, joins us. She has an Australian Chinese writer she'd like me to read. I thought Australians banned Chinese immigration. No, there're quite a few Chinese Australians in the cities. In one city they are so well established they've become a tourist attraction. She'll be interested in what I think of this writer. I'm about as anxious to read a Chinese Australian writer poetically ficting his Chinese Australian identity crisis as I am to bare my ass and hunker it over one of the wet holes in the cement floor of a Singapore public toilet and poop.

She comes back with a bowl of cold white stuff with granola in it. "What is that stuff?" I ask.

"I think it's called Muselix."

Frank Chin

Bette Greene asks Robert Drewe, a sharp-eyed, bald eagle of an Australian writer, to join us and convince me Chinese are not a despised minority. The English he speaks puts him in another movie. In one breath and one sentence he is complex, ironic, classic direct and tough, from another world of English. Another English of the Pacific Rim. He is a judge of the Singapore (English-language) short-story contest. Judges for the Chinese-language short story are from Taiwan. The Malay-language short-story judges are from Malaysia. Indonesian judges from Indonesia. Ah, Singapore geopolitics in action. It doesn't matter who wins or the literary merit of the writing. What matters is where the judges come from and how they are treated.

What Robert Drew calls the "traditional" Singapore short story is a pseudo-Dickensian tale of a bright Singapore lad who works very hard in school so he can go to Oxford and with an Oxford education make a lot of money and support his parents or get a good job in Australia or England. White racist kissass Gunga Din, like Christian Chinese American autobiographies of Pardee Lowe and Jade Snow Wong. Most of the stories in the contest are "traditional" Singapore short stories, and Robert Drew finds them tedious and disappointingly void of any literary ambition. However, at his suggestion—read insistence—the English-language short-story contest has two categories. And there will be two first-place prizes, one for the "traditional" and one for the "experimental" story. The story that caught his attention in the experimental category is an interesting mix of English and Chinese language, and ideas, and suicide, he says. By taking his suggestion, the National Arts Council may have legitimized the marketplace Singaporean English pidgin and set it free.

Bette Greene tells Robert Drew and me that her husband is balding like us and has started using Rogaine, and it works!

A Chinaman in Singapore

It grows hair. She says we would be better-looking men if we started using Rogaine. Robert Drew laughs politely, and we sneak looks at each other's hair and lack of hair.

"I've been drinking a bottle a day for months, and nothing's happened," I say.

MESSAGE

Message on my phone. Message under my door. The Wicked Witch. The police will not talk to me without me submitting my questions ahead of time. This again. No, thanks. I toss the message and think that's that. Then the Wicked Witch calls. She disagrees about this being the behavior of a professional dictatorship. "You might ask about classified information," she explains.

"Yes, I might, and if they are professional, they should be able to say they can't answer without asking permission and filling out forms. Welcome to the police-state bureaucracy."

TAMIL IS A LANGUAGE

A Tamil writer pulls up a seat next to me and says he agrees, yes, home is here and here, touching his head and his heart.

He tells me there are 100,000 plus Tamils in Singapore. Tamil is a language, not a religion. There are Tamils of every religion. Muslim, Christian, Sikh. Whooo, yeah, Tamil is not a religion. Not a race. A language. You mean they're fighting a bloody jungle terrorist war in Sri Lanka over a language? Yes, he grins. Skin the color of Hershey's chocolate with a dash of chili. Thick, straight black hair. Eyebrows like black puppy dogs' tails, and thick black mustache. Large black eyes. Tamils are all over Southeast Asia. They also are not a nation. A language. A people bound by a language. I don't understand it.

Frank Chin

They're not a race, not a nation, not a religion, not the usual force toward civil society and moral system. In the language alone, in the sound, the rhythms, the grammar, the vulgar, and the art of it is a moral force. They're willing to make war to save their language. They're willing to die fighting for a homeland for their language. Car bomb for a language. Yes, the Tamil can live anywhere in the world, speak English, the marketplace pidgin of business and law, and speak Tamil and write Tamil, which is all they really want to do, wherever they are, speak and write Tamil. In a nation of three million, 100,000 is pretty small. To the Tamil home really is in the head and the ear. Home is the tongue, home from the sea. Home is the language. That must be some language.

I'd think the speakers of a language to die for would all be like Max Von Sydow in a Bergman movie set in medieval Scandinavia. Dour, grim, doomedly biting off their words and gulping them down. No, it's a happy, snappy, lippy, and loping lingo anyone can see just makes these guys happy to speak and hear.

AMERICAN BREAKFAST

Bette Greene joins me for breakfast in the American restaurant around eight thirty. She hasn't slept, she says. Her room on the thirteenth floor is a disaster. She hates this hotel. It should have never opened. It's not finished. She wasn't going to come. They wanted to fly her economy class. She refused. Too uncomfortable. Business class or nothing. They flew her business class. Very comfortable. Good food. "I had a wonderful time last night. I took a cab to Little Arabia. I felt safe. I shopped. I had a wonderful dinner. Then back to my disaster of a room. The TV finally works. But I want another room. I have asked to see the manager, not an assistant man-

A Chinaman in Singapore

ager, but the manager." The assistant manager comes by the table to say the manager will not see her. Welcome to the police-state hotel.

Aritha van Herk introduces herself and asks if she can join us. Writers are basically shy people, she believes, and when writers get together and talk, the talk is just extraordinary, she says. The energy of shy people. Blonde. Perky. Dark eyes. She acts like she has dimples. I don't see any dimples. Can a girl from a small mining town in Canada, the daughter of Dutch immigrants, find happiness as a writer of the English language in Canada? Sure, she can.

Bette Greene tells her about her battle with the hotel over her room.

WHERE IS THE REAL SINGAPORE?

Dudley takes me for a drive to the border with Malaysia.

We drive past acres of jungle and plant life cut down and hauled away. We drive past massive building projects, cities of lookalike twenty-story buildings going up. Big monster buildings, crouching on the red earth of a freshly shaved jungle, all cement shoulders and necks, lined up skirmishers. A Chinese company is building a Chinese-looking condo complex. Chinese colors. Green. Yellow. Red. Tile touches. Chinese cliché. You want a two-bedroom condo: $850,000. Three bedrooms: $1 million. The Malaysian men who build them live in rusty steel containers stacked three high next to the scrap heap. The containers have windows and doorways cut in the steel. Air conditioners rattle in the cutout windows. The containers are stacked three high. Wooden staircases, and galleries tacked onto the stacked containers with a plywood roof built on top, each stack looks like Mississippi a riverboat, with dark-skinned men lounging on the decks in their underwear. This is on-site housing for the Malaysian workers. Singapore's Malaysian

Frank Chin

bachelor society. On Fridays they jump on their Suzuki two wheelers and buzz over the bridge home, Dudley says. There's a picture postcard here. Maybe two.

We look for the *kampongs,* the villages in the jungle, the Singapore of Dudley's childhood, the Singapore of just last year and it's gone. The orchid farm he remembers is a garbage dump. His jungles are stands of boxy high-rise uglies.

BREAKFAST PANEL

Kirpal Singh wears a different-colored turban everyday. In the light of the Malacca room, his turban glows a pastel green. "Today Aritha van Herk and Bette Greene share their experiences as women writers over breakfast," he says. Bette Greene and Aritha van Herk both look uncomfortable. They have no complaints about being either women or writers or their writing being punished or neglected or belittled because they are women. Their problems being women and writers, as they recall them, seem to have been a part of being young women and young writers.

Bette Greene, from Boston via a childhood in Arkansas, says girls were taught: "To be attractive to boys, they should be happy to be taken out to play miniature golf and let the boys win." Aritha van Herk, child of Dutch immigrant parents, from Calgary, Alberta, Canada, questions the holy quest of the individual to separate her identity from the history of her parentage and her parents' history and culture.

A young, grinning Singapore kid stands and makes a high preach for blazing new trails, making history, not following history, being a self free of culture, ethnicity, the past, history.

"You can't give up your roots," Aritha van Herk pleads. "You don't want to be Michael Jackson! Look at Michael Jackson! He's erased his roots, his sex, his nose. . . ."

"You're right!" Bette Greene says, and pats Aritha van

A Chinaman in Singapore

Herk's arm. "Oh, I'm so glad I thought of that!"

But they're wrong. This Chinese Singaporean writer wants to be Michael Jackson. He wants Singapore to be a nation of Michael Jacksons. A race of miracle synthetics. A machine-washable drip-dry culture. Entertainment for entertainment's sake. Singapore is high pop, industrial narcissism.

The discussion turns to "race" as a force in shaping culture.

"Yes, the Japanese are very good at it, aren't they!" this Australian white stiff upper lips.

"But the Brits were better at it in Asia, weren't they." I say. "They invented the unprovoked surprise attack in the Opium War, opiated and slaughtered millions from one end of Asia to the other, and then did it again, and again, and again, in the name of the white God and the white race. Oh, they're so much better at racism than the Japanese, don't you think?"

I walk Bette Greene and Aritha van Herk to the Raffles for lunch in the Writers Bar. Overhead, yellow paddles paddle back and forth against the white ceiling. Little brown boys in turbans and white uniforms used to crank the machinery that made these paddle-shaped rattan fans row the air together overhead. Ah, tradition! British white racist tradition. Colonial tradition. I feel so white sitting here in the Writers Bar. Bette and Aritha have Singapore slings. I'm an American and ask for their list of small-batch bourbons. They don't have any. Jack Daniels or Wild Turkey. That's it for American Bourbon sour-mash whiskey. Bette Greene has the delicatessen plate. I order the duck-leg confit. Aritha van Herk has something slight and drinks. She loves hotels. She's always on the phone home to her husband or her lovers, she says. Bette rises to the bait. "Lovers?"

Aritha grabs our hands; we all hold hands. "Let's swear to be friends, always!" she says. We swear, sounding a little short of sincere, but we're friends. I ask the waitress wrapped in silk for separate checks.

Frank Chin

The air war Operation Desert Shield has started. I am in Portland, on the road with my five-year-old son for an adventure during the Chinese New Year's season, when the TV tells me the ground forces of Operation Desert Storm are moving fast. One wants to start the new year right, home with the family. My home is the road. Interstate 5. So, while Mom works teaching school in California, and before Sam himself starts school, I strap our son into the tiny red '77 Honda and get a move on my home again.

The road's changed. America's changed. At first I don't take offense at people sticking their T-shirts in my face when I sit down with Sam after stacking our plates at the salad bar at the truck stops. I have gone from truck stop to truck stop for years after discovering they, of all the roadside cafés, take chicken-fried steak and the salad bar as serious American art for the stomach. Till this moment I'd found American truck stops to be road-opera idealizations of the naturally democratic old west out of a Sergio Leone spaghetti western. Check your guns, your drugs, your prejudices, and your grudges at the door. All shootouts and fistfights off the premises. No exceptions.

Pidgin Contest along I-5

The T-shirt hand silkscreened on 100 percent cotton with an American flag over a map of Saudi Arabia, Iraq, and Kuwait, with the words "THESE COLORS DON'T RUN!" in my face, doesn't bother me. It is the look on the man's face that goes along with the T-shirt that bothers me. I've been the only yellow in roadside restaurants before. I am often the only yellow for miles around. I'm used to it. I'm used to being mistaken for other yellows and other races. It never messes up my enjoyment of the local salad bar and search for the best chicken-fried steak in America.

No one has ever picked a fight with me with a T-shirt before. And all the eyes in the truck stop have never been hard on me, making a big deal of me before. "These colors don't run!" I read out loud. "Amen to that, brother. Where can I get one these righteous T-shirts?"

In a truck stop near Medford I look up from my salad bar and sirloin into an American flag, red, white, and blue, on a black T-shirt and, in belligerent red across the chest the legend "Try Burning This One, Asshole!"

I have an urge to introduce myself as an Iraqi cabdriver on vacation from New York but chicken out and say, "Boss T-shirt, brah! You think they got T-shirts like that in my son's size? Oooh, make my boy look sharp!"

We are admiring the hollow bronze man with an umbrella in Pioneer Courthouse Square in Portland. Sam has discovered sculpted animals, beavers and ducks in the planter boxes. Now he counts the nails in the heel of the bronze man's shoe. I look forward to stopping in the coffee hut on the corner for a cappuccino. Portland is a beautiful little city. Off the road. Out of the world. Then a kid in a black leather jacket, earrings, and no hair walks by and grumbles something.

"What did he say?" Sam asks.

"I don't know," I say. I have to think. "He said *foreigners*," I say. "Poor kid doesn't know how to cuss." Then I see we are

Frank Chin

surrounded by these funny-looking white kids who mean, mean, mean to be offensive, don't know how to cuss. As with the college kid who'd sneered "Literary conservative!" at me for saying texts do not change and the Marxist who'd meant "Cultural nationalist!" to wither me with contempt, I want to take the fuzz-headed boy aside and teach him how to swear. You want to rile me, kid, you call me a *Chink!* or you might call me a *Jap!* I'm not a Jap, but I'll know what you mean. But *foreigner!* Come on! That's too intellectual to really get me on the proper emotional level."

Then I see we are surrounded by these Clairol kids in black leather. I forget about the cappuccino and say, "Let's walk on out of here, Sam."

I see this need to teach our young how to properly cuss and offend with the specificity of a smart bomb as the first step toward full literacy and I-5 civility. You read to get the knowledge you need to win a fight, or, in this case, pick a fight, and avoid a fight.

On campus I seem to hear something else. I hear white kids on campus bitching about courses that teach nothing but hatred of whites and other kids talking PC. "Political correctness."

It's a shame white kids are sheltered by lingering white supremacy from the real world till they get to college. Nonwhite kids grow up in America despised by whites from birth, from history, from folklore, from their best friend the TV set. By the time they get to college they've learned to deal with it as a childhood disease. Either that, or it's fried their brains and turned them into gibbering Gunga Dins anxious to bugle the charge of white supremacy to white out their race and culture. Owooooo! Hear that wolf?

A multicultural America, a multicultural I-5, doesn't mean whites have to give up Christianity or hate themselves. It doesn't mean an orgy of mutual hostility either. Nor does it

Pidgin Contest along I-5

mean racial and cultural exclusivity. One thing it does mean—and I think PC is an attempt toward achieving this—is American standard English, the language all of us have to use to do business with each other, will be the one language reserved for civility, the one language we can speak without provoking each other. The American standard English of the newspapers and TV news, the language of the marketplace, will become more and more a pidgin, like pidgin in Hawai'i.

In pidgin Hawaiians, whites, Christians, pagans, Chinese, Japanese, Portuguese, did business with each other without giving up their identities, or their cultural integrity, or selling their children to monsters.

Political correctness seems to be a too serious and fascist, demagogic way of saying *civil language*. Of course, when civility is not our purpose, there are other languages and vocabularies available to us. With the need for a language of civility and doing business with strangers without betraying our secrets or slashing our wrists or starting a war in mind, I suggest PC stand for *pidgin contest*.

Civil language and tolerant behavior can't be imposed from the top without exercising heavy police-state censorship and driving everyone with a discouraging word underground. But in the bustling, competitive, passionate marketplace atmosphere of a port city or corner store, civil language and tolerant behavior are invented, or you go broke, brah.

In *The Movie about Me* there are pidgin contests held to encourage the use of the language to trade culture and lit. Pidgin is a live, up-front, face-to-face, present-tense language. The contestants tell heroic classics—*Chushingura, The Oath in the Peach Garden, Robin Hood, The Three Musketeers*—live. They compete with pidgin tellings of the fairy tales "Jack and the Beanstalk" and "Momotaro, the Peach Boy." On the way back home, driving I-5 South, Sam likes the idea. Yeah, it's

Frank Chin

better than punching somebody in the mouth and craving a many-fronted race war.

Then we walk back into the real world, a crowded resort restaurant around Lake Mount Shasta in Northern California, to get out of the nasty wind and rain.

"Did you tell them we're closed?" a middle-aged, crinkled-up woman bleats to another, taller, less crinkled-up white woman.

"We're closed," the taller woman says. For an instant I don't believe my ears. This has not happened to me since the South in the early sixties. Never in California.

"We're closed," the taller woman says again, and I can see she sees from the look in my eye I don't believe they are closed at all. I am not about to punch either of these old white ladies in the face. I look around for a customer to catch my eye and punch him in the face, and none does. Then I remember Sam, my five-year-old boy about to start school, is with me.

"They're closed, Sam," I say, take his hand, walk out, and wonder what I am teaching my kid letting skinheads and sixties-style white racists in California run us out of town. The winning of the Gulf War seems to have released an ugly brand of American patriotism that expresses itself as righteous white supremacy such as I have never seen before along the road between Seattle and LA I've called home for thirty years. I would have thought a nice cathartic victory would have released more winning sentiments on the road. What has happened to I-5?

HELLO, AMERICA, THIS IS LA

There are signs the times are freaking out. All over LA, wherever I drive, from Echo Park and Silver Lake to Hollywood to downtown and J-Town and Chinatown, I see magpies harass-

Pidgin Contest along I-5

ing hawks all over the sky. There are other signs of good times. There is an oriole, bright yellow and stark black on the wings and throat, in our weird tree flowering red fingers the morning of the day my friend the TV goes crazy with bad, bad news.

I pick up Sam from the school bus a little before three. He buckles himself in the backseat, and we're on our way to Chinatown for our usual after-school noodles when the news of the verdict acquitting the cops who'd beaten Rodney King comes between country songs and an appropriately remote broadcast from Hawai'i hyping travel over the LA FM country music station. "It's a bad day to be a cop or black man," I say.

My seven-year-old son knows Rodney King is the black man he'd seen beaten by LA cops on TV last March just after we're back home from a trip up and down I-5 to Seattle, through the Gulf War, and back down a road bristling a new, more blatant white racism. Skinheads in Portland. A resort restaurant in Northern California saying, "We're closed," when they were full of white people stuffing all manner of breakfast in their faces. And home to see Rodney King shot twice with a laser gun and beaten and beaten and beaten.

Between then and now black dislike for Koreans in little mom-and-pop groceries grows. The Korean groceries and liquor stores have all been broken into and/or robbed, and Mom and Pop have the same prejudice about blacks as the white Americans who taught it to them.

It might have helped if the blacks understood Korean manners and Korean culture have been toughened by a long history of being kicked around by the Chinese and the Japanese and a wartime society riddled with vicious spies, where being inquisitive about your neighbors and their personal lives is not necessarily a friendly gesture.

The tension breaks when a Korean grocer shoots a black

Frank Chin

teenage girl in the back and kills her. The grocer believed the girl was stealing a bottle of orange juice. The store's security camera that recorded the whole event on videotape shows the girl approaching the counter with money in her open hand as the grocer rages and screams at her.

The grocer is found guilty of voluntary manslaughter and given a suspended sentence. Blacks are outraged and are even now demanding the recall of the judge who let a Korean woman kill a black teenager without jailtime.

In response to the anger the Korean mom-and-pop grocers stop making change and throwing it at their customers and learn to smile and make Ozzie-and-Harriet Hollywood TV commercial small talk. I find it a little disconcerting. Smiling and small talk as a Korean martial art. The effort the Korean mom-and-pop stores are making to get along with the surrounding community is obvious all over LA. No doubt about it, they're willing to work at getting along. And the standard of getting along is hard-style Disneyland.

After our noodles in Chinatown we drive home past Dodger Stadium, see a hawk flap its wings over a line of palm trees, and see it's being run off by a pair of nagging magpies, see the same thing across the street from our house across our view of the HOLLYWOOD sign, and turn on our friend the TV set and see it is a bad day to be anybody in LA.

Korean mom-and-pops and generic LA minimalls are looter and pyro bait.

On the English-language LA channels some newspeople disconnect major sections of their brains. The pretty faces and trained voices who think they can do the news till the cows come home don't see the cows are home. One reporter has no idea the guns she was describing appearing in the hands of people are real guns, and when the police shove her out of the way, she reacts, not to the gunfire, but to the cop's rude shove.

Pidgin Contest along I-5

Back in the newsroom a million-dollar anchorman asks a pie-eyed, panic-stricken ninny chattering his teeth in the mike if most of the looters don't look like "illegal aliens."

The pretty face frozen on hold grabs the anchorman's question like a lifesaver and says, "Yes, most of the looters look like illegal aliens." To these fools, I would look like an illegal alien. They're so fried in their insight that if white-haired Barbara Bush, the president's wife, should be pushing a shopping cart, she'd look like an illegal alien.

Reporting the looting and burning of Korean stores working into Koreatown proper, the reporters for the English-language news run from pompous to melodramatic to thumb-sucking gibberers. It isn't until the newscopter sees the wave of looters charge in and out of Fedco, a huge warehouse discount store for government and state employees, that the newsies lose complete control. Mr. Purple Prose of the news-choppers gives up the morally loaded philosophical lingo and says it all in his voice going up and down out of breath as he blurts in amazement and moral outrage, "They're looting Fedco!" as if Fedco is a church or an orphanage.

My neighbors aren't among the looters. College educated. Liberal. Mixed marriages. Middle class. Still they act strange. As the smoke from the fires stuffs the air with the smell of burning rubber and electrical insulation and feathery black leaves of the ash fall on our houses and grass, I see some neighbors come out of their house with a portable TV, turn it on, and get into their outdoor Jacuzzi to what? Work off the tension of the day? Others start barbecuing in their backyard at sunset and invite friends, as if the curfew doesn't include them and the gunfire we hear clearly, a block or a mile away we can't tell, won't come any closer, and the smoke from burning LA won't flavor their meat.

The verdict from Simi Valley tells us all in LA there is no law. The looters don't read the news in the paper. They get it

Frank Chin

off the TV and the radio, their best friend, their storyteller. The looters are the children of the children who never had a childhood. Kids of kids who grew up alone, who never had a story told them by a live body, who grew up with TV as their storyteller. The black, white, Asian, and Latino kids and families out looting together are just acting like society on their TV acts when there is no law.

Had they a sense of myth that began with a live storyteller telling stories their people have valued through history, and if not those, then stories any people value—Greek myths, Bible stories, Br'er Rabbit, Hans Christian Andersen, the Peach Boy, the Boy born of Lotus—more people might look on themselves as more than the moral equivalent of consumer goods and stay away from the mob.

Then on TV there is a fake Spanish California mission-style minimall with a guard from a private Korean security outfit on the roof with an Uzi, a jumpsuit, a flak jacket, a baseball cap, and dark glasses.

The call had gone out on the channel that airs Korean programming for all good men to come to the aid of their Korea Town at the minimall, and they show up with shotguns, pistols of all kinds, Uzis, and AK-47s. The Alamo in Korea Town is a minimall.

In the race war that's started we're all going to choose up sides and appear at the appropriate minimall to man the barricades? The combined TV of LA with its two Spanish-language channels, and hours of Chinese, Japanese, Korean, Vietnamese, Farsi, and on and on programming, and visions of the action on the streets, is a vision of LA beyond *Bladerunner*, and not real, I think. It's all grotesque exaggeration. And it's impossible to choose up sides. The racially and culturally specific parts of towns, the barrios, the Chinatowns, Li'l Tokyo, Hollywood, Fairfax, blacks, Jews, white Christians, and even the dreamers and movie stars of LA, all are too interwoven

Pidgin Contest along I-5

into each other's business and loyalties to simply drop everything and Alamo up at our minimall behind barricades of rice sacks and shopping carts. We cannot blast and shoot each other into oneness. But we can agree on a common standard and language of civility. For a long time now, people on all sides, high and low, have and have not seemed to have accepted *business* as a synonym for *life*. Now we seem to agree the fire department is a good thing. It's a start. Whole civilizations have been started with less.

No school. Good. Sam's school is less than a mile from the downtown collection of courthouses and Parker Center police headquarters the TV news expects to go up in flames any second now. I take Sam out in the daylight, just down the hill to the Chinese bakery to order a cake for Dana's birthday. We pull open the door and walk in. The bakery is open. Still Mom and Pop the bakers freeze, and their eyes swirl and their breath gets short at the sight of me. "Hi," I say. "We'd like a cake."

They don't understand. They wait for me and my six-year-old son to stick 'em up, or loot 'em, or trash the joint. "We want to buy a cake," I say.

They don't move.

"We'd like it to say, 'Happy Birthday Mom,'" I say.

Poppa Chinese baker opens his mouth, and nothing comes out.

"Are you open?" I ask.

He nods his head. I start again. They understand.

While Mom and Pop are steaming the medium-sized two-layer cake into being for me, the door opens behind me. I turn and see a young Chinese woman in the doorway. She jumps back. "Are you open?" she asks.

"Yeah, come on in," I say.

"Mom, Dad? You okay?" she asks, and goes behind the counter. She's the daughter. This is her bakery, and she asks

Frank Chin

me if we're open? Is the young man in the car outside a cop? Welcome to Paranoid City.

We get the cake in a box and take it home.

Then George Bush declares war on LA, sounding as frustrated and pained as Alberto Fujimori ruling by mandate in Peru.

Sunday, the family cocooned up snug with our best friend the TV set, I drive to Chinatown along deserted streets in broad daylight. The streets are empty. I take a walk around the places I like to eat and walk into one. Empty. The Mexican kitchen help and the Chinese cooks in their kitchen whites and waiters sit and stand around a table where the owner sits and holds his head in his hands. It's around three in the afternoon. The sun shines outside. In here they don't know if they're opening or closing. Some of the tables are still stacked. Some of the tables on the floor have no tablecloths, no place mats with the lunar zodiac around the edges, no red napkin, fork, spoon, and wrapped chopsticks, no teacup and waterglass. The kitchen is cold. No one notices me.

"Are you open?" I ask.

The owner looks up; everyone looks up. The owner recognizes me as a frequent customer, tries to smile, and looks like he's going to cry. "First the riots. Now the curfew's killing us. We haven't had even one customer in two days till you walked in." Martial law seems to have worked.

On the way back I hear over the radio news of a huge peace rally in Korea Town. People are praying for forgiveness of the looters and peace in LA. Whole families show up. Others stop and join. Estimates range from 30,000 to a high of 100,000. It seems like good news, as I drive past stuff from the looting binge appearing for sale at yard sales. This is the America where reading is only good for reading signs and price tags. There is no story, no myth, no history, no art. Only TV. And

Pidgin Contest along I-5

now that the U.S. Marines and the army have had a taste of treating American streets like Panama and Grenada, I wonder if they can go home again.

Sam is down to sleep to be up early off to school in the morning tomorrow.

POLICE STATE

Every day after school, I pick Sam up at the bus and drive through Elysian Park, past the Dodger Stadium parking lot and the Marine Corps Naval Reserve Training Station, into Chinatown or Little Tokyo for noodles or sushi. Salmon egg sushi was Sam's first solid food. He doesn't like meat. Doesn't like veggies. He likes sushi, rice, and fish. Salmon eggs. Sea eel. softshell crab. Mackerel pike. Broiled smelt exploding with eggs. I tell Sam of trying to teach his half-sister, Betsy, how to drive in that parking lot and how she managed to drive into the only tree in this huge parking lot. True, it's a pitiful excuse for a tree, next to that pitiful little block house of a ticket office. Sam laughs every time he sees the tree and thinks of Betsy bumping into it.

This is a nice drive between our house and Chinatown and J-Town. We often see hawks perched in the tops of the trees of Elysian Park or cruising over the soft cliffs of Chavez Ravine, across the street from the Dodger Stadium parking lot.

It's a nice time of day. I break from staring at the blank page and screaming screen, do my mailing at the Chinatown or Little Tokyo contract postal station, walk around the town talking about life with Sam, watch the afternoon light reflect off glass walls of one building onto the textured concrete slab of another, snack, and shop for dinner. In Chinatown we walk by the square ponds full of fake rocks painted in fake colors, topped with the statues of Kwan Yin and the gods of wealth, happiness, and long life long ago broken off at the ankles. We

Frank Chin

look into the waters of one pond for the turtles and usually count more than a dozen basking on rocks and each other, swimming in the shallow water over pennies, and beaking at the puffy body of a dead goldfish. There are feeders grown large in these ponds. One has a golden carp. The other pond has crawdads.

In Little Tokyo there are the big granite boulders in Little Tokyo Village Sam likes to climb. There is the Amerasia Bookstore, where Irene, one of a group of Asian American UCLA students who call themselves Aisarema (Amerasia spelled backward) and are dedicated to saving the Amerasia Bookstore from closing, stands behind the cash register and folds little origami things for Sam. And all the sushi chefs at Frying Fish know Sam and call his name when we step inside.

One day, walking to sushi, we see National Guard Humvees parked all over the Honda Plaza parking lot. The Humvees are too big to fit in the marked parking spaces. They don't even try. Inside a J-Town fast-noodle shop we see the boys of the National Guard in their battle fatigues and flak jackets sitting down working chopsticks and noodles, with their M-16s leaning against the little tables. Sam and I are the only living things on the street. We look on the woman who runs the sushi bar and the chefs who call Sam by name as friends. We all cheer each other up, and I get my appetite back enough to eat.

Chinatown and Little Tokyo are dead. For days, for weeks after the riots, and waiting for the trials of the people arrested in the riots and the trials of the cops who beat up Rodney King to start, Sam and I are the only customers in our favorite J-Town sushi bar. Everyone else who walks in is a cop acting casual. Big guys in suits with guns under their jackets. They crouch over the pictures of the sushi and take a long time reading, looking, and choosing.

One day on our way home on the road past the Marine

Corps and Naval Reserve Training Station, we see the cops have set up a satellite dish, telephone lines, a couple of mobile booking stations, a fleet of unmarked pickup trucks in different colors, a fleet of motorcycles, a fleet of black-and-whites, a trailer serving as an on-site office, a phalanx of portable toilets. A command post. A base.

Two new, washed, gray or brown, nondescript four-door American-made Chevies waving several wire antennae like porcupine spines out of the trunks pass us on the inside bumper to bumper doing about sixty. Each car is full of four big men in dark glasses who don't give a thought to the likes of us in this flimsy little toy of a car. They know me before I know they're there. They know my every move before I make it, which is why it's easy for them to sneer their pursuit packages past me. "The Feds, Sam," I say. The two cars race by me bumper to bumper, at the next intersection two more cars swoop in front of the first two, and all continue racing at sixty in a kind of FBI automobile drill team. Sun Tzu the strategist says, Do not fuck with these guys. Even if he didn't say that, he should have, and I treat them like natural wildlife in the park.

For the next several days, we seem to drive home from sushi or noodles just when several pairs of motorcycle cops gurgle their machines toward us through Elysian Park and into the command post and the teams of Feds and local cops practice teaming up to trap cars in traffic and shove them over to the curb. Damn, it's a pretty sight. All these big new cars full of big square-jawed, uptight, muscular Americanismo diving and swooping as one out of Dodger Stadium parking lot, past the spiny green baobab trees by Barlow Respiratory Hospital, into shadows of impossibly tall and spindly palm trees in Elysian Park.

Sam enters his softshell crab phase. Every day he orders salmon eggs and a softshell crab appetizer. Miso soup with no

Frank Chin

tofu, no seaweed, no green onions, just soup. Coke to drink. He also likes the broiled mayonnaise sauce that tops the broiled New Zealand green mussels I order.

I see smoke rising from the corner of the Marine Corps Naval Reserve Training Center parking lot where the cops have set up a command post. "Oh, no, there's a fire at the command post," I say, and wonder how long ago it started. Is there anything about it on the radio? What happened? Has it started again?

As I roll past I see flames and smoke in the corner and cops in uniform, in their helmets and black leather jackets. They look like the bandits who threaten the village in Kurosawa's *The Seven Samurai,* but with paper plates instead of long weapons in their hands. It's a barbecue, not a bombing.

"It's a barbecue!" I say. "They're having a barbecue. They're roasting steaks and chicken and hotdogs on a barbecue. Whew." I laugh. Sam asks why I'm laughing. "I hope the cops have a fine long evening of barbecue. I never thought I'd ever say that before now." Owooooo! Hear that wolf?

Editor's Note

The essays in this collection originally appeared in various periodicals and have continued to evolve into their present form.

"I Am Talking to the Strategist Sun Tzu about Life When the Subject of War Comes Up" appeared in *Amerasia Journal* (17:1, 1991). "Confessions of a Chinatown Cowboy" first appeared in the *Bulletin of Concerned Asian Scholars* (no. 3, 1972). "Bulletproof Buddhists" was published in *San Diego's Weekly Reader* (July 27, 1995). "Lowe Hoy and the Strange Three-Legged Toad" appeared as "An Ugly Toad's Promise" in *San Diego's Weekly Reader* (March 5, 1994). "Pidgin Contest along I-5" was first published as "New Encounter along I-5: Bigotry" in the *Portland Oregonian* (March 4, 1992). In all cases, copyright held by Frank Chin.

DATE DUE

HIGHSMITH #45115